JOHN WEBSTER

a reference guide

A
Reference
Guide
to
Literature

James Harner
Editor

JOHN WEBSTER
a reference guide

SAMUEL SCHUMAN

G.K. HALL & CO.

70 LINCOLN STREET, BOSTON, MASS.

PR
3186
.S28
.5

Library of Congress Cataloging in Publication Data

Schuman, Samuel
  John Webster, a reference guide.

  (A Reference guide to literature)
  Includes index.
  1. Webster, John, 1580?-1625—Bibliography.
I. Title.   II. Series.
Z8961.3.S38   1985   [PR3186]   016.822'3   85-5570
ISBN 0-8161-8433-X

This publication is printed on permanent/durable acid-free paper
MANUFACTURED IN THE UNITED STATES OF AMERICA

Contents

The Author

Samuel Schuman is the Academic Dean of Guilford College
in Greensboro, North Carolina. He holds the B.A. from
Grinnell College, the M.A. from San Francisco State
University, and the Ph.D. from Northwestern University.
Dr. Schuman has taught English and world literature at
St. Mary's College, Northwestern University, and
Cornell College, and served as Director of the Honors
Program at the University of Maine at Orono. He is
the author of a previous publication in the G.K. Hall
Reference Guide series, <u>Vladimir Nabokov: A Reference
Guide</u>, as well as books on Renaissance dramatists John
Webster and Cyril Tourneur. His published articles and
papers at professional meetings have covered authors
from Chaucer to Nabokov, but focus mainly upon
Elizabethan and Jacobean playwrights.

Preface

It can be difficult, in a bibliographic survey such as this, to know exactly where to find the border between admirable inclusiveness and wearisome pedantry. I have tried to muster all my honesty and industry to find that demarcation, but will inevitably seem to some to have been overly inclusive, and to others to have been profligate in my exclusions. I have tried to list and annotate everything I or previous bibliographers could find written about Webster, with these exceptions:

--Student works below the level of Ph.D. dissertations are not included, save M.A. theses of outstanding interest.

--Works in foreign languages are annotated, but in a bit more sketchy fashion, particularly works in less accessible tongues (e.g., Danish, Japanese, Hebrew).

--Reviews of stage productions are included if, in my judgment, they include a component of scholarly criticism as well as topical and theatrical judgments.

--Anthologies, histories of literature and/or drama, and such works are included here only selectively to illustrate typical treatment of Webster in such works at any given time, or if their discussions seem noteworthy, eccentric in any way, or lengthy.

--General discussions of genre (comedy, tragicomedy, tragedy, satire, etc.), and general considerations of Renaissance literary and theatrical conditions and conventions that do not make specific and significant mention of Webster are not included.

--Also excluded are works on Webster's contemporaries, predecessors, or successors that simply mention his name or that of one of his works for illustrative or casual comparative purposes. I have tried to be fair to scholars by looking for works that seem to concentrate, however briefly, on Webster, rather than simply mentioning him in an off-hand manner while focusing elsewhere.

--Criticism on works probably not by Webster, but disputed, is included only if the critic believed himself to be discussing Webster, and that belief influenced his argument (e.g., finding a "Websterian" theme in a disputed work).

For the purposes of this study, attributions of works to Webster have been considered in a spirit that attempts to be generous and flexible, yet finally limited: a work that aimed to include everything written about every play that has, at one time or another, been assigned to Webster, would be nearly infinite (it would include most of Shakespeare's plays, for instance). I have concluded that Webster almost surely is responsible in whole or in part for: The White Devil, The Duchess of Malfi, The Devil's Law Case, Appius and Virginia, Northward Ho, Westward Ho, the induction to The Malcontent, A Cure for a Cuckold, and Sir Thomas Wyat. Somewhat less certain, in my opinion, are The Fair Maid of the Inn, Anything for a Quiet Life, The Honest Man's Fortune, The Thracian Wonder, and The Weakest Goeth to the Wall, but, where critics have written about these works assuming they are or might be by Webster, I have tried to include them. Monuments of Honour, A Monumental Column, and the additions to the Overburian Characters are also included. I have excluded what I judge to be the more whimsical attributions, e.g., The Revenger's Tragedy, or the claim by some of the anti-Stratfordians (e.g., Greenwood [1916.5]), that Webster was involved in a conspiracy to produce the works of Shakespeare. I have, though, occasionally annotated such words so as to indicate the range of attribution arguments that have swirled about the Webster canon.

Some additional specifications of the format in which the writings about John Webster are presented may usefully be cited by way of preface:

--Unrevised reprints of books are noted with the original entry, but are not accorded a separate entry. When only portions of books are reprinted, however, a separate, cross-referenced, entry will appear under the year of the subsequent version. Separate entries are provided for each reprint of periodical articles, with the annotation appearing with the original publication.

--Revised books will be cited both under the original publication and at the year of revision, and annotation on the revised portions will appear with the entries on the revised versions. All revisions will be cross-referenced.

--There was a profusion of Renaissance drama studies in the early years of this century that were simultaneously published and accepted as Ph.D. dissertations in German universities. These have been cited thus:

AUTHOR. "Title." Ph.D. dissertation, University. City of publication: Publisher, page reference.

This seems the simplest method of handling what seems a potentially confusing bibliographical anomaly.

--I have attempted to be sparing in my use of the word "passim," confining this designation to situations in which Webster is mentioned throughout a work or section intermittently.

--I have attempted to read all Ph.D. dissertations cited, but have occasionally relied upon <u>Dissertation Abstracts</u> or <u>Dissertation Abstracts International</u>. Annotations are offered on the basis of abstracts and are not specially designated. Often, in such cases, specific page references are not available; if so, I have cited the total number of pages in the dissertation.

--Entries preceded by an asterisk indicate items that have not been located. All such items have as annotation a citation of the source from whence the title was culled.

--Anonymous works are alphabetized by title under the year of publication.

In spite of my best efforts, I have inevitably missed some worthwhile discussions of the dramatist that should appear in these pages. To the author of any such piece, I sincerely apologize, and to any who know of works that should be cited herein, and are not, I invite correspondence: works of reference have been known to undergo periodic revision, and unfortunate errors may fortunately be corrected in subsequent editions.

With all due note taken of these exclusions and omissions, conscious and accidental, I nonetheless feel able to offer this work with sincere hope and some modest confidence that between its covers are recorded enough commentary on John Webster to satisfy the most thorough student of the Jacobean drama.

Acknowledgments

I am persuaded that a full and careful bibliography is no more likely to be a solitary effort than an equally comprehensive diction- ary—or, for that matter, an airplane or an economic policy. My work has been remarkably eased by the generosity and cooperation of several institutions and individuals. I am delighted to proclaim my deep and many debts to the libraries and librarians at the University of Maine at Orono, Guilford College, and the Greensboro and Chapel Hill branches of the University of North Carolina. Jim Harner, as my editor, showed infinite tact and patience in telling me what to do, and Barbara Ouellette and Nancy Settlemyre as my assistants, then did most of it. Ruby Cohn taught me much of what I know about bibliographical work; and Samuel Schoenbaum gave me more chances than I deserved to practice that knowledge. My deepest, most joyful, and constant debt is to Nancy, Daniel, and Leah.

Introduction

To survey critical responses to the Jacobean dramatist John Webster
is a task at once illuminating and voluminous. Studies of Webster can
be, on the one hand, a generalized introduction to changing fashions
in scholarly reactions to Renaissance drama, and on the other, extreme-
ly particularized reactions to a highly individualized, even idio-
syncratic, playwright. As there have been a number of excellent
chronological accounts of Webster criticism (e.g., Wang, 1975.31, or
Moore, 1966.19), the historical approach would probably not represent
a useful introduction to this volume. There is, though, a kind of
ordering of Webster studies that is logical rather than chronological,
and that should help make possible an overview of the hundreds of
entries that follow.

BIOGRAPHY AND BIBLIOGRAPHY

Many readers wish to know something about the life of a poet before
looking at his poetry. Those with such an impulse have always been
frustrated by Elizabethan and Jacobean dramatists, and will find Webster
particularly enigmatic: the known, or even hypothesized, facts of his
life might be described as hovering between miniscule and nonexistent.
Nevertheless, there have been two sorts of critical efforts to satisfy
the biographical impulse. First, many editions of individual plays,
or of the complete works, have attempted to survey what modest information is available concerning the playwright's life. For example,
F.L. Lucas, in his monumental four-volume edition of Webster's Works
(1927.11), manages to fill eight pages of his first volume with a section on "Webster's Life," but he does so only by virtue of allowing
such footnoted material as a listing of all known Jacobean "John
Websters" to overwhelm the text. The second source of commentary regarding Webster's biography has been a very small but steady trickle
of "Notes," invariably very short notices of very minor possibilities
regarding the poet's career. An illustration might be Robert Guy
Howarth's one-page article on John Webster's burial (1954.7) noting
a possible parish register reference that might suggest Webster was

neither impoverished nor a householder, and that he was dead by 1638.
The occasional "Webster" entry in encyclopedic collections of literary
biography (e.g., Kunitz and Haycroft, British Authors before 1800
[1952.14]) is useful only as a summary of what little has been previ-
ously discovered. More recent studies by Mary Edmond (1976.5) and
M.C. Bradbrook (1980.9) have restimulated interest in Webster's
biography.

What we know most about Webster's life, though, is that he wrote
plays, and when we turn from biography to bibliography, studies of our
author become more various and more numerous. The attempt to chronicle
what and when Webster wrote, though, is ultimately mired in as much uncertainty as the effort to document his existence: more raw material
seems only to have generated more confusion.

The first task of the descriptive bibliographer is attribution--
"who wrote what," or, in the case of Webster and his colleagues, more
often "who wrote which part of what." Although there has been little
doubt that Webster alone is responsible for The Duchess of Malfi and
The White Devil, there are a score of other works for which he has
been assigned part or whole authorship, and this process has generated
a considerable volume of criticism. Typical of such attribution studies
are "Authenticity and Attribution in the Jacobean and Caroline Drama,"
by G.E. Bentley (1943.7) which discusses Websterian authorship possibilities in The Thracian Wonder and The Revenger's Tragedy, or H.
Dugdale Sykes's articles on "A Webster-Middleton Play: Anything for
a Quiet Life" and "A Webster-Massinger Play: The Fair Maid of the Inn,"
collected in Sidelights on Elizabethan Drama (1924.9). Needless to say,
virtually all editors of Webster--and of most of his contemporaries--
have had to wade into the murky waters of attribution study. While
the early years of the twentieth century saw a great many enthusiasts
leaping into this particular intellectual pond with abandon, a spirit
of restraint, evident in the work of such scholars as Schoenbaum (e.g.,
1951.17) and Erdman (1959.4) has characterized the work of the past
several decades.

After plays are attributed, descriptive bibliographers attempt to
date them, and describe the process by which they move from the hand
of the author to the printed page. The latter sort of study is exempli-
fied in J.R. Brown's series of articles on "The Printing of John
Webster's Plays" (1954.2, 1956.4, and 1962.6), while the former is
illustrated by the same author's "On the Dating of Webster's The White
Devil and The Duchess of Malfi" (1952.4).

SOURCES AND INFLUENCES

Less neatly, questions of date are often intermingled with issues of
source and influence. For example, when Frederick E. Pierce (1927.15)

finds in The Duchess of Malfi an echo of John Davies's The Scourge of Folly, which dates from 1611, he can contend that Webster's play must be dated after that year. Studies of this sort are numerous: probably more short articles have been written on borrowings in Webster than on any other single subject. (Interestingly, there are also a few articles on borrowings from Webster, e.g., Marcia Lee Anderson's "Hardy's Debt to Webster in The Return of the Native" [1939.1].) Even Webster's contemporaries seem to have recognized him as an author who utilized an enormous amount of material from other works in his plays, and from the seventeenth century on, increasing evidence has shown the surprising extent to which Webster built original artistic structures with already used materials. These studies culminated in three major book-length works: R.W. Dent's John Webster's Borrowing (1960.12), and Gunnar Boklund's The Sources of "The White Devil" (1957.5) and "The Duchess of Malfi": Sources, Themes, Characters (1962.1).

It is perhaps necessary while discussing source and influence studies of Webster to take early note of what might be called the "reflexive Shakespeare comparison." Because all the non-Shakespearean Renaissance dramatists are, by definition, not Shakespeare, there is what seems to be an unavoidable tendency to remark over and over again on their subsidiary rank: the standard encyclopedia entry for Webster begins by noting that he was second only to Shakespeare in the field of Renaissance tragedy (that entry usually goes on to say that his works are marred by extravagant brutality, but rescued by flashes of brilliant poetry). The observation that Webster or any of his colleagues could never hope to achieve more than silver medalist status is no less boring for being true. It is also a much different thing than the serious study of the literary or theatrical relationship between Webster and Shakespeare (as, for example, in Stoll's Shakespeare and Other Masters [1940.10], where Iago and Bosola are compared).

CONVENTIONS

Just as Webster utilizes specific works and authors from his literary background as sources of his works, he also uses the literary tradition in a more general way--by employing and manipulating a variety of conventions and familiar motifs from both the theatrical and poetic inheritance. A number of important studies of Webster have concentrated upon his use of specific conventional materials. For example, Lily B. Campbell's "Theories of Revenge in Renaissance England" (1931.2) and Harold Jenkins's "The Tragedy of Revenge in Shakespeare and Webster" (1961.10) focus upon Webster's place in the tradition of the revenge drama, finding that he both employs and reverses some of the expected revenge motifs.

The revenge tradition is closely related to what has been called the Senecan tendency of Renaissance drama, and a number of authors,

for example G.K. Hunter ("Seneca and the Elizabethans" [1967.12]),
consider Webster's use of the Senecan tragic conventions.

A third important literary tradition--perhaps the subject of more
critical interest than the Senecan or the revenge motif--is that of
the "Italianate" drama, of which Webster is frequently cited as
the master. A number of general studies, such as The Italian Influence
in English Poetry by Lytton Sells (1955.24), cite Webster's works
as an important step in the development of this tradition, while
several works that are devoted specifically to Webster (e.g., Robert
Griffin's "John Webster: Politics and Italianate tragedy" [1966.10]),
show how the tradition is important in Webster. One dimension of the
Italianate tragedy is frequently seen as the Machiavellian character,
and a number of Webster's villains and tool villains--among them
Francisco and Flamineo in The White Devil and the Cardinal and Bosola
in The Duchess of Malfi--have been discussed as Machiavellians. Several
of these same characters have also been considered as "malcontent" types
(for example in John D. Jump's short book entitled "The White Devil" and
"The Duchess of Malfi" [1966.14], which presents Flamineo as a "malcontent") while other works have responded to the same constellation
of characters traits by focusing upon the traditional depiction of
"melancholy" and melancholic characters on the stage (see as a sample
Paul F. Saagpakk's "A Survey of Psychopathology in British Literature
from Shakespeare to Hardy" [1968.25], which treats Bosola as a melancholy villain, or L.C. Knight's "Seventeenth Century Melancholy"
[1933.9], which finds Flamineo, in his search for preferment without
the benefit of schooling, a common type of melancholic).

Needless to say, other critics have found in Webster's works, both
major and minor, a number of other stage conventions of the Jacobean
era. These range from conventional character types (e.g., physicians,
blacks, Jews, or widows) to structural or poetic devices. It is important to note, though, that most critics who focus upon the conventional
elements in Webster's drama, like most of those who concentrate on his
use of specific source materials, find that the highly derivative nature of his works, paradoxically, aids, rather than detracts from, their
originality. One of Webster's more interesting characteristics seems
to be his ability to construct plays that are unique within the canon
of the Renaissance drama--indeed, that many would claim are almost
flamboyantly idiosyncratic--while making maximum use of traditional
materials.

CRAFTSMANSHIP AND POETRY

It would be a distortion, however, to suggest that all literary
critics who have examined Webster's works have praised the craftsmanship with which they have been constructed--with which their parts,
such as source materials and conventional elements, have been assembled.

Indeed, since the seventeenth century there have been critics who have assaulted Webster for a lack of dramaturgical skill. As early as 1617, Henry Fitzjeffrey called Webster "crabbed," a description that certainly implies a lack of theatrical craft (1617.1). Perhaps the most notable attack upon Webster's skill as a dramatist, though, was that of William Archer, particularly in his much reprinted essay "The Duchess of Malfi" (1920.2). Archer lashes out at the "grisly absurdity" of Webster's works, the lack of character motivation, "cumbersome" plots, etc. He attacks those critics such as Lamb and Swinburne who, in the decades preceding, had praised Webster extravagantly and singled out specific passages as exemplifying especial poetic beauty (e.g., 1886.3). To Archer, such "specimen" collecting ignored the larger theatrical structure of the play, and in the case of Webster and most of the other non-Shakespearean Renaissance dramatists, that structure was ramshackle and laughable. Archer's attack on Webster as a shoddy dramatic craftsman is not without more contemporary echoes. Ian Jack, for example, repeats many of Archer's charges concerning ludicrous plotting and character construction (1949.6).

Scholars with a more favorable view of Webster have responded to these repeated charges of shoddy dramaturgy in two main ways. The earlier response was to concede major structural weaknesses within even the best of Webster's works but to argue that his poetic beauties redeem constructional faults. Perhaps the most common image in Webster criticism is that of "lightning flashes" of poetic brilliance, and to many critics those flashes are the major illumination of otherwise unimpressive works. Even as favorable a critic as Rupert Brooke in his major John Webster and the Elizabethan Drama (1916.1) sees lamentable gaps in the plotting of works such as The White Devil, but finds compensating virtues in moments of remarkable poetry. Other critics, somewhat less impressionistically, have also been struck by Webster's skill as a poet. In particular, there have been several interesting and worthwhile studies of his use of imagery and image clusters, such as Moody Prior's discussion of Webster in The Language of Tragedy (1947.8), which still sees the splendid poetic moments of the tragedies as compensating for structural deficiencies.

Another response to the Archerian charge of structural incompetence, however, has been the more positive assertion that Webster did build his works of art well and that they successfully achieve the ends he envisioned for them. In effect, such scholars argue on the basis of results: if the plays succeed in creating interest and meaning, then they must be well organized. To a large extent, then, the study of the themes of Webster's works is an overt or implied response to the accusation that those works are chaotic and pointless.

THEMATIC APPROACHES

Most studies that have focused upon the thematic level of Webster's works have seen the dramatist's meanings primarily in moral terms. The plays, especially the two major tragedies, raise questions of good and evil, specifically at three strata: the individual, the social, and the universal.

While there have been a number of notable dissenting voices, most Webster critics have found a structure of individual morality at work in his plays and, indeed, have seen that structure to be a major emphasis in The White Devil and The Duchess of Malfi. The organizing principle undergirding the ethical evaluation of individual characters in Webster's tragedies has overwhelmingly been found to be that of "integrity"--most scholars agree that Webster stresses the quality of heroic individualism, and admires the defiant and embattled person fighting to retain self-identity in a world which seeks to corrupt it. Studies such as Edwin Benjamin's "Patterns of Morality in The White Devil" (1965.2) derive a self-contained ethical pattern from Webster's development of the morality of individual "integrity of life." (In fairness, it must be noted that other students of literary ethical issues, such as J.A. Bastiaenen in The Moral Tone of Jacobean and Caroline Drama [1930.1], simply find Vittoria an evil adultress, whose much vaunted integrity is simply a bold assertion of immorality.)

Many critics have also concentrated on Webster's treatment of moral issues in human society. Studies in this area stress the role of Webster as a satirist, a student and critic of the follies and ills of the courtly world depicted in the major dramas. Webster's criticism of society is a major subject of works such as Joseph Stodder's Satire in Jacobean Tragedy (1974.23), Travis Bogard's The Tragic Satire of John Webster (1955.4) or Leonard Goldstein's "Three Significant Dramatists and Their Relation to the Moral Decadence of Jacobean and Caroline Drama" (1955.12). To many of these critics, an important issue is the manner in which Webster blends ethical criticism of society (satire) with moral affirmation of individual values (tragedy). A number of other studies have also focused upon social criticism and satire in Webster's minor works, especially The Devil's Law Case and the "Ho" plays (for example, Clifford Leech's "Three Times Ho and a Brace of Widows" [1973.19]).

A final group of critical studies concerns itself with the universal, cosmological, or theological morality explored in Webster plays, particularly the tragedies. These works ask if Webster's world is one of amoral bleakness, or if it demonstrates some universal ethical pattern. There seems a fairly even division of opinion over this question.

To some critics, such as Clifford Leech (1951.12) or J.R. Mulryne (1960.19), Webster, while a morally serious dramatist, depicts a world directed, as T.S. Eliot observed, towards chaos, one in which individuals may forge lives that we are forced to admire but that ultimately end "in a mist" of meaningless death within an amoral universe. Another group of critics counters this view, however, asserting that there is a coherent moral pattern to the Websterian cosmos. Thus, David Cecil (1949.2) sees Webster as depicting a world in which the forces of good and evil are engaged in a desperate spiritual struggle. Robert Ornstein (1960.21) sees Webster creating a world in which virtue and vice are real but irrelevant and impotent. But Irving Ribner (1961.15) finds an affirmation of human nobility, even in death, of characters like the Duchess, that imparts a moral order to experience.

HISTORY

Another body of Webster scholarship is less concerned with the plays themselves than with their reception. The 350-year life of the dramas has seen a number of interesting and revealing shifts in stage life, literary repute, and the like. Some critics have focused upon the theatrical history of Webster's dramas. Studies such as Frank Wadsworth's "Some Nineteenth Century Revivals of The Duchess of Malfi" (1967.26) or his "Webster, Horne, and Mrs. Stowe: American Performances of The Duchess of Malfi" (1970.30) can reveal a great deal about the theatrical tastes of an era and the perception of the nature of Webster's works within the matrix of those tastes. Another very closely related type of study focuses upon the conditions of performance in the Jacobean theater, illuminating the situations in which the plays were first produced and for which they were written. Such studies include some very specific topics ("Robert Johnson: King's Musician in His Majesty's Public Entertainment" by John Cutts [1955.8] or William Armstrong's "The Audience of the Elizabethan Private Theaters" [1959.2]) as well as very broad and general surveys, of which perhaps the most distinguished is G.E. Bentley's The Jacobean and Caroline Stage (1936.1).

Other writers have focused more upon the literary reputation than the theatrical history of Webster and his drama. Some very full surveys of Webster's rises and falls upon the literary stock market have provided an informative glimpse into the critical practices of Restoration, eighteenth-century, romantic, Victorian and twentieth-century scholars. Moore's and Wang's studies already cited are excellent examples. Some essays have focused upon some quite specific period or movement of Webster studies. For example, Earl Wasserman's "The Scholarly Origin of the Elizabethan Revival" (1937.11) discusses the relationship between Lamb's enthusiasm and more sedate eighteenth-century interest in Webster and his fellows. Robert D. Williams's "Antiquarian Interest in Elizabethan Drama before Lamb" (1938.16) focuses upon the same set of problems at the same time.

A small, but fascinating and related group of studies is concerned with an historical development both theatrical and literary: the adaptations and alterations of Webster's works so as to move them towards conformity with the critical dicta or popular expectations of a non-Jacobean era. A good example of this area of inquiry is R.K. Kaul's "What Theobald Did to Webster" (1961.12).

Another sort of historical study is, of course, that of which this work itself is a sample, the bibliography. Webster has been favored by the attentions of a number of good bibliographers, most exhaustively by Peter Mahaney (1973.23).

Most of these types of historical studies are at least touched upon in most editions of Webster's works, collected or individual, and in most of the larger volumes devoted to him.

This introduction has, obviously, been more selective than inclusive. I have ignored many fascinating nooks and crannies of Webster scholarship in the effort to note what seem to be the major areas of critical concern. A random glimpse into the entries that follow will reveal studies in such diverse areas as Webster's punctuation, his employment of criminal or medical motifs in the dramas, studies of his elegy and civic pageant, of his contribution to the "character" writing tradition, and the like. I have also not said, and should, that many larger or introductory sorts of studies straddle several of the critical areas of concern doubtlessly separated above with far too much neatness. The pages that follow will reveal, if not God's plenty, at least a panoply of critical styles, subjects, moods, tastes, and intelligences wide enough to convince most any discerning student that John Webster has inspired an enormous, fascinating, and articulate readership.

Writings by John Webster

I. DRAMATIC WORKS GENERALLY ATTRIBUTED, IN WHOLE OR IN PART, TO WEBSTER

Appius and Virginia. London: Nicholas Okes, 1612 (written 1612)
A Cure for a Cuckold. London: Thomas Johnson, 1661 (1625)
The Devil's Law Case. London: Augustine Matthews, 1623 (1617)
The Duchess of Malfi. London: Nicholas Okes, 1623 (1614)
The induction to The Malcontent. London: William Apsley, 1604
    (1604)
Northward Ho. London: G. Eld, 1607 (1605)
Sir Thomas Wyat. London: Thomas Archer, 1707 (1604)
Westward Ho. London: John Hodges, 1607 (1604)
The White Devil. London: Nicholas Okes, 1612 (1612)

II. NONDRAMATIC WORKS ATTRIBUTED TO WEBSTER

A Monumental Column. London: Nicholas Okes, 1624
Monuments of Honour. London: Nicholas Okes, 1613
Characters by Sir Thomas Overbury (additions to the 6th edition).
    London: Thomas Creede, 1615

III. WORKS OCCASIONALLY BUT DOUBTFULLY ATTRIBUTED TO WEBSTER

Anything for a Quiet Life. London: Francis Kirkman, 1662
The Fair Maid of the Inn. London: Robinson & Moseley, 1647 (The
    Beaumont and Fletcher First Folio)
The Honest Man's Fortune. London: Robinson & Moseley, 1647 (The
    Beaumont and Fletcher First Folio)
The Thracian Wonder. London: Thomas Johnson, 1661
The Weakest Goeth to the Wall. London: Thomas Creede, 1600

Writings about John Webster, 1602-1981

1602

1   HENSLOWE, PHILIP. "Henslowe's Diary." Manuscript. Dulwich
College, London. [Various reprints and editions include John
Payne Collier, ed., (London: Shakespeare Society, 1845); W.W.
Greg, ed. (London: A.H. Bullen, 1904-8); R.A. Foakes and R.T.
Rickert, eds. (Cambridge: Cambridge University Press, 1961);
and in Henslowe Papers, ed. W.W. Greg (London: A.H. Bullen,
1907), esp. pp. 66, 90.]
     Includes several entries recording payments to Webster, e.g.,
"Lent vnto the company the 22 of majj 1602 to geve vnto antoney
monday and michell drayton webester and the Rest mydelton in ernest
of a boocke called sesers ffale the some of . . . " and for 15
October 1602 a loan on "A playe called Ladey Jane. . . . "

1615

1   STOWE, JOHN. The Annales, or Generall Chronicle of England.
Continued by E. Howes. London: Adams, p. 811.
     Citation only in passing, but worth noting because of early
date.

1616

*1   PUDSEY, EDWARD. Unpublished commonplace book, written c. 1616,
p. 81.
     Records eight quotations from The White Devil. Source:
Wang, 1975.31.

1617

1   FITZJEFFREY, HENRY. "Notes from Blackfryers." In Certain
Elegies done by Sundrie Excellent Wits. Book 3. London: M.
Patrich, p. 17.

Terms the playwright "crabbed Websterio," a "Playwright-cartwright."

1618

*1   BUSINO, ORAZIO. "Anglopotrida." Unpublished letter.
        Describes the British dislike of Catholocism, citing The
Duchess of Malfi as an illustration. (Busino was a Venetian envoy
to England.) Source: Hunter and Hunter, 1969.17. See also 1913.8.

1623

1   FORD, JOHN. Prefatory Verse to The Duchess of Malfi. London:
        Nicholas Okes, A4^v.
        Notes Webster's debt to classical authors.

2   MIDDLETON, THOMAS. Prefatory Verse to The Duchess of Malfi.
        London: Nicholas Okes, A4^r.
        Argues the tragedy of the Duchess is Webster's monument; it
is a work of fame.

3   ROWLEY, WILLIAM. Prefatory Verse to The Duchess of Malfi.
        London: Nicholas Okes, A4^v.
        Suggests (in a conventional six-line ditty) that the Duchess
never spoke as well as in Webster's play.

1635

1   HEYWOOD, THOMAS. The Hierarchie of the Blessed Angells. Book
        4. London: A. Islip, p. 206.
        Contains a reference to Shakespeare and his contemporaries
that includes this couplet: "Fletcher and Webster of that learned
packe / None of the mean'st, yet neither was but Iacke. . . . "
The reference to Webster in the past tense is taken as evidence
of his death before 1635.

1648

*1   [NEEDHAM, WALTER?] [Mercurius Pragmaticus]. "To the Readers of
        my former Peece." Introduction to The Second part of Crafty
        Cromwell. London: n.p.
        Source: G.E. Bentley. Shakespeare and Johnson. Vol. 2.
Chicago: 1945, pp. 73-74. Ranks Webster along with "Johnson"
and Shakespeare as equal to Sophocles and Euripides.

1650

*1 WRIGHT, ABRAHAM. Unpublished commonplace book, c. 1650.
    British Museum MS. Add. 22608.
        Calls The Duchess of Malfi a good play, but with some flaws
    in language and plot. Finds The White Devil "an indifferent play
    to read, but for the presentments I believe good." The Devil's
    Law Case is indifferent. Source: Hunter and Hunter, 1969.17.
    Quoted in 1969.17; 1975.18.

1651

1   SHEPPARD, SAMUEL. "On Mr. Webster's Most Excellent Tragedy
    Called The White Devil." In Epigrams Theological, Philosophical,
    and Romantic. London: Thomas Bucknell, p. 27.
        Sets The White Devil above the efforts of Euripides and
    Sophocles: posterity will gaze at Webster's characters as if they
    were comets. (Webster is also mentioned in Sheppard's manuscript
    poem "The Fairy King" [1648-54]; see 1927.16.)

1655

1   COTGRAVE, JOHN. An English Treasury of Wit and Language.
    London: H. Mosley, 311 pp., passim.
        Culls quotations from Renaissance plays. Webster ranks sixth
    among all the dramatists used with 104 excerpts (after Shakespeare,
    Beaumont and Fletcher, Jonson, Chapman, and Greville). Quoted and
    discussed by G.E. Bentley, "John Cotgrave's English Treasure of
    Wit and Language and the Elizabethan Drama," Studies in Philology
    40 (April 1927):554 ff.

1656

1   ARCHER, EDWARD. An Exact and Perfect Catalogue. . . . [Printed
    with Philip Massinger et al., The Old Law.] London: E. Archer,
    pp. 1-16.
        Includes attributions to Webster of six plays: Appius and
    Virginia, The Devil's Law Case, The Duchess of Malfi, Guise, The
    White Devil, and Westward Ho. Discussed in 1975.31.

*2 [HOLLAND, SAMUEL?] Wit and Fancy in a Maze. London: Thomas
    Vere.
        Depicts Webster fighting in a mock-romantic battle of wits
    on the side of Shakespeare and Fletcher. Source: Wang, 1975.31.

3   ROGERS, RICHARD, and LEY, WILLIAM. An Exact and Perfect
    Catalogue. . . . [Appended to Goffe, Thomas, The Careles
    Shepherdess.] London: Rogers & Ley, pp. 77-82.

3

Does not mention Webster by name, but lists Appius and
Virginia, The Duchess of Malfi, The Devil's Law Case, Sir Thomas
Wyat and Westward Ho. Cited in 1975.31.

<u>1661</u>

1   KIRKMAN, FRANCIS. A True Perfect and Most Exact Catalogue. . . .
    [Appended to Tom Tyler and His Wife, 2d Impression.] London:
    F. Kirkman, 6 pp.
        Assigns Webster sole credit for Appius and Virginia, The
Devil's Law Case, The Duchess of Malfi and The White Devil. With
Rowley, he wrote A Cure for a Cuckold and The Thracian Wonder.
With Dekker, the "Ho" plays and Sir Thomas Wyat. Lists Guise
without an author. See also 1671.1; 1943.6.

2   PEPYS, SAMUEL. "Diary. 1661-1669." Manuscript, Magdalene
    College, Cambridge, passim. [First published: London: H.
    Colburn, 1848-49.]
        Mentions several performances of The White Devil, which
Pepys feels is a very poor play.

<u>1671</u>

1   KIRKMAN, FRANCIS. An Exact Catalogue of all the English Stage
    Plays. London: A. Johnson for F. Kirkman, 16 pp.
        Includes the same attributions as 1661.1. See also 1943.6.

<u>1675</u>

1   PHILLIPS, EDWARD. Theatrum Poetarum. Pt. 2. London: C.
    Smith, pp. 116-17.
        Includes an entry on Dekker, citing his collaboration with
Webster.

<u>1687</u>

1   WINSTANLEY, WILLIAM. The Lives of the Most Famous English
    Poets, or The Honour of Parnassus. London: Manship, pp.
    136-37, 140. [Facsimile reproduction, with an introduction by
    William Riley Parker. Gainesville, Fla.: Scholars' Facsimiles
    and Reprints, 1963.]
        Notes the Dekker/Webster collaboration on several "well
entertain'd" plays: Northward Ho, The Novel Stranger, New Trick
to Cheat the Devil, Westward Ho, The Weakest Goeth to the Wall,
Woman Will Have Her Will, and "Wiat's History." Also records
collaboration with Rowley on A Cure for a Cuckold and The Thracian
Wonder. Cites, in addition, the three "he wrote alone": The

Devil's Law Case (a tragicomedy) and The White Devil and The Duchess of Malfi (tragedies).

1691

1   LANGBAINE, GERARD. An Account of the English Dramatic Poets. Oxford: West & Clements, esp. pp. 508-10. [Facsimile repro- duction, with an introduction by David Stuart Rodes. Augustan Reprint Society, no. 150. Los Angeles: William Andrews Clark Memorial Library, University of California, 1971.]
        Describes Webster as "An author that liv'd in the Reign of King James the First; and was in those Days accounted an Excellent Poet." Makes exactly the same attributions as Kirkman (1661.1).

1694

1   WRIGHT, JAMES. Country Conversations. London: Henry Bonwick, pp. 54-55. [Reprint. London: Whibley, 1927.]
        Qoutes from Antonio's speech on "Ruins" from The Duchess of Malfi.

1696

1   HARRIS, JOSEPH. The City Bride. London: Roper & Wilkinson, 47 pp. [Facsimile reproduction, with an introduction by Vinton A. Dearny. Augustan Reprint Society, no. 36. Los Angeles: William Andrews Clark Memorial Library, University of California, 1952.]
        Adapts A Cure for a Cuckold, with some changes of name and much alteration of language; however, the structure remains pretty much unchanged.

1698

1   GILDON, CHARLES. The Lives and Characters of the English Dramatic Poets. London: Leigh & Turner, pp. 146-47.
        Repeat of 1691.1, adding that Webster was a clerk at St. Andrew's parish in Holborn.

1707

1   TATE, NAHUM. Injur'd Love. London: R. Wellington, 70 pp.
        Adapts and revises The White Devil, which remains recog- nizable in outline but is much altered in structure and language. Often changes Webster's lively prose to neat, if dull, verse.

5

1708

1   DOWNES, JOHN. Roscius Anglicanus: or, an Historical Review of
     the Stage from 1600 to 1706. London: H. Playford, passim.
     [Reprint. Edited by John Loftis. Augustan Reprint Society,
     no. 134. Los Angeles: William Andrews Clark Memorial Library,
     University of California, 1969.]
          Lists plays and actors of the Restoration stage, along with
     a history of the theater. Includes an account of The Duchess of
     Malfi in performance: "It fill'd the House 8 days Successively,
     it proving one of the Best of Stock Tragedies" (p. 25). Includes
     The White Devil in a list: "These being old plays, were acted but
     now and then, yet being well perform'd, were very Satisfactory to
     the Town" (p. 9).

1713

1   MEARS, W. A True and Exact Catalogue. . . . London: W. Mears,
     48 pp. [Reprinted and revised. 1715, 1719, 1726.]
          Lists six plays as Webster's, and, in the 1719 and 1726 edi-
     tions adds that The Duchess of Malfi and The Thracian Wonder were
     "Acted with applause."

1719

1   JACOB, GILES. The Poetical Register. Vol. 1. London: E.
     Curll, pp. 269-70. [Facsimile reproduction. New York:
     Garland, 1970.]
          Identifies Webster as a Clerk of St. Andrews in Holborn,
     "esteem'd a tolerable Poet in those Days" and cites as his works
     The White Devil, The Devil's Law Case, The Duchess of Malfi,
     Appius and Virginia, The Thracian Wonder, and A Cure for A Cuckold.
     The listing is based on Langbaine's in 1691.1.

1735

1   THEOBALD, LEWIS. The Fatal Secret. London: J. Watts, 57 pp.
          Adapts and much alters The Duchess of Malfi. Acknowledges
     the use of Webster as source, and cites his faults--excesses of
     horror and bombast, and no heed of the rules. Changes are con-
     siderable, including an ending in which all the major characters
     live on. A brief excerpt is published in 1969.18.
          In a 1731 letter to William Warburton, Theobald discusses
     his plans for this effort. Also noteworthy is Philip Frowde's
     prologue, citing the "rude old bard, if critic laws he knew, /
     From too warm imagination drew." Theobald's muse restrained this
     "wild luxuriance."

1738

1   HAYWARD, THOMAS, ed. The British Muse. 3 vols. London: F.
    Cogan, passim. [Republished as Beauties of the English Drama,
    1777.]
        Gathers quotations from plays on various subjects, including
    selections from The White Devil, The Duchess of Malfi, and The
    Devil's Law Case.

1744

1   DODSLEY, ROBERT, ed. A Select Collection of Old English Plays.
    Vol. 3. London: Dodsley, pp. 313-412.
        Includes The White Devil in this first collection of early
    drama. Later editions include some biographical data as well.

1747

1   MOTTLEY, JOHN. A List of All the Dramatic Authors. . . .
    [Appended to Thomas Whincop, Scanderbeg.] London: W. Reeve,
    pp. 87-315.
        Repeats the list of Jacob (1719.1), which is based on
    Langbaine (1691.1).

1750

1   CHETWOOD, W.R. The British Theatre. Dublin: P. Wilson, p. 38.
        Attributes to Webster The White Devil, The Duchess of Malfi,
    Appius and Virginia, The Thracian Wonder and A Cure for a Cuckold.
    Webster "was accounted a good poet, and well esteemed by his con-
    temporary authors." Based on Jacob, 1719.1 and Langbaine, 1691.1.

1753

1   CIBBER, THEOPHILUS, et al. The Lives of the Poets of Great
    Britain and Ireland to the Time of Dean Swift. Vol. 1. London:
    R. Griffiths, passim.
        Cites Webster often but has no section devoted specifically
    to him or his works.

1756

1   The Beauties of the English Stage. London: E. Withers, passim.
        Collects quotations from The Duchess of Malfi in this an-
    thology of notable passages.

1764

1   BAKER, DAVID ERSKINE. <u>Biographia Dramatica; or, A Companion</u>
     <u>to the Playhouse</u>. 3 vols. London: Rivingtons, 1:739; 3:
     passim. [Annotation based upon 1812 version. London: Longmans.]
        Includes a brief view of the rise and progress of the English
     stage--noting of Webster "he was accounted a tolerable poet." Vol.
     3 is an alphabetized list of plays, based on Chetwood (1750.1)
     which is in turn based on Langbaine (1691.1).

1783

1   CAPELL, EDWARD. <u>Notes and Various Readings to Shakespeare</u>.
     Vol. 3. London: E. & C. Dilley, pp. 113-15, 164. [Reprint.
     New York: Burt Franklin, 1970.]
        Cites publication and acting data for hundreds of old plays,
     ranking the works included. <u>A Cure for a Cuckold</u> is one of thirty-
     two evaluated as "good" while <u>The White Devil</u> is rated a rival of
     Shakespeare's excellence. Includes several passages from Webster
     in the section entitled "The School of Shakespeare."

1798

*1   DRAKE, NATHAN. <u>Literary Hours</u>. Sudbury: J. Burkitt, 529 pp.
        Ranks Webster next after Ford in talent, but notes that he
     had a predilection for the terrible and strange. Compared to
     Shakespeare, he seems labored, yet a genius. Source: Wang,
     1975.31.

1800

1   DIBDIN, CHARLES. <u>A Complete History of the Stage</u>. Vol. 3.
     London: Dibdin, pp. 217-72.
        Chapter 5 discusses Webster, Rowley, and "The Inferior
     Dramatic Poets." Presents Webster as a parish clerk who often
     collaborated--he found materials to which others gave form.

1807

1   BELOE, WILLIAM. <u>Anecdotes of Literature and Scarce Books</u>. Vol.
     1. London: Rivington, pp. 309, 332-33, 361.
        Cites title page data from copies of <u>The Malcontent</u>, <u>The</u>
     <u>White Devil</u>, <u>The Duchess of Malfi</u> and <u>Appius and Virginia</u> in the
     Garrick Collection and <u>Sir Thomas Wyat</u> in the Malone Collection.

1808

1   LAMB, CHARLES. Specimens of the English Dramatic Poets, Who
     Lived about the Time of Shakespeare: with notes. London:
     Longman, Hurst, Rees, & Orme, pp. 197-234.
     Includes one scene from The Devil's Law Case and one from
Appius and Virginia. From The Duchess of Malfi prints the court-
ship of the Duchess and Antonio and most of the fourth act. On
this "specimen," comments that the Duchess has lived among horrors
until she is not of this world. Webster was a master of fear and
horror unmatched by others whose "terrors want dignity." The White
Devil excerpts include the arraignment of Vittoria, where she pleads
with "an innocence-resembling boldness" that, in spite of her guilt,
is convincing. Cornelia's Dirge is also included. It embodies an
intenseness of feeling like the "ditty" in The Tempest.
     Lamb's Specimens is often credited with reviving interest in
Webster and his works after nearly two centuries of neglect. Reviewed: 1809.1-2. See also 1943.9.

1809

1   Review of Specimens of the English Dramatic Poets . . . , by
     Charles Lamb. Annual Review and History of Literature 3:568.
     Contends The Duchess of Malfi is not half so fine as Lamb
(1808.1) would have it: the play features absurd and monstrous
scenes of violence and pain. (Lamb thought that this review was
written by Coleridge.)

2   Review of Specimens of the English Dramatic Poets . . . , by
     Charles Lamb. Monthly Review 58:349-56.
     Expresses sharp dissatisfaction with Lamb's praise of Webster
(1808.1), especially his comparison of Webster and Shakespeare.
Finds Lamb's language is mock-heroic.

1810

1   BRYDGES, Sir SAMUEL EGERTON. The British Bibliographer. Vol.
     2. London: R. Triphock, p. 172.
     Prints the madmen's song from The Duchess of Malfi, indicat-
ing both the rise in Webster's repute, and increasing belief that
he is at his best in scenes of horror and grotesquerie.

2   [SCOTT, Sir WALTER?], ed. The Ancient British Drama. Vol. 3.
     Edinburgh: J. Ballantyne, pp. 1-46, 508-48.
     Includes The White Devil and The Duchess of Malfi; an im-
portant recognition of the growing critical reputation of the
tragedies.

1814

1   DILKE, CHARLES WENTWORTH, ed. Old English Plays. Vol. 6.
     London: Whittingham & Rowland, pp. 3-98.
       Prints Appius and Virginia. Demonstrates that Webster is
increasingly recognized as a major dramatist, even in his less ex-
citing works.

1817

1   DRAKE, NATHAN. Shakespeare and His Times. Vol. 2. London:
     T. Cadell & W. Davis, pp. 564-65.
       Depicts Webster as the author of striking but eccentric plays,
with a taste for the terrible and strange. He curdles the blood
with terror, especially in the death of the Duchess.

1818

1   M., H. "The Duchess of Malfi." Blackwood's Magazine 3 (March):
     656-62. [Excerpted: 1975.18.]
       Sees the chief merit of this play as the affection between
the Duchess and Antonio, which is mixed with much low and worthless
matter. In act 4, the wild, fantastic, and terrible grandeur of
Webster breaks forth, but act 5 is of no interest. Webster was a
man of truly original genius, fascinated by life's horrors.

2   _____. "The White Devil, or Vittoria Corombona." Blackwood's
     Magazine 3 (August):557-62.
       Finds the play "disjointed in its action," with "a mixture
of the horrible and the absurd." Mostly, therefore, it is just a
collection of great moments (several of which are quoted here).
Affirms that Webster's strength lies in his ability to evoke wild,
grotesque, fantastical and extravagant horror.

1819

1   CAMPBELL, THOMAS. Specimens of the British Poets. 3 vols.
     London: Murray, 1:133; 3:215-33. [Reprinted as Cyclopedia of
     English Poetry (Philadelphia: Lippincott, 1875), pp. 211-23.]
       Includes an historical survey, which notes Webster's gloomy
force of imagination and occasional beauty and pathos in the midst
of horrors. Also contains selections from Webster, with a brief
headnote commenting upon "his absurdities as a dramatist" and
Lamb's overeager criticism. Includes the arraignment of Vittoria
in The White Devil, and madmen, Duchess's death, and echo scenes
from The Duchess of Malfi. Based on Lamb's selections, 1808.1.

1820

1　COLLIER, JOHN PAYNE. The Poetical Decameron. Vol. 1.
　Edinburgh:　A. Constable, pp. 260-64.
　　　　Argues that Webster the dramatist is the same as the John
Webster who wrote Academiarum Examen in 1654.

2　HAZLITT, WILLIAM. Lectures Chiefly on the Dramatic Literature
　of the Age of Elizabeth. London:　Stodart & Steuart, pp. 57-84.
　[Excerpted:　1975.18.]
　　　　Lecture 3 is on "Marston, Chapman, Deckar [sic], and Webster."
Praises "the terrible graces of the obscure, forgotten Webster."
The Duchess of Malfi is not quite as spirited as The White Devil,
with its dazzling heroine.　It has the same kinds of beauties and
terrors, but the torture scenes exceed the bounds of poetry.

3　"John Webster." European Magazine 78 (October):301-4;
　(November):420-24.
　　　　Part of a series on Elizabethan dramatists which begins with
a general introduction praising the older writers, especially in
comparison with their French counterparts.　Surveys Webster's life
and works (he is identified as the churchman who wrote Academiarum
Examen and died c. 1660).　Finds the characters of Appius and
Virginia drawn in a bold and masterly style--specimens of the
beauty of this tragedy are presented.　Sees The White Devil as
the best of Webster's plays, with all the excellences of the early
dramatists:　it is irregular, yet lofty and pathetic.　The trial
scene, in particular, is masterly.　Also notes the "manly spirit"
of the preface to The White Devil.

1823

1　BUCHON, JEAN A. "Littérature étrangère:　Auteurs tragiques
　anglais depuis la naissance de l'art dramatique en Angleterre."
　Le Mecure du Dixneuvième Siècle 2:463-80.
　　　　Finds Webster comparable to Heywood, but more somber and
terrible.　Includes the Duchess/Antonio wooing scene as a specimen.

2　"Webster's Plays." Retrospective Review 7:87-120.
　　　　Laments the absence of biographical information on Webster.
Although he is not an especially great poet, "his excellence is
in the poetry of scenic action."　Quotes from the plays extensive-
ly, e.g., almost the entire arraignment of Vittoria.　Comments on
the plays:　The Devil's Law Case is a "tolerable play," but not as
good as The Duchess of Malfi and The White Devil.　The murder of
the Duchess is a fearful and terrible scene.　Appius and Virginia
is "the most finished and regular of all his plays," full of dramatic interest, although few scenes are as striking as those of
The White Devil or The Duchess of Malfi.　Of Webster's other works,
The Thracian Wonder is "vile," A Cure for a Cuckold is better, but

11

still inferior. Suggests Webster was not much for cultivating
the comic muse.

1830

*1   CHASLES, PHILARETE. "Des Auteurs dramatiques anglais con-
      temporaines de Shakespeare." Revue de Paris 17 (August):
      98-117; 18 (September):71-85.
      Source: Mahaney, 1973.23.

2   DYCE, ALEXANDER, ed. The Works of John Webster. 4 vols.
      London: Wm. Pickering, 1:319 pp.; 2:319 pp.; 3:368 pp.;
      4:311 pp. [Dyce's criticism excerpted: 1975.18.]
           For a long time, this was the standard edition of Webster's
      works. It is the first complete edition. Vol. 1: An account of
      John Webster and his writings, The White Devil, and The Duchess of
      Malfi; vol. 2: The Devil's Law Case, Appius and Virginia, Sir
      Thomas Wyat; vol. 3: "Ho" plays, A Cure for a Cuckold; vol. 4:
      The Malcontent, The Thracian Wonder, Monumental Column and poems.
           The introduction includes a brief collection of biographical
      and bibliographical data as well as critical commentary. The "Ho"
      plays are full of life and bustle. The White Devil is a play of
      extraordinary power with a confusing but interesting plot. Its
      high point is the character of Vittoria. The Duchess of Malfi is
      a highly affecting work. Appius and Virginia is simple and pa-
      thetic. Reviewed: 1830.3.

3   Review of The Works of John Webster, by Alexander Dyce. London
      Literary Gazette and Journal of the Belles Lettres, 17 April,
      p. 255.
           Concludes Dyce (1830.2) has created a worthy, and indispens-
      able edition of a celebrated dramatist, one of "our best painters
      of manners," who abounds in poetical beauties undebased by gross
      coarseness.

1831

1   COLLIER, JOHN PAYNE. The History of English Dramatic Poetry
      to the Time of Shakespeare, and Annals of the Stage to the
      Restoration. 3 vols. London: J. Murray, 490, 494, 604 pp.,
      passim.
           Frequently cites Webster in passing in vol. 3 of this en-
      cyclopedic work. In vol. 2, p. 476 Collier claims to have located
      Henslowe's record connecting Webster with The Guise. The Henslowe
      records, however, appear to be forgeries by Collier. See 1891.1;
      1906.10.

*2   DARLEY, GEORGE. Letter to Allan Cunningham, 22 May.
           Finds The White Devil is superior to any English poetry save

that of Shakespeare and Milton. Source: Hunter and Hunter,
1969.17.

1833

1   M., J. "The Early English Drama, III." Gentleman's Magazine
      103 (May):414-17.
          Ranks Webster high, but inferior to Jonson in comic humor,
    Fletcher in fancy and delicacy, and Massinger in consistency of
    plot and character. He surpasses them all in the depth of his
    pathos and his command of the sublime and the terrible. The White
    Devil has a weak plot and characters, but a deep theme. Its best
    scene is the divorce between Brachiano and Isabella ("as we read
    . . . the pages were wet with our tears") and the mourning of
    Cornelia.

1836

1   COLLIER, JOHN PAYNE. New Particulars Regarding the Works of
      Shakespeare. London: Rodd, pp. 28-29.
          Addressed to Dyce. Includes some (nonforged) notes regarding
    the dating of Webster's works, especially Monuments of Honour and
    some dedicatory poems. The book as a whole contains suspect mate-
    rial. See 1859.1.

1839

1   HALLAM, HENRY. Introduction to the Literature of Europe in the
      Fifteenth, Sixteenth, and Seventeenth Centuries. Vol. 3.
      London: J. Murray, pp. 619-21. [Reprint. New York: Harper,
      1868, 2 vols.]
          Suggests Webster possessed very considerable powers, and
    ranks next below Ford. Deep sorrows and terrors are his particular
    province, but his works are tainted with a savage taste of the
    Italian school. The scenes of The Duchess of Malfi are wrought
    with skill and the characters are well drawn, especially the Duchess.
    The White Devil has a more confusing plot. Webster's other plays
    are less interesting, although Appius and Virginia is not ineffec-
    tive.

2   KNIGHT, CHARLES, ed. The Pictorial Edition of the Works of
      Shakspere. 8 vols. London: C. Knight, passim. [Reprint.
      London: J.S. Vertu, 1873, 2 vols.]
          Admires Webster for his powerful passion, which approaches
    that in Shakespeare's plays, and the profoundness of the pathos
    of his characters.

3   NEELE, HENRY. <u>Lectures on English Poetry</u>. London: J. Thomas,
    229 pp., passim, especially lecture 4.
         Webster created in <u>The Duchess of Malfi</u> one of the most
    extraordinary compositions of our language. This play features
    a vivid poetic fancy and much power.

                              1843

1   COLLIER, JOHN PAYNE, ed. <u>The Alleyn Papers</u>. London:
    Shakespeare Society, pp. 14-15.
         Alleyn records a debt of fifteen shillings of "John Allein"
    and "Ed Allein" to John Webster "cytysen and merchaunt tayler of
    London" on 15 July 1591. Collier asserts that the debt was "doubt-
    less incurred in connection with the theater." Like all Collier's
    antiquarian discoveries, this is tainted by the possibility of
    forgery.

2   FAIRHOLT, FREDRICK W., ed. <u>Lord Mayor's Pageants</u>. Percy
    Society, no. 10. London: T. Richards, pt. 1, p. 51.
         Cites, briefly, Webster's 1624 Lord Mayor's show, <u>Monuments</u>
    <u>of Honour</u>.

                              1844

1   HUNT, LEIGH. <u>Imagination and Fancy</u>. London: Smith & Elder,
    p. 197.
         Includes selections from Webster, with critical notes, in
    the essay "What is Poetry?" Webster, with Dekker, is among the
    greatest of "Shakespeare's men," but he often overdoes his terror.

                              1847

1   S., L. "Notes on Old Plays by Bale, Marston, and Shakespeare."
    <u>Shakespeare Society Papers</u> 3:84-86.
         Includes a brief note on the induction to <u>The Malcontent</u>.

                              1848

1   TIECK, JOHAN LUDWIG. <u>Kritische Schriften</u>. Vol. 1. Leipzig:
    Brodhaus, p. 303.
         Comments very briefly on <u>The Thracian Wonder</u> in an essay on
    "the old theater." Tieck wrote a romantic novel about Vittoria
    Accorombona (1840), feeling that Webster had presented her un-
    fairly.

1849

1   SHAW, THOMAS B. Outlines of English Literature. London: J.
    Murray, pp. 137-38.
        Presents Webster as the most powerful and original of the
    dramatists "of the second order." His terrible and funereal muse
    was death, and the weakness and futility of human hopes was his
    theme. The Duchess of Malfi is his most celebrated work. Thinks
    mistakenly that "we possess Guise, or the Massacre of France,"
    that Webster employed "revolting" Italian action, and that he
    mangled prose and verse. This work went through several editions
    and titles, e.g., A Complete Manual of English Literature.

1850

1   "Horne's The Duchess of Malfi." Atheneaum, 7 December, pp.
    1272-73.
        Finds that in language and construction, Horne's version is
    close to the original. He has performed a questionable task with
    unquestioned skill. It is hard to tell the two writers' work
    apart. (See 1850.2 for a review of the theatrical production and
    Horne's adaptation; 1851.3 for the adaptation itself.)

2   "Horne's Version of The Duchess of Malfi at Sadler's Wells."
    Athenaeum, 23 November, pp. 1225-26.
        Concludes that Webster's drama, "though written evidently
    in a religious spirit, lacks that free humanity which looks so
    beautiful in Shakespeare." Webster is a gloomy believer in man's
    depravity, who creates in his works "the fetid atmosphere of the
    charnel." Although Horne's adaptation (1851.3) is done with tact,
    no pains can save the original from its clumsy structure. Webster
    is wholly unfitted for the modern stage.

1851

1   CHASLES, PHILARETE. Etudes sur W. Shakespeare, Marie Stuart,
    et l'Arétin. Paris: Amyot, pp. 106-30.
        Presents the irregular and remarkable Webster as an important
    predecessor of Shakespeare. The gorgon is his muse. Briefly dis-
    cusses The White Devil (a famous Protestant work of passion and
    popularity) and translates portions into French.

2   [DANIEL, GEORGE.] Preface to "The Duchess of Malfi":
    Reconstructed for Stage Representation. Adapted by R.H. Horne.
    London: Davidson, pp. i-ix.
        Asserts that the play's original moral is fine and has been
    preserved, but the "dross" has been expurged by Horne.

3   HORNE, R.H. "The Duchess of Malfi": Reconstructed for Stage
    Representation. London: Davidson, 59 pp.
        Adapts and moderately revises the tragedy. Argues, in prefa-
    tory material, that Webster's play excels in pity and terror but
    is ill-constructed and full of discrepancies. The adapter's task,
    therefore, was to rebuild the play, keeping its great scenes in-
    tact. Reviewed: 1850.1-2.

4   MILLS, ABRAHAM. The Literature and Literary Men of Great
    Britain and Ireland. Vol. 1. London: A. Low, pp. 344-48.
        Includes Webster in the fifteenth of a series of lectures.
    The White Devil and The Duchess of Malfi have divided the critics
    regarding their merits. Finds both powerful but overfilled with
    horrors.

                              1853

1   WHIPPLE, EDWIN PERCY. "Old English Dramatists." In Essays and
    Reviews. Vol. 2. Boston: Osgood, pp. 42-47.
        Presents The Duchess of Malfi and The White Devil as among
    the grandest productions of Shakespeare's contemporaries. Webster
    gazes steadily into the depths and emphasizes the element of death.

                              1854

1   WALKER, W.S. Shakespeare's Versification. London: J.R. Smith,
    296 pp., passim.
        Cites Webster to illustrate Elizabethan usage.

                              1856

1   [KINGSLEY, CHARLES.] "Plays and Puritans." North British
    Review 25 (May):1-25. [Reprinted in his Miscellanies, vol. 2
    (London: J. Parker, 1859), pp. 77-142; included in his Plays
    and Puritans (London: Macmillan, 1873). Excerpted: 1969.17;
    1975.18.]
        Maintains that the arts had been declining during the middle
    of the seventeenth century, and objections had been raised to them
    by non-Puritans, especially in the realm of the drama. Finds The
    White Devil all sin and horror, and with no development of the hu-
    man soul. The Duchess of Malfi is a better play but was written
    mostly for effect.

                              1857

1   HAZLITT, WILLAIM CAREW, ed. The Dramatic Works of John Webster.
    4 vols. London: J.R. Smith, 23+290, 282, 270, 305 pp.
        This edition, which supersedes Dyce (1830.2), contains all

Webster's acknowledged works as well as most of the conjectural
plays. In the introduction offers a brief biography of Webster,
focusing upon what his other occupation might have been (merchant-
taylor? teacher?), and briefly surveys his writings. Quotes ex-
tensively from Lamb's appreciations (1808.1) of The White Devil
and praises the nobility of The Duchess of Malfi.

1859

1   DYCE, ALEXANDER. Strictures on Mr. Collier's New Edition of
     Shakespeare, 1858. London: J.R. Smith, pp. 13, 16.
         In a response to Collier's attack on Dyce (1836.1), discusses
disagreements regarding The White Devil and emendations of Appius
and Virginia.

1860

1   HALLIWELL-PHILLIPPS, JAMES O. A Dictionary of Old English Plays,
     Existing either in Print or in Manuscript. London: J.R. Smith,
     296 pp., passim.
         Lists title page data, locations and availability and the
like for a multitude of Renaissance plays, including twenty cita-
tions of Webster's works. See 1889.3.

1863

1   EASY, BENJAMIN. "Shakespeare, Webster, and R. Perkins." Notes
     and Queries 28:366-67.
         Suggests that Richard Perkins acted the part of Flamineo in
the original production.

2   MEZIERES, A. Contemporains et successeurs de Shakespeare.
     Paris: Charpentier, pp. 236-75.
         Depicts Webster as a powerful, violent, and somber dramatist
whose taste runs towards dramatic and bloody effects. Finds
Flamineo, Bosola, and other characters skeptics and cynics. Trans-
lates numerous passages into French.

1864

1   TAINE, H. Histoire de la littérature anglaise. Vol. 2. Paris:
     Hachette, pp. 57-74. [Translated with less Webster material,
     by H. Van Laun, 4 vols. (London: Chatto & Windus, 1890). Re-
     print. New York: Colonial Press, 1960.]
         Pictures Webster as a somber man, whose thoughts live in
sepulchers and charnels. Recounts the story of The Duchess of
Malfi with extensive quotation. It is a play of extreme and

terrible actions. Finds The White Devil, which is also outlined and specimens presented, a deep exploration of diabolic nature.

2   TURNER, CHARLES EDWARD. Our Great Writers. Vol. 1. St.
    Petersburg: A. Munx, pp. 297-98.
        Find the plays unsurpassed for horror and gloom. Vittoria's hypocritical assumption of innocence makes her "one of the most unpleasing portraits a dramatist has ever sketched." But detached passages are of considerable beauty, as noted by Lamb.

1865

1   "The English Drama during the Reigns of Elizabeth and James."
    Cornhill Magazine 2:604-18, 706-16.
        Sees the Elizabethan-Jacobean drama as reflecting the transition out of the medieval period. Webster presents the exuberance and passion of the times in Italianate villains such as Flamineo and Bosola. Vittoria, too, has a death-defying energy.

1869

1   ROYER, ALPHONSE. Histoire universelle du théâtre. Vol. 2.
    Paris: A. Franck, pp. 496-503.
        Notes that Webster began his career as a collaborator. His later works have some relationship to those of Kyd and Marlowe in their violence, but are superior in their presentation of love and horror.

2   WHIPPLE, EDWIN PERCY. The Literature of the Age of Elizabeth.
    Boston: Fields, Osgood, pp. 119-56.
        Presents Webster as an "artist in agony" who accumulates horror on top of horror. Includes some long selections from The Duchess of Malfi. The White Devil shows "the satanic energy of purpose which may spring from the ruins of the moral will." Webster traces the moral confusion of the lovers in The White Devil with honesty and clarity. He is the most Shakespearean of Shakespeare's contemporaries.

1871

1   ALLIBONE, S.A. A Critical Dictionary of English Literature.
    Vol. 3. Philadelphia: Lippincott, pp. 2615-26.
        Includes the critical opinions of Dyce, Hazlitt, Hallam, and others, and describes Webster as "one of the greatest of the English Dramatists."

1873

1   NICHOLSON, BRINSLEY. "On the Dates of A Chaste Maid in
    Cheapside, Northward Ho, and The Northern Lass." Notes and
    Queries 47:317-19.
        Argues that a topical allusion in Northward Ho indicates a
    date for the play of 1601-4. For a response, see 1873.2.

2   STEPHENS, F.G. "On the Dates of A Chaste Maid, etc." Notes
    and Queries 47:386.
        A response to 1873.1. The play's depth of anti-Spanish
    feelings suggests a date around 1620.

1874

1   GOSSE, EDMUND. "John Webster." Fraser's Magazine 9:620-34.
    [Reprinted in his Seventeenth-Century Studies (London and New
    York: Dodd, Mead, 1883), pp. 47-80.]
        After a brief biographical sketch, remarks that there are
    but four dramas solely Webster's, yet he ranks just after Jonson,
    who comes after Shakespeare. Reacts to the individual works: in
    The White Devil, Vittoria has grace and subtlety, implacable warm
    passions, wit and duplicity. The theme of The Duchess of Malfi is
    that nobility of character is revealed when one is forced to act
    and suffer alone. The Devil's Law Case is an extremely faulty
    production, with beautiful lines and a stupid plot. Appius and
    Virginia is his most popular effort. It is classical--and cold.
    A Cure for a Cuckold can be divided into Webster and Rowley scenes,
    which can be assigned "without a shadow of a doubt."

2   MINTO, WILLIAM. Characteristics of English Poets. London:
    William Blackwood, pp. 462-66.
        Discusses Webster in chapter 8, "Shakespeare's Contemporaries
    and Successors." Webster is strikingly different than his jolly
    collaborator Dekker. Finds among his characteristics a penetrating
    grasp of character, well-constructed scenes, and a judicious han-
    dling of terrible situations. His plots, save in Appius and
    Virginia, are winding, yet the plays are stage-worthy. Webster's
    strength lies in scenes of darkness in which characters are moved
    by grand passions and illuminated in "a sudden flash."

1875

1   WARD, ADOLPHUS WILLIAM. A History of English Dramatic Literature
    to the Death of Queen Anne. Vol. 2. London: Macmillan, pp.
    249-62. [Rev. ed. 1899.]
        Sees Webster as a genius of commanding originality, though
    not very versatile. Surveys his career and early collaborative
    efforts. The White Devil is a most remarkable work, although not

Webster's best. A highly elaborated, but ill-proportioned play,
its chief flaw is that all the main characters inspire a "sicken-
ing combination of awe and loathing." The Duchess of Malfi is
more mature and is a moving experience in the theater; The Devil's
Law Case is a romantic comedy; Appius and Virginia is uneven, but
powerful. Finds Webster's general characteristics include theatrical power and an insight into human nature. He has fine poetic
feeling and humor, but little moral purpose is at work in his
plays.

1878

1   PATER, WALTER. Appreciations. London and New York: Macmillan,
    p. 110.
        Cites Lamb as "the best critic, almost the discoverer of
    Webster, a dramatist of genius so sombre, so heavily coloured, so
    macabre."

1879

*1   KELTIE, JOHN S. The Works of the British Dramatists. Edinburgh:
    W.P. Nimmo, pp. 316-45.
        Source: Mahaney, 1973.23.

*2   NICHOLSON, BRINSLEY. "The Insatiate Countess: The White Devil."
    Notes and Queries 61:222; 63 (1881):106.
        Source: Mahaney, 1973.23.

1882

*1   BALDWIN, JAMES. An Introduction to the Study of English
    Literature and Literary Criticism. Vol. 1. Philadelphia:
    J.E. Potter, p. 238.
        Source: Mahaney, 1973.23.

2   PAGET, VIOLET [Vernon Lee]. "The Italy of the Elizabethan
    Dramatists." British Quarterly Review 75:295-323. [Reprinted
    in her Euphorion, vol. 1 (Boston: Roberts, 1884), pp. 57-108.]
        Argues the crimes of Italy fascinated Elizabethan Englishmen
    and furnished the subjects of a good half of the tragedies of the
    era of James I, among them The White Devil. Finds Webster reacted
    to Italian horror with "ineffable sadness, unmarred by cynicism,
    but unbrightened by hope." His villains and heroes alike are
    doomed, in a world with no justice and no Christianity. He has
    sympathy for oppressed virtue, but that sympathy does not lead to
    hope. There is some truth to Webster and his fellows' image of
    Renaissance Italy.

3   WELSH, ALFRED H. The Development of English Literature and
    Language. Vol. 1. Chicago: S.C. Griggs, pp. 422-25.
        Sees Webster as a specialist in depicting agony and the most
    Shakespearean of the later dramatists. Outlines the plots of both
    tragedies, and gives extensive quotations from each.

1883

1   PHIPSON, EMMA. The Animal Lore of Shakespeare's Time. London:
    Kegan Paul, 476 pp., passim.
        An encyclopedic treatment, arranged by animal and topic.
    Cites Webster (along with a vast array of other dramatists and
    authors) for his use of these motifs--but with no analysis. As
    an example, quotes Flamineo's story in The White Devil in the sec-
    tion on crocodiles.

2   SYMONDS, JOHN ADDINGTON. Italian Byways. London: Smith,
    Elder, pp. 155-93. [Also published in his Sketches and Studies
    in Italy and Greece, vol. 2 (London: Smith, Elder, 1898), pp.
    89-125.]
        Tells the historical tale of Vittoria, based on Henri Beyle's
    Chroniques et novelles, and recounts briefly other versions. Sum-
    marizes the alterations made by Webster, e.g., changes in the
    characters of Camillo, Lodovico, Flamineo and Vittoria. Finds
    Webster's plays dense and difficult, revealing the gloom of a
    sixteenth-century spirit. Webster brooded upon horrors, and hence
    was naturally drawn to the lurid crimes of Renaissance Italy. He
    added a northern intellectual knowledge of sin to southern villainy,
    so his characters know their own guilt. Webster's plays are less
    true to the historical Italy of his time than to the impression
    made by that area on a northern imagination.

1884

1   FLEAY, F.G. "John Webster: Annals of His Career."
    Shakespeariana 1, no. 10 (August):248-50.
        Chronicles Webster's career in order to show him the con-
    temporary of Shakespeare rather than his successor (as Dyce be-
    lieves). Thus, dates Appius and Virginia 1607, The White Devil
    1608, The Devil's Law Case 1609-10, and The Duchess of Malfi 1612.

2   "Her Grace, The Duchess." Theater 4 (September):131-44.
        Finds the Duchess a noble and admirable character. The woo-
    ing scene between her and Antonio is especially fine. Defends the
    final scenes of The Duchess of Malfi as showing the Elizabethan
    concern with "consequences."

3   MASKELL, J. "Allusions in Webster's White Devil." Notes and
    Queries 69:108.

Two brief queries regarding allusions to gallows in the Low
Countries and servants carrying glasses.

4   SYMONDS, JOHN ADDINGTON. Shakspere's Predecessors in the English
     Drama. London: Smith, Elder, pp. 387-98. [Reprint. 1900.]
        Includes Webster in the discussion of the "Tragedy of Blood."
     He, along with Marston and Tourneur, utilized Kyd's conventions--
     ghosts, court villains, assassins, lustful princes, etc.

                              1885

1   LEE, SIDNEY. "John Webster." In Dictionary of National
     Biography. Edited by Leslie Stephen. Vol. 55. London: Smith,
     Elder, pp. 120-25. [Reprint. London: Oxford University Press,
     1921.]
        Begins by stressing Webster's close relationships with other
     dramatists, especially his enduring alliance with Dekker, but notes
     that his genius found full expression only when freed from partner-
     ship, with The White Devil. Finds Appius and Virginia a less not-
     able piece, but of substantial merit. Webster regained the highest
     level of his tragic art in The Duchess of Malfi. Notes the sources
     of that play and Lamb's enthusiastic comments. Discusses doubtful
     attributions and lost plays. Concludes with some general observa-
     tions: Webster is a disciple of Shakespeare and approaches him
     more nearly than do any of his fellows, but at times discipleship
     comes close to plagiarism. He lacks Shakespeare's sureness of
     touch in characterization, and he concentrates his chief energies
     on repulsive themes and characters. Yet he had a true artistic
     sense and a high poetic spirit.

2   SPRING-RICE, S.E. Love's Graduate. Oxford: H. Daniel, 69 pp.
        A version of A Cure for a Cuckold that eliminates the
     "Compass" portions, presumably by Rowley.

                              1886

1   FLEAY, F.G. "On the Chronology of the Plays of Fletcher and
     Massinger." Englische Studien 9:12-35.
        Attempts to date (within two years) fifty-five Fletcher and
     forty-two Massinger plays. No metrical tests are used. Discusses
     A Cure for a Cuckold, The Thracian Wonder, The Fair Maid of the
     Inn and The Honest Man's Fortune.

2   FURNIVALL, F.J. Some 300 Fresh Allusions to Shakespeare: From
     1594-1694. New Shakspere Society Publications, 4th ser., no.
     3. London: New Shakspere Society, 372 pp., passim. [Reissued
     1909, 1932, 1970. The 1932 edition is retitled The Shakespeare
     Allusion-Book with a preface by E.K. Chambers.]
        Includes a number of Webster passages, especially from The

White Devil and The Duchess of Malfi, which imitate Shakespeare
and echo specific Shakespearean lines.

3   SWINBURNE, ALGERNON CHARLES. "John Webster." Nineteenth
    Century 19 (June):861-81. [Reprints. Eclectic Magazine 108
    (1886):226-40; Littell's Living Age 170 (July 1886):67-79;
    and in his The Age of Shakespeare (New York and London: Harper,
    1908), pp. 15-59. Excerpted: 1969.18; 1975.17.]
        An enthusiastic survey that ranks Webster just next to
    Shakespeare: like Shakespeare, he makes his characters say what
    they must have said. His characters have a streak of heroism that
    preserves them from hatefulness. Comments on The Devil's Law Case
    (a weak plot, but some nice verse) and Appius and Virginia (a far
    more workmanlike effort). In the two great tragedies fate seems
    the subject of chance: the heroes die "in a mist," but they are
    indomitable figures. Finds that Webster's special features in-
    clude a command of terror and the creation of nobility of spirit
    in his characters.

4   _____. "Thomas Middleton." Nineteenth Century 19 (January):
    138-53. [Reprinted in The Age of Shakespeare (New York and
    London: Harper, 1908), pp. 150-86.]
        Compares the "perfect and living figure of De Flores" to
    Webster's characters and notes that Anything for a Quiet Life in-
    cludes "good stuff in the plot" but weak workmanship.

                            1887

1   RUSHTON, WILLIAM LOWES. Shakespeare an Archer. Liverpool:
    Lee & Nightengale, 118 pp., passim.
        In an examination of Shakespeare's use of archery language
    and imagery, cites Webster occasionally, e.g., Vittoria says "I
    am at the mark, sir: I'll give aim to you, and tell you how near
    you shoot."

2   SAINTSBURY, GEORGE. A History of Elizabethan Literature.
    London: Macmillan, pp. 273-79.
        Classifies Webster with several other dramatists as belong-
    ing to a period not yet decadent, still creative, but with a new
    flavor. Finds Appius and Virginia a classic work, but by a romantic
    author; The Devil's Law Case "hopelessly undigested"; The White
    Devil the best of the tragedies--a picture of female vice contrasted
    with The Duchess of Malfi's view of female virtue.

                            1888

1   ARNOLD, THOMAS. A Manual of English Literature, Historical and
    Critical. London: Longmans, p. 231.
        Presents Webster as "the author of a famous tragedy called

The Duchess of Malfi" as well as seven other plays, and offers a synopsis of The Duchess of Malfi.

2   MARSTON, WESTLAND. Our Recent Actors. Vol. 1. Boston: Roberts, pp. 124-26.
    Discusses Sheridan Knowles in a collection of biographies and sketches of famous actors, and includes praise for his version of Appius and Virginia.

3   Review of Webster and Tourneur, by John Addington Symonds. Spectator, 1 December, pp. 1681-82.
    An appreciative reaction to Symonds's introduction (1888.5), which ranks Webster ahead of Tourneur. The former is a better poet, displaying a saner philosophy, but Tourneur is powerful and bitter. Notes the nobility of Webster's thought, his command of terror and pity, his somber and powerful imagination and the picture he presents of the triumph of heroic souls over physical humiliation and torture.

4   SWINBURNE, ALGERNON CHARLES. "John Webster." In The Encyclopedia Britannica. Vol. 24. Edinburgh: A.C. Black, pp. 473-74. [Reprinted in his Studies in Prose and Poetry (London: Chatto & Windus, 1894), pp. 49-52.]
    Finds Webster "the greatest of Shakespeare's contemporaries or successors." Surveys his works, including the curious and vivacious induction to The Malcontent and the lively and humorous collaborations with Dekker. The White Devil established him as a poet and dramatist of the foremost rank. The Duchess of Malfi is "one of the imperishable and ineradicable landmarks of literature," offering sustained terror and pity, transcendent imagination and impassioned sympathy, thus making it the most tragic of tragedies save King Lear. The Devil's Law Case is ill-constructed, Appius and Virginia is competent, and A Cure for a Cuckold is a doubtful attribution.

5   SYMONDS, JOHN ADDINGTON, ed. Webster and Tourneur. London: Unwin, 432 pp. [Reprinted as Four Plays (New York: Hill & Wang, 1956). Introduction excerpted: 1969.17; 1975.18.]
    Symonds's introductions claims that Webster blends tenderness and pity with the exhibition of acute moral anguish. He is not strong in plot or character but is good with dramatic situations, particularly the struggle of the human soul to deal with sin and fate. The Duchess of Malfi and The White Devil are mosaics of luminous parts, but they lack breadth. Brief lightning flashes of self-revelation illuminate the midnight darkness of lost souls. Webster has a natural bias towards the dreadful, and he is often melodramatic, yet he shows a firm grasp of diseased and guilty human nature. While his style gives everything a sinister twist, he is morally noble.

*6   VOPEL, C. "John Webster. His Life and Dramas." Ph.D. disser-
      tation, University of Zurich. Bremen, 31 pp.
         Source: Mahaney, 1973.23.

                              1889

1   AITKEN, GEORGE A. "John Webster and Thomas Adams." Academy
      35:133-34.
         Discusses Thomas Adams, a seventeenth-century preacher, who
      called a sermon of 1613 "The White Devil," probably playing with
      the title of Webster's earlier play of the same name. The sermon
      deals with Judas Iscariot.

*2   GRIFFITHS, LEMULE M. Evenings with Shakespeare. Boston and
      London: Arrowsmith, 365 pp.
         Source: Mahaney, 1973.23.

3   HAZLITT, WILLIAM CAREW. "Bibliographical and Literary Notes
      on the Old English Drama." Antiquary 20:14-17, 61-63, 106-11,
      192-203, 256-59.
         Additions and corrections, touching upon matters Websterian,
      to Halliwell-Phillipps's Dictionary (1860.1).

                              1890

1   FLEAY, F.G. A Chronicle History of the London Stage, 1559-1642.
      London: Reeves & Turner, 424 pp., passim.
         Discusses the chronological evolution of the English
      Renaissance drama by periods (e.g., 1587-1593) with sections on:
      court performances, companies, theaters, authors, general stage
      history, intercalatory items, etc. Cites Webster appropriately
      throughout, e.g., in a list of Lord Mayor's shows, in lists of
      plays, under general stage history of 1603-14, etc. Includes no
      criticism, just lists, charts, and the like.

2   GOLDEN, WILLIAM ECHARD. A Brief History of the English Drama
      from the Earliest to the Latest Times. New York: Welch,
      Fracker, pp. 138-40.
         Finds Webster is a genius of surpassing and original--
      although not very versatile--talents. The Duchess of Malfi is
      his masterpiece. Its characteristics include accumulated murders,
      a love of the horrible, investigation of the terrible side of human
      nature, fine poetic feelings, strong situations, and the lack of a
      high moral purpose.

3   MITCHELL, DONALD GRANT. English Lands, Letters and Kings.
      Vol. 2. London: Low, Marston, Searle & Rivington, pp. 88-90.
         Contends Webster, Ford, and others "may be counted in liter-
      ary significance only as the trail to that grander figure which

                               25

swung so high in the Elizabethan heavens." Webster lost favor in
the eighteenth century until Lamb revived interest in him, Dyce
edited, and Swinburne praised his works. Webster is judged
"dolorous." He depicts blood-curdling scenes of crime with
"wondrous flashes of dramatic power" but with little brightness--
he even puts flowers to sad offices.

4   OLIPHANT, E.H.C. "The Works of Beaumont and Fletcher."
     Englische Studien 14:53-94; 15 (1891):321-60; 16 (1892):180-200.
        Discusses the attribution of the Beaumont and Fletcher canon
     (see his book on the same subject, 1927.14). Does not credit
     Webster with any part in any of the Beaumont and Fletcher plays,
     including The Fair Maid of the Inn, The Honest Man's Fortune, etc.

5   RUMBAUR, O. Geschichte von Appius and Virginia in der englischen
     Literatur. Ph.D. dissertation, University of Breslau. Breslau:
     Brehmer & Minuth, 48 pp.
        Surveys the story of Appius and Virginia from Livy and the
     Romance of the Rose through English versions beginning with Gower
     and Chaucer. Considers the drama by "R.B.", then Webster's play--
     its date, and exact sources. Discusses post-Renaissance versions
     including those of Dennis, Moncreiff, Brooke, and Knowles.

                              1891

1   FLEAY, F.G. A Biographical Chronicle of the English Drama,
     1559-1642. Vol. 2. London: Reeves & Turner, pp. 268-73.
     [Reprint. New York: B. Franklin, 1962.]
        Includes a list of Webster's plays and coproductions (in-
     cluding some rather dogmatic assertions about his share in col-
     laborations) within a series of alphabetically ordered biographies
     of playwrights. Assigns The Revenger's Tragedy to Webster on the
     basis of its likeness to The White Devil. See 1906.1 for discus-
     sion of Fleay's attribution of The Thracian Wonder.

2   "Meetings of Societies: Clifton Shakespeare Society." Academy
     39:328.
        Reports papers read by Mrs. C.I. Spencer, "A Criticism of
     The Duchess of Malfi," and Mr. John Taylor, "A Note on Mr.
     Swinburne's Statement of the Case 'Euripides v Webster.'"

                              1892

1   "Amalfi and The Duchess of Malfi." Theatre 20 (October):148-53.
        Suggests the place and the play are both "entirely mediaeval"
     --the drama gives dramatic shape to a triumphantly wicked time and
     place in its depiction of spies, assassins, and torturers, such as
     Bosola. Renaissance Italians did not see themselves as criminals,
     but Englishmen, such as Webster, did.

2   DILLON, ARTHUR. "The Duchess of Malfi--A Note." Library Review
     1 (October):519-21.
           Argues it would be difficult, but worthwhile, to adapt the
     extravagant and Marlovian The Duchess of Malfi for the modern stage,
     as Webster is both like and unlike Shakespeare. Many questions
     raised by the play are unanswered. Poel has prepared a new acting
     version.

3   KOEPPEL, EMIL. Studien zur Geschichte der italienischen Novelle
     in der englischen Litteratur des sechzehnten Jahrhunderts.
     Quellen und Forschungen, 70. Strasbourg: Karl J. Trübner,
     100 pp., passim.
           Includes a discussion of the relation between Bandello,
     Painter, and Webster regarding the story of The Duchess of Malfi.

4   LOWELL, JAMES RUSSELL. "Webster." Harper's Monthly Magazine
     85 (August):411-18.
           (First delivered as a lecture in 1887.) Finds Webster, un-
     like Shakespeare, not a master of "form," since his plots are
     miscellaneous and his characters motiveless. Further, he presents
     crime as a spectacle, not a means of self-examination. Sees The
     Devil's Law Case as particularly weak, although it contains some
     savage grandeur in speech and occasional humor, while Appius and
     Virginia is a "spirited, well-constructed play," as good as any
     non-Shakespearean Roman drama. The tragedies show Webster's fas-
     cination with crime. They are full of horrors, yet move the audi-
     ence also to pity.

5   "Meetings of Societies: Elizabethan Society." Academy 42:
     339-40.
           Reports a general, somewhat negative paper by William Poel,
     finding flaws in plot and composition, but single scenes of great
     and powerful passion, in both tragedies.

6   STEADMAN, EDMUND CLARENCE. The Nature and Elements of Poetry.
     Boston and New York: Houghton Mifflin, pp. 108, 249.
           Sees in The Duchess of Malfi the "triumphs and dangers of
     dramatic fury": construction runs riot; some characters are well
     conceived, others are not; language is "fantastic"; yet the tragedy,
     passion, and imagery are Shakespearean.

*7   SWINBURNE, ALGERNON CHARLES. Unpublished letter to William
     Poel, 27 October.
           Congratulates Poel for a fine production of The Duchess of
     Malfi. Source: Hunter and Hunter, 1969.17.

                                 1893

1   ARCHER, WILLIAM. "Webster, Lamb, and Swinburne." New Review
     8 (January):96-106. [Included in 1969.17; 1975.18.]

Attacks Lamb's overenthusiasm for the poetry of Elizabethan
drama at the expense of coherent dramatic structure. Webster's
violence and physical horrors in The Duchess of Malfi and The White
Devil cannot be excused solely on the basis of imagistic skill.
Sees these two plays as "loose-strung, go-as-you-please romances
in dialog." Webster is a great poet, who wrote haphazard dramatic
or melodramatic romances for an eagerly receptive but semibarbarous
public. See 1920.2, 1924.1 for later similar discussions.

2   BAHLSEN, LEO. "Spanische Quellen der dramatischen Litteratur,
     besonders Englands zu Shakespeares Zeit." Zeitschrift für
     Vergleichende Litteraturgeschichte, n.s. 6:151-59.
          Studies the Spanish influence on Elizabethan and Jacobean
     drama. Comments upon the relationship between Webster's The Duchess
     of Malfi and Lope de Vega's Mayordomo de la Duquesa de Almalfi.

3   CUNLIFFE, JOHN W. The Influence of Seneca on Elizabethan
     Tragedy. London: Macmillan, pp. 109-112. [Reprints. New
     York: G.E. Stechart, 1907. Hamden, Conn.: Archon Books,
     1965.]
          Describes Seneca's works and various English translations.
     The second half of the book lists authors, including a section on
     Webster and Tourneur, and their use of Senecan material.

4   MEINERS, MARTIN. Metrische Untersuchungen über den Dramatiker
     John Webster. Ph.D. dissertation, University of Halle. Halle:
     C. Colbatzky, 40 pp.
          Summarizes Webster's inflectional system, word choice, rhyme
     patterns (e.g., tables on the use of weak endings), and the like.

5   POEL, W. "A New Criticism of Webster's Duchess of Malfi."
     Library Review 2:21-24. [Excerpted: 1969.17; 1975.18.]
          Responds to Archer, 1893.1. Poetry can not be separated
     from drama. An understanding of the Elizabethan Italianate con-
     vention is necessary for understanding Webster. His characters
     are true to Italian "types," e.g., Bosola is a "familiar" who is
     also a humanist.

6   WATSON, WILLIAM. Excursions in Criticism. London and New York:
     Mathews & Lane, pp. 1-22.
          In chapter 1, "Some Literary Idolatries," describes
     Swinburne's, Lamb's, and Hazlitt's enthusiasm and praise of
     Webster's and Shakespeare's contemporaries. Webster's language
     is an echo of Shakespeare's, and his plays are filled with "filch-
     ings"; Webster has a morbid imagination and lacks Shakespeare's
     moral vision, offering only cynicism, disgust, and despair. Bosola
     in The Duchess of Malfi is "a kind of human gangrene, infecting the
     whole body of the play." Argues Shakespeare's contemporaries are
     not his coequals but foils to set off his superior talents.

1894

1   GOSSE, EDMUND. The Jacobean Poets. New York: Scribner's,
    pp. 164-73.
        Assigns Webster a major portion of the "Ho" plays. Describes
    The Duchess of Malfi as his masterpiece and the "finest tragedy in
    the English language outside the works of Shakespeare"--a great,
    irregular, and sublime poem for the study, not the stage. It is
    not dramatic, but Webster aimed at more than the entertainment of
    the groundlings; therefore, the movement of the whole is sacrificed
    to brilliant passages. Unlike Lamb and Swinburne, does not find
    the play's horrors valid. Sees The White Devil as much rougher,
    with Vittoria the play's only fully developed feature. Presents
    Appius and Virginia as the best constructed of Webster's plays,
    but The Devil's Law Case is several steps backwards--incoherent,
    but with many verbal felicities. Concludes Webster was more a
    romantic poet than a dramatist.

1895

1   CARPENTER, FREDRIC IVES. Metaphor and Simile in the Minor
    Elizabethan Drama. Chicago: University of Chicago Press, pp.
    73-94. [Reprint. New York: Phaeton Press, 1967.]
        Describes Webster as a powerful and careful craftsman of
    language. His characteristic form is the short, blazing simile,
    often with classical sources dwelling on moral subjects. Also
    notes Webster's use of the sententious couplet, proverbs, and per-
    sonifications. A catalog of his images includes material from
    nature, human life (e.g., the body and its parts, sports and
    amusements), and the like.

2   CORBIN, JOHN. The Elizabethan "Hamlet": A Study of the Sources
    and of Shakespeare's Environment, to Show that the Mad Scenes
    Had a Comic Aspect, Now Ignored. London: E. Mathews, pp. 58-62.
        Finds that The Duchess of Malfi includes, in its madmen,
    gruesome comedy designed to amuse its audience and to provide a
    laughing spell to relieve the tragic tension.

3   FLETCHER, ROBERT. "Medical Lore in the Older English Dramatists
    and Poets (Exclusive of Shakespeare)." Bulletin of the Johns
    Hopkins Hospital 6:73-84.
        Considers the general medical conditions of the Elizabethan
    period and the low estimation in which doctors were held. The
    works of the period including Webster's are filled with references
    to venereal disease and to miscellaneous curiosities of therapeu-
    tics.

4   KIESOW, KARL G. "Die verschiedenen Bearbeitungen der Novelle
    von der Herzogin von Amalfi des Bandello in den Literaturen des
    XVI. und XVII. Jahrhunderts." Anglia 17:199-258.

Discusses Webster's use of Painter's <u>Palace of Pleasure</u> as a source in <u>The Duchess of Malfi</u>.

5   SCOTT, MARY AUGUSTA. "Elizabethan Translations from the Italian." <u>PMLA</u> 10:249-93. [Included in 1916.7.]
      Cites some of Webster's Italian source materials.

6   SWINBURNE, ALGERNON CHARLES. "John Webster." <u>Bibelot</u> 1:171. [Reprinted in <u>The Poems of Algernon Charles Swinburne</u>, vol. 5 (New York: T.Y. Crowell Co.), p. 307.]
      An impressionistic sonnet: "Earth cries out from all her graves . . . / Shapes here and there of child and mother pass." Quoted in 1969.17.

1896

1   BATES, KATHERINE L., and GODFREY, LYDIA B. <u>English Drama: A Working Basis</u>. Boston: Wellesley College Press, pp. 90-91.
      Includes basic bibliographical data on collections of old plays, authors, individual plays, and other references for pre-Elizabethan through nineteenth-century drama.

2   DEIGHTON, KENNETH. <u>The Old Dramatists: Conjectural Readings</u>. Westminster: A. Constable, pp. 196-203.
      Suggests emendations for <u>The White Devil</u>, <u>The Devil's Law Case</u>, <u>Appius and Virginia</u>, <u>Sir Thomas Wyat</u> and the "Ho" plays.

*3   KING, F.G. "John Webster." <u>Columbia Literary Monthly</u> 5 (November):56-69.
      Source: Mahaney, 1973.23.

4   LEWES, G.H. <u>Dramatic Essays</u>. Edited by William Archer and Robert Lowe. London: Scott, pp. 118-22.
      Argues that anyone with more than second-hand familiarity with old dramatists knows their plays to be poor in artistic and theatrical construction--poor characterization, violent plots, and the like. Affirms that a regard for Lamb and Hazlitt led to the misapprehension that old English drama was worthy of study. These plays are actually dreary and foolish. <u>The Duchess of Malfi</u> as produced by Horne has its absurdities lessened, but it is still poor, ludicrous and wearisome, feeble and foolish. Webster holds a mirror up to Madame Tussaud, not to nature, and his play is a nightmare, not a tragedy. Horne is a better dramatist than Webster.

5   SEAGER, HERBERT WEST. <u>Natural History in Shakespeare's Time</u>. London: E. Stock. 358 pp. [Reprint. New York: AMS Press, 1971.]
      An encyclopedically organized listing and explanation of the "quaint theories about natural history accepted by Shakespeare and his contemporaries." Cites Webster, for example, under "Hare": "Like your melancholy Hare, feed after midnight."

<u>1897</u>

1   BROOKE, STOPFORD A. <u>English Literature</u>. New York: Macmillan,
    p. 146.
        Feels that Webster's genius was not well served by the plot
    conventions that governed his works. Yet his works are redeemed
    by intensity of imagination and a power to sound the depths of
    the human heart. His worst characters have some redeeming touch,
    and this poetic pity brings him nearer to Shakespeare than his
    contemporaries.

*2 EDWARDS, WALTER S. "The Dumbshow in Elizabethan Drama." Ph.D.
    dissertation, Columbia University.
        Source: Mahaney, 1973.23.

3   MEYER, EDWARD. <u>Machiavelli and the Elizabethan Drama</u>. Ph.D.
    dissertation, University of Heidelberg. Litterarhistorische
    Forschungen, no. 1. Weimar: E. Felber, 180 pp., passim.
        Notes Webster calls Florence a Machiavellian in <u>The White
    Devil</u> and seems to refer to <u>Il Principe</u>, since Francisco uses
    Machiavellian maxims and Brachiano "has much of the Florentine in
    him."

4   SMITH, HOMER. "Pastoral Influence in the English Drama."
    <u>PMLA</u> 12, no. 3:355-460.
        Considers the nature of the pastoral and the sources of
    English pastoral drama. English plays affected but not dominated
    by the pastoral mode include <u>The Thracian Wonder</u>, in which pastoral
    elements are subordinated.

5   SWITHIN, STEPHEN. "Pearles in <u>The Duchess of Malfi</u>." <u>Notes
    and Queries</u> 95 (20 February):146.
        Proposes that the Duchess' dream of pearls may have been
    suggested by the story that Mary, Queen of the Medicis, dreamed
    of pearls before the assassination of Henry IV of France in 1610.

<u>1898</u>

1   SHIPMAN, ADA A. "The Duchess of Malfi." <u>American Shakespeare
    Magazine</u> 4:44-46.
        Believes Webster's true field is tragedy: he studied
    Shakespeare closely and blended tragedy with pathos, pity with
    terror in a way that has never been surpassed. At the beginning
    of the play, sees the Duchess as a "wanton widow" and Antonio a
    "presumptuous upstart," but finds the audience condones "her many
    sins" due to the gracious constancy of her love. Concurrently the
    brothers move from champions of family honor to vulgar assassins.
    Bosola is "one of the most subtle and profound creations" of the
    English drama.

2   WURZBACH, WOLFGANG VON. "John Webster." Shakespeare-Jahrbuch
     34:9-51.
         Surveys at length the relationship between the dramatist and
the author of Academiarum Examen. Discusses Webster's plays indi-
vidually, with an emphasis on attribution problems.

                                1899

1   COOK, GRACE L. "English Tragedy in the Reign of King James I."
     Wellesley Magazine 8 (February):233-43.
         Argues that Jacobean tragedy features intense poetry and
thematic deformation. It avoids nobility and tends to overempha-
size plot at the expense of character. The Duchess of Malfi is
one of the few plays that show someone resisting evil. Favorably
compares it to The Revenger's Tragedy and Fletcher's Bonduca.

2   LAUSCHKE, JOHANNES. John Websters Tragödie "Appius and
     Virginia." Eine Quellenstudie. Ph.D. dissertation, University
     of Leipzig. Potsdam: R. Müller, 64 pp.
         Traces Webster's sources and borrowings in Appius and Virginia,
with special reference to his use of Painter.

3   McLAUGHLIN, TOMPKINS. "A So-Called Pessimist of the Old Drama:
     John Webster." New Englander and Yale Review 51:175-88.
         Notes Webster is usually associated with powerful expression,
incomparable gloom, and a few strong characterizations. But there
are quiet touches of Christian morality and love in the plays, de-
nouncing pride and ambition and pleading for honesty. Thus, family
pride destroys an admirable marriage in The Duchess of Malfi.
Webster also creates characters of piety and virtue (Cornelia,
Isabella, and Giovanni). His imagery also suggests his love of
birds. The death of Bosola demonstrates that Webster believes in
an afterlife of both reward and punishment, while the death of the
Duchess is one of Christian affirmation.

4   SIMPSON, PERCY. "Perseus as 'Masculine Virtue' in The White
     Devil." Notes and Queries 100 (October):286.
         Argues that the source of Vittoria's line regarding Perseus
as masculine virtue is Jonson's Masque of Queens, 1609.

5   SMALL, ROSCOE ADDISON. The Stage Quarrel between Ben Jonson
     and the So-Called Poetasters. Forschungen zur Englischen
     Sprache und Litteratur, vol. 1. Breslau: M. & H. Marcus, p.
     56.
         Demonstrates how Northward Ho satirizes Chapman, but suggests
the play is too late to be related to the quarrel between Jonson
and the poetasters. (Originally a Harvard dissertation, 1897.)

6   SWINBURNE, ALGERNON CHARLES. "Prologue to The Duchess of Malfi."
     Nineteenth Century 45 (January):90-91.

A panegyric, e.g.: "Half Shakespeare's glory, when his hand sublime / Bade all the change of tragic life and time / Live, and outlive all date of quick and dead / Fell, rested, and shall rest on Webster's head."

1900

1   GREG, W.W. A List of English Plays Written before 1643 and Printed before 1700. London: Bibliographical Society, pp. 34, 117-19.
        Lists editions with title page data.

2   _____. "Webster's White Devil: An Essay in Formal Criticism." Modern Language Quarterly 3 (December):112-25.
        Compares possible (Italian) documentary sources to demonstrate that when Webster altered history he did so as a conscious artistic choice. The play's division into acts and scenes is arbitrary, not Webster's, and not good. There is, though, a pattern of alteration between inner stage and outer stage, leading to the climax of the play in the scene in the house of convertites.

1901

1   BYRON, GEORGE GORDON, Lord. Letter to John Murray. In The Works of Lord Byron. Edited by R.E. Prothero. Vol. 5. London: Murray, p. 47.
        Byron affirms, in this letter written 6 July 1820, that he left England "for one woman": Vittoria Carambona (sic) or the white devil.

2   HAMILTON, CLAYTON M. "The Duchess of Malfi Considered as a Tragedy of Blood." Sewanee Review 9 (October):410-34.
        Argues that The White Devil is more poetic and refined than earlier examples of the tragedy of blood, but the play's structure is weak. The Duchess of Malfi is the greatest work in this genre. Bosola rises above the hired rogue role; Antonio is morally noble and the Brothers are twin Machiavellians, subtly differentiated. Finds the torment of the Duchess the greatest single act in an English play except for Othello, 3. It consists of psychological, not physical, torture. Sees Webster as, in general, careful, scholarly, neither falsely modest nor very versatile. His sympathy overcomes pessimism, and his lyricism overcomes his gloom. Webster carried the tragedy of blood to its ultimate perfection.

*3   PATRICK DAVID, ed. Chamber's Cyclopaedia of English Literature. Vol. 1. London: Chambers, pp. 426-29. Rev. ed. 1938.
        Notes that Webster's life is obscure, and he achieved little success until Lamb. Yet his tragedies are nearest to Shakespeare's. He had great penetration into the troubled sources of human emotion

and showed the pursuit of moral beauty in works of crime and horror.
Quotes from The White Devil and The Duchess of Malfi at length.
(The 1901 edition is not available: this annotation is based upon
the 1938 revision.)

4   SCOTT, Sir WALTER. Letter to Alexander Dyce, 31 March 1831.
     In Memoirs of the Life of Sir Walter Scott. Edited by John G.
     Lockhart. Vol. 9. Boston: Houghton Mifflin, p. 41.
     Calls Webster "one of the best of our ancient dramatists."

5   WENDELL, BARRETT. William Shakespeare. New York: Scribner's,
     pp. 407-11.
         Cites The White Devil as an example of the "crushing sense
     of limitations" that led to the degeneration of the Jacobean drama
     and an illustration of what the stage was like after Shakespeare;
     it is a morbidly horrible story, studiously realistic.

                                   1902

1   BALLMANN, OTTO. "Chaucers Einfluss auf das englische Drama im
     Zeitalter der Königin Elisabeth und der beiden ersten Stuart-
     Könige." Anglia 25:1-85.
         Studies Chaucer's influence on Renaissance drama with a brief
     section on Webster. Finds a few verbal parallels in Monuments of
     Honour and The White Devil, and notes Appius and Virginia's obvious
     use of "The Physician's Tale."

2   LANDAU, MARCUS. "Vittoria Accoramboni in der Dichtung im
     Verhältnis zu iher wahren Geshichte." Euphorion 9:310-16.
         Compares the historical facts regarding Vittoria with
     Webster's version.

*3   MOODY, WILLIAM VAUGHN, and LOVETT, R.M. A History of English
     Literature. New York: Scribner's. [Several eds., through
     1956. 7th ed., F.B. Millet, pp. 153-54.]
         Depicts Webster as a great poet, devoting himself to melo-
     drama of the most gory and unrestrained description. He created
     the tragedy of blood in its most developed form. But, while his
     subject matter appalls modern taste, his characters and poetry
     keep his fame intact. (The earliest edition available is the
     seventh, here annotated.)

4   MORRIS, J.E. "John Webster." Fortnightly Review 77:1065-78.
         Notes that Webster inspired a wide range of critical estima-
     tion, and that he was probably the best of Shakespeare's contempo-
     raries. He had a somber, morbid tendency of mind and a habit of
     protesting the unearned claims of the highly born. Webster's hor-
     rors are powerful and strip life of its amenities with a lurid
     brilliance. Analyzes The White Devil, 2.1, to show Webster's
     conscious art.

5   SCHELLING, FELIX E. The English Chronicle Play: A Study in
    the Popular Historical Literature Environing Shakespeare. New
    York: Macmillan, pp. 228-31.
        Discusses Sir Thomas Wyat as a collaboration between Dekker
    and Webster, and finds it a coherent piece, not too badly mangled,
    but singularly colorless in its political and religious allusions.
    Remarks that the subject--toppling a legitimate monarch--is a
    "delicate" one. The story of Lady Jane and her lover/husband is
    touching, but the work is below the best efforts of either of its
    authors.

6   SIMONDS, WILLIAM E. A Student's History of English Literature.
    Boston: Houghton Mifflin, p. 151.
        Describes Webster with other "lesser dramatists": "they
    were all university men, strong intellectually and in artistic
    power, but the over-topping genius of Shakespeare is never so
    conspicuous as when his works are placed in contrast to theirs."

7   THORNDIKE, ASHLEY H. "The Relation of Hamlet to Contemporary
    Revenge Plays." PMLA 17, no. 2:125-220.
        In a discussion of the additions to The Spanish Tragedy,
    notes that Webster developed the figure of the accomplice villain
    in his plays "notably."

1903

1   HOBBINS, J.H. "Some Women of the Early Dramatists." Papers
    of the Manchester Literary Club 29:93-101.
        Compares Vittoria to Tamyra in Chapman's Bussy d'Ambois:
    both are faithless, but Vittoria is a better drawn character who
    evokes our sympathy in spite of her sins. The Duchess in The
    Duchess of Malfi is equally gripping. She begins the play mani-
    festing animal affections but grows in our sympathy.

2   MATTHEWS, BRANDER. The Development of the Drama. New York:
    Scribner's, pp. 186-226.
        Finds flagrant faults of taste and structure but also vigor
    and vitality in The Duchess of Malfi. Webster was "a gloomy soul
    in revolt," but he had a strange power. He was not a born drama-
    tist but turned to the stage for his "own pecuniary needs."

3   SCHELLING, FELIX E. "Some Features of the Supernatural as
    Represented in Plays of the Reigns of Elizabeth and James."
    Modern Philology 1, no. 1 (June):31-47.
        Shows that the miraculous and blood-curdling echo in The
    Duchess of Malfi is at the end of a long sequence of Elizabethan
    dramatic witches, devils, fairies, etc.

*4 SCHENKER, A. "John Webster's Weissen Teufel und Ludwig Tieck's
    Vittoria Accorambona." Ph.D. dissertation, University of Vienna.
        Source: Mahaney, 1973.23.

5   SECCOMBE, THOMAS, and ALLEN, J.W. The Age of Shakespeare
     (1579-1631). Vol. 2, The Drama. London: G. Bell, pp. 182-87.
         Surveys Webster's career, and finds that his fame rests on
     the two tragedies that display rare and intense imaginative power,
     a murky atmosphere of gloom and cynicism, unrestrained passion and
     pride, and that have no real moral. His peculiar genius reaches
     its most intense expression in The Duchess of Malfi, 4. Although
     Webster was a conscious imitator of Shakespeare, both plays are
     very defective in constructional skill.

6   SYMMES, HAROLD S. Les Débuts de la critique dramatique en
     Angleterre jusqu'a mort de Shakespeare. Paris: Ernest Leroux,
     pp. 195-97.
         Argues that the preface to The White Devil shows that Webster
     knows, and chooses not to keep, the rules of the ancients. He is
     one of the founders of the English romantic drama as a separate
     genre.

                              1904

1   ADAMS, W. DAVENPORT. A Dictionary of the Drama. Philadelphia:
     Lippincott, 627 pp., passim.
         Cites Webster and his major works, including stage history,
     critical opinions, and reviews.

2   CRAWFORD, CHARLES. "John Webster and Sir Philip Sidney."
     Notes and Queries 110:221-23, 261-63, 303-4, 342-43, 381-82.
     [Reprinted: 1906.6.]
         Finds The Duchess of Malfi, The Devil's Law Case, and A
     Monumental Column all borrow heavily from Sidney's Arcadia.

3   GARNETT, RICHARD, and GOSSE, EDMUND. English Literature: An
     Illustrated Record. Vol. 2. New York: Macmillan, pp. 333-36.
         Presents Webster as one of a group of dramatists catering
     to a popular taste for stage horrors. Webster was the most out-
     standing of this group: he had magnificent ideas, but poor crafts-
     manship. Suspects he was driven to the stage and was a natural
     poet. Presents some extracts, mostly from The Duchess of Malfi.

4   GREENOUGH, CHESTER NOYES. "Studies in the Development of
     Character Writing in England." Ph.D. dissertation, Harvard
     University, 124 pp., passim.
         Finds that although Webster is the author of thirty-two
     Overburian "Characters," the "Characters" in his plays are not
     Theophrastan. (Boyce's The Theophrastan Character [1947.1] was
     based upon Greenough's notes.)

5   OTT, ADELE. Die italienische Novelle im englischen Drama, von
     1600 bis zur Restauration. Zürich: Zürcher & Furrer, pp. 87-90.
         Considers the importance of Bandello's Novelle in The Duchess

of Malfi and also cites his influence on A Cure for a Cuckold and
that of Ser Giovanni Fiorentino on Appius and Virginia.

6   SAMPSON, M.W., ed. "The White Devil" and "The Duchess of
    Malfi." Boston: D.C. Heath, 422 pp.
        Introductory material includes a life and a critical intro-
    duction: finds Webster fine of mind and strange of soul; difficult,
    but repaying study. He is characterized by an intensity, especially,
    of likes and dislikes, and of sorrow. His comedy is bitter. Sug-
    gests that at times he resembles Shakespeare in his creation of
    dramatic moments. Notes that his women are brilliantly depicted
    and, indeed, all his characters are well drawn.

7   STOTSENBURG, JOHN H. An Impartial Study of the Shakespeare
    Title. Louisville: J.P. Morton, pp. 503-9. [Reprint. Port
    Washington, N.Y.: Kennikat Press, 1970.]
        Argues that Shakespeare's plays were written by collaborators,
    among them John Webster, not to mention Drayton, Dekker, Porter,
    Chettle, Heywood, Munday, Bacon, etc. Finds Webster's hand in
    Coriolanus 1. 1, the fable of the body (which is like the fables
    in The White Devil), Lady Macbeth's hand washing scene, and perhaps
    in Hamlet and the Roman plays as well.

8   WENDELL, BARRETT. The Temper of the Seventeenth Century in
    England. New York: Scribner's, pp. 85-88.
        Contends Webster's art is inhibited, and therefore his imagin-
    ation crushed by literal facts. Both tragedies seem crabbed and
    to have demanded a conscious effort. His Italy is accurately local
    and corrupt.

                                1905

*1 BRERETON, JOHN Le GAY. "Webster's Twin Masterpieces." Hermes,
    22 November. [Reprinted: 1909.2; 1948.4.]
        Source: Moore, 1966.19.

2   CRAWFORD, CHARLES. "Montaigne, Webster, and Marston: Dr.
    Donne and Webster." Notes and Queries 112:41-43, 121-23, 201-3,
    302-3; 113 (1906):301-2, 382-83; 114 (1906):22-24, 122-24,
    242-44. [Reprinted: 1907.1.]
        Finds the influence of Florio's translation of Montaigne on
    Webster's The White Devil and The Duchess of Malfi was strong.
    Marston and Webster borrowed from Montaigne independently, as il-
    lustrated in many passages.

3   HUME, MARTIN. Spanish Influence on English Drama. London:
    E. Nash, p. 277.
        Asserts that "Webster's gloomy play The Duchess of Amalfi
    [sic] was either taken direct from Bandello's Italian novel of the
    same name, or Lope de Vega's dramatization of it."

4   ROBERTSON, JOHN MACKINNON. Did Shakespeare Write "Titus Andronicus?" London: Watts, p. 54.

      Cites The Devil's Law Case in support of the notion that much legalism found its way into Elizabethan plays that were not written by lawyers.

5   SAINTSBURY, GEORGE. A Short History of English Literature. New York: Macmillan, pp. 346-48.

      Presents The White Devil and The Duchess of Malfi as two great plays, displaying a remarkable tendency toward gloom, the supernatural, terror--and no cheerfulness. The action of The White Devil is very compressed and at its best in the scenes of Cornelia's madness and of Vittoria's murder. The Duchess of Malfi's real excellence is confined to the fourth act.

6   STOLL, ELMER EDGAR. John Webster: The Periods of His Work. Boston: A. Mudge, 216 pp. [Reprint. New York: Gordian Press, 1967. Excerpted: 1968.23.]

      Begins by surveying the dates and authorship of dubious plays, then dates the major works: The White Devil, 1612; The Duchess of Malfi, printed 1623, acted 1617; The Devil's Law Case, printed 1623, written 1620-22; Appius and Virginia, 1623-39. Considers authorship questions regarding A Cure for a Cuckold, The Thracian Wonder and The Weakest Goeth to the Wall. Surveys the three periods of Webster's career:

      1. Apprenticeship. Discusses Sir Thomas Wyat as a chronicle play, the largest part of which is Dekker's, and comments on the induction to The Malcontent. Considers the sources of the citizen comedies and grants Dekker the largest share of these plays, including the theatrical satire.

      2. Revenge plays. Finds the sources and plots of the tragedies are drawn from Italian life. The plays are alike in characterization, plot, sources, etc. Discusses the Kydian, Senecan influence on Webster and his contribution to the genre, namely, that his revengers are villains, not heroes. Webster's style minimizes the brutality of his stories, as does the fact that his characters are humanized.

      3. The Fletcherian and eclectic period. Outlines the sources of the late plays, and influences upon them (especially Fletcherian construction, morals, and characters). In this period, Webster breaks with the style of his prime and yields to other influences. Overall, no dramatist was ever more influenced than Webster. Reviewed: 1907.3

7   WOLFF, MAX J. Shakespeare, der dichter und sein Werk. 2 vols. Munich: C.H. Beck, 487, 489 pp., passim.

      Cites Webster often, never at length, usually in comparison with Shakespeare.

<u>1906</u>

1   ADAMS, JOSEPH QUINCY. "Greene's <u>Menaphon</u> and <u>The Thracian</u>
    <u>Wonder</u>." <u>Modern Philology</u> 3 (January):317-25.
        Finds <u>The Thracian Wonder</u> is based on Greene's work, as re-
    vealed by a comparison of dramatic <u>personae</u> and borrowed passages.
    Questions Fleay's attribution to Heywood (1891.1). See 1906.5.

2   ANKENBRAND, HANS. <u>Die Figur des Geistes im Drama der englischen</u>
    <u>Renaissance</u>. Leipzig: A. Deichert, pp. 58-62.
        Briefly discusses the ghosts of <u>The White Devil</u> (Brachiano
    appearing to Flamineo and Isabella to Francisco).

3   BAYLEY, HAROLD. <u>The Shakespearean Symphony</u>. London: Chapman
    & Hall, 393 pp., passim.
        Collects short quotations on various subjects (e.g., medi-
    cine, classicism, and assorted similitudes) and cites several of
    Webster's plays frequently.

4   BORMANN, HERMANN. <u>Der Jurist im Drama der elisabethanischen</u>
    <u>Zeit</u>. Halle: H. John, pp. 28-32.
        Notes, and comments upon, lawyers and the law in <u>Appius and</u>
    <u>Virginia</u>, <u>A Cure for a Cuckold</u>, and <u>The Devil's Law Case</u>.

5   BRERETON, JOHN Le GAY. "The Relation of <u>The Thracian Wonder</u>
    to Greene's <u>Menaphon</u>." <u>Modern Language Review</u> 2 (October):
    34-38.
        Contends than <u>The Thracian Wonder</u> is little more than a
    dramatic adaptation of Greene's work, as proven by parallel pas-
    sages and similar plot and characters. See 1906.1.

6   CRAWFORD, CHARLES. <u>Collectanea</u>. 1st Series. Stratford-on-
    Avon: Shakespeare Head Press, pp. 20-47.
        Reprint of 1904.2.

7   GRIERSON, HERBERT J.C. <u>The First Half of the Seventeenth</u>
    <u>Century</u>. New York: Scribner's, pp. 110-19. [Reprint. Folcroft,
    Pa.: Folcroft Press, 1969.]
        Argues that Webster's two tragedies are of the melodramatic,
    Senecan, Machiavellian type, with Senecan morality and Machiavellian
    characterization. <u>The White Devil</u> is a swifter and more intense
    play, but the character of the Duchess is supreme.

8   HADOW, G.E., and HADOW, WILLIAM CAREW. <u>The Oxford Treasury of</u>
    <u>English Literature</u>. Vol. 2. Oxford: Clarendon Press, pp.
    11-50.
        Prints selections from <u>Vittoria Carambona</u> as an example of
    "Romantic Tragedy." The introduction focuses upon the "wonderful
    figure" of Vittoria. Finds she puts power in the place of love.
    All the play's other characters are seriously flawed.

9   MORELLI, DOMENICO. <u>Giovanna d'Aragona duchessa d'Amalfi</u>.
     Cesena: Vignuzzi, 93 pp.
          Presents the historical Duchess and evaluates the accuracy
     of Bandello (Webster's source). Reviewed: 1907.2.

10   SMITH, ARTHUR HAROLD. <u>Les Evénements politique de France dans</u>
     <u>le théâtre anglais du siècle d'Elisabeth</u>. Paris: Larose,
     166 pp., passim.
          Believes that Webster's <u>Guise</u> (as cited in the prologue to
     <u>The Devil's Law Case</u>) dealt with French history. Collier found--
     or perhaps forged--an entry in Henslowe recording an advance to
     Webster for this play (1831.1). Fleay (1891.1) accused Collier
     of inserting "Webster" in this entry. Suggests the piece to which
     Henslowe actually referred was Marlowe's <u>Massacre at Paris</u>.

11   STOLL, ELMER EDGAR. "The Influence of Jonson on Dekker."
     <u>Modern Language Notes</u> 21, no. 1 (January):20-23.
          In <u>Sir Thomas Wyat</u> and the citizen comedies, sees Webster
     and Dekker influenced by some of Jonson's jolly and swaggering
     characters. Contends that Dekker was closer to the bourgeois in-
     terests of Jonson than to the sublime ghastliness of Webster.

12   STURGE, L.J. "Webster and the Law: A Parallel." <u>Shakespeare-</u>
     <u>Jahrbuch</u> 42:148-57.
          In spite of his weird, somber, and morbid imagination, finds
     Webster was in some ways typically Elizabethan in his use of the
     law. His knowledge of legal matters was quite full, e.g., the
     Duchess' wedding is legal; the plays are full of legal language,
     images, and concepts; and the trial scenes are important in
     Webster's plays.

13   WEULKER, R. <u>Geschichte des englischen literature</u>. Vol. 1.
     Leipzig: Bibliographisches Institut, pp. 355-58.
          Surveys Webster's major works briefly, focusing upon the
     character of Vittoria in <u>The White Devil</u> and the relationship be-
     tween Bosola and the Duchess in act 4 of <u>The Duchess of Malfi</u>.
     Also cites <u>A Cure for a Cuckold</u> and <u>The Devil's Law Case</u>.

                              <u>1907</u>

1   CRAWFORD, CHARLES. <u>Collectanea</u>. 2d Series. Stratford-on-Avon:
     Shakespeare Head Press, pp. 1-63.
          Reprint of 1905.2.

2   GREG, W.W. Review of <u>Giovanna d'Aragona duchessa d'Amalfi</u>, by
     Domenico Morelli. <u>Modern Language Review</u> 2, no. 4 (July):
     373-74.
          Judges Morelli's biography (1906.9) to be of considerable
     interest to students of the Jacobean drama. It is an effort to
     present historical facts in the life of the Duchess, in relation
     to Webster's source, Bandello, who seems fairly accurate.

3   _____. Review of John Webster . . . , by Elmer Edgar Stoll.
      Modern Language Review 2, no. 1 (October):73-74.
           Describes Stoll's book (1905.6) as a very elaborate and very
      careful piece of work, although it does not add much to our major
      knowledge of the dramatist. Disagrees with Stoll's sense of
      Webster's dependence upon the work of others and with some of his
      attributions, but admires his perseverance and energy.

*4   LIEBE, CARL. Der Arzt im elisabethanischen Drama. Ph.D. dis-
      sertation, Halle. Halle: R. Espehhahn, 50 pp.
      Source: Mahaney, 1973.23.

*5   SCHRÖDER, OTTO. Marlowe und Webster. Halle: S. John, 32 pp.
      Source: Mahaney, 1973.23.

6   SIMPSON, PERCY. "An Allusion in Webster." Modern Language
      Review 2, no. 2 (January):162-63.
           Argues that although Vittoria's citation of Perseus during
      the scene of her trial is often emended, it should not be: it
      alludes to a Jonsonian masque in which Perseus typifies "heroic
      virtue."

7   TISCHNER, F. Die Verfasserschaft der Webster-Rowley Dramen.
      Ph.D. dissertation, University of Marburg. Marburg: K.
      Gleiser, 76 pp.
           Discusses the Webster-Rowley authorship of A Cure for a
      Cuckold and The Thracian Wonder, and considers the general charac-
      teristics of Webster's personality and works (theme, verse, etc.).

                              1908

1   GILDERSLEEVE, VIRGINIA C. Government Regulation of the
      Elizabethan Drama. New York: Columbia University Press, p. 217.
           Sees the civic pageants of Webster and others as signs that
      there were sometimes good relations between the city and the stage.

2   GREENWOOD, GRANVILLE GEORGE. The Shakespeare Problem Restated.
      London: J. Lane, pp. 397-405. [Reprint. Westport, Conn.:
      Greenwood Press, 1970.]
           One of Greenwood's many anti-Stratfordian tracts. Cites
      Webster as part of a discussion of Shakespeare's legal knowledge
      in comparison to that of the author of The Devil's Law Case (a
      play that actually contains no law at all, only an absurd travesty
      of a trial).

3   KRUSIUS, PAUL. Eine Untersuchung der Sprache John Webster's.
      Ph.D. dissertation, University of Halle. Halle: Wischan &
      Burkhardt, 217 pp.
           Studies the language patterns of The White Devil, The Duchess
      of Malfi, The Devil's Law Case and Appius and Virginia, including

metaphors, personifications (furies, gods, devils, muses), alle-
gories, synecdoche, metonymy, rhetorical figures, euphuisms, etc.
Arranged by play, with a section on lesser works.

4   SAINTSBURY, GEORGE. A History of English Prosody. Vol. 2.
     London: Macmillan, pp. 76-77.
         Finds the prosody of the two great romantic tragedies very
     irregular. Appius and Virginia is very regular, and The Devil's
     Law Case in between.

5   SCHELLING, FELIX E. Elizabethan Drama, 1558-1642. Vol. 1.
     Boston: Houghton Mifflin, pp. 587 ff.
         Presents The White Devil as a master study of womanhood in
     its deadliest perversity, wherein Vittoria and Brachiano are
     masterpieces of portraiture; The Duchess of Malfi as a romantic
     tragedy on the theme of womanly pride, virtue, and constancy; and
     Appius and Virginia as a careful work that shows calm and restraint.

6   SCHÜCKING, LEVIN L. Shakespeare im literarischen Urteil seiner
     Zeit. Heidelberg: Carl Winter, 196 pp., passim.
         Mentions Webster in passing, e.g., his praise for Shakespeare
     in the preface to The White Devil.

7   THOMPSON, ELBERT N.S. "Elizabethan Dramatic Collaboration."
     Englische Studien 40:30-46.
         Discusses Webster as part of the "intimate world" of the
     Elizabethan theater, replete with vast and often curious collabora-
     tive efforts, sometimes perplexing to modern scholarship. Notes
     various ways of dividing collaborative assignments.

8   THORNDIKE, ASHLEY H. Tragedy. Boston: Houghton Mifflin, pp.
     202-3, 217-19.
         Discusses Webster with "later revenge plays" in this history
     of tragedy in England to the mid-nineteenth century. His works
     abound in theatrical horrors, but they are impressive in both
     poetry and morality. Like Shakespeare, he recognized moral values:
     there is no confusion of good and evil in his plays, yet his view
     of life is cynical.

9   WALLACE, CHARLES W. The Children of the Chapel at Blackfriars,
     1597-1603. University of Nebraska Studies, vol. 8, nos. 2, 3.
     Lincoln: University of Nebraska, pp. xv, 164. [Reprint. New
     York: AMS Press, 1970.]
         Announces that there exists, yet to be published, "voluminous
     sources of hitherto unknown plays by Chapman, Dekker, Webster, Ford,
     Rowley, and others." Also notes the discovery of "the sources of
     hitherto unknown dramas" including Websters. (Originally a Freiburg
     dissertation, 1906.)

1909

1   ALBRIGHT, VICTOR E. The Shaksperian Stage. Ph.D. dissertation,
     Columbia University. New York: Columbia University Press, pp.
     56-57, 59-60, 111.
        Notes the need for a traverse in The Duchess of Malfi, 4. 1,
     as evidence of the use of hangings and second curtains on
     Renaissance stages; Flamineo's discovery, in The White Devil, of
     Cornelia mourning shows the use of the outer and inner stages and
     traverse.

*2   BRERETON, JOHN Le GAY. Elizabethan Dramatists. Sidney:
     University Library Publications.
        Source: Moore, 1966.19. See 1948.4; 1905.1.

3   Calendar of State Papers. Venetian, XV (1617-1619). London:
     Longmans, p. 134.
        A description of England's "disastrously modified" religion,
     including an account in the entry for 7 February 1618 of the
     Cardinal in The White Devil--an act of "derision of ecclesiastical
     pomp."

4   CALISCH, EDWARD N. The Jew in English Literature. Richmond,
     Va.: Bell, p. 90.
        Notes Jewish characterization in The White Devil and
     Romelio's disguise in The Devil's Law Case.

*5   GOUCH, CHARLES EDWARD. The Life and Characters of Sir Thomas
     Overbury. Norwich: n.p.
        Source: Mahaney, 1973.23.

6   JUSSERAND, J.J. A Literary History of the English People.
     Vol. 3. New York: Putnam, pp. 410-21. [English translation
     of Histoire littéraire du peuple anglais, vol. 2 (Paris: Didot,
     1904).]
        Affirms that horror was Webster's speciality, along with
     lust and murder. The dramatist barely avoids making the audience
     laugh at the conclusion of The White Devil, but The Duchess of
     Malfi is much better, with real characters and some beautiful
     poetry.

7   KETTLER, FRANZ. "Lateinische Zitate in den Dramen namhafter
     Zeitgenossen Shakespeares." Ph.D. dissertation, University
     of Strasburg. Bremen: H.M. Hauschild, pp. 109-13.
        Comments upon Latin citations in eight authors, including
     Webster, who utilizes Ovid, Virgil, and Horace, as well as mili-
     tary, theological, judicial, and university Latin.

8   PIERCE, FREDERICK E. The Collaboration of Webster and Dekker.
     New York: Henry Holt, 159 pp.
        Finds the Webster-Dekker collaboration was probably a

shoulder-to-shoulder alliance against lifelong poverty. Discusses
the "Ho" plays and Sir Thomas Wyat in an effort to assign scenes
to each author on the basis of various tests, concluding that a
few scenes in the "Ho" plays are Webster's and that Webster wrote
most of Sir Thomas Wyat.

9   REYHER, PAUL. Les Masques anglais. Paris: Hachette, p. 245.
     [Reprint. New York: B. Blom, 1964.]
         Notes the Webster/Dekker character Monopoly in Westward Ho
is a typical--careful--topical reference.

10   SHEAVYN, PHOEBE. The Literary Profession in the Elizabethan
     Age. Publications of the University of Manchester, English
     Series, no. 1. Manchester: Manchester University Press, pp.
     124-26 and passim. [Reprint. New York: Haskell House, 1964;
     revised by J.W. Saunders (Manchester: Manchester University
     Press, 1967).]
         Notes Webster's dedication of The Duchess of Malfi as part
of a discussion of patronage. Also, finds the evidence suggests
that Webster had cordial relations with his fellow dramatists.

11   WALLACE, CHARLES W. "Shakespeare in London: Fresh Documents
     on the Poet and His Theatres, the Globe and the Blackfriers
     [sic]." Times (London), 2 October, p. 9.
         Describes recently uncovered documents including material
on the actor Osteler (who appeared in The Duchess of Malfi) that
fixes the date of the play at no later than 16 December 1614, when
he died.

12   WATT, LAUCHLAN M. Attic and Elizabethan Tragedy. New York:
     E.P. Dutton, pp. 330-33. [Reprint. Port Washington, N.Y.:
     Kennikat Press, 1968.]
         Argues that The White Devil has some great passages, espe-
cially Vittoria's defense and Cornelia's dirge. The Duchess of
Malfi is a full house of tragic emotions. It featured a dangerous
plot for the period, but treated the relationship between the
Duchess and her steward with great delicacy.

                              1910

1   COURTHOPE, W.J. A History of English Poetry. Vol. 4. London:
     Macmillan, pp. 256-66.
         In chapter 9 ("The Dramatic Taste of the City: Melodrama"),
finds Webster refines and elevates melodrama. His works show some
bad taste, but they are powerful and affecting; for example act 4
of The Duchess of Malfi is a monument of horror and pity. In spite
of Webster's literary and philosophical talents, his plays lack a
unity of action: they aren't tragedies, but a succession of scenes.

2   MATTHEWS, BRANDER. A Study of Drama. Boston: Houghton
    Mifflin, p. 236.
        Describes Webster as an awkward dramatist--a poet, beyond
    question, but not a born playwright.

3   MURRAY, JOHN TUCKER. English Dramatic Companies, 1558-1642.
    Vol. 2. Boston: Houghton Mifflin, pp. 146-48.
        Discusses the list of the King's Men found in The Duchess of
    Malfi, 1623, with several parts listed with two actors (those of
    the first production and the revival). Notes there are some puz-
    zles in the list, e.g., actors who don't seem able to have per-
    formed at the same time.

4   RISTINE, FRANK HUMPHREY. English Tragicomedy: Its Origin and
    and History. New York: Columbia University Press, 247 pp.,
    passim.
        Considers The Devil's Law Case in relation to the fashion
    for tragicomedies. It has a plot of Italian intrigue, with few
    attractive characters, ending in a trial producing light punish-
    ments. Furthermore, the device of the stabbing cure is an absurdi-
    ty. The preface to The White Devil suggests that audiences de-
    manded mirth mixed with tragedy.

5   SCHEFFLER, WILLIBALD. "Thomas Dekker als Dramatiker." Ph.D.
    dissertation, University of Leipzig. Leipzig: Borna, pp. 18,
    27, 31.
        Discusses Dekker's life and work and notes the place of the
    "Ho" plays within the chronology of his dramatic production but
    does not analyze them.

6   SCHELLING, FELIX E. English Literature during the Lifetime of
    Shakespeare. New York: Henry Holt, pp. 261-64.
        In the chapter entitled "Shakespeare, Webster, and the Heyday
    of Romantic Tragedy," observes that The Devil's Law Case offers "no
    striking excellence," that Appius and Virginia is very restrained,
    and that Webster's reputation is based on the two tragedies. Brief-
    ly discusses the sources of the plays. Finds the presentation of
    the torture and heroism of the Duchess among the finest things in
    tragic literature.

7   STORK, CHARLES. William Rowley: His "All's Lost by Lust,"
    and "Shoemaker, a Gentleman": With an Introduction on Rowley's
    Place in the Drama. University of Pennsylvania Studies in
    Philology and Literature, 13. Philadelphia: University of
    Pennsylvania Press, pp. 7-68.
        An edition of the two plays, with an introduction. Discusses
    Kirkman's attribution (1661.1) to Rowley and Webster of The Thracian
    Wonder and A Cure for a Cuckold, finding Webster had nothing to do
    with the first, but the second was a genuine collaboration.

8   VAUGHAN, C.E. "Tourneur and Webster." In <u>The Cambridge History</u>
     <u>of English Literature</u>. Edited by A.W. Ward and A.R. Waller.
     Vol. 6, <u>The Drama to 1642</u>, Part Two. Cambridge: Cambridge
     University Press, pp. 188-211.
          Sketches Webster's life and the three periods of his work
     (collaboration, tragedies, tragicomedies). Considers authorship
     and text issues in <u>Lady Jane</u>, the induction to <u>The Malcontent</u>,
     and the citizen comedies (mostly Dekker). <u>The White Devil</u> is an
     incalculable advance on his previous work with some awkwardness
     of plot, but much powerful poetry. Finds <u>The Duchess of Malfi</u> a
     more mature work focusing upon the graciousness and firmness of a
     noble woman. The play goes on too long and loses some tragic
     effect after the Duchess' death. Concludes Webster's unique quali-
     ties are a knowledge of human character, a tragic sense of life
     derived from the heroic resistance to assault, and great poetry
     that lingered on images of mortality.

                                1911

1   BROOKE, C.F. TUCKER. <u>The Tudor Drama</u>. Boston: Houghton
     Mifflin, pp. 221, 415, 417, 445.
          Cites Webster's "stale and acrid . . . decadent Italianism"
     as an example of the beginning of the end of Elizabethan drama.

2   HUNT, MARY LELAND. <u>Thomas Dekker: A Study</u>. Ph.D. dissertation,
     Columbia University. Columbia University Studies in English,
     2d ser., no. 17. New York: Columbia University Press, 213 pp.,
     passim.
          Attempts to distinguish Dekker's and Webster's parts in vari-
     ous collaborations. Stresses the intimacy of their collaboration:
     they had many interests in common, including a preoccupation with
     life after death. Although the "vexed question" of Webster's part
     in the "Ho" plays remains unsettled, assigns him "the more unusual,
     subtle, or abnormal elements."

3   OLIPHANT, E.H.C. "Problems of Authorship in Elizabethan Dramatic
     Literature." <u>Modern Philology</u> 8 (January):411-59.
          Defines authorship problems including anonymity, early mis-
     attributions, and the like. Categorizes types of attribution situ-
     ations and the plays that fall into them. <u>Anything for a Quiet</u>
     <u>Life</u>, <u>Appius and Virginia</u>, and <u>A Cure for a Cuckold</u> merit recon-
     sideration regarding Webster's part--he isn't "obvious."

4   ROBIN, PERCY ANSELL. <u>The Old Physiology in English Literature</u>.
     London: Dent, 184 pp., passim.
          Cites Webster for such features as: descriptions of melan-
     choly in <u>The Devil's Law Case</u>; the relation of the liver to love
     and lust; and the like.

1912

1   BULAND, MABLE. The Presentation of Time in the Elizabethan
    Drama. New York: Henry Holt, pp. 167-69. [Reprint. New
    York: Haskell House, 1966.]
        Studies the ways in which Elizabethans deal with the issue
    of "double time." Finds in Webster's tragedies a surprising dis-
    regard for the unity of time. The White Devil lasts a week or ten
    days, The Duchess of Malfi nearly four years. Yet, the dramatic
    situation of the Duchess seems nearly continuous.

2   FOSTER, FRANCES A. "Dumbshow in Elizabethan Drama before 1620."
    Englische Studien 44:8-17.
        Discusses the dumb show in general, with reference to
    Webster's The White Devil.

*3 GROESBECK, K. "Comedy Dumbshow in Elizabethan Drama." Ph.D.
    dissertation, Columbia University.
        Source: Mahaney, 1973.23.

4   LANG, ANDREW. A History of English Literature from "Beowulf"
    to Swinburne. London: Longmans, Green, pp. 215-59.
        Notes Webster is best known by Lamb's extracts from The White
    Devil and The Duchess of Malfi. Finds him a much overrated drama-
    tist: for example, Camillo's murder is "about as subtle as the
    blowing up of Darnley with gunpowder."

5   LAWRENCE, WILLIAM J. "Irish Types in Old-Time English Drama."
    Anglia 35:347-56.
        Notes recurring allusions to Ireland in The White Devil, a
    play set in Italy.

*6 WANN, LOUIS. "Oriental Matter in Elizabethan Drama." Ph.D.
    dissertation, Columbia University, 49 pp.
        Source: Mahaney, 1973.23. See 1915.6. (The Comprehensive
    Dissertation Index, vol. 37 [Ann Arbor, Mich., 1973], p. 741 lists
    this as a 1919 University of Wisconsin dissertation.)

1913

1   ANSCOMBE, ALFRED. "'Castle' in Shakespeare and Webster."
    Notes and Queries 127:394.
        Discusses the etymology of the use of the word "castle" to
    mean "helmet." (See also 1913.2, 10.)

2   BAYLE, A.R. "'Castle' in Shakespeare and Webster." Notes and
    Queries 127:253.
        Argues "castle" was used by the Elizabethans to mean "helmet."
    (See also 1913.1, 10.)

3   BROOKE, RUPERT. "The Authorship of the Later Appius and
     Virginia." Modern Language Review 8:433-53. [Reprinted as an
     appendix: 1916.1.]
          Asserts the play does not seem to fit Webster's character-
     istics--it is cool, smooth, classical. The characters and meter
     are not Websterian, nor is the language. On the other hand, the
     title page, parallel lines and early attributions all argue for
     Webster. Brooke's candidate is Thomas Heywood, with Webster as
     a possible reviser.

4   _____. "A Note on John Webster." Poetry and Drama 1:27-32.
          Notes Webster made much use of notebooks. Often, even when
     he does not change a source he improves it by superior use.
     Webster makes material from Sidney, Montaigne, and Donne more
     visual, more concrete.

5   LAWRENCE, WILLIAM J. "Light and Darkness in the Elizabethan
     Theater." Englische Studien 45 (September):182-200. [Reprinted
     in his The Elizabethan Playhouse (Stratford-upon-Avon:
     Shakespeare Head Press, 1913), pp. 1-22.]
          Demonstrates that there was no artificial illumination in
     public theaters with the aim of improving visibility--only for
     symbolizing night scenes. Observes that the scene in The Duchess
     of Malfi, 5.4, is supposed to be wholly in the dark, with Bosola
     unable to see Antonio.

6   PARRY, G.A. "Vittoria Carombona." Notes and Queries 127:326.
          Notes Brachiano's line on leaving the hall of justice about
     bringing his own stool with him is paralleled by a story from the
     "Percy Anecdotes" about the father of William the Conquerer.

7   ROBERTSON, JOHN MACKINNON. The Baconian Heresy. London: H.
     Jenkins, pp. 157-73.
          Opposes Greenwood and the anti-Stratfordians. Deals with
     the question of how much law Webster includes in his plays--actu-
     ally, quite a bit in The Devil's Law Case and Appius and Virginia.
     See 1908.2 and 1916.5 for the anti-Stratfordian case.

8   SMITH, G.C. MOORE. "Webster's Duchess of Malfi." Notes and
     Queries 128 (1 November):355; (29 November):424-25.
          Finds a possible description of some of the Cardinal scenes
     of The Duchess of Malfi in a letter from a Venetial from London
     on 7 February 1618. (The second of these notes observes that this
     is not a new discovery. 1618.1 records this letter.)

9   SYKES, H. DUGDALE. "An Attempt to Determine the Date of
     Webster's Appius and Virginia." Notes and Queries 127:401-3,
     422-24, 466-67.
          Argues that, since the play appears on a list of 1639, it
     predates that year but probably postdates the 1623 preface to The
     White Devil, where it is not cited. Resemblances to other works

of Jonson, Rowley, and Heywood, especially in the field of vocabu-
lary, point to a post-1630 date. Concludes the play was probably
done before 1635, when Webster may have died.

10 _____. "'Castle' in Shakespeare and Webster." Notes and
     Queries 127:165-66.
          Asks if "castle" meant "helmet" in Titus Andronicus and
     Troilus and Cressida. It seems used in this manner in Webster's
     Appius and Virginia, which would support such a reading. See
     1913.1, 2 for other notes on this usage.

11 _____. "Date of Webster's Play The Devil's Law Case." Notes
     and Queries 127:106-7.
          Since the play borrows from Jonson's The Devil Is an Ass
     (written in 1616), argues that it must be later than that date.

12 _____. "Date of Webster's Play The White Devil." Notes and
     Queries 127:342-43.
          Finds this play must have been written after Jonson's Masque
     of Queens (2 February 1609) and before its publication in 1612.

13 _____. "'Night-Cap.'" Notes and Queries 127:68.
          Comments that the term "night cap" is used to describe a
     person twice in Webster. (As a reference to the barrister's cap
     or coif, it was a contemptuous name for a lawyer.)

14 _____. "Webster and Sir Thomas Overbury." Notes and Queries
     128:221-23, 244-45, 263-65, 282-83, 304-5.
          Believes Webster used Overbury's "Characters" as a source.
     Thus, The Duchess of Malfi has a late date--post-1615. Cites many
     parallels. See 1915.4 for Sykes's later opinion on this subject.

15 ZEITLIN, JACOB. Hazlitt on English Literature. New York:
     Oxford University Press, pp. 421-22.
          Reports that Hazlitt said he would like to have seen Webster,
     "with his melancholy yew trees and death's heads." Also notes
     Hazlitt's discussion of Webster in the third lecture of The Age
     of Elizabeth, where he compares Webster to Dekker (1821.1).

                              1914

1 ALDEN, RAYMOND M. "The Use of Comic Material in the Tragedy of
     Shakespeare and His Contemporaries." Journal of English and
     Germanic Philology 13:281-98.
          Notes that in Shakespeare's day there was a general comming-
     ling of serious and comic dramatic materials and finds "The blend-
     ing of serious and comic is most striking in the two great trage-
     dies of Webster's."

2   B., C.C. "John Webster and the N.E.D." Notes and Queries 129:
     398-99.
         Additions to 1914.5. Believes that, as suggested in The
     Devil's Law Case, the actual medicinal use of fox lung was prac-
     ticed in Webster's time.

3   BOURGEOIS, A.F. "John Webster a Contributor to Sir Thomas
     Overbury's Characters." Notes and Queries 130:3-6, 23-24.
         Offers as proof of Webster's authorship of the "Characters"
     added to Overbury's collection, the tremendous number of parallels
     between them and Webster's work: he is self-plagiarizing. See
     1915.1 for a clarification and 1913.14 for another discussion of
     this issue.

4   _____. "John Webster: The Probable Date of The Devil's Law
     Case." Notes and Queries 130 (19 July):41-42.
         Doubts Fleay's date of 1610, which was based on internal evi-
     dence (1890.1). The notorious law suit on which the play is based
     took place in 1618-19 and it is cited in the play's subtitle; hence,
     1618-19 is a probable date of composition.

5   _____. "Webster and the N.E.D." Notes and Queries 129:302-4,
     324-25, 343-44; 130 (1915):165-66, 182-83.
         Finds over 100 words in Webster are not cited in the N.E.D.
     as occurring prior to 1625. See 1914.2 for additional items.

6   BOYER, CLARENCE VALENTINE. The Villain as Hero in Elizabethan
     Tragedy. London: G. Routledge, pp. 151-64. [Reprint. New
     York: Russell & Russell, 1964. Excerpted: 1975.18.]
         Finds Marlowe's villain-heroes were an important influence
     on subsequent Elizabethan dramatists, including Webster. Bosola
     is such a hero-villain, especially after the death of the Duchess.
     He is not a Machiavellian, but a poor gentleman trying to live,
     combining malcontent, tool villain, and reverger. Bosola's con-
     version, albeit unsuccessful, gives us back some confidence in
     human nature.

7   FORSYTHE, ROBERT STANLEY. The Relation of Shirley's Plays to
     the Elizabethan Drama. New York: Columbia University Press,
     pp. 185-90, and passim. [Reprint. 1965.]
         Cites Webster often throughout and notes the "too tangible
     and fundamentally physical nature of many of his horrors." The
     Duchess of Malfi strongly influenced Shirley's The Cardinal, but
     while they touch at several points, there is no plagiarism.
     Webster's The Duchess of Malfi probably also influenced Shirley's
     romantic comedy The Brothers.

8   GAYLEY, CHARLES MILLS. Francis Beaumont, Dramatist. London:
     Duckworth, 445 pp., passim.
         Characterizes Webster's works as filled with "poisoned ex-
     halations, the wildering of sympathy, and the disproportioned

art. . . . " Finds The Duchess of Malfi lurid, miasmatic, and
stupefying.

*9   OERTER, M. "Thomas L. Beddoe's Literary Relation to John
      Webster and Cyril Tourneur as Evident in his Death's Jest Book."
      Ph.D. dissertation, University of Southern California.
      Source: Mahaney, 1973.23.

10   PEERS, EDGAR ALLISON. Elizabethan Drama and Its Mad Folk.
      Cambridge: W. Heffer, pp. 18, 25, 46, 51, 103-5.
          Cites The Duchess of Malfi's mad scene as typical, e.g.,
      singing and shouting, use of the mad for "sport," etc. While
      Webster's use of lunacy is "inane" and "disfigures" act 4 of The
      Duchess of Malfi, Ferdinand's insanity has great force and passion.
      Also discusses insanity in Northward Ho.

11   SCHELLING, FELIX E. English Drama. London: Dent, pp. 140-42.
          Discusses Webster in the chapter "Height of Tragedy": he is
      remembered for his power in romantic tragedy, as seen in his two
      masterpieces. Praises especially the characterization in The
      White Devil. The Duchess of Malfi includes the same atmosphere
      of intrigue--again, with good characters, especially the Duchess
      in her torture scenes.

12   SYKES, H. DUGDALE. "Webster's Share in Cure for a Cuckold."
      Notes and Queries 129:404-5, 443-45, 463-64.
          Finds the greater part of this play (subplot and main love
      story as well) is Webster's, as Kirkman claimed. It has the same
      sources as familiar Webster pieces and a similar unusual vocabu-
      lary. The few scenes not by Webster are by Rowley.

                                1915

1   BOURGEOIS, A.F. "John Webster and Overbury's Characters."
      Notes and Queries 132:282-83.
          Clarifies 1914.3: Webster wrote only the last thirty-two
      of the additions to the 1615 edition of the Characters.

2   FREEBURG, VICTOR OSCAR. Disguise Plots in Elizabethan Drama:
      A Study in Stage Tradition. New York: Columbia University
      Press, 241 pp., passim. [Reprint. New York: Benjamin Blom,
      1965.]
          Mentions a number of plays in which Webster may have had a
      hand. Discusses the disguise of Westward Ho, in which the suspi-
      cious Justiano confirms his wife's fidelity: "The motivation and
      action in this scene will not bear close scrutiny, but the stage
      business was doubtless vital to the gaping groundlings, who pre-
      ferred the sensational to the subtle."

3   LOCKERT, LUCY. "Marston, Webster, and the Decline of the
    Elizabethan Drama." Sewanee Review 27:62-81.
        Finds late Jacobean dramatists show a loose coordination of
    passions and of theme. This dissolution was well begun before its
    usually assigned onset--the era of Beaumont and Fletcher. Actually,
    seeds of Renaissance dramatic degeneration were present from the
    beginning. Webster never achieved genuine dramatic construction
    since his only real unity is one of atmosphere. Thus, his best
    works are merely collections of scenes with picturesque and power-
    ful verse.

4   SYKES, H. DUGDALE. "Was Webster a Contributor to Overbury's
    Characters?" Notes and Queries 131:313-15, 335-37, 355-57,
    374-75.
        Since Webster knew some of the 1615 "Characters" before they
    appeared in print (they appear in The Duchess of Malfi), argues
    that while he could not have written all the additions, he may
    have written some. See 1913.14 for Sykes's earliest opinion.

5   _____. "A Webster-Massinger Play: The Fair Maid of the Inn."
    Notes and Queries 131:134-37, 155-57, 175-77, 196-98. [Re-
    printed: 1924.9.]
        Using vocabulary tests, phraseology, etc., finds "conclusive"
    evidence that Webster collaborated with Massinger on this play.

6   WANN, LOUIS. "The Oriental in Elizabethan Drama." Modern
    Philology 12:423-47.
        Includes The White Devil in the corpus of plays studied in
    terms of sources, types of plays, etc. Comments that the portrait
    of Zanche constitutes a typical Renaissance depiction of a lustful
    Moor. See 1912.6 for a previous version.

7   WHITMORE, CHARLES E. The Supernatural in Tragedy. Cambridge,
    Mass.: Harvard University Press, pp. 259-62. [Reprint.
    Mamaroneck, N.Y.: P.P. Appel, 1971.]
        Considers Webster's use of the supernatural to evoke an at-
    mosphere of tense, abnormal horror. The White Devil includes the
    ghosts of Isabella (who may be real or imaginary) and Brachiano
    (an omen of evil to Flamineo). The Duchess of Malfi has no actual
    material horrors--just portents, hints, etc.

                              1916

1   BROOKE, RUPERT. John Webster and the Elizabethan Drama. New
    York: John Lane, 282 pp. [Reprint. New York: Russell &
    Russell, 1967. Reprints 1913.3 as appendix A. Excerpted:
    1968.23; 1969.17; 1975.18.]
        Finds Webster's work is quite ordinary, save for the two
    tragedies. Even there, his talents are more literary than the-
    atrical. In The White Devil Vittoria is wicked, but her enemies

are wicked and mean as well, and her spirit of resistance is as-
tonishing. The Duchess of Malfi is a better play: its language
is more dramatic, and it shows Webster's supreme gift, the depiction of some intense state of mind at a crisis. The Devil's Law
Case, while debased, is still totally Webster's and it contains
good features.
     Describes some general characteristics of Webster: in his
best moments, he plays directly on the nerves with scenes of intense, horrible vigor. His blank verse is very free. His dramaturgy is awkward and slow, e.g., the old-fashioned use of couplets
to end scenes. The fables are also old-fashioned and out of place,
as are the soliloquies and asides. They reveal a tendency to
generalize, especially at the ends of the plays. He borrowed heavi-
ly, often improving his sources, and probably composed with a notebook. Webster's world consists of people blindly driven like ani-
mals, an atmosphere of foul and indestructible vitality, like "the
feverish and ghastly turmoil of a nest of maggots."
     In appendices, discusses dating, authorship, collaboration,
and sources of Appius and Virginia, The Thracian Wonder, Monuments
of Honour, Sir Thomas Wyat, the "Ho" plays, The Malcontent, The
White Devil, The Duchess of Malfi, Monumental Column, The Devil's
Law Case, A Cure for a Cuckold, and nonextant plays. Reviewed:
1916.6; 1918.1.

2   BUTLER, PIERCE. "Stage Mad-Folk in Shakespeare's Day."
     American Journal of Insanity [now American Journal of Psychiatry]
     73:19-42.
         Finds insanity was used for comedy and for horror in
     Shakespeare and Webster. Specifically comments on The White Devil's
     depiction of Isabella's reaction to the death of one son, killed
     by another, and her later mourning scene, which creates intense
     pathos. Also, Brachiano's madness when poisoned is noteworthy.
     Argues that in The Duchess of Malfi the dance of madmen probably
     produced a comic effect.

3   CLARK, JOHN SCOTT, and ODELL, J.P. A Study of English and
     American Writers. Chicago: Row, Peterson, pp. 62-66.
         Describes Webster's characteristics as including the por-
     trayal of horror and agony, epigrammatic terseness (especially in
     The White Devil), realistic portraiture and faithful characteriza-
     tion, and spasms of dramatic fury.

4   CREIZENACH, WILHELM. The English Drama in the Age of Elizabeth.
     Translated by Cecile Hugon. London: Sidgwick & Jackson, pp.
     67, 92.
         Discusses Webster's early, collaborative career.

5   GREENWOOD, GRANVILLE GEORGE. Is There a Shakespeare Problem?
     London and New York: John Lane, 613 pp.
         Another anti-Stratfordian tract that argues that when
     Webster cites Shakespeare in the preface to The White Devil, he

refers only to the works, not the man. Contends that all Renaissance
dramatists are involved in the Shakespeare biography controversy.
For a refutation of such works, see 1913.7.

6   Review of John Webster and the Elizabethan Drama, by Rupert
     Brooke. Times Literary Supplement, 10 November, p. 571.
         Finds Brooke's study (1916.1) intelligent but tainted with
a "note of frenzied immaturity." Agrees that Webster is a genius:
the virtue of the plays is not in their morality or in their sudden
flashes of fine writing, but in their emotional and intellectual
vitality and intensity, and in characters who are glorious and indestructible.

7   SCOTT, MARY AUGUSTA. Elizabethan Translations from the Italian.
     Vassar Semi-Centennial Series. Boston: Hougton Mifflin, pp.
     4, 12, 16, 42, 45, 83, 106.
         Includes and expands material from 1895.5, focusing mainly
upon Westward Ho.

8   STONEX, ARTHUR B. "The Usurer in Elizabethan Drama." PMLA 31:
     190-210.
         Observes that the character Security in Eastward Ho combines
the roles of procurer and usurer and that usurers are cuckolded in
both "Ho" plays. Westward Ho's Tenterhooke is one of the very few
sympathetic usurers depicted in the drama of the period.

9   THORNDIKE, ASHLEY H. Shakespeare's Theatre. New York:
     Macmillan, p. 85.
         Cites Webster (with Dekker) as the author of the "Ho" plays.
Also notes Webster's description of his audience as "ignorant
asses."

1917

1   ADAMS, JOSEPH QUINCY, ed. The Dramatic Records of Sir Henry
     Herbert. New Haven: Yale University Press, pp. 24, 117.
         Herbert was Master of the Revels, 1623-73. The entry for
September 1624 includes "A new tragedy called A Late Murther of
the Sonne upon the Mother: written by Forde, and Webster"; another
entry records a December 1661, production of "Vittoria Corumbana."

*2   BUTLER, E.M. "The Masterpieces of John Webster." Ph.D. dis-
     sertation, Columbia University.
         Source: Mahaney, 1973.23.

1918

1   DRINKWATER, JOHN. "Rupert Brooke on John Webster." In Prose
     Papers. London: E. Mathews, pp. 193-98. [Reprint. Freeport,

N.Y.: Books for Libraries Press, 1969.]
In a review of 1916.1, says Brooke assesses a large and difficult subject with skill and a poet's understanding. His analysis
of Webster's genius is perfect. Finds the chief charm of the book
is not in its criticism, but in its general temper--robust, positive, and eager.

1919

1   BAKER, GEORGE P. Dramatic Technique. Boston: Houghton,
    Mifflin, 531 pp., passim.
       In this textbook on writing plays, discusses Webster under
    "motivation" (the Cardinal in The Duchess of Malfi) and "character-
    ization" (both tragedies) and elsewhere intermittently.

2   COLBY, ELEBRIDGE. "The Echo Device in Literature." Bulletin
    of the New York Public Library 23, no. 11:683-713; no. 12:
    783-804. [Slightly revised: 1920.3.]
       Finds the echo scene in The Duchess of Malfi "Without a
    doubt . . . is the most dignified and serious use of the echo de-
    vice in all of English literature."

3   ELIOT, T.S. "Whispers of Immortality." In Poems. Richmond,
    Eng.: L. & V. Woolf, Hogarth Press, [pp. 77-8].
       Includes the oft-cited lines: "Webster was much possessed
    by death / And saw the skull beneath the skin."

4   LAWRENCE, WILLIAM J. "The Date of The Duchess of Malfi."
    Athenaeum, 21 November, pp. 1235-36.
       Observes that since the cast of the play is given in the
    1623 quarto and includes William Osteler as Antonio, we know that
    performance preceded the actor's death in 1614. The masque of mad-
    men is a response to a theatrical fad of 1613, so a date of spring
    1613, or between February 1613, and November 1614, is likely.

5   MUNCASTER, MARIE. "The Uses of Prose in Elizabethan Drama."
    Modern Language Review 14, no. 1 (January):10-15.
       Presents Webster's two tragedies as great examples of vari-
    ation between prose and poetry in the speeches of Flamineo and
    Bosola.

6   TARN. "The Duchess of Malfi." Spectator 122 (29 November):
    720-21.
       A review of the Stage Society production at the Lyric Theatre,
    Hammersmith. Comments that readers of Webster have been able to
    be selective, but in production some things are revealed unavoid-
    ably. For example, the theatrical construction of the play is
    "abominable," but Webster was a good poet. This production does
    not capture the poetry and fails with the theatre as well.

<u>1920</u>

*1   ALDEN, ROSE. "The Tragedy of Revenge." Ph.D. dissertation,
      Cornell University.
          Source: Mahaney, 1973.23.

2   ARCHER, WILLIAM. "The Duchess of Malfi." <u>Nineteenth Century</u>
     87 (January):126-32. [Excerpted: 1968.23.]
          Finds <u>The Duchess of Malfi</u> a "fundamentally bad" play, a
     coarse and sanguinary melodrama. It was glorified in Swinburne's
     "passage worship," which ignored structural efects such as the
     total absence of a motive for the Aragonian brothers' warnings to
     the Duchess; a cumbersome underplot; the delay in the brothers'
     revenge; the "grisly absurdity" of the severed hand; and the wax
     figures ("the device of a dramatist whose imagination works on the
     level of a Tussaud Chamber of Horrors"). Believes Swinburne, Lamb
     et al. went wrong because criticism must pay attention to dramatic,
     as well as poetic, characteristics. For the evolution of this
     thesis see also 1893.1; 1924.1.

3   COLBY, ELBRIDGE. <u>The Echo Device in Literature</u>. New York:
     New York Public Library, 61 pp.
          Slightly revised version of 1919.2.

4   CRUICKSHANK, ALFRED HAMILTON. <u>Philip Massinger</u>. Oxford:
     B. Blackwell, 228 pp., passim.
          Compares Massinger to Webster and finds Webster's tragedies
     are comparable only to Shakespeare's--"a great, a subtle, a well-
     studied mind, he produces isolated tragic effects of the most
     poignant kind; he is a master of atmosphere." Suggests that
     Webster does have some affinities with Massinger.

5   ELIOT, T.S. "<u>The Duchess of Malfi</u> at the Lyric: And Poetic
     Drama." <u>Art and Letters</u> 3 (Winter):36-39.
          Reviews a bad performance that seems to justify Archer's
     derision of Webster and the Elizabethan drama (1920.2) but that
     actually constitutes an indictment of the modern stage. Contempo-
     rary actors are ill at ease with poetry meant to be spoken: they
     insist on "interpreting" poetry, and ruining it as drama. It
     should just be "transmitted." Modern actors cannot do this be-
     cause they are too interested in themselves.

6   GROSSMANN, RUDOLF. <u>Spanien und das elisabethanische Drama</u>.
     Hamburgische Universität, Abhandlunger aus dem Gebeit der
     Auslandskunde, 4. Hamburg: L. Friederichsen, 138 pp., passim.
          Mentions Webster in discussing Spanish literature, politics,
     culture, society, and language in Renaissance drama.

7   NEILSON, WILLIAM ALLEN, and THORNDIKE, ASHLEY H. <u>A History of</u>
     <u>English Literature</u>. New York: Macmillan, pp. 129-40.
          Advanced high school text that cites Webster as a successor

of Shakespeare. Finds The White Devil "a horrible tragedy . . . in which a woman passes from crime to crime, still imperturbable, self-possessed, and glorying in her sin."

1921

1   BRADFORD, GAMALIEL. "The Women of Middleton and Webster." Sewanee Review 29:14-29. [Reprinted in Elizabethan Women, ed. H.O. White (Boston: Houghton-Mifflin, 1936), pp. 131-39.]
     Comments that women play a chief part in both Webster's major works. In The White Devil, Vittoria has a splendid and "masculine" intellect, but we do not know how guilty she is. The Duchess in The Duchess of Malfi is far more winning. She seeks the domestic life Vittoria flees.

2   CLARK, ARTHUR M. "The Authorship of Appius and Virginia." Modern Language Review 16:1-17.
     Claims Appius and Virginia is Heywood's companion piece to The Rape of Lucrece, with revisions by Webster, including the trial scene.

3   GREENLAW, EDWIN. A Syllabus of English Literature. Chicago: Sanborn, p. 106.
     College text that cites Webster's works as examples of the "end of the romantic drama."

4   INGERSLEBEN, IRMGARD von. Das elisabethanische Ideal der Ehefrau bei Overbury, 1613. Coethen: Otto Schultz, 108 pp.
     Considers Overbury's characters in general, especially his virtuous ones. Compares his characterizations of virtuous women to similar portraits, e.g., Thomas Elyot's.

*5 OWSLEY, R.N. "The Attitude Towards Death of Shakespeare, John Webster, and Thomas Dekker." Ph.D. dissertation, Columbia University.
     Source: Mahaney, 1973.23.

*6 ROSS, C.R. "The Machiavellian Man in Elizabethan Drama." Ph.D. dissertation, Columbia University.
     Source: Mahaney, 1973.23.

7   STRONG, ARCHIBALD J. A Short History of English Literature. London: Oxford University Press, pp. 119-51.
     Considers Webster in the chapter on "The Age of Shakespeare." Finds The Duchess of Malfi merits a place beside Shakespeare's tragedies. It is a greater play than The White Devil, producing intense tragic feeling and manifesting subtle psychology, sinister imagination, and a strange beauty.

8   SYKES, H. DUGDALE. "A Webster-Middleton Play: Anything for a
     Quiet Life." Notes and Queries 141:181-82, 202-4, 225-26, 300.
     [Reprinted: 1924.9.]
         Finds the main action is Webster's, the secondary plot is
     Middleton's. The attribution is based on "conclusive evidence"
     of style, vocabulary, borrowing patterns, and passages paralleling
     acknowledged plays. See responses: 1922.7, 11; 1928.1.

9   WALKLEY, ARTHUR B. Pastiche and Prejudice. New York: Knopf,
     pp. 178-83.
         Includes an essay titled "Vicissitudes of Classics," inspired
     by the Phoenix Society's production of The Duchess of Malfi, which
     demonstrated that the play's violence is dated.   The performance
     provoked titters.

                                   1922

1   BARTLETT, HENRIETTA C. Mr. William Shakespeare: Original and
     Early Editions of his Quartos and Folios, His Source Books, and
     Those Containing Contemporary Notices. New Haven: Yale
     University Press, pp. 149, 172-73.
         Lists Webster's preface to The White Devil as a "Contemporary
     Notice" of Shakespeare.

2   GREG, W.W. "Notes on Old Books." Library, 4th ser. 2:49-57.
         Discusses the printing practices involved in the three edi-
     tions of The Malcontent, including the third printing that included
     Webster's additions.

*3   HOWARTH, ROBERT GUY. "The Dramatic Art of John Webster." Ph.D.
     dissertation, University of Vienna.
         Source: Mahaney, 1973.23.

4   LAWRENCE, WILLIAM J. "Assembled Texts in the First Folio."
     Times Literary Supplement, 12 January, p. 28.
         Criticizes a thesis that claims the text of Merry Wives of
     Windsor is a collation of actors' versions since entrances are
     listed in opening stage directions.   This is also the arrangement
     of the text of The Duchess of Malfi, which is clearly not an as-
     sembled text.

5   LUCAS, F.L. Seneca and Elizabethan Tragedy. Cambridge:
     Cambridge University Press, pp. 117, 132. [Reprint. New York:
     Haskell House, 1969.]
         In chapter 5, contends that Webster's tragedies fall within
     the Senecan revenge play tradition.   Many of the lines in The White
     Devil also are Senecan.

                                   58

6   MARTINENGO-CESARESCO, EVELYN. "Webster's White Devil." Times
     Literary Supplement, 20 April, p. 261.
          Claims that Webster has the story of The White Devil garbled.
     Perhaps his source was a ballad. (The writer of this note lives
     in the house where the real Brachiano was killed.)

7   OLIPHANT, E.H.C. "Anything for a Quiet Life." Notes and Queries
     142:11.
          Divides act 5 into two scenes and also raises some questions
     regarding the authorship of Appius and Virginia. (A reply to
     1921.8 and in turn answered in 1922.11.)

8   SISSON, CHARLES JASPER. Le Goût public et le théâtre élisabéthain
     jusqu'à la mort de Shakespeare. Dijon: Darantière, pp. 65, 147.
          Briefly cites The Duchess of Malfi in regard to its physical
     and psychological "horrors."

9   SPENS, JANET. Elizabethan Drama. London: Methuen, pp. 131-43.
          Considers Webster along with Massinger, Middleton, and Ford
     in the chapter on "The Decadents." Finds Webster interested in
     the corrupting power of wealth, especially on the upper classes.
     The Duchess of Malfi has a "marked democratic tendency."

10   SUMMERS, MONTAGUE. Review of Donne's Sermons, ed. Logan P.
     Smith (Oxford: Clarendon Press, 1919). Modern Language Review
     70, no. 1 (January):88-90.
          Comments upon the similar imaginations of Donne and Webster:
     funeral metaphors, sepulchral properties, dreams of churchyards,
     mock friars, mocking death, etc. Suggests Webster remains morally
     noble in spite of this dark background of spiritual ruin and despair.

11   SYKES, H. DUGDALE. "Anything for a Quiet Life." Notes and
     Queries 142:50.
          In response to 1922.7, expresses pleasure that Oliphant
     corroborates the partial attribution of Anything for a Quiet Life
     to Webster.

12   THALER, ALWIN. Shakspere to Sheridan: A Book about the Theatre
     of Yesterday and Today. Cambridge, Mass.: Harvard University
     Press, pp. 22, 234, 298, 300-304. [Reprint. New York: B.
     Blom, 1963.]
          Stresses the continuity of seventeenth- and eighteenth-century
     theater. Cites Webster in relation to Henslowe's practices, al-
     though the emphasis in the book is on a later period.

                              1923

1   CHAMBERS, E.K. The Elizabethan Stage. Vol. 3. Oxford:
     Clarendon Press, pp. 507-12.
          Contains a wealth of general material about the court, the

control of the stage, the boy and adult companies, public and
private theaters and staging, the printing of plays, playwrights,
plus appendices and indexes. The section on Webster as a playwright includes the known facts of his life and collaborative efforts, a bibliography of collections of his works and of criticism,
a chronological list of plays with notes regarding dates, authorship, etc.

2   NICOLL, ALLARDYCE. A History of English Drama, 1660-1900.
     Vol. 1. Cambridge: Cambridge University Press, pp. 93, 296,
     303, and passim.
        Cites Webster often in passing, and especially as an influ-
ence upon Restoration dramatists. Also notes revivals and revisions of his plays during this period.

3   SCHELLING, FELIX. Foreign Influences on Elizabethan Plays.
     New York and London: Harpers, pp. 63-67, 72.
        Calls the plot of The White Devil an example of "the lure of
Italy." Asks where Webster found his version of Vittoria's story.
The sources and parallels of the story of The Duchess of Malfi
"would take us through half the literatures of Europe." Notes
that the actual Italian nobles mixed horrible cruelty with great
civility.

                              1924

1   ARCHER, WILLIAM. The Old Drama and the New. Boston: Small,
     Maynard, 396 pp.
        (Fourteen lectures on the history of the drama, generally
aimed to debunk the non-Shakespearean Elizabethans.) Since Webster
stood closest to Shakespeare, investigates The Duchess of Malfi in
light of the idolatry of Lamb and Swinburne. The major discussion
of Webster is the same as 1920.2. See also 1893.1. Reviewed:
1925.11. Archer is quoted in 1968.23; 1969.17; 1975.18.

2   BULLEN, A.H. Elizabethans. London: Chapman & Hall, pp. 73-94.
     [Reprint. New York: Russell & Russell, 1962.]
        Includes a brief discussion on the bustle and life of the
"Ho" plays.

3   CAMP, CHARLES W. The Artisan in Elizabethan Literature.
     Columbia University Studies in English and Comparative Literature.
     New York: Columbia University Press, pp. 16-17. [Reprint. New
     York: Octagon Books, 1972.]
        Remarks that Monuments of Honour glorifies John Hawkwood, a
merchant taylor.

4   ELIOT, T.S. "Elizabethan Dramatists: A Preface." Criterion
     2, no. 6:115-23. [Frequently reprinted, e.g., in Selected
     Essays, 1917-1932 (London: Faber & Faber, 1932) and Elizabethan

Essays (London: Faber & Faber, 1934).]
Notes that Lamb's Specimens created enthusiasm for the
Elizabethan drama but separated theater from literature. These
positions are now those of Swinburne and Archer, who oppose each
other, yet both believe in the distinction between poetry and drama.
Finds the weakness of the Elizabethan drama is not its lack of
realism but its lack of convention and its aim for realism. The
art of the Elizabethans is impure; it demands too much intrusion
of the actors' personalities, and there is not enough guidance
from stage conventions. Webster is "an interesting example of a
very great literary and dramatic genius directed toward chaos."

5 HARRISON, G.B. The Story of Elizabethan Drama. Cambridge:
   Cambridge University Press, pp. 126-27. [Reprint. New York:
   Octagon Books, 1973.]
   An introduction to the Elizabethan drama for beginners. Cites
Webster only as a dramatist of the next generation, writing for a
different audience under different conditions.

6 LEGOUIS, EMILE, and CAZAMIAN, LOUIS. Histoire de la littérature
   anglaise. Paris: Hachette, 1312 pp. [English translation.
   A History of English Literature. Vol. 1, The Middle Ages & the
   Renascence (650-1660), trans. Helen Douglas Irvine (New York:
   Macmillan, 1927), pp. 486-91. (Reissued 1964).]
   Discusses Webster as a contemporary of Shakespeare, lauded
by the romantics, and most noted for his tragedies. The White
Devil is one of a series of dramatic studies of courtesans (The
Maid's Tragedy, etc.) and also employs Italianate conventions.
The Duchess of Malfi is more closely knit and focuses upon the
theme of persecuted virtue. It is full of Shakespearean echoes
but aims at pathos, not psychology. "Not until Edgar Poe was there
another genius as completely morbid as Webster"--a painful artist,
who raised melodrama to true poetry. (The annotation is based
upon the English version.)

7 LUCAS, F.L. "The Duchess of Malfi." New Statesman 22:602-3.
   Comments that the source of the play is "fact" as well as
Bandello and Painter. Webster is often attacked by those who de-
mand realism and sermons, but he sought poetry and dramatic situation. Finds the fascination of Webster's work is in the intensity
of atmosphere and the passionate personality of his deep despair.
There is strength, beauty, and courage in his work as well.

8 P., A.W. Review of Sidelines on Elizabethan Drama, by H.
   Dugdale Sykes. Library, 4th ser. 5:366-71.
   Notes that Sykes (1924.9) bases his attributions on "frequency," and vindicates Webster's authorship of Appius and Virginia
as opposed to Rupert Brooke's support of Heywood on the basis of
similar evidence (1916.2). Praises Sykes for enlarging our appa-
ratus for attributing authorship.

9   SYKES, H. DUGDALE. Sidelights on Elizabethan Drama. Oxford:
     Clarendon Press, 237 pp. [Reprint of 1915.5 (pp. 140-58);
     1921.8 (pp. 159-62).
         In "Webster's Appius and Virginia: A Vindication" (pp.
     108-39), rejects Brooke's assertion that the play is not Webster's
     (1916.1); concludes that Appius and Virginia is mostly Webster's
     and written late in his career. Reviewed: 1924.8; 1925.3; 1927.6.

10   WELLS, HENRY W. Poetic Imagery Illustrated from Elizabethan
     Literature. Ph.D. dissertation, Columbia University. Columbia
     University Studies in English and Comparative Literature. New
     York: Columbia University Press, pp. 121-37. [Reprint. New
     York: Russell & Russell, 1961.]
         Studies types of images (e.g., decorative, "radical," etc.).
     Cites Webster under "radical" imagery.

11   WULCKO, CHARLES T. "The Webster Family." Notes and Queries
     148:29.
         Raises two queries: Is there a painting of "Shakespeare and
     his friends" that includes Webster? Is there a stained glass me-
     morial window featuring the Webster family?

                              1925

1   AGATE, JAMES. The Contemporary Theater. London: L. Parsons,
     pp. 144-46. [Reprinted: 1943.2.]
         Describes Webster's world in The White Devil as one of total
     evil, governed strictly by chance. His virtues include a mastery
     of horror, vigor of characters, and language. "To descend from
     Shakespeare to Webster is to walk out of air into the grave."

2   CARDOZO, JACOB LOPES. The Contemporary Jew in Elizabethan Drama.
     Amsterdam: H.J. Paris, pp. 78-79, 130-33. [Reprint. New York:
     Franklin, 1967.]
         Argues that there were probably very few Jews in England dur-
     ing the Renaissance. In The Devil's Law Case, Romelio imitates
     Machiavelli and Marlowe's Barabas when he disguises himself as a
     Jewish doctor. Cites The White Devil to show how some Renaissance
     references to Jews and Judaism have no real relationship with re-
     ligion.

3   GREG, W.W. Review of Sidelines on Elizabethan Drama, by H.
     Dugdale Sykes. Modern Language Review 20, no. 2 (April):
     195-200.
         Remarks that Sykes (1924.9) plays the game of parallelography
     with skill. His work is of some value in Elizabethan dramatic au-
     thorship attribution, but the method itself is doubtful: it is
     all superstructure and no foundation.

4   MURPHY, GWENDOLEN. A Bibliography of English Character-Books,
    1608-1700. Supplement to Biographical Society Transactions, no.
    4. Oxford: Oxford University Press for the Bibliographical
    Society, pp. 15-26.
        Describes the contents of the successive versions of the
    Overbury Characters, from 1614 to 1869, tracing which "Characters"
    were added, and when.

5   _____. A Cabinet of Characters. London: Oxford University
    Press, 437 pp., passim.
        An anthology of "Characters" from Theophrastus through
    Galsworthy that includes some of Webster's additions to Overbury.
    In the introduction describes the attribution of thirty-two
    "Characters" to Webster.

6   NICOLL, ALLARDYCE. British Drama. London: Harrap, 497 pp.
    [Rev. ed. New York: Crowell, 1933, pp. 101-15, 184-85. Re-
    printed through a 5th ed. (New York: Barnes & Noble, 1963).]
        Describes Webster's two tragedies as inhabiting a world of
    intense evil. Vittoria is a female counterpart of the Marlovian
    hero--prepared to indulge in any crime to satisfy her ambitions.
    The Duchess, however, is noble, but entrapped by evil. Evaluates
    Webster as a "half-genius": he creates masterful scenes, but the
    plays are less satisfying as wholes--his vision flags.

7   _____. An Introduction to Dramatic Theory. London: Harrap,
    pp. 36, 109, 129. [Revised as The Theory of Drama (London:
    Harrap, 1931).]
        Cites Webster as stressing the spiritual (in The Duchess of
    Malfi) and as a creator of a form: "horror tragedy."

8   OLIVERO, FEDERICO. "La Duchessa de Amalfi di John Webster."
    Rivista d'Italia 28:329-45.
        Reviews Webster's life and the general characteristics of
    his career. Discusses the characters of The Duchess of Malfi and
    compares the play to The White Devil and other Renaissance trage-
    dies. Translates several passages into Italian.

9   RÉBORA, PIERO. L'Italia nel dramma inglese (1558-1642). Milan:
    Modernissima, pp. 198-206.
        Discusses Webster in the chapter on "La Vita italiana nella
    tragedia romantica inglese." Finds The White Devil is based on a
    true and passionate story of Italy. The Duchess of Malfi is a
    nobler work that also recounts a true story.

10 SCHELLING, FELIX. Elizabethan Playwrights. New York: Harper,
    pp. 169-72.
        Describes Webster's works as showing three periods, of which
    only the middle one demonstrates artistic power. Webster belongs
    to the arrogant, scholarly, and satirical school of Jonson et al.
    Although some of his mannerisms are old-fashioned, his speeches

are brisk and often racy, and The Duchess of Malfi's torture scenes
are "overpowering."

11   STOLL, ELMER EDGAR. "The Old Drama and the New." Modern
      Language Review 20, no. 2 (April):147-57.
            In reviewing 1924.1 notes that Archer does away with vener-
      ation of the Elizabethans, but he goes too far: Shakespeare was
      not a wild exception to his time. Archer, unfairly, presents
      Webster as a lyric poet, not as the creator of structured dramas.
      Archer's praise of modern realism is overzealous.

12   SUGDEN, EDWARD H. A Topographical Dictionary to the Works of
      Shakespeare and His Fellow Dramatists. Manchester: University
      of Manchester Press, 580 pp., passim.
            A dictionary of Renaissance dramatic place names, including
      those in Webster's plays, e.g., "Malfi: A port on the E. shore of
      the Adriatic in Dalmatis, 7 miles N.W. of Ragusa. It is the scene
      of the earlier part of Webster's The Duchess of Malfi."

                              1926

*1   CHELLI, MAURICE. Etude sur la collaboration de Massinger avec
      Fletcher et son groupe. Paris: Les Presses Universitaires de
      France, 310 pp.
            Source: Mahaney, 1973.23.

2   DUKE, WINIFRED. "The Law in Drama." Juridicial Review 38:
      55-69.
            Argues that while the law is dramatic, most dramatists do
      not treat the law with credibility and accuracy. Webster employs
      law in the tragedy of The White Devil and the comedy of The Devil's
      Law Case. Some of the legal material in The Devil's Law Case is
      oddly modern, yet the play as a whole is excessively Elizabethan.

3   KOHLER, HENRY CHARLES. "The Frenchman in Elizabethan Drama."
      Ph.D. dissertation, Ohio State University.
            Finds some slight references to Frenchmen in Westward Ho.
      Several Webster plays refer to venereal disease as a French afflic-
      tion. Cites other remarks, passim.

4   LANDA, MYER JACK. The Jew in Drama. London: King, pp. 90-91,
      122. [Reprint. New York: KTAV Publishers, 1969.]
            Cites Webster (noted for his horrors and his lack of humor)
      for verbal references to Jews in The Duchess of Malfi and The
      White Devil, and the disguising of a Jew as a Christian in The
      Devil's Law Case, wherein "the vicious influence of Marlowe is
      discernible."

5   LUCAS, F.L. "An Unexplained Allusion in Webster and Rowley."
      Times Literary Supplement, 15 April, p. 283.

                              64

Explains a reference to the "Ballad of Flood" in A Cure for a Cuckold that has to do with a pamphlet concerning a blackmailer, published in 1623 (helping to date this play 1624-26).

6 _____. "Vincentio Lauriola." Notes and Queries 151:27.
Asks about the origin of the name given the "famous wax sculptor" in The Duchess of Malfi. One possible candidate is Cardinal Vincentio Laureus in De Thou's History.

7 MACKENZIE, AGNES MURE. The Playgoer's Handbook to the English Renaissance Drama. New York: Macmillan, pp. 122-28.
Presents Webster as a bridge between the Elizabethans and the decadents: his plays feature horror, but are never mere horror. Surveys individual works: Appius and Virginia and The Devil's Law Case have nice moments but are second rate. Both Italianate trage-dies are powerful, but The Duchess of Malfi has a weak beginning and end. The White Devil is his greatest work with lurid and powerful action and characters. The play "has strange lights through it like a meteor in a tempest." Notes some professional and amateur performances in the appendices.

8 PASSMANN, HANS. Der Typus der Kurtisane im elisabethanischen Drama. Leipzig: Noske, pp. 24-26, 39-43.
Discusses Lucy and Doll Hornet in the Dekker/Webster Westward Ho and Northward Ho, and considers Vittoria's role as a courtesan in The White Devil--reviews her accusation, refutation, and the facts of her trial. Another Webster courtesan is Julia, the Cardinal's mistress in The Duchess of Malfi.

9 POLLARD, A.W., and REDGRAVE, G.R. A Short-Title Catalogue of Books Printed in England, Scotland, & Ireland and of English Books Printed Abroad, 1475-1640. London: Bibliographical Society, p. 587. [Rev. ed. by W.A. Jackson, F.S. Ferguson, and Katharine F. Pantzer, vol. 2, I-Z (London: Bibliographical Society, 1976), pp. 443-44, adds one listing.]
Includes editions of The Devil's Law Case, A Monumental Column, Monuments of Honor, The Duchess of Malfi, and The White Devil. See 1951.23 for a continuation.

10 SHUSTER, GEORGE N. English Literature. Boston: Allyn & Bacon, p. 123.
Finds that realism and gracefulness are missing in Webster's powerful plays of horror, but he is a master of language.

11 TRENEER, ANNE. The Sea in English Literature from "Beowulf" to Donne. Liverpool: University Press of Liverpool; London: Hodder & Stoughton, p. 291.
Discusses images of storms, ships, galley slaves, and por-poises in The White Devil and The Duchess of Malfi. "Webster does not say much about the sea, but what he does say can never be for-gotten."

*12   WECTER, D. "The Literary Indebtedness of John Webster to John
       Donne." Ph.D. dissertation, Yale University.
           Source: Mahaney, 1973.23.

 13   WINSLOW, OLA ELIZABETH. Low Comedy as a Structural Element in
       English Drama from the Beginnings to 1642. Chicago: University
       of Chicago Press, pp. 134-48.
           Cites the "Ho" plays for incorporating low comedy in "Comedy
       of Manners."

                                   1927

  1   ALBRIGHT, EVELYN MAY. Dramatic Publication in England, 1580-
       1640. London: Oxford University Press, pp. 205-14.
           Studies the printing, selling, and performing of literary
       works, including dramatic ones. Finds Webster did oversee some
       publication of his own works, noting especially the comments in
       the preface to The White Devil.

  2   BALDWIN, THOMAS WHITFIELD. The Organization and Personnel of
       the Shakespearean Company. Princeton: Princeton University
       Press, pp. 365-66.
           In appendix 3, discusses The Duchess of Malfi as a play with
       assigned parts for specific actors for both the 1613 first per-
       formance and the 1623 revival. Also cites Webster passim.

  3   _____. "Posting Henslowe's Accounts." Journal of English and
       Germanic Philology 26 (January):42-90.
           Explicates the accounts of Henslowe's diary according to the
       principles of Elizabethan dramatic financing in order to reveal
       much of the history of the Admiral's Men, with some information
       relevant to Webster studies.

  4   BELLINGER, MARTHA F. A Short History of the Drama. New York:
       Henry Holt, pp. 242-43.
           Finds that Webster's few surviving plays are of "commanding
       quality." Webster is a somber, powerful dramatist, "full of grandi-
       ose poetic fury," occasionally crude and a touch obscure.

  5   BRETTLE, ROBERT E. "Bibliographical Notes on Some Marston
       Quartos and Early Collected Editions." Library, 4th ser. 8:
       336-48.
           Includes some information on the first, and subsequent,
       editions of The Malcontent.

  6   BRIGGS, WILLIAM DINSMORE. Review of Sidelights on Elizabethan
       Drama, by H. Dugdale Sykes. Modern Language Notes 42, no. 8
       (December):545-46.
           Finds Sykes's book (1924.9) is entirely devoted to authorship
       questions, and most of his conclusions are based on language.

Doubts can be raised about Sykes's methods: "anonymous" remains an attractive attribution.

7 GRAY, HENRY D. "Appius and Virginia: By Webster and Heywood." Studies in Philology 24, no. 2 (April):275-89.
    Concludes that, in reading, some scenes are obviously Heywood's, some are unclear, and some are clearly Webster's (e.g., the trial scene, 4.1). Splits the play accordingly, using such evidence as characteristic contractions, metrical characteristics, etc. Notes also the possibility of other collaborators early (c. 1603-4) in Webster's career. See 1916.1, 1924.9 for additional discussions of this issue.

8 GRAY, HENRY DAVID. "A Cure for a Cuckold by Heywood, Rowley, and Webster." Modern Language Review 22, no. 4 (October): 389-97.
    Gives most of the play to Rowley, with three scenes by Webster and four by Heywood, on the basis of considerations of style. See 1905.6, 1914.12 for other considerations of this subject.

9 HAWORTH, PETER. English Hymns and Ballads, and Other Studies in Popular Literature. Oxford: B. Blackwell, pp. 71-148.
    Discusses Webster and his works in five sections:
    1. Traces classical and "Miltonic" traits in Webster and notes the absence of any comic spirit in his works. Finds grave defects in all his works (e.g., he did not seem to finish his plays), concluding that Webster was a literary artist forced into the drama.
    2. Presents The White Devil as a study of a sympathetic heroine. Her love is sincere, and her attitude in the trial is not "innocence-resembling boldness." Her sins are simply a more concentrated version of the Duchess of The Duchess of Malfi, and her love gives the play heart and meaning.
    3. Discusses The Duchess of Malfi: to Elizabethan audiences the Duchess' remarriage below her station was courting disaster; thus, her persecutors would seem less inhumane to them. The play presents a conflict between her femininity and her nobility. Like Vittoria, she is the whole heart of her play, and after she dies, the glory of the drama is gone. The Duchess' death is a true catharsis--it robs death of its sting.
    4. Presents The Devil's Law Case as Webster's most personally "revealing" work. The characters are appropriate for tragedy, but the action is comic.
    5. Finds that most critics ignore the un-Websterian Appius and Virginia and concludes that this play is not Webster's.

10 LAWRENCE, WILLIAM J. Pre-Restoration Stage Studies. Cambridge, Mass.: Harvard University Press, 435 pp., passim.
    Cites Webster intermittently, e.g., he uses light skillfully; the madmen's dance in The Duchess of Malfi is a species of the

stage jig; The White Devil demands splendid costuming, even for
performance in the low class Red Bull theater.

11   LUCAS, F.L., ed. The Complete Works of John Webster. 4 vols.
      London: Chatto & Windus, 1:288 pp.; 2:372 pp.; 3:339 pp.;
      4:274 pp. [Reprint. New York: Gordian Press, 1966. Intro-
      ductory material excerpted: 1975.18. The Duchess of Malfi
      and The White Devil reprinted with additions and revisions:
      1958.17, 18.]
          The first modern--and still definitive--complete edition of
      Webster's works.
      Vol. 1--Preface; Bibliography; General Introduction; Webster's
          Imitation; and The White Devil.
      Vol. 2--The Duchess of Malfi; The Devil's Law Case.
      Vol. 3--Collaborations: A Cure for a Cuckold; Appius and Virginia;
          Minor works: Short poems; A Monumental Column, induction to
          The Malcontent; Monuments of Honour.
      Vol. 4--Conjectural Works: Characters; Anything for a Quiet Life;
      The Fair Maid of the Inn; Collaborations with Dekker; Spurious
      Plays; Additions to The Spanish Tragedy; Metrical Material; Index.

          In the general introduction, reviews accusations that Webster
      is incompetent and immoral. But, conceding ill construction and
      crudities, finds his work is fascinating: he creates great situ-
      ations, ablaze with pageantry and passion. The inconsistencies
      are not important, especially in stage production, since the
      poetry justifies the plots. He is the master of brooding atmosphere
      and sudden flashes. Also finds Webster's poetry and his satire
      praiseworthy. He rises to his highest in the somber splendor of
      death, creating a world of despair, in which virtue is rewarded no
      more than evil. Also discusses Webster's life and his borrowings.
          Believes that The White Devil comes close to the real Italy
      of the Renaissance--people actually did those things. Webster
      creates magnificent characters amid the ruins. They have little
      virtue, but great will, spirit, and splendor, especially Brachiano
      and Vittoria, while Flamineo is a cold, clear, intellectual
      Machiavellian, cynical but engaging. This is Webster's greatest
      play.
          Finds The Duchess of Malfi is a sadder, tenderer, less vio-
      lent play, with less fire and a twilight tone. With less vigor,
      it has more grace. The Duchess has the endurance of a martyr,
      not the spirit of a fighter like Vittoria. The play is pervaded
      by the spirit of melancholy. Reviews and analyzes the play's
      plot and characters.
          Suggests The Devil's Law Case presents life as a bitter
      comedy. The play is obscure and weakly motivated, with a few
      superb scenes. Still, it has a cleverness and vividness, espe-
      cially the trial.
          Judges A Cure for a Cuckold (with Rowley and Heywood) better
      than Anything for a Quiet Life, but still the product of a decayed
      dramatist--frivolous without being lighthearted, with an obscure

plot and improbable characters.

   Appius and Virginia (with Heywood) is a very worthy piece
that reverts to a direct and simple style. It is competent, but
with no flicker of genius.

   Says of Anything for a Quiet Life (with Middleton) "It would
have given me great pleasure to suppress this play: it has certainly given me none to edit it."

   Finds The Fair Maid of the Inn (with Massinger, Fletcher,
Rowley, and others) has an improbable plot, but some vigorous
comedy and one lovable character. Reviewed: 1928.2, 7.

12   LUCAS, F.L. "Did Dr. Forman Commit Suicide?" Times Literary
     Supplement, 7 April, p. 250.
        Reports, in Webster's portion of The Fair Maid of the Inn,
     an allusion to the well-known astrologer and physician, Simon
     Forman.

13   MACKENZIE, AGNES MURE. The Playgoer's Handbook to the English
     Renaissance Drama. New York: Macmillan, pp. 122-28. [Reprint.
     New York: Cooper Square Publishers, 1971.]
        Sees Webster as bridging the true Elizabethans and the
     Decadents. His greatest two plays utilize the machinery of the
     earlier revenge plays. They have a "superb dark spaciousness that
     glimmers now and then with royal pity." Recounts the plots and
     analyzes the characters of both works. The Duchess of Malfi, in
     which Bosola is the chief character, is inferior to The White Devil.
     Finds the latter play derives its unity and reason from its three
     main figures, and that the entire piece "has strange lights through
     it."

14   OLIPHANT, E.H.C. The Plays of Beaumont and Fletcher: An
     Attempt to Determine Their Respective Shares and the Shares of
     Others. New Haven: Yale University Press, pp. 92-94, 276-77,
     383-91, 463-72.
        Surveys Webster's particular qualities, especially character-
     istic verse patterns, as he is a candidate for authorship of some
     plays in the Beaumont and Fletcher canon. Concludes that The
     Honest Man's Fortune is by five authors, including Webster, who
     is seen most in the prose, especially the railing passages. The
     Fair Maid of the Inn includes among its authors Webster, Fletcher,
     Ford and Massinger. See 1928.8, 1930.7 for further studies in this
     area.

15   PIERCE, FREDERICK E. "Some Literary Echoes." Modern Language
     Notes 42, no. 1 (January):27-29.
        Suggests that Webster's citation of glowworms in The Duchess
     of Malfi 4.2 comes from John Davies's The Scourge of Folly (1611)--
     although the reference could be proverbial.

16   ROLLINS, HYDER E. "Samuel Sheppard and His Praise of Poets."
     Studies in Philology 24, no. 4 (April):509-55.

Reports that in his "Fairy King" (1648-54), book 5, canto 6
(1651.1), Sheppard praises Webster's three tragedies as greater
than Jonson's ("thou shallt bee / read longer, and with more
Applause than hee").

*17   SIMRELL, VIVIAN EARLE. "Studies in Elizabethan Drama: John
       Webster." Ph.D. dissertation, Stanford University.
            Source: Mahaney, 1973.23.

18   STOLL, ELMER E. Shakespeare Studies. New York: Macmillan,
       502 pp., passim.
            Mentions Webster often, usually in relation to Shakespeare,
       e.g., Webster is the only dramatist who singled out Shakespeare
       as especially valuable. Compares Shakespeare's ghosts to the
       spirit of Brachiano in The White Devil.

19   WELSFORD, ENID. The Court Masque: A Study in the Relationship
       between Poetry & the Revels. Cambridge: Cambridge University
       Press, pp. 293-301. [Reprint. New York: Russell & Russell,
       1962.]
            Discusses Webster in the chapter on "The Influence of the
       Masque on Drama." Examples of that influence include the lyrical
       episode of Cornelia's lamenting dirge with its elaborate pomp in
       The White Devil, and The Duchess of Malfi's "masque of madmen
       where the white clad Duchess is surrounded by howling lunatics."

                                    1928

1   DUNKEL, WILBUR D. "The Authorship of Anything for a Quiet Life."
       PMLA 43:793-99.
            Responds to Sykes (1921.8), who overstates Webster's role:
       Middleton is the chief author. The borrowings are not exclusively
       Websterian, the characterization is Middleton's, as is the satire,
       language, etc. Suggests that perhaps Webster revised a Middleton
       comedy.

2   ELIOT, T.S. "Mr. Lucas' Webster." Criterion 8 (June):155-58.
            In a review of 1927.11, finds Lucas's work a monument of
       editing, but expresses some disagreements with the critical intro-
       duction: Lucas treats Webster too much in isolation from his con-
       temporaries. Still, his criticism is better than that of either
       Archer or Swinburne.

3   HENDY, E.W. "John Webster--Playwright and Naturalist."
       Nineteenth Century 103 (January):111-23. [Excerpted: 1968.23.]
            Finds Webster's biological knowledge shows him a keen ob-
       server of wildlife, especially birds. His most prolific nature
       imagery is in the tragedies--most often in the speeches of Flamineo
       or Bosola, and in central scenes of the plays. Songs, dirges, and
       the like also contain much nature imagery. "Shakespeare and

Webster must have been acquainted, and it is legitimate for us to imagine them meeting at the 'Mermaid' and chaffing each other over their little lapses in scientific accuracy."

4   LUCAS, F.L. Tragedy: Serious Drama in Relation to Aristotle's "Poetics." New York: Harcourt, Brace & Co., 160 pp., passim. [Rev. ed. London: Hogarth Press, 1957.]
     Cites Webster frequently in a general study of Aristotle's definition of tragedy and its application through the ages. Notes, for example, Webster's ability to manipulate plot to create tension and the importance of women characters as initiators of his actions.

5   PRAZ, MARIO. "Machiavelli and the Elizabethans." Proceedings of the British Academy 14:49-97. [Reprinted with minor revisions in his The Flaming Heart (New York: Doubleday, 1958), pp. 90-145. Also printed as Machiavelli e gl'inglesi dell'epoca elisabettiana (Florence: Vallechachi, 1930), and revised as Machiavelli in Inghilterra ed altri saggi (Rome: Tumminelli, 1943).]
     Finds that in The White Devil Flamineo is a Machiavellian: so is Romelio in The Devil's Law Case, and Bosola in The Duchess of Malfi is an "extreme development" of the character of the villain.

6   SISSON, CHARLES JASPER. The Elizabethan Dramatists Except Shakespeare. London: Benn, pp. 58-59.
     Describes The White Devil as a sensational drama of sinister Italian crime. Finds the tragic theme of The Duchess of Malfi in the persecution of the Duchess. In general, Webster's works include lapses into sensation and sheer despair, but they are lightened by occasional splendors of dramatic poetry.

7   SQUIRE, J.C. "Webster." Observer, 12 February, p. 4.
     Judges Lucas's edition (1927.11) vivacious and competent: it shows great labor. Some of Lucas's attributions, especially Anything for a Quiet Life, are questionable.

8   SYKES, H. DUGDALE. Review of The Plays of Beaumont and Fletcher . . . , by E.H.C. Oliphant. Review of English Studies 4, no. 16 (October):465-63.
     Agrees with Oliphant's (1927.14) attribution of part of The Fair Maid of the Inn and The Honest Man's Fortune to Webster. See 1930.7.

9   THORP, WILLARD. The Triumph of Realism in Elizabethan Drama, 1558-1612. Princeton Studies in English, 3. Princeton: Princeton University Press, pp. 81-120. [Reprint. New York: Gordian Press, 1970.]
     Contends that the Elizabethan dramatic evolution from romance to realism was caused by, among other things, a loss of didactic purpose. Illustrates this thesis in a discussion of the

realistic depiction of the relationship between the sexes in The
White Devil.

10 TURNER, CELESTE. Anthony Mundy: An Elizabethan Man of Letters.
    University of California Publications in English, vol. 2, no.
    1. Berkeley: University of California Press, pp. 140-44.
        Cites Webster throughout, especially for his "verses" to
Mundy, attached to Palmerin of England, III (1602). (Originally
a University of California, Berkeley, Ph.D. dissertation, 1928:
"Anthony Mundy: A Study in the Elizabethan Profession of Letters".)

1929

1 ARONSTEIN, PHILIPP. Das englische Renaissancedrama. Leipzig
   and Berlin: B.G. Teubner, pp. 214-16, 259-63, 278-80.
       Discusses the "Ho" plays (under Children's Companies), The
White Devil, and The Duchess of Malfi. Also considers general
characteristics of Jacobean drama and mentions Appius and Virginia.

2 BASKERVILL, CHARLES READ. The Elizabethan Jig and Related Song
   Drama. Chicago: University of Chicago Press, p. 160.
       Mentions the dance of madmen in The Duchess of Malfi as a
type of comic or antic dance.

3 ECKHARDT, EDUARD. Das englische Drama der Spätrenaissance.
   Berlin and Leipzig: Walter de Gruyter, pp. 112, 118.
       Discusses the minor works and attribution problems, and out-
lines the stories and sources of the tragedies, including Appius
and Virginia.

4 FOSS, KATHERINE A. "A Study of the Ideas Reflected in the
   Plays of John Webster." M.A. thesis, University of Cincinnati.
       Discusses major concepts, religious and classical in origin,
in Webster's works, focusing especially on stoicism and the inde-
pendence of reason. Finds his religious ideas are hard to pin-
point: he sees evil in the formalism of the Church, and has doubts
about immortality. But the classical virtue of friendship is very
important.

5 GRIERSON, HERBERT J.C. Cross Currents in English Literature
   of the Seventeenth Century. London: Chatto & Windus, p. 104.
       Considers Webster briefly in the chapter on tragedy. He
creates a welter of crime, especially murder, making it impossible
to contemplate with sympathy any of his characters.

6 HOLMES, ELIZABETH. Aspects of Elizabethan Imagery. Oxford:
   B. Blackwell, pp. 102-28. [Reprint. New York: Russell &
   Russell, 1966.]
       Emphasizes Elizabethan drama as a predecessor of metaphysical
poetry. Thus, it is philosophical, a mixture of passion and

thought, etc. Marston, Tourneur, and Webster share a capacity to
suggest overpowering darkness and gloom. Webster presents the
beauty of tragic but indestructible human passion. His imagery
is in close touch with this tragic conception, creating a dark and
shut-in scene.

7   NICOLL, ALLARDYCE, ed. The Works of Cyril Tourneur. London:
    Fanfrolico Press, pp. 47-49. [Reprint. New York: Russell &
    Russell, 1963.]
        Describes The White Devil as one of the three most powerful
non-Shakespearean plays of its age. Also discusses Tourneur's
share in The Honest Man's Fortune.

8   OLIPHANT, E.H.C. "How Not to Play the Game of Parallels."
    Journal of English and Germanic Philology 28:1-15.
        Surveys authorship studies by Sykes and others, asking if
parallel passages prove authorship, borrowing, or nothing at all.
Notes a number of pitfalls, e.g., citing trite parallel passages.
In Appius and Virginia studies, Sykes seems to fit the facts to
his arguments. The play probably is not all Webster's, but a
collaboration. See 1924.9 for a collection of studies by Sykes.

9   PRAZ, MARIO. "The Italian Element in English." Essays and
    Studies 15:20-66.
        Surveys the use of Italian words in English literature,
especially in Elizabethan plays, including Webster's.

10 SPIVEY, GAYNELL CALLAWAY. "Elizabethanisms in Victorian Poetic
    Drama." Ph.D. dissertation, University of North Carolina,
    271 pp., passim.
        Focuses upon Swinburne and his use of Vittoria as a model
Mary Stuart. Also notes that Browning was familiar with Webster's
work.

11 THORNDIKE, ASHLEY H. English Comedy. New York: Macmillan,
    pp. 152, 159, 219, 221.
        A broad history, from the beginnings to 1900, that finds
Webster/Dekker's "Ho" plays realistic, gross, and coarse, and The
Devil's Law Case a "rather unsuccessful tragicomedy."

                              1930

1   BASTIAENEN, JOHANNES A. The Moral Tone of Jacobean and
    Caroline Drama. Amsterdam: H.J. Paris, 198 pp., passim.
    [Reprint. New York: Haskell House, 1966.]
        Studies the moral flaws in Shakespeare and Jonson, and the
lesser, "less excusable" dramatists of the period. Cites Webster
often. In a section dealing with adultery in The White Devil, notes
that in the play "gratification of lust on the one hand, and of am-
bitious aspirations on the other, are the ruling passions. . . . "

Also cites Webster as the author of <u>Bussy d'Ambois</u> in the section on "Lust."

2   EATON, WALTER P. <u>The Drama in English.</u> New York: Scribner's, pp. 130-35.
       Contends that although <u>The Duchess of Malfi</u> has been hailed as a masterpiece, it isn't. Among its weaknesses are the time lapse between acts 2 and 3 and Bosola's failure to tell the brothers whom the Duchess married ("Could anything be more absurd, or more destructive to dramatic illusion?"). A modern audience would laugh at Webster's dramatic ineptness and sheer stupidity. Closely follows Archer: <u>The Duchess of Malfi</u> is not a masterpiece but "a clumsy, overwrought, illogical 'shocker.'"

3   FENTON, DORIS. "The Extra-Dramatic Moment in Elizabethan Plays before 1616." Ph.D. dissertation, University of Pennsylvania, 125 pp., passim.
       Studies direct addresses to audiences, a device used in some of the conjectured Webster plays and in the dying didactic addresses in <u>The Duchess of Malfi</u>.

4   GASPARETTI, ANTONIO. "Giovan Battista Giraldi e Lope de Vega." <u>Bulletin Hispanique</u> 32:372-403.
       Considers the relationship of <u>El Mayordomo de la Duquesa de Amalfi</u>, Bandello, and <u>The Duchess of Malfi</u>.

*5   HÖHNA, HEINRICH. <u>Der Psysiologus in der elisabethanischen Literatur</u>. Erlangen: Höfer & Limmert, 96 pp.
       Source: Mahaney, 1973.23 (cites pp. 42-57).

6   LINTHICUM, M. CHANNING. "Gingerline." <u>Philological Quarterly</u> 9, no. 2 (April):212-13.
       Suggests the word "gingerline" is used in <u>Anything for a Quiet Life</u> to mean a kind of reddish color.

7   OLIPHANT, E.H.C. "The Plays of Beaumont and Fletcher: Some Additional Notes." <u>Philological Quarterly</u> 9:7-22.

8   TAYLOR, JOSEPH RICHARD. <u>The Story of Drama</u>. Vol. 1. Boston: Expression Co., pp. 468-69.
       Discusses Webster with "Shakespeare's Predecessors." <u>The White Devil</u> and <u>The Duchess of Malfi</u> stand out among contemporary plays and are often presented in anthologies as "Tragedies of Blood." <u>The Devil's Law Case</u>, however, is scorned by modern critics. His other works are involved in a maze of collaboration.

*9   WHITTAKER, W.H. "Conjectures on the Relationship of the Two 'White Devils' of the Seventeenth Century." Ph.D. dissertation, Columbia University.
       Source: Mahaney, 1973.23.

<u>1931</u>

1   BALD, R.C.   "'Assembled' Texts." <u>Library</u>, 4th ser. 12:243-48.
        Comments on the text of <u>The Duchess of Malfi</u>, especially its
stage directions at the head of each scene, as well as some other
related textual curiosities (e.g., a repeated stage direction that
suggests the restoration of an earlier cut).

2   CAMPBELL, LILY B.   "Theories of Revenge in Renaissance England."
    <u>Modern Philology</u> 28, no. 3 (February):281-96.
        Finds God's vengeance for sin and the forbidden nature of
human revenge is the great theme of Elizabethan tragedy. Contends
that human revengers, such as those in <u>The Duchess of Malfi</u> or <u>The
White Devil</u>, would be considered evil.

3   CLARK, ARTHUR MELVILLE.   <u>Thomas Heywood, Playwright and
    Miscellanist</u>. Oxford: B. Blackwell, 356 pp., passim.
        Mentions Webster often in a study of Heywood's life and work.
Discusses the relationship between the two dramatists in the authorship of <u>Sir Thomas Wyat</u> and <u>Appius and Virginia</u>: Webster perhaps revised Heywood's manuscript of the latter play. They were
members of the Queen's Men and coauthors of elegies on the death
of Prince Henry (1613).

4   GREG, W.W.   <u>Dramatic Documents from the Elizabethan Playhouses</u>.
    Vol. 1. Oxford: Oxford University Press, pp. 288-93.
        Describes the manuscript of <u>The Honest Man's Fortune</u>, includ-
ing a list of all stage directions.

5   LINDABURY, RICHARD VLIET.   <u>A Study of Patriotism in the
    Elizabethan Drama</u>. Princeton: Princeton University Press,
    218 pp., passim.
        Includes multiple references to some of Webster's conjectural
works: in <u>Sir Thomas Wyat</u> the Spanish are accused of being very
proud and that play's anti-Catholicism is noteworthy.

6   McMILLAN, ADDIE TOWNSEND.   "The Ghost as a Medium of Revenge,
    in the Elizabethan Drama Outside Shakespeare's Works, 1585-
    1625." M.A. thesis, University of Oklahoma, 109 pp., passim.
        Believes Webster helped to develop the "sepulchral type of
revenger ghost." Notes his use of ghosts include the voice from
the tomb in <u>The Duchess of Malfi</u> and the visible spirit of
Brachiano in <u>The White Devil</u>. Webster employs the supernatural
for moral ends. Outlines both plays and describes supernatural
visits and visions therin.

7   MYERS, AARON MICHAEL.   <u>Representation and Misrepresentation of
    the Puritan in Elizabethan Drama</u>. Philadelphia: University of
    Pennsylvania Press, 151 pp., passim, esp. pp. 27-39.
        Finds the "Ho" plays contain some fairly gentle and casual
belittlement of Puritans, who are also satirized in <u>The Devil's
Law Case</u>. (Originally a Ph.D. dissertation.)

8   ODELL, GEORGE C.D. <u>Annals of the New York Stage</u>. Vol. 7.
      New York: Columbia University Press, p. 5.
         Notes a 5-10 April 1858 production of Horne's version of
<u>The Duchess of Malfi</u> with Mr. and Mrs. Waller. Advertisements for
this version quoted Lamb, Hazlitt, and "other enthusiasts."

9   PIETZKER, ANNEMARIE. <u>Der Kaufmann in der elisabethanischen</u>
      <u>Literatur</u>. Quakenbrück: C. Trute, pp. 16-17.
         Briefly considers Webster's merchants, especially Romelio
in <u>The Devil's Law Case</u> and Rochefield in <u>A Cure for a Cuckold</u>.
(Originally a Freiburg dissertation.)

10   SHAW, GEORGE BERNARD. <u>Our Theatre in the Nineties</u>. 3 vols.
      London and New York: Wise, 1:133-40; 2:191; 3:333-37.
         In vol. 1, remarks, on the occasion of a revival of <u>Macbeth</u>,
on the "insane and hideous rhetoric" that Shakespeare shares with
"Jonson, Webster, and the whole crew of insufferable bunglers and
dullards whose work stands out as vile even at the beginning of
the Seventeenth Century when every art was corrupted to the marrow
by the orgie called the Renaissance. . . . "
         In vol. 2 comments that nature can produce no murderer cruel
enough for Webster.
         In vol. 3 notes, in a review of <u>The Coxcomb</u> by Beaumont and
Fletcher, "the opacity that prevented Webster, the Tussaud laureate,
from appreciating his own stupidity."

11   THOMAS, PERCY G. <u>Aspects of Literary Theory and Practice 1550-</u>
      <u>1870</u>. London: Heath, Cranton, pp. 175, 197. [Reprint. Port
      Washington, N.Y.: Kennikat Press, 1970.]
         Cites Webster in the section concerning Lamb's resurrection
of Elizabethan authors and, later, for his ability, like that of
Dickens, to draw tears.

12   WAGNER, BERNARD M. "New Verses by John Webster." <u>Modern</u>
      <u>Language Notes</u> 46, no. 6 (June):403-5.
         Describes seven "emblematical" verses found on an engraving
in the British Museum that may be added to Webster's works. The
engraving is titled "The Progenie of the Most Renowned Prince James
King of Great Britaine France and Ireland" and is dated 1624-25.

13   WRIGHT, LOUIS B. "Madmen as Vaudeville Performers on the
      Elizabethan Stage." <u>Journal of English and Germanic Philology</u>
      30 (January):48-54.
         Offers several examples of insanity as extraneous entertain-
ment in regular Elizabethan play performances, including the
Bedlamites in <u>Northward Ho</u>, 4. These seem created simply for
audience amusement. In <u>The Duchess of Malfi</u>, modern audiences
see the madmen as intensifying the play's horror: Elizabethans
may have found them comic relief. See 1932.6 for an opposing
view.

14 ZEYDEL, EDWIN HERMANN. Ludwig Tieck and England. Princeton: Princeton University Press, pp. 9, 113, 139.
Discusses Webster and Tate as sources for Tieck's Vittoria Accorombona.

1932

*1 "Article IX--English Tragedy." Edinburgh Review 38 (February): 197-98.
Mahaney, 1973.23, cites this article as dealing with The Duchess of Malfi, but no such piece appears in 1932, 1832, or vol. 38.

2 BRADBROOK, MURIEL C. Elizabethan Stage Conditions. Cambridge: Cambridge University Press, 148 pp., passim. [Reprint. 1968.]
Charts the construction of Shakespeare's stage and discusses its effect upon the structure of Elizabethan plays. Cites Webster in passing: The White Devil is his best effort; he borrows from Sidney; his style is epigrammatic, and so on.

3 GUHA, P.K. Tragic Relief. London: Oxford University Press, 233 pp., passim.
Defines the subject as "the artistic palliative of the pain of tragic art" (not just comedy). Revenge tragedies, including Webster's, degenerate into tragedies of horror in which the relief is absent. Among the "mechanical devices of tragic relief" are ghosts such as those of The White Devil and supernatural premonitions.

4 HART, ALFRED. "The Time Allotted for Representation of Elizabethan and Jacobean Plays." Review of English Studies 8, no. 32 (October):395-413.
Based on line count and internal references within the plays, finds certain authors and companies specialized in two-hour plays, while others went longer. Notes Webster's complaint about acting The White Devil on a "dull" day--night hits London around 4:30 in the winter, so plays and performances longer than two and a half hours were in trouble if they began at 2:00. There was probably much abridgement to get within the two-hour limit.

5 HARVEY, Sir PAUL. The Oxford Companion to English Literature. Oxford: Oxford University Press, p. 877. [4th ed. rev. by D. Eagle (Oxford: Clarendon Press, 1967).]
Judges Webster nearest in tragic power to Shakespeare.

6 HAYAKAWA, SAMUEL ICHIYE. "A Note on the Madmen's Scene in Webster's The Duchess of Malfi." PMLA 47, no. 3 (September): 907-9.
Contrary to several critics (e.g., 1931.13), finds this scene does not have any comic import. It is meant to be horrible

and tyrannical, and is part of a carefully calculated series of
increasingly horrible events--the dead man's hand, waxworks, madmen, dirge, and strangling--that point out the splendid courage
of the Duchess.

7   MARTIN, MARY FOSTER. "If You Know Not Me You Know Nobodie and
     The Famous Historie of Sir Thomas Wyat." Library, 4th ser. 13:
     272-81.
         Doubts both these works are part of the "Lady Jane" to which
     Henslowe refers. But parts of both were written by Heywood, and
     this accounts for some textual similarities.

*8   SCHMIDT, MIKLOS. Webster Tragikus Muveszte. Budapest.
     Source: Mahaney, 1973.23.

9   STEVENS, THOMAS WOOD. The Theatre: From Athens to Broadway.
     New York: D. Appleton, p. 114.
         Notes Webster's sudden and passionate phrases.

10   SUMMERS, MONTAGUE. "Webster and Cardano." Notes and Queries
     163:424.
         Finds a section of The Duchess of Malfi (5.2) borrows from
     Cardano's De Rerum Varietate.

1933

1   d'EXIDEUIL, PIERRE. "Vengeance." Cahiers du Sud 10:67-76.
     [Reprinted: 1941.5.]
         Surveys the Senecan tradition, especially in The Duchess of
     Malfi--a culminating point in the revenge tragedy line. Comments
     upon the hateful and monstrous persecutors of the Duchess.

2   EDWARDS, W.A. "John Webster." Scrutiny 11:12-23. [Excerpted:
     1969.17. Reprinted in Determinations, ed. F.R. Leavis (London:
     Chatto & Windus, 1934), pp. 155-78.]
         Believes Lamb and Swinburne exaggerate--but so does Archer.
     Sees Webster's tragedies as dramatic poems, not historical docu-
     ments. Their style is epigrammatic, with striking images, many
     oxymorons, and set piece "characters," but it is a conceited and
     fantastical style. Sometimes Flamineo especially seems to deliver
     maxims and sentences not especially called-for. This is not the
     best of styles for a drama. Both tragedies are also "incompetent-
     ly" plotted--with many unrelated incidents, much melodrama, popu-
     lar pornography, etc. Webster broods over the sinister and the
     morbid with an "oppressive monotony."

3   ELTON, OLIVER. The English Muse. London: Bell, pp. 186-88.
     [Reprint. 1950.]
         Describes Webster's language as richly figurative and sardon-
     ic. His poetic diction is spare, concentrated and full of strange-
     ness. His poetry blazes, but interest is not sustained consistently.

*4   FRIENDLY, D.E. "An Historical Production of The Duchess of
      Malfi." Ph.D. dissertation, Yale University.
          Source: Mahaney, 1973.23.

5   FROHBERG, GEORGE. "Das Fortleben des elisabethanischen Dramas
      in Zeitalter der Restauration." Shakespeare-Jahrbuch 69:61-86.
          Lists Restoration productions of Renaissance plays, by author.
      Notes a Betterton production of Appius and Virginia, and versions
      of A Cure for a Cuckold, The Duchess of Malfi, The White Devil and
      the Tate The White Devil of 1707.

6   HOWARTH, ROBERT GUY. "John Webster." Times Literary Supplement,
      2 November, p. 751.
          Suggests that although Lucas's edition does not mention it,
      there is some possibility Webster was related (a brother?) to a
      cart-wright. This would help clarify Fitzjeffrey's satire in
      Notes from Blackfryers (1617.1).

7   ISAACS, JACOB. Production and Stage-Management at the
      Blackfriars Theatre. London: Oxford University Press for the
      Shakespeare Association, 28 pp., passim.
          Cites The Duchess of Malfi as an illustration several times
      in this general study of private theater conditions. For example,
      the actual configuration of the masque of madmen is left for the
      production staff.

8   JALOUX, EDMUND. "L'Esprit élizabéthain." Cahiers du Sud 10:
      7-20. [Reprinted: 1941.5.]
          Surveys the Elizabethan dramatists, noting especially
      Webster's views on death.

9   KNIGHTS, L.C. "Seventeenth Century Melancholy." Criterion 13
      (October):97-112.
          Examines the causes and manifestations of Jacobean melancholy,
      citing Flamineo as an example of those with schooling who lack pre-
      ferment--a common class of melancholics.

*10   LEOPOLD, H. "John Webster, le dramaturge." Ph.D. dissertation,
      University of Paris.
          Source: Mahaney, 1973.23.

11   RIBEMONT-DESSAIGNES, G. "A propos de Webster et de quelques
      femmes." Cahiers du Sud 10:44-49. [Reprinted: 1941.5.]
          Offers a brief look at several Webster females, especially
      Vittoria.

12   SIBLEY, GERTRUDE MARIAN. The Lost Plays and Masques, 1500-1642.
      Cornell Studies in English, vol. 19. Ithaca, N.Y.: Cornell
      University Press, 205 pp., passim. [Reprint. New York:
      Russell & Russell, 1971.]
          An alphabetical index, citing all that is known about lost

items. Notes as Webster works of this sort <u>Caesar's Fall</u>,
<u>Christmas Comes but Once a Year</u>, <u>The Guise</u>, <u>Lady Jane Grey</u>, pts.
1 and 2, and <u>The Late Murder of the Son Upon the Mother, or Keep
the Widow Waking</u>.

13   SILBERSTEIN, PAULA E. "The Theory of the Assembled Texts: A
      Critique." Ph.D. dissertation, Columbia University, pp. 39-40,
      70.
          Deals with textual problems in <u>The Duchess of Malfi</u>.

14   SMET, ROBERT de [Romain Sanvic]. "Jugement sur Philip
      Massinger." <u>Cahiers du Sud</u> 10:281-88. [Reprinted: 1941.5.]
          Compares Massinger to Webster in the realm of the tragic
      dramatists. His Domita rivals Vittoria in nerve and cynicism.

15   STARNES, D.T. "Barnabe Riche's 'Sappho Duke of Mantona': A
      Study in Elizabethan Story-Making." <u>Studies in Philology</u> 30:
      (July):455-72.
          Argues Riche's story is the source of <u>The Weakest Go to the
      Wall</u>, and his "love" theme is based on Painter's adaptation of
      Bandello's story of the Duchess of Malfi.

16   WALLEY, HAROLD R. "The Dates of <u>Hamlet</u> and Marston's <u>The
      Malcontent</u>." <u>Review of English Studies</u> 9, no. 36 (October):
      397-409.
          Since these plays are related, notes it is important to be
      sure which came first. Webster's additions to the second (1604)
      edition of Marston's work is part of the argument, since the
      induction gives some clues to the first performance. (Finds
      <u>Hamlet</u> predates <u>The Malcontent</u>.) See 1935.13 for a rejoinder.

17   YEARSLEY, PERCIVAL MACLEOD. <u>Doctors in Elizabethan Drama</u>.
      London: Bale, 128 pp., passim.
          Notes physicians as characters and a number of allusions to
      doctors, medicine, and anatomy in Webster's tragedies.

1934

*1   FLUCHERE, HENRI. <u>Reflexions sur le théâtre élisabéthain</u>.
      Marseille: Le Foyer Universitaire.
      Source: Mahaney, 1973.23.

2   GILBERT, ALLAN H. "Seneca and the Criticism of Elizabethan
      Tragedy." <u>Philological Quarterly</u> 13, no. 4 (October):370-81.
          Finds Webster's relatively low appraisal of Shakespeare in
      the preface to <u>The White Devil</u> reflects his preference for more
      Senecan dramatists. In <u>The Duchess of Malfi</u>, act 5 exists to serve
      the political end of Senecan tragedy--punishment of the brothers
      as rulers. Also, <u>The White Devil</u> includes much political material
      and many Senecan <u>sententiae</u>.

3   HOFFMAN, JOHANNES. Die Gerichtsszenen im englishchen Drama von
     Shakespeare bis zur Schliessung der Theater (1642). Breslau:
     Grufischer Grossbertrieb, pp. 68-74.
          Discusses the use of the courts in Shakespeare and seven
     other Elizabethan dramatists, including Webster. Considers the
     law case in The Devil's Law Case, the trial scene in The White
     Devil, and typical English judicial language in the Roman senate
     in Appius and Virginia.

4   JENKINS, HAROLD. The Life and Works of Henry Chettle. London:
     Sidgwick & Jackson, 276 pp., passim.
          Traces Chettle's career with Henslowe and, hence, his asso-
     ciation with the group that included Webster. Chettle is an im-
     portant link between the Senecan tragedy of Kyd and that of Webster
     and Tourneur. Makes an attempt to explain where Chettle fits in
     the attribution of Lady Jane, Sir Thomas Wyat, and other doubtful
     plays.

5   SCHMUCK, THOMAS K. A Footnote to "The Devil's Law Case." New
     York: Published privately, 27 pp.
          "A running commentary to the play, especially its legal
     aspects." Explicates legal language and references and discusses
     the trials (which are recounted, in prose, at great length) in the
     play. Finds Webster's drama captures the reality of lawyers and
     law courts.

6   SPENCER, HAZELTON. "Tate and The White Devil." Journal of
     English Literary History 1:235-49.
          Describes Injured Love (Tate's version of The White Devil)
     act by act. Tate's verse is alliterative "in the style of Pyramus
     and Pistol." The trial scene is not one of a tiger at bay, but of
     an innocent besieged. Describes, and suggests reasons for, several
     other changes, such as the omission of profanity.

7   WESTON, HAROLD. Form in Literature: A Theory of Technique and
     Construction. London: Rich & Cowan, p. 170. [Reprint.
     Folcroft, Pa.: Folcroft Library Editions, 1970.]
          Finds Webster's "Vittoria Corombona an encyclopaedia of
     tertiary matter"--material that has nothing to do with the plot,
     but is introduced for its own sake, not even for the sake of
     illustration.

8   WRIGHT, LOUIS B. "The Reading of Plays during the Puritan
     Revolution." Huntington Library Bulletin 6 (November):73-108.
          Cites Appius and Virginia, printed by Moseley in 1659, to
     illustrate how plays were printed and read during the Revolution,
     even though performances were forbidden.

1935

1   AGATE, JAMES. "Webster and the Modern Mind." In More First
    Nights. London: V. Gollancz, pp. 89-95. [Reprinted: 1943.2.]
        Finds The Duchess of Malfi wildly improbable, but this im-
    probability bothers neither Renaissance nor modern playgoers very
    much.

2   BROADUS, EDMUND K. The Story of English Literature. New York:
    Macmillan, pp. 113-15.
        Describes Webster as an "extraordinary flare-up of power,"
    especially in The Duchess of Malfi, which is not a melodrama, but
    a story of courage, love, and a beauty that shines through horrors.

*3 FELLHEIMER, JEANETTE. "The Englishman's Conception of the
    Italian in the Age of Shakespeare." Thesis, University of
    London.
        Source: Mahaney, 1973.23.

4   GASSNER, JOHN W., and MANTLE, R.B., eds. A Treasury of the
    Theatre. New York: Simon & Schuster, pp. 326-62.
        Includes The Duchess of Malfi with a brief introduction that
    presents Webster as the most powerful post-Shakespearean dramatist.
    He views humanity with cynicism and horror and is morbidly obsessed
    with death. He points to the ruthlessness of power in a dark world
    that permits only the nobility of integrity.

5   JENKINS, SADIE FRANKLIN. "The Treatment of Tyranny in
    Elizabethan History Plays." Ph.D. dissertation, University of
    North Carolina, pp. 190-92.
        Finds Sir Thomas Wyat reflects Renaissance attitudes towards
    usurpation and rebellion. The play supports the principle of the
    inalienability of kingship.

6   LAWRENCE, WILLIAM J. Those Nut-Cracking Elizabethans: Studies
    of the Early Theatre and Drama. London: Argonaut Press, p. 188.
        Cites The White Devil as combining a short title with a long
    descriptive one in the chapter on "Double Titles in Elizabethan
    Drama."

7   MILLETT, FRED B., and BENTLEY, G.E. The Art of the Drama.
    New York: Appleton-Century, 253 pp., passim.
        Comments on Webster intermittently, e.g., for The Duchess of
    Malfi's use of melodrama; his ability to create lively characters;
    and his fine ear for language.

8   PEARN, B.R. "Dumb Show in Elizabethan Drama." Review of
    English Studies 11, no. 44 (October):385-405.
        Defines the dumb show (action without words where they would
    normally be) and briefly considers its history. Among the func-
    tions of this convention: in The White Devil, among others, to

represent dreams and visions; in Thracian Wonder, and most plays,
to advance the action. Notes also that in The Duchess of Malfi
there are some scenes without words.

9 SARGEAUNT, MARGARET JOAN. John Ford. Oxford: B. Blackwell,
   232 pp., passim.
       Cites Webster occasionally, for example, in a discussion of
   the date, authorship, and nature of A Late Murder of the Son upon
   the Mother. Also finds Ford's use of women parallels Webster's,
   and his use of madness comparable to that of The Duchess of Malfi.

10 SEATON, ETHEL. Literary Relations of England and Scandinavia
    in the Seventeenth Century. Oxford: Clarendon Press, pp. 28,
    36, 97, 285. [Reprint. New York: B. Blom, 1972.]
        Notes that Webster cites Scandinavian events and images occa-
    sionally in his plays, for example, the phrase "this is my tribute:
    custom is not more truly paid in the Sound of Denmark."

11 SHARPE, ROBERT B. The Real War of the Theaters: Shakespeare's
    Fellows in Rivalry with the Lord Admiral's Men, 1594-1603.
    Modern Language Association of America Monograph Series, 5.
    Boston and London: D.C. Heath, pp. 126, 138, 239.
        Observes that Webster reached his greatness after breaking
    with Henslowe.

12 SIMPSON, PERCY. The Theme of Revenge in Elizabethan Tragedy.
    Annual Shakespeare Lecture of the British Academy. London:
    H. Milford, 38 pp. [Reprinted in his Studies in Elizabethan
    Drama (Oxford: Clarendon Press, 1955), pp. 138-78.]
        Surveys the conventions and history of revenge plays by Kyd,
    Shakespeare, Marston, Chapman, Chettle, and Tourneur. Notes The
    Duchess of Malfi is not a revenge play, but one in which revenge
    is an important motif. The Duchess is a victim.

13 STOLL, ELMER EDGAR. "The Date of The Malcontent: A Rejoinder."
    Review of English Studies 11, no. 41 (January):42-50.
        In a rejoinder to 1933.16, defends 1600 as the date for the
    composition of The Malcontent, thus leaving as a possibility some
    influence of that play on Hamlet.

14 WHITE, HAROLD OGDEN. Plagiarism and Imitation during the
    English Renaissance: A Study in Critical Distinctions. Harvard
    Studies in English, vol. 12. Cambridge, Mass.: Harvard
    University Press, pp. 174-79.
        Notes Webster's "Character" of "An Excellent Actor" attacks
    John Stephen's "A Common Player" as "imitating"--meant pejoratively,
    although Webster was certainly not above imitation. (Based on his
    Harvard dissertation, "Plagiarism and Imitation in English
    Literature, 1558-1625," 1930.)

15   WRIGHT, LOUIS B. Middle-Class Culture in Elizabethan England.
     Chapel Hill: University of North Carolina Press, 733 pp.,
     passim.
          Cites Webster often, especially with Dekker for the "Ho"
     plays and their depiction of London daily life. The dramatist's
     merchant-taylor background and his pageantry on behalf of the mer-
     chants make him a "city-poet."

16   ZEYDEL, EDWIN H. Ludwig Tieck, the German Romanticist: A
     Critical Study. Princeton: Princeton University Press, pp.
     318-22.
          Discusses the novel Vittoria Accorombona, 1840, which used
     Webster and also Tate as a source. Tieck elevated the heroine
     and criticized Webster for debasing her.

                                   1936

1   CRAIG, HARDIN. The Enchanted Glass. New York: Oxford
     University Press, 293 pp., passim.
          Cites Webster frequently, e.g., he and his fellows' plays
     are difficult in language and thought, and yet they were popular.
     Briefly discusses The Duchess of Malfi: it has a psychological
     depth to its characterization lacking in its source (Painter).
     Webster creates complex characters, based on the doctrine that
     everyone can succumb to the passions. His characters are full
     and consistent with this psychological philosophy.

2   ELLIS-FERMOR, UNA. The Jacobean Drama. London: Methuen, pp.
     170-191. [Rev. ed. 1958. Excerpted: 1968.23; 1969.17;
     1975.18.]
          Finds Webster marks a movement from the darkest of the
     Jacobeans to those who can glimpse possibilities of serenity. The
     Duchess seems his only character who sees beyond the "mist" of
     death. There is a conflict between Webster's belief in nobility
     and conventional morality. The imagery of the plays and subtle
     shifts of mood give the audience some imaginative relief from the
     tension between these two codes or visions. Reviewed: 1938.14.
     See also 1973.18.

3   GLEN, ENID. "Webster and Lavater." Times Literary Supplement,
     11 April, p. 316.
          Suggests that the Cardinal's "thing armed with a rake" in
     The Duchess of Malfi may come from a 1572 translation of Lavater's
     Of Ghosts and Spirites Walking by Nyght.

*4   HEYMSFELD, J.A. "Ludwig Tieck's Vittoria Accorombona and John
     Webster's The White Devil: A Chapter in English and German
     Literary Relations." Ph.D. dissertation, Columbia University.
     Source: Mahaney, 1973.23.

5   HOLZKNECHT, KARL J. Outlines of Tudor and Stuart Plays, 1497-
     1642. New York: Barnes & Noble, pp. 302-14.
         Includes an annotated list of characters and a plot outline
     for each play. Webster's tragedies are melodramas, filled with
     mental and physical horror, and amorous and political intrigue.
     The White Devil is an even more intense treatment of unconventional
     virtue, suffering, and diabolical revenge.

6   SILVETTE, HERBERT. "The Doctor on the Stage: Medicine and
     Medical Men in Seventeenth Century English Drama." Annals of
     Medical History 8:520-40; 9 (1937):62-87, 174-88, 264-79,
     371-94, 482-507.
         Cites Webster often, including the character of Quacksalver
     in the "Characters," and the mad doctor in the masque in The
     Duchess of Malfi. Finds that, while Webster was no medical man,
     his stock of medical and surgical information is astonishingly
     large and well digested. Webster uses much medical lore in many
     of his plays, and satirizes the medical profession in The Devil's
     Law Case. See 1967.22.

7   SISSON, CHARLES JASPER. Lost Plays of Shakespeare's Age.
     Cambridge: Cambridge University Press, pp. 80-124.
         Comments upon Keep the Widow Waking by Dekker, Rowley, Ford,
     and Webster. Reveals through court records and ballads the story
     of the actual events (involving one Anne Elsdon) that inspired
     this lost play.

8   SPENCER, THEODORE. Death and Elizabethan Tragedy. Cambridge,
     Mass.: Harvard University Press, 288 pp., passim. [Reprint.
     New York: Pageant Books, 1960.]
         Cites Webster frequently. Flamineo and Bosola suggest death
     as the final bitterness of a life without moral values against the
     meaningless horror of which we can only defend ourselves with wry
     and mocking jokes. Webster's two tragedies are filled with dark
     yet fiery pessimism. He creates a black and oppressive atmosphere,
     and a morally meaningless universe, thus making death almost a
     relief from the horrors of life. Reviewed: 1938.9.

1937

1   ANDERSON, MARCIA LEE. "John Webster's The White Devil and The
     Duchess of Malfi: A Critical Study." Ph.D. dissertation, Duke
     University, 304 pp.
         Contends Webster is not a careless dramatist. An examination
     of the known facts and of his method of composition, which relies
     largely on imitation, reveals the care with which he wrote. He
     worked in an atmosphere of mutual influence with other dramatists
     and was interested in nondramatic literature as well. Includes
     as an appendix a checklist of borrowings in The White Devil and
     The Duchess of Malfi.

2   BALD, R. "The Chronology of Middleton's Plays." <u>Modern
     Language Review</u> 32, no. 1:33-43.
          Attributes <u>Anything for a Quiet Life</u> to Middleton and argues
     for a composition date of 1621.

3   BOWERS, FREDSON THAYER. "The Audience and the Poisoners of
     Elizabethan Tragedy." <u>Journal of English and Germanic Philology</u>
     36:491-504.
          Asks two questions: how realistic did the poisonings seem
     to an Elizabethan audience when presented as Italian? Did the
     audience believe such events took place in England? Offers a brief
     history and description of available poison types. Generally,
     Elizabethan Englishmen believed Italians were masters of poison,
     but they themselves used it only rarely. Still, they believed it
     a constant threat, esepcially in the court. Thus, poisonings in
     Italianate dramas such as <u>The White Devil</u> would seem quite realis-
     tic.

4   BREEN, ROBERT S. "A Production of John Webster's <u>The Duchess
     of Malfi</u>." M.A. thesis, Northwestern University, 201 pp.
          Describes a thesis production of <u>The Duchess of Malfi</u> at
     Northwestern. Includes sections on the staging of the play and
     a copy of the director's script, with stage directions, scene,
     costume, stage, lighting designs, etc.

5   DREW, ELIZABETH. <u>Discovering Drama</u>. London: J. Cape, 252 pp.,
     passim.
          A general introduction that cites Webster frequently, e.g.,
     for his "flaming figures of evil, Vittoria Corombona and her
     brother." Also takes slight notice of his use of poetry and song.

6   HUGHES, A.I. "The Women of the Elizabethan Domestic Tragedies."
     M.A. thesis, University of Arizona, 99 pp.
          Compares the heroine of <u>The Duchess of Malfi</u> to Lady Macbeth
     as a motivating factor in a domestic tragedy. Webster's play fea-
     tures a legion of murders, the cause of which is the Duchess stoop-
     ing to propose to her steward.

7   KNIGHTS, L.C. <u>Drama and Society in the Age of Jonson</u>. London:
     Chatto & Windus, pp. 233-34, 280, 330.
          Mentions Webster as responsible for the better satiric
     touches of <u>Westward Ho</u> and notes his use of the malcontent figure
     in Flamineo.

8   MILLS, LAURENS J. <u>One Soul in Bodies Twain: Friendship in
     Tudor Literature and Stuart Drama</u>. Bloomington, Ind.:
     Principia Press, pp. 332-35.
          Finds Webster and Rowley's <u>A Cure for a Cuckold</u> a refinement
     of the themes of Massinger's <u>The Parliament of Love</u>: the demands
     of (unworthy) love against friendship. The play is based on a
     verbal quibble over "friend" and "kill a friend." It is one of
     several dramas that develop this conflict.

9   PRUVOST, RENE. Matteo Bandello and Elizabethan Fiction.
     Bibliothèque de la Revue de litterature comparée, 113. Paris:
     H. Champion, pp. 19, 23, 122, 140.
          Traces the influence of Bandello in England, from Brooke's
     Romeus and Juliet through Painter, Belleforest, etc. Discusses
     the evolution of source material for The Duchess of Malfi.

10   SQUIRE, TOM. "Webster." Theater Arts Monthly 21, no. 12
     (December):981-84.
          Finds Webster exceptional, the creator of the bloodiest of
     the tragedies of blood, whose reputation has vacillated wildly.
     He tries to use horrors to attract attention to his themes. The
     White Devil is a bit mechanical; The Duchess of Malfi is more
     passionate; but The Devil's Law Case is dull.

11   WASSERMAN, EARL R. "The Scholarly Origin of the Elizabethan
     Revival." Journal of English Literary History 4, no. 3
     (September):213-44. [Incorporated in 1947.12.]
          Believes Lamb did not really restore interest in the minor
     Elizabethans single-handedly. There was, instead, a slowly widen-
     ing pre-Lamb interest. Early scholars such as Theobald and Dodsley
     combatted the Augustan distaste for the "wild" Elizabethans.

12   WITHINGTON, ROBERT. Excursions in English Drama. New York:
     Appleton-Century, p. 169.
          Comments that while The Duchess of Malfi has its great poetic
     moments, they do not redeem inadequate characterization and poor
     plot development.

                              1938

*1   ARMBRISTER, VICTOR S. "The Origin and Function of Subplots in
     Elizabethan Drama." Ph.D. dissertation, Vanderbilt University,
     195 pp.
          Discusses the comic relief subplot of The Thracian Wonder.
     Source: Mahaney, 1973.23.

2   BALD, R.C. Bibliographical Studies in the Beaumont and Fletcher
     Folio of 1647. Supplement to the Transactions of the Biblio-
     graphical Society, no. 13. Oxford: Oxford University Press,
     114 pp., passim.
          Deals with the text, transmission, and authorship of The
     Honest Man's Fortune and The Fair Maid of the Inn.

3   CAWLEY, ROBERT R. The Voyagers and Elizabethan Drama. MLA
     Monograph Series, 8. Boston: D.C. Heath, 428 pp., passim.
     [Reprint. New York: Kraus Reprint, 1966.]
          (This book is arranged by areas of the world and their char-
     acteristic products, discovery, etc., then references in specific
     works noted.) Cites Webster throughout, e.g., The Devil's Law Case

reference to the "Indian Pox" is noted in book 4 (The West),
chapter 3 (Indians), the section on "customs." See 1940.3 for a
related study.

*4   EASTON, JUDITH M. "An Amateur Bibliography of the Works of
      John Webster the Dramatist." Ph.D. dissertation, The University
      of London.
          Source: Mahaney, 1973.23.

5   GREG, W.W. "Authorship Attribution in the Early Play-Lists,
      1656-1671." Edinburgh Bibliographical Society Transactions 2
      (1938-45):305-29.
          Considers the validity of the attributions of the early play-
      lists. Rogers and Ley (1656.3), who include many odd spellings,
      are probably generally wrong. Archer's list (1656.1) is based
      upon, but is better than, its predecessor. (He records the Guise
      as a comedy, attributed to John Webster.) Kirkman (1661.1; 1671.1)
      is based on Archer, but again an advance. (He calls Guise a trage-
      dy and drops the Webster attribution.)

6   IWATSUKI, JACHIWO. "On the Changing Literary Modes in the
      Development of Renaissance Tragedy." Studies in English
      Literature (Japan) 18:486-505.
          Contends that certain rhythms recur in the great streams of
      literary development--from a crude experimental period through
      decadence. This pattern is followed in Renaissance tragedy, from
      Kyd and Marlowe through Shakespeare's various phases. The Duchess
      of Malfi and The White Devil fall into a period of "aftermath,"
      before decadence set in. The White Devil exhibits intensely vil-
      lainous cynicism, cruelty, lust, and treachery, while The Duchess
      of Malfi seems to include too much straining after the horrible.

7   KELLETT, E.E. "John Webster." In Encyclopaedia Britannica.
      14th ed. Vol. 23. London: Encyclopaedia Britannica Co.,
      pp. 472-73.
          Proclaims Webster one of the great tragic writers of English
      literature. His tragedies combine the tragedy of blood with the
      Machivaellian play. Webster suffers from serious defects in
      dramaturgy but also possesses stupendous merits.
          (Note: The 9th and subsequent editions feature a portrait
      by Swinburne, 1888.4, while the 1978 version has only a brief ci-
      tation to the effect that Webster is a paramount seventeenth-
      century English tragedian.)

8   KIRSCHBAUM, LEO. "A Census of Bad Quartos." Review of English
      Studies 14, no. 53 (January):20-43.
          Finds Sir Thomas Wyat exists in no good text, only in what
      appears to be a "reported" text. It has been attributed to Dekker,
      Chettle, Wentworth Smith, and Webster.

9   MATTHIESSEN, F.O. "Towards our Understanding of Elizabethan
    Drama." Southern Review 4:398-428.
        Notes that Spencer's Death and Elizabethan Tragedy (1936.8)
    "makes a revelatory contrast between Webster and Shirley."

10 McGINN, DONALD JOSEPH. Shakespeare's Influence on the Drama
    of His Age, Studied in "Hamlet." Rutgers University Studies
    in English. New Brunswick: Rutgers University Press, pp.
    91-92, 160, 168, 186.
        Uses Hamlet as a touchstone to measure Shakespeare's influ-
    ence on his contemporaries. Webster is influenced in the parallel
    Cornelia/Ophelia mad scenes and in Shakespearean verbal echoes in
    Appius and Virginia, The White Devil, and The Devil's Law Case.

11 OTIS, WILLIAM BRADLEY, and NEEDLEMAN, MORRISS. A Survey-History
    of English Literature. New York: Barnes & Noble, pp. 245-46.
        Reports Webster is traditionally regarded as the finest
    tragedian next to Shakespeare. He wrote tragedies of horror, full
    of beautiful phraseology, and imaginative intensity. His flaws
    include a lack of restraint and of unity. The White Devil is a
    tragedy of blood, with effective characterization and the famous
    trial scene and dirge, while The Duchess of Malfi, a more somber
    play, is highly dramatic, but less poetic and plausible. Appius
    and Virginia features a singleness of plot and coherence of struc-
    ture. It contains some remarkable passages.

12 PINTO, V. de SOLA. The English Renaissance, 1510-1688.
    Introductions to English and American Literature, vol. 2.
    London: Cressett Press, pp. 293-94.
        Cites Webster's works, editions, and a few works of criticism.
    He is also cited passim elsewhere, e.g., The Duchess of Malfi illus-
    trates an Elizabethan sense of the greatness of the human spirit
    as it nears death.

13 SCHÜCKING, LEVIN L. The Baroque Character of the Elizabethan
    Tragic Hero. London: H. Milford, p. 23. [Also published in
    Proceedings of the British Academy, 1938 (London, 1939), pp.
    85-111.]
        Observes that Vittoria in The White Devil is absolutely
    heartless, a criminal courtesan who is forgiven in the face of her
    heroic attitude in the trial scene. She accepts death with glori-
    fied self-aggrandizement. (The British Academy Annual Shakespeare
    Lecture, read 27 April 1938.)

14 TILLOTSON, GEOFFREY. Review of The Jacobean Drama, by Una
    Ellis-Fermor. Review of English Studies 14, no. 53 (January):
    94-97.
        Finds Ellis-Fermor's book (1936.2) complete and stimulating.
    Some differences between reviewer and author concern Webster:
    Ellis-Fermor's discussion of Webster seems to assume that his
    plays, like a nineteenth-century poet's works, reflect his opinions.

But at other times, she assumes that the characters have their
own personalities and hence don't speak for the author.

15   WILLIAMS, ROBERT D.   "Antiquarian Interest in Elizabethan Drama
     before Lamb."   PMLA 53 (June):434-44.
         Beileves Lamb's Specimens (1808.1) was not solely responsible
     for reviving popular or scholarly interest in the Elizabethans, in-
     cluding Webster.

                                   1939

1   ANDERSON, MARCIA LEE.   "Hardy's Debt to Webster in The Return
     of the Native."   Modern Language Notes 54:497-501.
         Reveals Hardy owned and carefully annotated Hazlitt's edition
     of Webster. Some parallels exist between book 5, chapter 3 of The
     Return of the Native and The White Devil, 4.2.

2   "Webster's Debt to Guazzo."   Studies in Philology 36:192-205.
         Finds Webster borrowed images and ideas from Stephano Guazzo's
     La Civil Conversatione, translated by Pettie in 1581.

3   De La MARE, WALTER.   "Dream and Poetry."   Saturday Review 20,
     no. 15 (5 August):4-5, 14.
         Comments that "Webster is reputed to have been a sexton by
     trade. That, in any case, was the secret occupation of his mind."

4   GREG, W.W.   A Bibliography of the English Printed Drama to the
     Restoration.   Vols. 1 and 2 (1951). London: Bibliographical
     Society. [Reprint. 1970.]
         A standard bibliography of all editions to 1700. Includes
     The White Devil (1:446-48, no. 306); The Devil's Law Case (2:535,
     no. 388); The Duchess of Malfi (2:535-37, no. 389); Appius and
     Virginia (2:844-45, no. 733).

5   HALSTEAD, W.L.   "Note on the Text of The Famous History of Sir
     Thomas Wyat."   Modern Language Notes 54, no. 8 (December):585-89.
         Attempts, unsuccessfully, to determine the shares of Dekker
     and Webster in this play. There may have been up to five authors,
     and only a bad text has survived.

6   KNIGHT, G. WILSON.   The Burning Oracle.   London: Oxford
     University Press, pp. 19-58.
         Includes several comparisons between Shakespeare and Webster,
     e.g., Shakespeare's impressionism is less second-hand than Webster's,
     which relies on stock reactions based on abstract and universal
     impressions inherited from the medieval era.

*7   OUTRAM, A.E.   "Some Conventions of Elizabethan Drama."   Ph.D.
     dissertation, Oxford University.
         Source: Mahaney, 1973.23.

8   PRAZ, MARIO. Studies in Seventeenth Century Imagery. London:
     Warburg Institute, pp. 223-24. [Reprint. Rome: Edizione di
     Storia e Letteratura, 1964.]
          Studies emblems and devices in seventeenth-century life and
     literature. Webster's use of the word "emblem" argues the specifi-
     cally emblematic intent of his imagery. Also, he uses "mottos,"
     e.g., "Inopem me copia fecit," in The White Devil 2.1. See 1969.29.

9   REINHALTER, MARY A. [Sister Berchmans]. "An Interpretation of
     Webster's Duchess of Malfi According to the Norms of Aristotle's
     Poetics." Ph.D. dissertation, Boston College, 186 pp.
          Applies terminology and definitions from Aristotle to The
     Duchess of Malfi. The play keeps the forms of the revenge tragedy,
     but for non-Kydian uses. Cites Marston, Tourneur, Shakespeare as
     important influences on Webster.

10   SMITH, JAMES. "The Tragedy of Blood." Scrutiny 8 (September):
     265-80. [Excerpted: 1969.1.]
          Considers The White Devil as a dramatic whole, not just a
     collection of "flashes." Analyzes the first two scenes, showing
     that Webster's speeches, scenes, and even acts do not "develop"
     but show different sides of the same thing simultaneously. Thus,
     there is no central point of view or character.

11   WELLS, HENRY W. Elizabethan and Jacobean Playwrights. New
     York: Columbia University Press, pp. 45-49.
          Discusses The White Devil and The Duchess of Malfi as
     "tragedies of evil" (a genre in which sin serves as inspiration
     for didactic melodrama). Both works celebrate the bravery of a
     defiant woman surrounded by a Machiavellian court. Stresses
     Webster's moral or satirical intent, seen most clearly in the
     choral characters of Flamineo and Bosola. Finds something almost
     sentimental in The Duchess of Malfi, and prefers the greater vigor
     of The White Devil.

12   WEST, ROBERT H. The Invisible World: A Study in Pneumatology
     in Elizabethan Drama. Athens: University of Georgia Press,
     275 pp., passim.
          Studies the spirit-action in non-Shakespearean drama and
     cites Webster often. Discusses the ghosts in The White Devil and
     some possible demons in The Duchess of Malfi. Asks if play's
     lycanthropia, echo, and the Cardinal's vision in the fish pond
     are demonic or simply manifestations of guilt.

                                   1940

1   BAX, CLIFFORD. The Life of the White Devil. London: Cassell,
     pp. 204-30.
          An account of the actual and melodramatic life of this par-
     ticular Renaissance Italian "aesthetic gangster," including a

section on Webster's play. Suggests Webster's version of the story must have been based on hearsay because of his "extraordinary mistakes." Discusses the play itself and its critical repute. Reviewed: 1940.7.

2   BOWERS, FREDSON THAYER. Elizabethan Revenge Tragedy, 1587-1642.
    Princeton: Princeton University Press, 288 pp., passim, esp.
    177-83. [Excerpted: 1968.23; 1975.18.]
        Surveys the general background and development of the revenge
    motif in English law and literature. One variation includes the
    depiction of villainy and horror, in which Webster excels. Sees
    The Duchess of Malfi as a play in which revenge is taken upon the
    hero by the villains. The White Devil is Webster's real master-
    piece of a villain play. Again, our sympathies are with the vic-
    tim of revenge. This play's value lies chiefly in its characteri-
    zation: the victims and the revengers alike are neither black nor
    white, but morally gray. Webster combines the Kydian revenge motif
    with the Marlovian villain hero.

3   CAWLEY, ROBERT R. Unpathed Waters: Studies in the Influence
    of the Voyagers on Elizabethan Drama. Princeton: Princeton
    University Press, pp. 199-201. [Reprint. New York: Octagon
    Books, 1967.]
        Cites Webster in a study of the impact of the tradition of
    maritime voyages on Elizabethan literature, e.g., his use of poi-
    sons derives from travelers' accounts, especially tales of uni-
    corns. Also finds Webster utilizes marine images and supersti-
    tions. See 1938.3 for a related study.

4   CRAIG, HARDIN. "The Shackling of Accidents: A Study of
    Elizabethan Tragedy." Philological Quarterly 19, no. 1
    (January):1-19.
        Mentions Webster in passing in this essay on the influence
    of Seneca.

5   GASSNER, JOHN W. Masters of the Drama. New York: Random
    House, pp. 258-63.
        Includes Webster in the chapter entitled "Ben Jonson and the
    'Noble Brood,'" describing him as the last Elizabethan: he had a
    demonic, tragic outlook. The plays exhibit slipshod workmanship
    but also dynamic characters and sublime evil depicted in poetry
    of the highest order. Webster was a master of pity and terror.
    But not all his characters are evil or doomed. The White Devil
    features a remarkable woman and Brachiano is equally splendid--a
    passion-swept man. The Duchess of Malfi shows greater pathos,
    since the main characters are innocent, but it is inferior to The
    White Devil in spite of its moments of pity and terror worthy of
    Shakespeare. The Devil's Law Case is an amiable second-rate work.

*6 OLMSTED, STERLING P. "The Development of the 'Induction' in
    English Drama." Ph.D. dissertation, Yale University, 199 pp.
        Source: Mahaney, 1973.23.

7   Review of The Life of the White Devil, by Clifford Bax. Times
     Literary Supplement, 25 May, p. 256.
          Wonders why the story of Vittoria, which is "rather sordid,"
     has continued to attract attention.

8   REYNOLDS, GEORGE F. The Staging of Elizabethan Plays at the
     Red Bull Theater, 1605-1625. London: Oxford University Press,
     193 pp., passim.
          Finds Webster's prefatory remarks to The White Devil suggest
     that the Red Bull Theater (where it was performed) had a reputation
     that was "scarcely first class." Also cites The Devil's Law Case
     throughout, e.g., in a list of plays with bed scenes.

9   SOBEL, BERNARD. The Theater Handbook. New York: Crown, pp.
     811-39. [Reprinted as The New Theater Handbook and Digest of
     Plays (New York: Crown, 1959).]
          Presents Webster as a conscientious craftsman, a master of
     pathos, and the portrayal of gloom, grisly horror, and sardonic
     humor. Also mentions Webster in the entry for "English Drama."

10   STOLL, ELMER EDGAR. Shakespeare and Other Masters. Cambridge,
     Mass.: Harvard University Press, pp. 279-80.
          Cites Webster frequently, most often in the chapter on Iago
     where Webster's villains are compared to Shakespeare's.

                              1941

1   ALLEN, DON CAMERON. The Star-Crossed Renaissance. Durham, N.C.:
     Duke University Press, pp. 157, 177, 187, 191.
          Notes Webster's use of stars, natal stars, portentous comets,
     and the like: Webster portrays astrologers as madmen in The Duchess
     of Malfi.

2   BABB, LAWRENCE. "Melancholy and the Elizabethan Man of Letters."
     Huntington Library Quarterly 4, no. 3 (April):247-61.
          Discusses The Duchess of Malfi's Bosola as one of the many
     melancholy scholars presented on the Elizabethan stage.

3   _____. "The Physiological Conception of Love in the Elizabethan
     and Early Stuart Drama." PMLA 61:1020-35.
          Notes that in The Devil's Law Case erotic passion is seen as
     a disease.

4   BATESON, F.W., ed. The Cambridge Bibliography of English
     Literature. Vol. 1, 600-1660. Cambridge: Cambridge University
     Press, pp. 629-30. [Revised: 1974.26.]
          The Webster bibliography entry includes primary works and
     some secondary sources. In the Supplement, ed. George Watson
     (1957), the Webster entry appears on p. 303.

                               93

5   CAMILLE, GEORGETTE, and d'EXIDEUIL, PIERRE, eds. Le Théâtre
     élizabéthain. Paris: Cahiers du Sud & J. Corti, 331 pp.
         Reprint of 1933.1, 8, 11, 14; includes 1941.13.

6   CLARK, ELENOR GRACE. Raleigh and Marlowe: A Study in
     Elizabethan Fustian. New York: Fordham University Press,
     488 pp., passim. [Reprint. New York: Russell & Russell,
     1965.]
         Cites Webster in passing. For example: The Duchess of
     Malfi may contain anti-Buckingham satire in scene 1, and perhaps
     Appius and Virginia's description of starving troops is also an
     attack on Buckingham.

*7   DURFEE, JOSEPH. "A Study of Expectation and Surprise in
     Tragedy, Especially Elizabethan and Jacobean." Ph.D. disserta-
     tion, University of Colorado, 445 pp.
         Source: Mahaney, 1973.23.

8   ELIOT, T.S. "The Duchess of Malfi." Listener, 18 December,
     pp. 825-26. [Excerpted: 1968.23.]
         Argues that a period of artistic greatness has three phases--
     rise, height, decline. Webster represents the last phase of
     Elizabethan drama. Finds The Duchess of Malfi his greatest play:
     it includes much sensationalism, romance, and novelty, but should
     be remembered for certain scenes--the wooing, bed chamber, and tor-
     ture ones in particular. Webster is unlike Shakespeare in that
     he can produce great scenes but not whole plays, but he is also
     better than his contemporaries in that he can maintain a tone, if
     not plot and character, throughout a work. Furthermore he is moral-
     ly and artistically serious, and he had the gift of style. Right
     and wrong still had meaning in his world.

9   FULLER, EDMUND. A Pageant of the Theatre. New York: Thomas
     Crowell, p. 125.
         A history of the theater that mentions Webster as active
     during Shakespeare's lifetime.

10   FREEDLEY, GEORGE, and REEVES, JOHN A. A History of the Theater.
     New York: Crown, p. 688.
         A typical history text for undergraduate students. Presents
     gloomy John Webster as primarily a writer of melodrama, but a cer-
     tain lyric quality sometimes raises his work to tragedy. Sees The
     Duchess of Malfi, as a "study of evil and unhappiness," and The
     White Devil is "awesome." His other plays are unimportant.

11   HARBAGE, ALFRED B. Shakespeare's Audience. New York: Columbia
     University Press, p. 122.
         Surveys the size, social composition, behavior, aesthetic and
     intellectual capacity of Shakespeare's audience. Notes Webster's
     address to the readers of The White Devil describing the poor the-
     atrical conditions of that play's performance and the audience's
     ignorance.

12   LEECH, CLIFFORD. "Catholic and Protestant Drama." Durham
     University Journal 33:171-87.
        Compares Spanish and English seventeenth-century plays.
     Notes that both Webster and Lope de Vega assert that public taste
     must be served before classical precedent.

13   MATTHEY, P.L. "Le Demon blanc de John Webster." In Le Théâtre
     élizabéthain. Edited by Georgette Camille and Pierre d'Exideuil.
     Paris: Cahiers du Sud & J. Corti, pp. 172-76.
        Translates the trial of Vittoria into French.

14   REUL, PAUL de. Présentation du théâtre jacobéen de Marston à
     Beaumont et Fletcher (1600-1625). Anvers: Buschmann, pp.
     31-50.
        Finds Webster superior to Marston and Tourneur and other
     tragedians of blood, but his beauties are hidden behind grotesquerie
     and melodrama. His tragedies are his only important work: they are
     here extensively outlined and sections are translated into French.

15   SAMPSON, GEORGE. The Concise Cambridge History of English
     Literature. Cambridge: Cambridge University Press, pp. 319-21.
     [Revised: 1970.26.]
        Presents Tourneur and Webster as a pair of dramatists re-
     markable for their somber and macabre genius. Webster's debt to
     Shakespeare is great, but he was an original contributor to the
     tradition of revenge tragedy. The White Devil shows evil revengers
     and good victims, a situation that is even clearer in The Duchess
     of Malfi.

16   TANNENBAUM, SAMUEL. John Webster (A Concise Bibliography).
     Elizabethan Bibliographies, no. 19. New York: Samuel A.
     Tannenbaum, 38 pp. [Reprint. Port Washington, N.Y.: Kennikat
     Press, 1967.]
        A once useful bibliography, now out of date. The 629 items
     include plays and adaptations, poems and characters, collected
     works, selections, and biography and commentary. Includes work
     through the 1930s. For a supplement, see 1967.5.

1942

1   CLARKSON, PAUL S., and WARREN, CLYDE. The Law of Property in
     Shakespeare and the Elizabethan Drama. Baltimore: Johns
     Hopkins University Press, 346 pp., passim.
        Finds that Webster seems to know the law: he cites numerous
     statutes in all his plays, including The Duchess of Malfi and The
     White Devil and, especially, The Devil's Law Case. Refers to
     Webster's plays intermittently.

2   DELATTRE, FLORIS. La Littérature de l'Angleterre puritaine
     1603-1660. Paris: Didier, pp. 26-27.

Very briefly cites The Duchess of Malfi and The White Devil
as historically important in the development of the Jacobean stage.

3   GREG, W.W. The Editorial Problem in Shakespeare. Oxford:
    Clarendon Press, 210 pp., passim.
        Mentions Webster in passing, especially in the context of
some of the problems raised in the induction to The Malcontent.

4   REESE, GERTRUDE C. "The Question of the Succession in
    Elizabethan Drama." University of Texas Studies in English
    22:59-85.
        Discusses several plays, from Gorbuduc on, dealing with the
succession issue. Finds Sir Thomas Wyat substantiates Mary Tudor's
claim until her marriage to the Catholic Philip, then takes the
conservative Protestant position, favoring the next-in-line claim-
ant. Notes the strong anti-Spanish element of the play.

5   STEWART, BAIN TATE. "The Renaissance Interpretation of Dreams
    and Their Use in Elizabethan Drama." Ph.D. dissertation,
    Northwestern University, 221 pp., passim.
        Cites Webster often, e.g., discusses Vittoria's dream as the
motivation of the whole action of The White Devil. The dream is
constructed with care and realism.

6   THOMPSON, ALAN R. The Anatomy of Drama. Berkeley: University
    of California Press, p. 378. [Reprint. Freeport, N.Y.: Books
    for Libraries Press, 1968.]
        Notes that Webster's famous lines (e.g., "Cover her eyes:
mine eyes dazzle; she died young") derive their beauty from their
dramatic context, not for any intrinsic lyric qualities.

                                1943

1   ADAMS, HENRY HITCH. English Domestic or Homiletic Tragedy
    1575-1642. Columbia University Studies in English and Compara-
    tive Literature, no. 159. New York: Columbia University Press,
    pp. 78-80, 90.
        Considers Webster's Appius and Virginia as a domestic drama
exploring pathos. The play is an improvement over "R.B.'s" earlier
version. It focuses upon the contrast between the tranquility of
family life and public strife. Finds that as both a domestic and
a regular tragedy, the play reveals no particular aesthetic theory
of Webster's.

2   AGATE, JAMES. Brief Chronicles. London: J. Cape, 311 pp.
    [Reprint. New York: B. Blom, 1971.]
        A collection of columns, most from the Sunday Times, includ-
ing 1925.1 and 1935.1.

3   BABB, LAWRENCE. "Melancholic Villainy in the Elizabethan
     Drama." Papers of the Michigan Academy of Science, Arts, and
     Letters 29:527-35.
          Shows that one type of melancholic villain is the malcontent,
often a Machiavellian. Gives Bosola as an example of this species.

4   _____. "Scientific Theories of Grief in Some Elizabethan Plays."
     Studies in Philology 40:502-19.
          Finds Webster utilizes the Renaissance physiology of grief
in The Devil's Law Case. He also pictures psychological disturb-
ances, e.g., lycanthropia with its hallucinations in The Duchess
of Malfi.

5   _____. "Sorrow and Love on the Elizabethan Stage." Shakespeare
     Association Bulletin 18:137-42.
          Finds appearance and deportment of actors portraying sorrow
and love was formal (disordered clothing, arms folded, etc.), not
natural. Webster employs this convention in The Devil's Law Case
and Appius and Virginia, wherein "melancholy" is used as a descriptive stage direction.

6   BALD, R.C. "Francis Kirkman, Bookseller and Author." Modern
     Philology 41 (August):17-32.
          Chronicles Krikman's career as collector, author, seller,
and publisher--including publication of some Webster-related materials. See 1661.1; 1671.1.

7   BENTLEY, G.E. "Authenticity and Attribution in the Jacobean
     and Caroline Drama." In English Institute Annual, 1942. New
     York: Columbia University Press, pp. 101-18. [Reprinted:
     1966.8 (pp. 179-87).]
          Discusses the problems and some principles for attribution
of plays like The Thracian Wonder (ascribed to Webster) or The
Revenger's Tragedy (given to Tourneur). Notes also court records
documenting Webster's participation in some collaborations. Pleads
for good sense and logic in a field rampant with zeal and folly.

8   _____. "John Cotgrave's English Treasury of Wit and Language
     and the Elizabethan Drama." Studies in Philology 40 (April):
     186-203.
          Describes Cotgrave's work as a miscellany. Unlike many, it
includes material from the drama, including The Duchess of Malfi,
The White Devil, and The Devil's Law Case. Argues that the number
of entries suggests the tastes of the author and his audience:
Webster has 104 quotations, preceded only by Shakespeare (159),
Beaumont and Fletcher (112), Jonson, Chapman, and Greville out of
some 50 dramatists. The Duchess of Malfi is the third most frequently cited play.

9   BOAS, F.S. "Charles Lamb and the Elizabethan Dramatists."
     Essays and Studies 29:62-81.

Reviews Lamb's treatment (in 1808.1) of various dramatists, including Webster, about whose tragedies Lamb wrote "in his most exquisitely felicitous strain."

10   COLEMAN, EDWARD DAVIDSON. The Jew in English Drama: An
      Annotated Bibliography. New York: New York Public Library,
      p. 52. [Reprinted with the addition of "The Jew in Western
      Drama: An Essay and Checklist" (New York: Publishers Library,
      1968).]
          Cites The Devil's Law Case for its depiction of a Christian
      disguised as a Jew.
          Some of this bibliography appeared between November 1938 and
      November 1940 in The Bulletin of the New York Public Library.

11   PARROTT, J.M., and BALL, R.H. A Short View of Elizabethan Drama.
      New York: Scribner's, pp. 222-36.
          Presents The White Devil as an Italianate drama, based upon
      unknown sources, the strength of which is to be found in single
      scenes, not the entire structure, and featuring powerful characters,
      especially Vittoria and Flamineo. The Duchess of Malfi's plot is
      pathetic rather than tragic. Webster's sympathy is wholly with
      the Duchess, while the Cardinal is a fox and Ferdinand a wolf.
      Both plays are based upon, but vary, the revenge tradition.

                                    1944

1   AKRIGG, G.P.V. "The Anatomy of Websterian Tragedy." Ph.D.
      dissertation, University of California, 557 pp.
          Studies the "scheme of tragedy which underlies" The White
      Devil and The Duchess of Malfi. Finds Webster's thought has a sub-
      stratum of medievalism. At the same time, he inherits Renaissance
      ideals and was much influenced by contemporary Italy. Particularly
      Jacobean is Webster's mood of disillusion and his emphasis on court
      vices. Finally, he incorporates elements of metaphysical skepti-
      cism and empiricism in his works.
          The products of these influences are tragedies in which there
      is a conflict between "good"--virtue, honor, innocence, justice and
      stoic fortitude (not specifically Christian)--and "evil"--presented
      as physically loathsome, often "beastly." The tool villains are
      the focus of this conflict.

2   GREENE, GRAHAM. "British Dramatists." In Impressions of English
      Literature. Edited by W.J. Turner. London: Collins, pp. 101-42.
          Presents The White Devil as the work of an erratic genius, a
      play with no moral center, depicting a world lost in darkness.
      Thus, Vittoria is conceived as a devil, yet emerges as a heroine
      in the trial scene. But The Duchess of Malfi is finer, displaying
      true tenderness and heroism. Webster has an unmistakable tone--
      one of "odd" dialogue, expressing the night side of life.

                                    98

3   GRIERSON, HERBERT J.C., and SMITH, J. A Critical History of
    English Poetry. London: Chatto & Windus, pp. 41-44, 135.
    [Reprint. 1947.]
        Considers Webster second to Shakespeare in tragedy. Like
    Shakespeare, he believed that the wages of sin is death, but his
    plots are more clumsy, none of his characters is sympathetic, and
    his horrors wring our nerves but not our hearts.

4   KERNODLE, GEORGE R. From Art to Theater: Form and Convention
    in the Renaissance. Chicago: University of Chicago Press,
    255 pp., passim.
        Studies the visual dimension in Renaissance theater--paint-
    ings, tableaux vivants, architecture, emblems, Italian illusion
    and perspective, etc. Cites several Webster scenes, among them
    the scene at the shrine at Loretto in The Duchess of Malfi and
    symbolic mourning tableau in The Devil's Law Case 3.3.

*5 McCOLLOM, WILLIAM GILMAN. "Illusion and Formalism in
    Elizabethan Tragedy." Ph.D. dissertation, Columbia University,
    pp. 232-74.
        Source: Mahaney, 1973.23.

6   TILLYARD, E.M.W. The Elizabethan World Picture. New York:
    Macmillan, pp. 17-18, 20.
        Finds The Duchess of Malfi illustrates "sin" since the
    Duchess knows she is straying by courting Antonio and disrupting
    social order. Webster likes her, but she is guilty. Bosola too
    lives in a world that is filled with violent crime, yet loyal to
    a theological scheme.

7   WELLS, HENRY W. "Senecan Influence on Elizabethan Tragedy:
    A Re-Estimation." Shakespeare Association Bulletin 19:71-84.
        Believes Seneca was probably best understood by the satirical
    dramatists such as Webster. It is wrong to say that Seneca influ-
    ences only a few closet dramas, or that he influences only the
    worst traits of Elizabethan plays. Actually, Senecan influence
    on plays like The White Devil is "almost entirely salutary."

                              1945

1   AVERY, EMMETT L. "A Tentative Calendar of Daily Theatrical
    Performances, 1660-1700." Research Studies of the State College
    of Washington 13:225-83. [Reprint. PMLA 63 (March 1948):
    114-80.]
        Lists Restoration play performances, on a day-by-day basis,
    including several performances of Webster's plays.

*2 BARNHART, THEARLE A. "An Index of the Characters in Caroline
    Drama." Ph.D. dissertation, Ohio State University, 292 pp.
        Source: Mahaney, 1973.23.

3   BROOKE, DONALD. The Romance of the English Theatre. London:
     Rockliff, p. 36.
          Notes that a recent production of The Duchess of Malfi showed
     the power of Webster.

4   BUSH, DOUGLAS. English Literature in the Earlier Seventeenth
     Century, 1600-1660. Oxford History of English Literature, vol.
     5. Oxford: Clarendon Press, pp. 200-201. [Rev. ed. 1962.]
          Discusses Webster as the author of additions to Overbury's
     Characters.

*5   JOSEPH, BERTRAM LEON. "Lewis Theobald and Webster."
     Comparative Literature Studies 17-18:29-31.
          Source: Mahaney, 1973.23.

6   PARR, JOHNSTONE. "The Horoscope in Webster's The Duchess of
     Malfi." PMLA 60, no. 3 (September):760-65. [Included in
     Tamberlaine's Malady and Other Essays on Astrology in
     Elizabethan Drama (University: University of Alabama Press,
     1953).]
          Shows Webster understood astrological technicalities. Ex-
     plains the terms involved in the horoscope in The Duchess of Malfi,
     2, wherein Webster gives to Antonio's son a very bad prognostica-
     tion. Although the son survives the play, perhaps Webster means
     us to be skeptical regarding his ultimate chances. Astronomically,
     the horoscope is not that of any early seventeenth-century year:
     Webster constructed a hypothetical situation to meet his require-
     ments.

7   WEBSTER, JOHN. The Duchess of Malfi. London: Sylvan Press,
     88 pp.
          Includes the Lucas text (1927.11), essays by George Rylands
     (pp. v-xiv) and Charles Williams (pp. xv-xxii), and autolithographs
     by Michael Ayrton. In "On the Production of The Duchess of Malfi,"
     Rylands divides the play into three movements: the first intro-
     duces the characters and plot, the second presents the martyrdom
     of the Duchess, and the third is an anti-climax. It has acting
     problems: the characters do not always have a consistent psycholo-
     gy; Jacobean language must be learned; the verse is irregular; the
     whole effect is startling and tragic. In "On the Poetry of The
     Duchess of Malfi," Williams finds the play was written just as
     Elizabethan tragic poetry was beginning to lose force. The play
     has a "shape," but it is not an organic whole, except in "its
     spasmodic and convulsive movements of great poetry." It comes to
     life as Bosola presides over the death of the Duchess.

8   WEISINGER, HERBERT. "The Seventeenth Century Reputation of the
     Elizabethans." Modern Language Quarterly 6 (March):13-21.
          Argues Lamb did not rediscover the Elizabethans; they had
     always been appreciated, partly because of an admiration of
     Elizabeth and her reign.

9   WILSON, F.P. Elizabethan and Jacobean. London: Clarendon
     Press, pp. 98-108.
        Suggests that Webster's preoccupation with death is not ab-
     normal. We share his feelings and should not, therefore, be put
     off by his morbid apparatus.

                              1946

1   BOAS, F.S. An Introduction to Stuart Drama. London: Oxford
     University Press, pp. 193-209.
        Discusses Webster's poetic imagination, especially in the
     tragedies: The White Devil has vivid characters, especially
     Vittoria with her forceful will and intellect. Her trial scene
     is a high point of Elizabethan drama. The Duchess of Malfi pre-
     sents murders and lust from a different angle than The White Devil.
     There is a certain tender pathos and charm in the relationship of
     the Duchess and Antonio. The Devil's Law Case is set in a gloomy
     world, illuminated by flashes of genius, but less consistent than
     the tragedies. Notes that all three plays feature a woman who de-
     fies the world to get what her heart is set on.

2   WILSON, ELKIN C. Prince Henry and English Literature. Ithaca,
     N.Y.: Cornell University Press, pp. 139, 144, 157.
        Notes and discusses Webster's, Tourneur's, and Heywood's
     elegies for the Prince. A Monumental Column laments the loss of
     Henry's support for literature and science.

                              1947

1   BOYCE, BENJAMIN. The Theophrastan Character in England to 1642.
     Cambridge, Mass.: Harvard University Press, pp. 117, 136, 141,
     222. [Reprint. New York: Humanities Press, 1967.]
        Studies the "character" in classical and the native English
     traditions through Hall. Accepts Webster's authorship of thirty-
     two characters added to the sixth edition (1615) of Overbury's col-
     lection. Especially noteworthy is his depiction of "The Common
     Player." See 1904.4 for a related study.

2   BRADBROOK, M.C. "Two Notes Upon Webster." Modern Language
     Review 42, no. 3 (July):281-94. [First note reprinted: 1961.3;
     1968.23; 1969.17.]
        1. "Fate and Chance in The Duchess of Malfi." Finds that
     the horror of this play depends upon a sense of the supernatural
     combined with skepticism. Therefore, curses are important in the
     play, as are lycanthropy, diabolism, etc. Fortune, opportunity,
     and chance (i.e., accident) are recurring motifs. The play, thus,
     involves two possible interpretations, with accidental and determin-
     istic readings never directly clashing.
        2. "Chapman and Webster." Comments upon parallels and

                              101

thematic similarities between The Conspiracy and Tragedy of Byron
and The Duchess of Malfi: notes common passages and both authors'
use of the "notebook method."

3   CLARK, BARRETT H.   European Theories of the Drama.   Rev. ed.
     New York: Crown, pp. 3-64, 517-58.
          Includes a section of Webster's preface "To the Reader" of
     The White Devil as an illustration of dramatic criticism by
     Elizabethan dramatists.

4   DAVENPORT, A.   "Dekker's Westward Ho and Hall's Virgidemiae."
     Notes and Queries 192:143-44.
          Finds several echoes of Hall's work in the Dekker/Webster
     play--all in scenes usually assigned to Dekker.

5   GREENOUGH, CHESTER NOYES.   A Bibliography of the Theophrastan
     Characters in English with Several Portrait Characters.
     Cambridge, Mass.: Harvard University Press, pp. 23-25.
          Includes bibliographical data on the Overburian Characters.
     (Interestingly, on the same page as the discussion of Overbury is
     Thomas Adams's "The White Devil or The Hypocrite Uncased.")

6   LEECH, CLIFFORD.   "The Implications of Tragedy."   English 6:
     177-82. [Included in 1950.10.]
          Asserts that Webster, like other Renaissance tragedians,
     makes us ask what kind of justice operates in the universe.   The
     Duchess of Malfi shows the framework of the tragic idea--a deaf
     universe grinding down the individual ("Look you, the stars shine
     still") and the basic enobling tragic response ("I am Duchess of
     Malfi still").

7   MORGAN, F.C.   "A Deed of Gift (1624) and John Webster."   Notes
     and Queries 192:496.
          Notes a document that names John Webster.

8   PRIOR, MOODY.   The Language of Tragedy.   Bloomington: Indiana
     University Press, pp. 44, 196.
          Observes that Webster has become an illustration of the mer-
     its and defects of Elizabethan tragedy, especially as regards
     structure and splendid poetry.   His intense and figurative language
     is second only to Shakespeare.   The design of the whole of The
     Duchess of Malfi is clumsy, but its diction and imagery are har-
     monious and consistent, especially as regards the play's melancholy
     and clouded characters.   Thus, for example, Ferdinand's imagery is
     violent, featuring natural upheavals, physical violence, animals,
     disease, etc.   In the play as a whole, recurrent images include
     animals and birds, demonic forces, fire, storm, witchcraft, battle
     and warfare, disease, foulness, decay, and dramas and the theater.
     There are also some individual images of great power.

9   REED, A.W. "Erasmus and John Webster." Times Literary
     Supplement, 14 June, p. 295.
          Believes Brachiano's death scene in The White Devil is based
     upon a death scene in Erasmus's Funus--Webster has quoted the Latin
     original in virtually verbatim translation.

10   SCHÜCKING, LEVIN L. Shakespeare und der Tragödienstil seiner
     Zeit. Bern: A. Franck, 184 pp., passim.
          Cites Webster often, particularly the development of char-
     acters in The White Devil, but offers no lengthy analysis.

11   WALLIS, LAWRENCE B. Fletcher, Beaumont and Company: Enter-
     tainers to the Jacobean Gentry. New York: Kings Crown, 315 pp.,
     passim.
          A re-examination of tragicomedy that mentions Webster, The
     White Devil, and The Duchess of Malfi throughout, but does not
     consider The Devil's Law Case.

12   WASSERMAN, EARL R. Elizabethan Poetry in the Eighteenth Century.
     Illinois Studies in Language and Literature, vol. 32, nos. 2-3.
     Urbana: University of Illinois Press, 291 pp., passim.
          Studies the neglect and revival of Elizabethan literature,
     including Webster, in the eighteenth century. Part 5 includes
     most of 1937.11. (Based on his University of Illinois disserta-
     tion, "The Elizabethan Revival: Its Background and Beginning,"
     1937.)

13   "Webster's Women." Times Literary Supplement, 1 February, p. 65.
          On the occasion of a Vision Press edition of Webster, comments
     that Webster was a "metaphysic wit" and had a very strong and medi-
     tative mind.

                              1948

1   AKRIGG, G.P.V. "A Phrase in Webster." Notes and Queries 193:
     454.
          Suggests that The Duchess of Malfi, 4.2. 362 ("off my painted
     honour") means Bosola will no longer keep up the pretense of love
     for Ferdinand.

2   _____. "Webster and Raleigh." Notes and Queries 193:427-28.
          Connects a reference to "brittle evidence" (The White Devil
     3.2. 93-95) with the robbery of Raleigh's estate of Sherbourne.

3   BOWERS, FREDSON THAYER. "The First Series of Plays Published
     by Francis Kirkman in 1661." Library, 5th ser. 2:289-91.
          Describes A Cure for a Cuckold and The Thracian Wonder as
     among Kirkman's first published works. Reproduces and comments
     upon Kirkman's prefatory remarks, and raises some questions regard-
     ing dating of these early editions.

4   BRERETON, JOHN Le GAY. Writings on Elizabethan Drama.
     Collected by Robert Guy Howarth. Melbourne: Melbourne
     University Press, p. 52.
          A posthumous collection that praises Webster's "intensity
     of imagination and the sympathy and psychic insight" that charac-
     terize his works. Includes some material from 1905.1 and 1909.2
     not available elsewhere.

5   BROOKE, C.F. TUCKER. "The Renaissance (1500-1660)." In A
     Literary History of England. Edited by Albert C. Baugh. New
     Appleton-Century-Crofts, pp. 547-51. [Notes revised by M.A.
     Shaaber (New York, 1967), pp. 547-51.]
          Surveys Webster's life and collaborations, then comments
     upon individual works: The White Devil emphasizes the brutal
     irrationality of life, with its plethroa of lawless deaths punctu-
     ated by small and moving moments. The Duchess of Malfi, a better
     work, contains as much terror and more pity. Act 4 is the greatest
     death scene in Elizabethan literature.

6   ELLIS-FERMOR, UNA. The Frontiers of Drama. London: Methuen,
     154 pp., passim. [Rev. ed. 1964.]
          Cites Webster frequently, e.g., he, like Shakespeare and
     other Jacobeans, considers the inner pattern of conduct to be of
     supreme importance; he uses the imagery of his opening scenes to
     foreshadow the rest of the play and to reveal character quickly.
     See 1973.18 for a general reaction to the work.

7   EVANS, Sir BENJAMIN IFOR. A Short History of English Drama.
     Harmondsworth: Penguin Books, pp. 86-105. [Reprint. Boston:
     Penguin, 1965.]
          Presents Webster as the first Jacobean and markedly different
     from Shakespeare and their contemporaries. Love and revenge moti-
     vate his characters, within a cruel world. Webster's somber
     spirit and poetic powers raise melodrama to tragedy. His plots
     have little smooth development but many moments of great passion,
     giving his plays a certain brutal force. Evil is ever present,
     but what the characters lack in virtue they regain in great ges-
     tures.

8   FLUCHERE, HENRI. Shakespeare, dramaturge élisabéthain.
     Marseille: Cahiers du Sud, 868 pp., passim.
          Notes Webster exemplifies the spirit of joyous cynicism that
     characterized the age; comments on his interest in Machiavelli
     and his use of a variety of dramatic elements (dumb show, mono-
     logues, songs).

9   FREEMAN, ROSEMARY. English Emblem Books. London: Chatto &
     Windus, pp. 12, 100-101. [Reprint. New York: Octagon Books,
     1966.]
          Discusses Webster's use of emblems to embody and give cur-
     rency to conventional allegory and imagery. He also includes them

for rhetorical interest, e.g., Flamineo's tale of the crocodile and the emblematic dream of the yew tree in The White Devil. See 1969.29.

10 McCULLEN, JOSEPH J. "The Functions or Uses of Madness in Elizabethan Drama between 1590 and 1638." Ph.D. dissertation, University of North Carolina, pp. 74-76, 113-16, 151-54, 266-72, 291-302.
    Finds Brachiano's madness in The White Devil shows some satiric coloring, and there is also a comic element in the madmen's masque in The Duchess of Malfi. Cornelia's madness, on the other hand, is pathetic, while Ferdinand's insanity shows his mind as a slave of passion. See 1951.13 for a revised version of chapter 2 dealing with madness in The White Devil and The Duchess of Malfi.

*11 MOORE, FREDRICK H. "John Webster." Ph.D. dissertation, Columbia University.
    Source: Mahaney, 1973.23.

12 SEVERS, KENNETH. "Imagery and Drama." Durham University Journal, n.s. 10:24-33.
    Discusses the imagery of Eliot's The Wasteland, very briefly citing Eliot's use of The White Devil.

13 TREWIN, J.C. The English Theatre. London: Paul Elek, p. 13.
    Sees Webster as "first gravedigger of the Jacobeans," an author of towering tragedies. Comments on the Gielgud productions of The Duchess of Malfi of 1945 and The White Devil of 1947.

14 URE, PETER. "On Some Differences between Senecan and Elizabethan Tragedy." Durham University Journal, n.s. 10:17-23. [Included with other related essays in 1974.25.]
    Suggests that understanding Seneca does help us place plays such as Appius and Virginia in an appropriate context, but the Latin dramatist was probably not a major influence.

15 WILLIAMS, PHILIP. "The Compositor of the 'Pied Bull' Lear." Studies in Bibliography 1 (1948-49):59-68.
    Compares the composition of Lear to two other productions of Nicholas Okes, including the first quarto of The White Devil.

16 WILSON, EDWARD M. "Cervantes and the English Literature of the Seventeenth Century." Bulletin Hispanique 50:27-52.
    Shows The Fair Maid of the Inn was influenced by Cervantes's Exemplary Novels.

17 WITHINGTON, ROBERT. "What 'War of the Theaters'?" College English 10, no. 3 (December):163-64.
    Notes that Webster's descriptions of his fellow dramatists in the preface to The White Devil are not casually chosen--as the remarks of others, such as Jonson, may have been.

1949

*1   BEJBLIK̂, ALOIS. "Poznamkyk Websterove hre The White Devil." Slovesna Veda (Prague) 2:243-44.
      Source: Mahaney, 1973.23. In Czech.

2   CECIL, DAVID. Poets and Storytellers. New York: Macmillan, pp. 25-43.
      Comments that Webster is probably unappreciated and is usual-ly seen as a barbaric genius saved by the intensity of his scenes and language. While it is true his plays do reflect the tastes of a popular audience, they are also more. Webster expresses a vision of a conflict between right and wrong, sin and its conse-quences. Webster is a stern and careful moral teacher, who reveals his moral message in extravagant gestures and symbols.

3   GARDNER, HELEN. "Milton's 'Satan' and the Theme of Damnation in Elizabethan Tragedy." English Studies [now Essays & Studies] 1948, n.s. 1:46-66.
      Comments upon some of the theological implications of the Renaissance interest in evil. Frequently mentions, in passing, Webster's villains.

*4   HILL, NEVILLE V. "Some Aspects of the Style of John Webster." Ph.D. dissertation, University of Birmingham.
      Source: Mahaney, 1973.23.

5   HYDE, MARY C. Playwriting for Elizabethans, 1600-1605. Columbia University Studies in English and Comparative Literature, no. 167. New York: Columbia University Press, pp. 28, 32-33, 64-80.
      Attempts to recreate the theatrical basis of Elizabethan drama, based on actual plays, including Sir Thomas Wyat and the "Ho" plays.

6   JACK, IAN. "The Case of John Webster." Scrutiny 16:38-43.
      Finds Webster presents a world in ruins and disintegration. He did not have a balanced view of life; thus, his sententiae point to a stoical, Senecan philosophy, but the action does not. "There is no correspondence between the axioms and the life represented in the drama. This disassociation is the fundamental flaw in Webster." Believes Webster insincerely lets Machiavellianism sub-stitute for order, and his characters have only the pagan courage of hell--the virtue of despair. The plays' characters have no motives for their crimes. Finds something ridiculous in Webster's decadent plethora of horrors.

1950

*1   ADAMS, MARTIN. "Webster--A Museum Piece?" Arts Quarterly 1:50-52.
      Source: Mahaney, 1973.23.

2   AKRIGG, G.P.V. "The Name of God and The Duchess of Malfi."
     Notes and Queries 195:231-33.
          Argues that the absence of the word "God" in The Duchess of
     Malfi suggests censorship, similar to that of Shakespeare's First
     Folio (also published in 1623).

3   CASSAGNAU, M. "P.J. Joulet et John Webster." Revue de
     Littérature Comparée 24:575.
          Believes that in The White Devil 3.1 (Vittoria's trial) the
     Cardinal may derive part of his accusation from Contre rime LIV
     of P.J. Joulet.

4   CRAIG, HARDIN. A History of English Literature. Vol. 2, The
     Literature of the English Renaissance, 1585-1660. London:
     Oxford University Press, pp. 172-74.
          Within a chapter on Webster, Tourneur, and Middleton includes
     a brief review of the tragedies: both are revenge plays, mixed
     with horror.

5   DENT, ROBERT W. "John Webster's Debt to William Alexander."
     Modern Language Notes 65:73-82.
          Contends that Webster borrowed from Alexander's Monarchicke
     Tragedies (1607) and cites several parallels. See 1952.7 for addi-
     tional related material.

6   DOWNER, ALAN S. The British Drama. New York: Appleton-Century-
     Crofts, pp. 119-24.
          Shows that in Webster's major plays the revenge convention
     is used to depict a decadent world where moral order must be re-
     stored. The traditional revenge pattern is de-emphasized in favor
     of complex characterization.

7   FARNHAM, WILLARD. Shakespeare's Tragic Frontier: The World of
     His Final Tragedies. Berkeley: University of California Press,
     pp. 27-30.
          Believes Webster, with Chapman, helps to illustrate the
     Jacobean quality of Shakespeare's last plays: they share an in-
     terest in deeply flawed but noble-spirited characters. Vittoria
     is such a Jacobean tragic heroine. She is a guilty but an admir-
     able great spirit. Reviewed: 1951.16.

8   KRZYŻANOWSKI, J. "Conjectural Remarks on Elizabethan Drama-
     tists." Notes and Queries 195:400-402.
          Proposes some possible emendations of The Weakest Goeth to
     the Wall.

9   LEBEQUE, R. "Corneille et le théâtre anglais." Revue de la
     Société d'Histoire du Théâtre 2:200-202.
          Finds Corneille appropriated the necromancer/dumb show scene
     from The White Devil, the only instance of his borrowing from
     Webster.

10   LEECH, CLIFFORD. Shakespeare's Tragedies and Other Studies in
      Seventeenth Century Drama. London: Catto & Windus, 232 pp.,
      passim.
          Includes 1947.6 and mentions Webster frequently in other
      essays.

11   MASON, E.C. "Satire on Women and Sex in Elizabethan Tragedy."
      English Studies 30:1-10.
          Argues that Elizabethan and Jacobean ravings against women--
      often to the point of madness--are actually directed against the
      sex drive and human nature. Even in Vittoria, fascination is
      balanced by abhorrence.

12   NICOLL, ALLARDYCE. World Drama from Aeschylus to Anouilh.
      New York: Harcourt & Brace, pp. 285-86.
          Presents Webster as a "dark genius," whose tragedies stand
      above his earlier works. His stage becomes cluttered with in-
      essentials and a plethroa of horrors, but an atmosphere of courtly
      evil is momorably created.

13   PARKES, H.B. "Nature's Diverse Laws: The Double Vision of the
      Elizabethans." Sewanee Review 58:402-18.
          Argues that Elizabethans lived after the medieval belief in
      God's universe and before Newton's substitute cosmology; thus,
      they suffered a conflict between naturalism and religion. This
      confusion is echoed in Flamineo's dying "in a mist." The natural-
      ists maintain human and animal society is based on force, not ethics.

*14   QUINN, SEABURY. "Lope de Vega's Duchess of Malfi Play." Ph.D.
      dissertation, Columbia University.
          Source: Mahaney, 1973.23.

15   ROBB, DEWAR M. "The Canon of William Rowley's Plays." Modern
      Language Review 45, no. 2 (April):129-41.
          Finds the Rowley who collaborated with Webster on A Cure for
      a Cuckold in 1625 had developed into a mature artist. Assigns
      specific scenes to Rowley and Webster, and the possible third hand
      of Heywood, on the basis of distinctive stylistic traits.

16   ROBY, ROBERT C. "T.S. Eliot and the Elizabethan and Jacobean
      Dramatists." Ph.D. dissertation, Northwestern University,
      196 pp., passim.
          Describes Eliot's high respect for the dramatic art of the
      Renaissance dramatists but negative reactions to their thought and
      attitude, particularly in tragedies of blood such as The Duchess
      of Malfi. Eliot's poetic allusions include many to Webster.

17   ROSSITER, A.P. English Drama from Early Times to the Elizabethans.
      London: Hutchinson, pp. 151, 159.
          Compares Shakespeare to Webster: Webster seems scornful of
      the commoners in his audience (especially in the preface to The
      White Devil).

18   TYNAN, KENNETH. <u>He That Plays the King</u>. London: Longmans,
     Green, pp. 68-71.
          Comments on Margaret Rawlings's Vittoria in Benthall's pro-
     duction of <u>The White Devil</u> at the Duchess Theatre (the production
     was "terrifying" and Rawlings stirring). Finds <u>The White Devil</u> a
     prodigious and gripping play of rapacious men and savage women,
     barbaric morals, and an exquisitely civilized attitude toward
     death. It is a masterpiece because its poetry is somber, realis-
     tic, and ragged; it is less a tragedy than a poem on death (which
     was, for Webster, a constant presence).

19   WALLERSTEIN, RUTH. <u>Studies in Seventeenth-Century Poetic</u>.
     Madison: University of Wisconsin Press, pp. 86-91.
          Believes <u>A Monumental Column</u> parallels Donne in thought and
     expression. Compares the poem to several other elegies on Prince
     Henry.

20   WEDGWOOD, C.V. <u>Seventeenth-Century English Literature</u>.
     London: Oxford University Press, pp. 34-38.
          Ranks Webster high among Jacobean dramatists on the strength
     of his lightning flashes of poetry and sense of the theater.

21   WESTLAND, PETER. <u>The Teach Yourself History of English Literature</u>.
     Vol. 2. London: English Universities Press, pp. 200-219.
          Suggests that like Beaumont, Webster was partial to collabo-
     ration, yet <u>The White Devil</u> and <u>The Duchess of Malfi</u> are his only
     good works. Believes <u>The White Devil</u> has more freshness and in-
     tensity of passion.

                                    1951

1   BABB, LAWRENCE. <u>The Elizabethan Malady: A Study of Melancholia</u>
     <u>in English Literature from 1580 to 1642</u>. East Lansing: Michigan
     State College Press, pp. 70-71, 83-90, 110-13, 154.
          Shows that Webster seemed to have considerable physiological,
     pharmaceutical, and psychiatric learning. Bosola, the tool-villain,
     driven to his melancholy by others, represents a malcontent type
     falling out of fashion by the time of <u>The Duchess of Malfi</u>. He de-
     velops in the play from discontent to remorse. In both tragedies,
     melancholy is associated with visions and optical hallucinations,
     e.g., Ferdinand's lycanthropic delusion.

2   BOWDEN, W.R. <u>The English Dramatic Lyric, 1603-42</u>. Yale Studies
     in English, vol. 118. New Haven: Yale University Press, 219
     pp., passim.
          Examines the roles and functions of song in Stuart plays.
     Discusses two songs in <u>Appius and Virginia</u>, one in <u>The Devil's Law</u>
     <u>Case</u>, the ditty in <u>The Duchess of Malfi</u> 3.4, the dirge that pre-
     cedes the murder of the Duchess, and three songs from <u>The White</u>
     <u>Devil</u>.

*3   BROWN, JOHN RUSSELL. "The Plays of John Webster Considered in
      the Light of Contemporary Stage Conditions." Ph.D. disserta-
      tion, Oxford University.
          Source: Index to Theses Accepted for Higher Degrees by the
      Universities of Great Britain and Ireland and the Council for
      National Academic Awards 2:9, item 180.

4   CRANE, MILTON. Shakespeare's Prose. Chicago: University of
      Chicago Press, pp. 54-59.
          Finds Webster comes nearest to Shakespeare in the intricate
      beauty of his prose, almost all of which is spoken by Flamineo and
      Bosola. These prose characters are grim clowns, and their use of
      prose contributes to a sinister atmosphere that pervades the plays.

5   EISLER, ROBERT. Man into Wolf. London: Spring Books, p. 162.
          In an anthropological interpretation of sadism, masochism,
      and lycanthropy, notes Webster's use of lycanthropy in The Duchess
      of Malfi.

6   HARTNOLL, PHYLLIS, ed. The Oxford Companion to the Theatre.
      London: Oxford University Press, p. 1001.
          Notes that Webster's reputation is based upon the tragedies,
      which compound crude horror and sublime poetry, and provide scope
      for great acting; his other works are unimportant.

7   HEWITT, RAY S. "Foreshadowing in Elizabethan Tragedy." Ph.D.
      dissertation, University of California, pp. 118-35.
          Sees Webster among the best of the post-Shakespeareans in
      his use of foreshadowing. Instances of foreshadowing in The White
      Devil include Brachiano's ghost and skull, and the narration of
      Flamineo's childhood; in The Duchess of Malfi, the language of the
      wooing scene.

*8   HOUSMAN, JOHN E. "Parallel Plots in English and Spanish Drama
      of the Early Seventeenth Century." Ph.D. dissertation,
      University of London.
          Source: Index to Theses Accepted for Higher Degrees by the
      Universities of Great Britain and Ireland and the Council for
      National Academic Awards 2:174.

9   HUNTER, G.K. "The Marking of Sententiae in Elizabethan Printed
      Plays, Poems, and Romances." Library, 5th ser. 6:171-88.
          Shows The White Devil, A Monumental Column, and The Duchess
      of Malfi had, in their first editions, gnomic pointing of sententiae,
      generally a sign of authors aiming to exhibit learning.

10   JACQUOT, JEAN. George Chapman (1559-1634). Paris: Les Belles
      Lettres, pp. 39, 167, 275.
          Discusses Eastward Ho in relation to the "Ho" plays of
      Webster and Dekker, and notes, as well, Webster's citation of the
      full and heightened style of Chapman in the preface to The White

Devil. Briefly compares the two dramatists in terms of language
and scenic structure.

11   JOSEPH, BERTRAM LEON. Elizabethan Acting. London: Oxford
     University Press, pp. 143-44.
        Cites Webster often, including the Character of "An Excellent
     Actor," and notes the appropriateness of speech to character in The
     White Devil. Also observes that Webster says in the prefatory re-
     marks to The Devil's Law Case that much of the grace of the play
     was in performance.

12   LEECH, CLIFFORD. John Webster: A Critical Study. London:
     Hogarth Press, 122 pp.
        In the introduction, sketches the few facts of Webster's
     life. He seemed esteemed by his contemporaries, then not recog-
     nized again until Lamb. Offers a brief bibliography and stage
     history, including Restoration productions of the tragedies, early
     eighteenth-century adaptations, mid-nineteenth-century revivals,
     Horne's adaptation of The Duchess of Malfi, and modern productions
     beginning with Poel (1892).
        The White Devil. Suggests that the opening symbolizes the
     absence of order in Webster's universe. All his characters are
     evil, although Vittoria is persuasive during her trial. She is
     more obviously acting in the convertites scene, and she dies with
     authority. Beside her, Brachiano is smaller and "blacker."
     Flamineo is perhaps the most interesting figure, the least de-
     ceived, a Machiavellian with no glory about him. He is used as
     a chorus and at his death, his defiance is the play's strongest.
     What comes after life is uncertain, but in The White Devil, evil
     is sure and Vittoria and Flamineo face it with nobility.
        The Duchess of Malfi. Finds the play collects great scenes
     but lacks coherence. The last act is anticlimactic, and there
     are structural inconsistencies and thematic confusion (e.g., what
     do we make of the Duchess?). By the torture scenes of act 4, the
     question of guilt becomes irrelevant: integrity and survival are
     all.
        Comments upon Webster as a dramatic poet: the motivations
     of his characters are often confused, especially in late plays.
     This is prefigured by Ferdinand in The Duchess of Malfi. Inequali-
     ties of style are seen elsewhere, too, including the nondramatic
     works. Webster has a tendency toward the generalized utterance
     and at times he can be crude and insensitive. His short, not his
     long, speeches impress us. The plays excel in their passionately
     apprehended major characters and their flashes of great verse.

13   McCULLEN, JOSEPH J. "Madness and the Isolation of Characters
     in Elizabethan and Early Stuart Drama." Studies in Philology
     48, no. 2 (April):206-18.
        Defines madness as a withdrawal into one's own mind.
     Webster's plays show that abandonment to evil subjects a person
     to the isolation of madness. This is especially clear in the

Brachiano death scene ("solitariness of dying princes") and the
isolation of Ferdinand in The Duchess of Malfi. Other characters,
like Cornelia, are driven into mad isolation even though innocent.
(Based upon Ph.D. dissertation, 1948.10.)

14   MINER, WORTHINGTON. "Shakespeare for the Millions." Theater
      Arts 35 (June):58, 94.
          Finds Coriolanus strikingly similar to The Duchess of Malfi,
      and hence wants to ascribe it to Shakespeare and Webster.

*15   POPKIN, HENRY. "Dramatic Theory of the Elizabethan and Jacobean
      Playwrights." Ph.D. dissertation, Harvard University, 184 pp.
          Source: Doctoral Dissertations Accepted by American
      Universities 18:226.

16   ROTH, ROBERT. "Another World of Shakespeare." Modern Philology
      49, no. 1:42-61.
          Reviews 1950.7, observing Farnham finds Webster sympathetic
      to Vittoria, which seems an oversimplification.

17   SCHOENBAUM, SAMUEL. "Internal Evidence and the Attribution of
      Elizabethan Plays." Bulletin of the New York Public Library
      65:102-24. [Reprinted: 1966.8; expanded as chapter 3 ("Avoid-
      ing Disaster") of 1966.22.]
          Examines the methodology of attribution of Elizabethan plays,
      citing several that have been, at times, attributed to Webster.

18   STAMM, RUDOLF. Geschichte des englischen Theaters. Bern: A.
      Francke, pp. 60-78 and passim.
          Considers The Duchess of Malfi and The White Devil as revenge
      tragedies. Also discusses Webster's association with theater com-
      panies and revivals of The Duchess of Malfi in the eighteenth cen-
      tury.

*19   TRIENENS, ROGER. "The Green-eyed Monster: A Study of Sexual
      Jealousy in the Literature of the English Renaissance." Ph.D.
      dissertation, Northwestern University, 184 pp.
          Sources: Doctoral Dissertations Accepted by American
      Universities 18:228; Summaries of Doctoral Dissertations . . .
      Northwestern University 19:45-49.

20   VENEZKY, ALICE S. Pageantry on the Shakespearean Stage. New
      York: Twayne, pp. 22, 25, 112.
          Notes that the high points of Sir Thomas Wyat were the royal
      pageants; in The White Devil the dumb show was used to "indicate
      important incidents omitted from the regular action"; and Webster
      utilized ambassadors with lavish costumes in The White Devil's
      trial scene. (Originally a Columbia University dissertation,
      1951.)

21   WADSWORTH, FRANK W. "The White Devil: An Historical and
     Critical Study." Ph.D. dissertation, Princeton University,
     403 pp.
          Finds The White Devil is often misunderstood, especially by
     those who too readily classify it (e.g., as a revenge play). Dis-
     cusses Webster's use of conventions, such as those governing the
     depiction of villains and courtesans.
          Suggests that the stagecraft of The White Devil is more skill-
     ful than often assumed. Characters are consistent and effectively
     drawn and the imagery creates an atmosphere of gloom, yet at times,
     it is beautiful.

22   WILLIAMSON, AUDREY. Theatre of Two Decades. London: Rockliff,
     pp. 283-89.
          Discusses twentieth-century productions of the tragedies as
     reflections of the political instability of our time, and our
     sense, shared with the Jacobeans, of futility and spiritual degra-
     dation. We are also Jacobean in our taste for sex, crime, and
     Machiavellianism.

23   WING, DONALD. A Short-Title Catalogue of Books Printed in
     England, Scotland, Ireland, Wales, and British America and of
     English Books Printed in Other Countries, 1641-1700. Vol. 3.
     New York: Index Society, p. 460.
          Includes entries on Webster in this continuation of 1926.9.

*24 WU, CHI-HWEI. "Elements of Conflict in Elizabethan Tragedy."
     Ph.D. dissertation, Cornell University, pp. 182-232.
          Source: Doctoral Dissertations Accepted by American
     Universities 18:224.

                                   1952

1   BAKER, HERSCHEL. The Wars of Truth. Cambridge, Mass.: Harvard
     University Press, pp. 53-58.
          Surveys the deterioration of Christian humanism in the early
     1600s, citing Webster as an example of "the literature of disen-
     chantment." Webster's characters are pure evil, existing in a
     world without moral value, humanistic moderation, or rational self-
     control, confronting the "leering masks of sex and death."

2   BAMBOROUGH, J.B. The Little World of Man. London: Longmans,
     Green, pp. 99-103, 114-15. [Reprint. Darvey, Pa.: Arden
     Library, 1980.]
          Studies the psychological theories that prevailed in
     Shakespeare's day--the Great Chain of Being, and man as a microcosm.
     The White Devil illustrates the melancholic imagination.

3   BRADBROOK, MURIEL C. Themes and Conventions of Elizabethan
     Tragedy. 2d. ed. Cambridge: Cambridge University Press, pp.
     186-212.

In this general discussion of acting, stage, reading, speaking and similar conventions, followed by discussions of specific dramatists, argues that Webster can be too literary, resulting in a perfection of detail at the expense of overall structure. Unlike Tourneur, his characters blur their good and evil sides. For example, Vittoria is guilty, but surrounded by a suggestion of innocence. Similarly, Brachiano is poisonous and damned, yet noble. Flamineo, Florence, and Lodovico are also mixed characters. The play is held together only by the tone of its writing. In The Duchess of Malfi, the action hovers between the natural and the supernatural. The marriage of the Duchess would meet with the disapproval of the audience, but the actions of her brothers are clearly "diabolical." Finds the last act impressionistic: the scenes are not unified and show the weakness of Webster's notebook method of composition.

4   BROWN, JOHN RUSSELL. "On the Dating of Webster's The White Devil and The Duchess of Malfi." Philological Quarterly 31, no. 4 (October):353-62.
     Argues that The White Devil should be dated early 1612 or winter, 1612-13 (old style) based on a Dekker allusion and Webster's reference to winter in the preface, support by some related lines and parallels. Using evidence derived from topical references, suggests The Duchess of Malfi was written c. 1612-14 and revived in 1617-18.

5   CAMDEN, CHARLES CARROLL. The Elizabethan Woman. London and Houston: Elsevier Press, pp. 90, 179, 183.
     Cites the espousal procedure of the Duchess and Antonio to illustrate the "de praesenti" ceremony and also briefly discusses some references to cosmetics in the "Ho" plays.

6   CUTTS, JOHN P. "Two Jacobean Theater Songs." Music and Letters 33, no. 4:333-34.
     Reports that the song "O let us howle" from The Duchess of Malfi is included in British Museum Additional MS. 29481. This is the only known setting. The song helps create an atmosphere of pain, doubt, and perplexity that is part of the torture of the Duchess. It was probably written by Robert Johnson (see 1955.8).

7   DENT, ROBERT W. "John Webster's The White Devil: A Critical Introduction and Commentary." Ph.D. dissertation, University of Chicago, 132 pp.
     Includes three short chapters of general introduction (on the play's structure, characterization, and value system) followed by a "commentary" (notes to specific lines in the Lucas text). Deals with Webster's borrowing in two appendices, including material on William Alexander discussed in 1950.5.

*8   FOAKES, R.A. "Imagery in Elizabethan and Jacobean Drama." Ph.D. dissertation, University of Birmingham.

Source: Index to Theses Accepted for Higher Degrees by the
Universities of Great Britain and Ireland and the Council for
National Academic Awards 2:163.

*9 GREENFIELD, THELMA N. "The Use of the Induction in Elizabethan
     Drama." Ph.D. dissertation, University of Wisconsin, 199 pp.
        Cited in Doctoral Dissertations Accepted by American
     Universities 19:231. See 1969.14 for a book by this author on
     the same subject.

10 HALLIDAY, FRANK ERNEST. A Shakespeare Companion, 1550-1950.
     New York: Duckworth, pp. 176, 692-93. [Revised. 1969.]
        An alphabetical encyclopedia. Includes entries for "Webster"
     (after Shakespeare, perhaps our greatest dramatic poet, although
     almost forgotten until rediscovered by Lamb) and "The Duchess of
     Malfi" (title page data).

11 HARBAGE, ALFRED B. Shakespeare and the Rival Traditions. New
     York: Macmillan, 393 pp., passim.
        In this general study of Shakespeare and the public and
     coterie theaters cites Webster intermittently, e.g., his lament
     about Red Bull audiences for The White Devil and his reduction of
     the sordidness of his sources for The White Devil for public thea-
     ter production.

12 HELTON, TINSLEY. "The Concept of Woman's Honor in Jacobean
     Drama." Ph.D. dissertation, University of Minnesota, 371 pp.
        Demonstrates that Elizabethans stressed chastity as the key
     to woman's honor. In the first years of the seventeenth century,
     some unchaste women were also depicted as admirable by Chapman,
     Heywood, Marston, Shakespeare (e.g., Cleopatra), and most clearly
     by Ford and Webster. Vittoria and the Duchess, like Cleopatra,
     are resolute, and their resolve and wit eclipse moral judgment.
     See Dissertation Abstracts 12 (1952):795.

*13 HONEYFORD, BRUCE N.M. "Problems of Good and Evil in Jacobean
     Tragedy." Ph.D. dissertation, University of Toronto, pp. 329-61.
     Source: Mahaney, 1973.23.

14 KUNITZ, STANLEY JASPOON, and HAYCROFT, HOWARD. British Authors
     before 1800. New York: H.W. Wilson, pp. 555-56.
        Includes a small section on Webster's life and reputed work
     habits. Presents him as a great tragic poet, but not much of a
     dramatist as far as plot construction is concerned. His works
     fall into three periods: apprenticeship and collaboration, the
     two tragedies, and decline. Believes Webster should be judged by
     The White Devil and The Duchess of Malfi, plays of tragic sense
     and bitter wrath that present a catastrophe of horror.

15 McCULLEN, JOSEPH J. "The Functions of Songs Aroused by Madness
     in Elizabethan Drama." In A Tribute to George Coffin Taylor.

Edited by Arnold Williams. Chapel Hill: University of North
Carolina Press, pp. 185-96.
Finds the song by the mad bawd in Northward Ho creates a
mood of sexual abandon. In The Duchess of Malfi the madmen's gro-
tesqueries make the torture of the Duchess more terrifying; and
in The White Devil, Cornelia's song is pathetic, giving vent to
grief and helplessness.

*16 MARGESON, JOHN M.R. "Dramatic Irony in Jacobean Tragedy."
      Ph.D. dissertation, University of Toronto.
      Source: Doctoral Dissertations Accepted by American
Universities 19:231.

17 NAGLER, A.M. Sources of Theatrical History. New York: Theatre
    Annual, pp. 126-27.
      The section on Elizabethan acting includes the character,
"An Excellent Actor," described as "perhaps written with Burbage
in mind."

18 REED, ROBERT R. Bedlam on the Jacobean Stage. Cambridge, Mass.:
    Harvard University Press, 190 pp., passim. [Reprint. New York:
    Octagon Books, 1970.]
      Studies non-Shakespearean mad folk and Bethlehem hospital in
the Jacobean drama. Webster was one of those who produced Bedlamites directly on stage, especially in Northward Ho (an accurate
depiction), and The Duchess of Malfi (a more stereotyped depiction
used to further the atmosphere of mental terror and provide a
brief spell of comic relief). Duke Ferdinand is a memorable delineation. Takes some note also of Webster's use of Renaissance
psychological theories. The malcontent, melancholy Bosola is a
classic--pseudo-mad, he comments on social immorality.

19 SHAW, PHILLIP. "Sir Thomas Wyat and the Scenario of Lady Jane."
    Modern Language Quarterly 13:227-38.
      Argues that by tracing the sources of Wyat, we can determine
its relation to Lady Jane. Attempts to reconstruct Lady Jane plays
that lie behind Wyat. The abridged version was written by more
men than Webster and Dekker--probably three additional hands.

20 WAITH, EUGENE M. The Pattern of Tragicomedy in Beaumont and
    Fletcher. Yale Studies in English, vol. 120. New Haven: Yale
    University Press, 214 pp., passim.
      Cites Webster throughout, often with Shakespeare, to compare
tragic style with the comic and tragi-comic. The Duchess of Malfi
offers a look at a "fundamental problem of the nature of man."
Also briefly discusses Webster's use of aphorisms.

1953

1   BALDINI, GABRIELE. <u>John Webster e il linguaggio della tragedia</u>.
     Rome: Edizione dell'Ateneo, 300 pp. [Pp. 95-104, translated
     by Lorraine Whithead, Judy Rawson, and G.K. Hunter, appear in
     1969.17 as "John Webster and the Language of Tragedy."]
          Surveys Webster's theatrical language. Covers the early
collaborations with Dekker and the additions to <u>The Malcontent</u>,
finding the "Ho" plays works of poetic apprenticeship. Webster's
language in <u>The White Devil</u> has the violence of a bolt of lightning,
enhanced by the use of epigrams, fables, borrowings, and the like,
while <u>The Duchess of Malfi</u> moves towards melodrama and away from
tragedy. <u>The Devil's Law Case</u> is considered as a tragicomedy. Includes also appendices on Webster's reputation from 1615 to 1808;
Webster and Lamb; the lost play <u>The Late Murder</u> and the vaulting
horse of Flamineo. Reviewed: 1953.5.

2   CLARK, JOHN E. "<u>The White Devil</u>: A Critique." <u>Manitoba Arts
     Review</u> 8, no. 2:22-28.
          Finds the actions of the play are based upon those of a so-
ciety with no moral code. It contains typical Jacobean imagery--
animal, disease, etc.--that degrades humankind, especially in its
sexual nature. This imagery contrasts with the strength and de-
termination of the characters. Believes <u>The White Devil</u> is a
tragedy because we admire Vittoria, even though she is evil--her
evil is caused by a rotten society.

3   DENT, ROBERT W. "Pierre Matthieu: Another Source for Webster."
     <u>Huntington Library Quarterly</u> 17:75-82.
          Discusses the relationship between <u>The Duchess of Malfi</u> and
Grimeston's translation of Matthieu's <u>Histoire de la mort . . . de
Henry III</u> (Paris, 1611). See 1960.12 for Dent's book-length study
of Webster's borrowing.

4   HOWARTH, ROBERT GUY. <u>Literature of the Theater: Marlowe to
     Shirley</u>. Sydney, Australia: Halstead Press, 14 pp.
          Believes actual theatrical staging is important. Suggests
that <u>The Spanish Tragedy</u> leads to <u>The Duchess of Malfi</u>, which is
about revenge for the fancied crime of marriage below one's class.

5   LUCAS, F.L. Review of <u>John Webster e il linguaggio della
     tragedia</u>, by Gabriele Baldini. <u>Letterature Moderne</u> 5:478-80.
          Finds Baldini's loving study of Webster (1953.1) a welcome
feat of international scholarship. Lucas's only disagreements are
on matters of opinion.

6   MERLE, ROBERT. "S'explique sur Falmineo." <u>Les Nouvelles
     Litteraires</u>, 22 October.
          A letter contesting charges by René Lalou (in the same
journal, 1 October 1953) concerning the translation of Webster.

7   PELLEGRINI, GUILIANO. Barocco inglese. Messina: G. d'Anna,
     pp. 49, 87, 107.
         Cites Webster's malcontent characters and Italianate settings.

8   WADSWORTH, FRANK W. "Webster's The White Devil, III. ii. 75-
     80." Explicator 11:Item 28.
         Suggests Webster's reference to a "holy whore" is an echo of
     Edward IV's remark about one of his mistresses as cited in Thomas
     More's History of King Richard III.

9   WARD, ALFRED CHARLES. Illustrated History of English Literature.
     Vol. 2. New York: Longmans, Green, pp. 15-16. [Reprinted with
     insignificant alterations as English Literature, Chaucer to
     Bernard Shaw (New York: Longmans, Green, 1958).]
         Describes The White Devil as a conventional adultery-murder-
     revenge play, and The Duchess of Malfi as less hackneyed. Concludes
     that Webster displays only intermittent poetic power.

10   WILSON, EDWARD M. "Family Honour in the Plays of Shakespeare's
     Predecessors and Contemporaries." Essays and Studies, n.s. 6:
     19-40.
         Notes that The Duchess of Malfi is the most famous case of
     a brother's vengeance on his own sister. It is paralleled by
     Webster's other plays, especially The White Devil and The Devil's
     Law Case. Webster shows the effects of a wrongly conceived sense
     of honor on a criminal man.

                                1954

1   AKRIGG, G.P.V. "John Webster's 'Devil in Crystal.'" Notes and
     Queries, n.s. 1:52.
         Suggests that the image of the "devill in christall" in The
     White Devil may come from crystal saints' shrines popular during
     that period.

2   BROWN, JOHN RUSSELL. "The Printing of John Webster's Plays
     (I)." Studies in Bibliography 6:117-40.
         Part 1 of an intensive bibliographical and textual study,
     continued 1956.4; 1962.6. Discusses the facts behind the authori-
     tative text of The White Devil published by Nicholas Oakes in 1612.
     The Duchess of Malfi also appears in one good text, published by
     Oakes in 1623. The Devil's Law Case was printed by Augustine
     Mathewes in 1623 in a virtually error-free version. See 1969.15
     for a supplementary article.

3   DORAN, MADELEINE. Endeavors of Art: A Study of Form in
     Elizabethan Drama. Madison: University of Wisconsin Press,
     482 pp., passim.
         Attempts to understand the literary values of Renaissance
     drama historically. Cites Webster prominently throughout.

                                118

Discusses The White Devil and The Duchess of Malfi as Italianate
tragedy; the relationship of the plays to fortune; and the theatrical and philosophical values of the dramas.

4   ELLRODT, ROBERT. "Les Poètes anglais et la psychologie de
     l'enfant." Revue de la Mediterranée 14:641-56.
         A general study based on the assumption that the most pro-
found elements of humanity are universal, especially so where
children are concerned. Finds Giovanni in The White Devil is one
of the most attractive of stage children.

*5   EKEBLAD, INGA-STINA. "The Function of Imagery in the Plays of
     Webster, Tourneur, and Middleton." M.A. thesis, Sheffield
     University.
         Source: Index to Theses Accepted for Higher Degrees by the
     Universities of Great Britain and Ireland and the Council for
     National Academic Awards 5:9.

6   HOWARTH, ROBERT GUY. "Dramatists' Namesakes and Milton's
     Father." Notes and Queries, n.s. 1:83.
         Shows that a lawsuit in 1622/3 of "Webster vs Rowley" does
not involve John Webster the dramatist.

7   _____ . "John Webster's Burial." Notes and Queries, n.s. 1:
     114-15.
         Suggests that a burial entry in the parish register of
March 1638, at the Church of St. James, Clerkenwell, is probably
for the dramatist. It shows him as neither impoverished nor a
householder.

*8   _____ . "John Webster's Classical Nescience [sic]." Sydney
     University Union Recorder, 14 October, pp. 224-26.
         Source: Mahaney, 1973.23.

9   JARRETT, HOBART SIDNEY. "The Character-Writers and Seventeenth
     Century Society: 1608-1658." Ph.D. dissertation, Syracuse
     University, 215 pp.
         Finds the character writers, including Webster, constructed
prototypes that embody class traits, for the purpose of moral in-
struction. Most of the character writers were conservative, theo-
centric, and tried to preserve traditional social patterns and the
great-chain-of-being hierarchy of souls and society. They urged
moderation, the careful following of good models, and the rule of
reason. See Dissertation Abstracts 15 (1955):260-61.

10   PRAZ, MARIO. "The Duchess of Malfi." Times Literary Supplement,
     18 June, p. 393.
         Argues that although Lucas and Charles Crawford cite the
Arcadia as a source of the mock corpses and dead man's hand scene
of The Duchess of Malfi, the source is actually Herodotus' History
(2.121).

11   _____. "Shakespeare's Italy." Shakespeare Survey 7:95-106.
      The story of The Duchess of Malfi is an example of the lurid,
   exotic appeal of Italy: "Webster is the supreme exponent of a
   school of Italianate horrors." Shakespeare's Italy is more gentle.

12   WALTON, CHARLES E. "The Impact of the Court Masque and the
      Blackfriars Theatre upon the Staging of Elizabethan-Jacobean
      Drama." Ph.D. dissertation, University of Missouri, 196 pp.
      Studies the impact of the court masque upon the theater.
   This influence was especially strong after the 1608 opening of
   the Blackfriars Theater. Webster's plays were among many in this
   period that featured masque-like spectacle. See Dissertation
   Abstracts 14 (1954):136-37.

                              1955

1   ABRAMS, SHERWIN F. "The Tragic Impulse." Ph.D. dissertation,
      University of Wisconsin, 325 pp.
      Suggests that Elizabethan plays, including The Duchess of
   Malfi, heighten our awareness of man's material and physical
   boundaries, and, more positively, of his spiritual and creative
   possibilities. See Dissertation Abstracts 15 (1955):2596.

2   AXELRAD, ALBERT JOSÉ. Un Malcontent élizabéthain. John Marston
      (1576-1634). Paris: Didier, 351 pp., passim.
      Mentions Webster in passing, especially his creation of a
   malcontent, cynical and criminal, in Bosola.

3   BOGARD, TRAVIS. "A Preface to Websterian Tragedy: A Critical
      Study of The White Devil and The Duchess of Malfi." Ph.D. dis-
      sertation, Princeton University, 348 pp.
      Finds nineteenth-century critics compared Webster to
   Shakespeare, leading to such distortions as the notion that Webster
   was a great poet but a bad dramatist, or that he was immoral.
   Rupert Brooke and modern criticism have recognized his integrity
   as an artist. Contrary to the claim of William Archer, Webster
   was a skillful dramatist. His characters don't develop like
   Shakespeare's: their stories are of the struggle to maintain their
   integrity of life. Webster employs the techniques of Elizabethan
   satire, mixed with tragedy, thus obtaining a double perspective
   and subjecting the actions of the drama to satiric irony. The
   satire strips all illusion from men, revealing what makes them
   truly great. The White Devil is a realistic study of society and
   the evils of court life. The Duchess of Malfi is a deeper inquiry
   into the nature of evil. Mortality threatens to make both good
   and evil meaningless. Only by the preservation of integrity of
   life can such forces be fought. See 1955.4 and Dissertation
   Abstracts 15 (1955):411-12.

4   _____. The Tragic Satire of John Webster. Berkeley:
        University of California Press, 158 pp. [Excerpted: 1961.3;
        1968.23; quoted in 1969.17; 1975.18.]
            Essentially the same work as 1955.3.

5   BORINSKI, LUDWIG. "Die tragische Periode der englischen
        Literatur." Die neueren Sprachen 4:289-307.
            Considers a great number of the major tragedies produced be-
        tween 1599 and 1608, including Shakespearean and non-Shakespearean
        plays (among the latter The White Devil).

6   BOWERS, FREDSON THAYER. On Editing Shakespeare and the
        Elizabethan Dramatists. Philadelphia: University of Pennsylvania
        Press, pp. 17-18.
            Deals with problems of editing Elizabethan plays including
        those of Webster. Cites The White Devil as posing a number of prob-
        lems due to the form in which it appears to have been transmitted
        to the printer.

7   CURRY, JOHN V., S.J. Deception in Elizabethan Comedy. Chicago:
        Loyola University Press, pp. 60, 84.
            Briefly considers the theme of deception in Westward Ho
        (Justiano as a deceiver) and Northward Ho (the Bellemont/Greenshield
        hoax).

8   CUTTS, JOHN P. "Robert Johnson: King's Musician in His
        Majesty's Public Entertainment." Music and Letters 36, no. 2
        (April):110-25.
            Discusses Robert Johnson, who wrote stage music for plays by
        Shakespeare, Middleton, Tourneur, Beaumont and Fletcher, Johnson,
        and Webster. Notes especially the madmen's song "O let us howle,"
        used in the original production of The Duchess of Malfi. The song
        is raucous, frightening, and pathetic, and Webster's use of it is
        both subtle and serious. See 1952.6 for a related discussion.

9   DENT, ROBERT W. "Webster's Borrowings from Whetstone." Modern
        Language Notes 70 (December):568-70.
            Notes a parallel between The Duchess of Malfi and Heptameron
        of Civill Discourses. (See 1960.12 for Dent's book-length study
        of Webster's borrowing.)

10   EKEBLAD, INGA-STINA. "Webster's 'Wanton Boyes.'" Notes and
        Queries, n.s. 2:294-95.
            Suggests Webster's use of this phrase is not, perhaps, bor-
        rowed from Shakespeare, but from Whitney's emblem book.

11   FOAKES, R.A. Review of The Tragic Satire of John Webster, by
        Travis Bogard. English 10:227-28.
            Discusses Bogard's thesis (1955.4) that Webster's success
        lies in his fusion of tragedy and satire. Finds the discussion of
        the relation of Webster, Chapman, and Marston especially interesting.

But the treatment of Webster's morality is contradictory: it
moves between objective moral judgments and purely internal standards of consistency.

12   GOLDSTEIN, LEONARD. "Three Significant Dramatists and Their
      Relation to the Moral Decadence of Jacobean and Caroline Drama."
      Ph.D. dissertation, Brown University, 223 pp.
          Studies post-Elizabethan drama, including Chapman, Ford, and
      Webster, to show how the morals of the court clash with the family
      values of the rising middle class. Webster describes courtly deca-
      dence and expresses despair. The other two playwrights attempt
      rationalizations. In their pessimism, all three are ideologues
      of the court, approving the status quo. See Dissertation Abstracts
      15 (1955):1386-87.

13   HERRICK, MARVIN T. Tragicomedy: Its Origin and Development in
      Italy, France, and England. Illinois Studies in Language and
      Literature, vol. 39. Urbana: University of Illinois Press,
      pp. 80-83.
          Comments upon Webster as the author of the induction to The
      Malcontent (termed a tragicomedy in the Stationers' Register) and
      his defense of impure tragedy in the preface to The White Devil.
      Of all the leading Elizabethan dramatists, Webster seems least
      interested in tragicomedy, since The Devil's Law Case was his only
      effort in this genre.

14   HOSKINS, FRANK LAWRENCE, Jr. "Master-Servant Relations in Tudor
      and Early Stuart Literature." Ph.D. dissertation, Columbia
      University, 294 pp.
          Discusses disturbed master-servant relations in non-
      Shakespearean drama, including the misalliance theme, as in The
      Duchess of Malfi where lower class men seek to marry above them-
      selves. See Dissertation Abstracts 15 (1955):1387.

15   HOWARTH, ROBERT GUY. "Webster's Vincentio Lauriola." Notes
      and Queries, n.s. 2:99-100.
          Suggests the name of the "master wax worker" in Webster is
      invented, but perhaps based on Vincentio Saviolo, who is mentioned
      by Dekker.

16   IRGAT, MINA. "Disease Imagery in the Plays of John Webster."
      Studies by Members of the Istanbul University English Department
      2:1-26.
          Webster's interest in the morbid is a critical commonplace.
      Finds that "disease" is the principal motif of his imagery. Images
      of torture, decay and animals are also important. The White Devil
      reminds us that the human body is subject to decay and pain. The
      Duchess of Malfi has even more images of disease (sixty), half of
      which are spoken by Bosola. The Devil's Law Case has thirty allu-
      sions to disease, including the central surgical plot device.
      While A Cure for a Cuckold has only few and commonplace disease

images, <u>Appius and Virginia</u> has more such figures, and more striking ones, though not as many as the tragedies. Concludes Webster
equals Shakespeare in the use of iterative imagery. Summarized
in <u>Seventeenth-Century News</u> 14 (1955):5.

17   LAIRD, DAVID. "The Inserted Masque in Elizabethan and Jacobean
     Drama." Ph.D. dissertation, University of Wisconsin, 196 pp.
        In a history of the masque from the 1580s through 1633, con-
     tends that in <u>The Duchess of Malfi</u> the masque has a symbolic role,
     functioning as a grotesque parody that heightens the horror of the
     torment of the Duchess. See <u>Dissertation Abstracts</u> 15 (1955):2527.

18   LEECH, CLIFFORD. "Presuppositions of Tragedy." <u>Essays in
     Criticism</u> 5:178-81.
        A response to J.C. Maxwell's reaction to Leech, 1950.10, and
     the thesis that tragedy is incompatible with Christianity. Re-
     affirms the concept that tragedy itself is a-Christian, but may be
     written by and for Christians. We know nothing of Shakespeare's
     or Webster's beliefs, but our thoughts are not directed to God by
     the end of <u>Othello</u> or <u>The Duchess of Malfi</u>.

19   LIEVSAY, JOHN LEON. Review of <u>The Tragic Satire of John Webster</u>,
     by Travis Bogard. <u>Shakespeare Quarterly</u> 6, no. 4 (Autumn):
     472-73.
        Notes Bogard (1955.4) denies that Webster's greatness is in
     his verse. Finds Webster morbidly satiric and his works full of
     "hothouse abnormalities."

20   MACGOWAN, KENNETH, and MELNITZ, WILLIAM. <u>The Living Stage</u>.
     Englewood Cliffs, N.J.: Prentice-Hall, pp. 143-52.
        Standard college-level textbook that describes <u>The Duchess
     of Malfi</u> as a revenge play that has been revived in the twentieth
     century. It is "the best poetic tragedy since Shakespeare."

21   OLIVER, HAROLD JAMES. <u>The Problem of John Ford</u>. Carlton,
     Victoria: Melbourne University Press; New York: Cambridge
     University Press, pp. 23, 25, 30, 41-45, 64-65, 70, 80-81.
        Discusses the problems of the Ford/Webster collaboration on
     <u>Keep the Widow Waking</u> and <u>The Fair Maid of the Inn</u>. Also observes
     that Ford echoes Webster in <u>Loves Sacrifice</u>.

22   PRICE, HEREWARD T. "The Function of Imagery in Webster."
     <u>PMLA</u> 70:717-39.
        Finds <u>The White Devil</u> and <u>The Duchess of Malfi</u> employ similar
     clusters of images. Webster is distinguished by a double construc-
     tion of figure in action and figure in language, uniquely integrated.
     He uses imagery to convey the contrast between outward appearance
     and inward substance. Images of poison, the devil, and evil covered
     by a semblance of good are common. Dumb shows and the trial scene
     feature figures of appearance vs. reality. This polarity dominates
     <u>The White Devil</u>. The system of linked action and language figures

is brought to perfection in The Duchess of Malfi in its motif of
hidden corruption. A scene-by-scene analysis of the play shows
these images of evil hidden by fair show in action and language.

23   SCHOENBAUM, SAMUEL. Middleton's Tragedies: A Critical Study.
     Columbia University Studies in English and Comparative
     Literature, no. 168. New York: Columbia University Press,
     275 pp., passim.
         Cites Webster several times in passing as a point of compari-
     son of imagery and style, etc. Also notes that The Revenger's
     Tragedy is occasionally attributed to Webster, as well as
     Middleton and Tourneur. Reviewed: 1956.5.

24   SELLS, ARTHUR LYTTON. The Italian Influence in English Poetry.
     London: Allen & Unwin, pp. 114, 336.
         Finds Webster's tragedies full of Machiavellianism, as
     Renaissance England conceived it. His "Italian" works helped de-
     fine "Italy" for Shakespeare's contemporaries.

25   SMET, ROBERT de [Romain Sanvic]. Le Théâtre élizabéthain.
     Collections Lebegue et nationale, no. 114. Brussels: Office
     de Publicité, pp. 99-105.
         Finds Webster's works especially attractive to the modern
     audience. The preface to The White Devil tells more about him
     than any biographical material we have. Briefly recounts the
     plots of the tragedies and translates some of the more famous
     speeches into French. Although Webster claims to disdain the pub-
     lic, both his major plays seem aimed at popular taste, and they
     continue to hold the stage occasionally.

26   STYPHER, WYLIE. Four Stages of Renaissance Style. Garden City,
     N.Y.: Doubleday, pp. 103-4, 120-23, 177, 185.
         Describes Webster's "disassociated" and dissolving world as
     sordid but dazzling, i.e., mannerist. Webster and his fellows
     approach things from unusual angles, defying proportion to present
     a subjective view of reality. They create a sense of the unrelated-
     ness of things, including character and action. Compares the dark-
     ness of the world of The Duchess of Malfi to Renaissance paintings.
     Webster is a passionate mannerist.

1956

1   BENTLEY, G.E. The Jacobean and Caroline Stage. Vol. 5. Oxford:
     Clarendon Press, pp. 1239-56.
         Includes, in the section on Webster, biographical and biblio-
     graphical information, the attribution and chronological order of
     the works, and allusions to him by others. There are bibliographi-
     cal sections for the Jacobean plays.

*2   BERRY, RALPH T. "Webster's Interpretation and Treatment of
      Machiavelli." M.A. thesis, University of London, External.
          Source: Index to Theses Accepted for Higher Degrees by the
      Universities of Great Britain and Ireland and the Council for
      National Academic Awards 6:9.

3   BRADNER, LEICESTER. "The Rise of Secular Drama in the
      Renaissance." Studies in the Renaissance 3:7-22.
          Compares Webster's tragedies to Cinthio's to show how the
      Italians were lifeless and unrealistic in relation to the English
      drama.

4   BROWN, JOHN RUSSELL. "The Printing of Webster's Plays (II)."
      Studies in Bibliography 8:113-27. [Continuation of 1954.2;
      continued: 1962.6.]
          Lists press variants of the first quartos of The White Devil,
      The Duchess of Malfi, and The Devil's Law Case and presents more
      evidence that Ralph Crane was the transcriber of The Duchess of
      Malfi. The article is mostly lists and charts. See 1969.15 for
      a supplementary table.

5   BRYANT, J.A. "Four Critics of Drama, Academic and Otherwise."
      Sewanee Review 64:508-20.
          In reviewing 1955.4, finds Bogard feels that Webster created
      a world of chaos, meaningless and terrible, save for a few charac-
      ters who triumph through integrity. But the plays don't support
      this, e.g., the Duchess dies humble, repudiating the world, as do
      Flamineo and Vittoria. The Duchess of Malfi is a picture of a
      society gone wrong, but good is still good, and evil, evil.
      (Also briefly reviews 1955.23.)

6   BUSH, GEOFFREY. Shakespeare and the Natural Condition.
      Cambridge, Mass.: Harvard University Press, pp. 10-12.
          Compares Webster and Chapman together to Shakespeare. Their
      plays are comprehensive statements about the natural condition.
      Webster believes that the natural life is removed from meaning.
      The soul is caged in the body, heaven is distant, and the life
      is a long war in the midst of a mist of error, in which men may
      approach virtue only in the manner by which death in encountered.

7   CROSS, GUSTAV. "A Note on The White Devil." Notes and Queries,
      n.s. 3:99-100.
          Suggests Webster's title perhaps comes from The Revenger's
      Tragedy 3.5 (an image of Vindici). There is a literally white
      devilish character in The Devil's Law Case: the wanton nun
      Angelica dressed in white robes.

8   _____. "Ovid Metamorphosed: Marston, Webster, and Nathaniel
      Lee." Notes and Queries, n.s. 3:244-45.
          Discusses an image--a city with a thousand gates--that is
      used in The Duchess of Malfi, Marston's Antonio and Mellida, and

Lee's Oedipus, and derives from Ovid's Metamorphoses. See also
"Ovid Metamorphosed" (Notes and Queries, n.s. 3:508-9) in which
Cross adds a possible Virgilian use of the image.

9   DENT, ROBERT W. "John Webster and Nicolas de Montreux."
     Philological Quarterly 35 (October):418-21.
        Suggests Robert Tofte's translation of Nicholas de Montreux's
     Bergeries de Juliette (a "wearisome" book) as a minor source for
     The White Devil, especially that play's metaphorical sententiae.

10   DUNKLE, ANNA BARRETT. "A Concordance to Three Plays of John
     Webster." Ph.D. dissertation, University of Wisconsin.
        A concordance to The Duchess of Malfi, The White Devil, and
     The Devil's Law Case. See Summaries of Doctoral Dissertations,
     University of Wisconsin 16:534-35.

11   EKEBLAD, INGA-STINA. "Storm Imagery in Appius and Virginia."
     Notes and Queries, n.s. 3:5-7.
        Finds a chain of storm images in the play's central scenes
     that works just like the chains of imagery in The White Devil and
     The Duchess of Malfi. This strengthens Webster's claim to author-
     ship and certainly suggests he was no hasty reviser.

12   _____. "Webster's Villains. A Study of Character-Imagery in
     The Duchess of Malfi." Orpheus 3, no. 3:126-33.
        Asserts Webster's villains are Italianate machiavels incarn-
     ate: he did not strive for plausibility. Offers Duke Ferdinand
     in The Duchess of Malfi as an example of Webster's poetic and non-
     realistic goals. He surrounds his evil characters in this play
     with storm and animal images that become real, as in the wolf mo-
     tif. Finds the play is consistent as a poem, not a psychological
     study.

13   FELDMAN, A. BRONSON. "The Yellow Malady: Short Studies of
     Five Tragedies of Jealousy." Literature and Psychology 6:38-52.
        Examines Othello, Women Beware Women, The Maid's Tragedy, The
     Broken Heart, and The White Devil in terms of marital infidelity,
     or the fear of it, that springs from a contempt of the opposite
     sex. Compares the ridiculous jealousy of Camillo to the titanic
     jealousy of Brachiano, which approaches that of Othello.

14   HALLIDAY, FRANK ERNEST. Shakespeare in His Age. New York:
     Thomas Yoseloff, pp. 235, 275, 278, 286, 312-13, 334-35.
        Finds The White Devil replete with melancholy and corruption,
     great poetry, and dramatic, grotesque, characters. Suggests The
     Duchess of Malfi is, next to Shakespeare's dramas, the greatest
     Jacobean tragedy.

15   HENN, T.R. The Harvest of Tragedy. London: Methuen, 304 pp.,
     passim.
        Cites The White Devil and The Duchess of Malfi often in a

general inquiry into the values and forms of tragedy. Believes
Webster's tragedies create an illusion of freedom, but the action
is finally inexorable.

16   HOY, CYRUS. "The Shares of Fletcher and his Collaborators in
      the Beaumont and Fletcher Canon." Studies in Bibliography 8:
      129-46; 9 (1957):143-62; 11 (1958):85-106; 12 (1959):91-116;
      13 (1960):77-108; 14 (1961):45-68; and 15 (1962):71-90. [Par-
      tially reprinted: 1966.8.]
          Attempts to sort-out and attribute various hands in the fifty-
      four plays of the Beaumont and Fletcher canon, on the basis of
      "linguistic forms." Denies Webster a share in The Honest Man's
      Fortune, but assigns him a part (with Fletcher, Massinger, and
      Ford) in The Fair Maid of the Inn.

17   LUCAS, F.L. "The Duchess of Malfi." Times Literary Supplement,
      13 July, p. 423.
          Asks why the Duchess worried about her children before she
      died and after she had seen the (wax) corpses. Suggests that per-
      haps the corpses are just of Antonio and their oldest child and the
      two young ones are still alive and imprisoned with her.

*18   LUTZE, LOTHAR. "John Websters Tragödienstil als Ausdruck der
      Leidenschaftlichkeit." Ph.D. dissertation, Berlin.
      Source: Mahaney, 1973.23. See 1980.30.

19   MARTIN, MARY FOSTER. "An Early Use of the Feminine Form of the
      Word "heir.'" Modern Language Notes 71 (April):270-71.
          Notes the word "heires" (i.e., "heiress") is used in Sir
      Thomas Wyat.

20   MILL, ADAIR. "John Webster as a Moralist." Litera 3:15-34.
          Argues that critics have confused the dark philosophy of
      Webster's characters with the accuracy of the world he creates,
      making it difficult to explain the overt moral stance of his
      sententiae. Actually, Webster depicts sinners who are fascinating
      in their abnormality, but are set against a background of conven-
      tional morality that is Webster's true world. Sees there is no
      doubt about what is good or evil in Webster, unlike Marlowe, who
      is genuinely ambiguous. Webster accepts the conventional world
      and weaves his pattern before it.

21   MULLER, H.J. The Spirit of Tragedy. New York: Alfred Knopf,
      pp. 153, 197-99, 201. [Excerpted: 1968.23; 1975.18.]
          Suggests Webster's works shows a desperation that proves he
      was not a master of the tragic tradition. He could not see evil
      within a larger frame. Finds his pessimism not medieval, but a
      disenchantment with the Renaissance, especially the growth of po-
      litical Machiavellianism and materialism.

22   PETER, JOHN D. Complaint and Satire in Early English
      Literature. Oxford: Clarendon Press, 323 pp., passim.
           In a study of medieval complaint and Renaissance satire,
      with special focus upon the drama of Marston, mentions Webster in
      passing, e.g., Antonio's thumbnail sketch of Bosola at the begin-
      ning of The Duchess of Malfi is a satiric portrait.

23   PRAZ, MARIO. "John Webster and The Maid's Tragedy." English
      Studies 37, no. 6:252-58.
           Suggests Beaumont and Fletcher's The Maid's Tragedy is like
      modern cinema in its subject, but better in its poetry. It takes
      scenes from many other works and sticks them together: it is
      "synthetic." In turn, Webster is indebted to The Maid's Tragedy
      in The Duchess of Malfi, which is similar in terms of the basic
      plot of brotherly revenge for family dishonor. Many parallels of
      specific passages are also clear.

24   Review of The Tragic Satire of John Webster, by Travis Bogard.
      Times Literary Supplement, 17 February, p. 102.
           Notes that Webster's reputation varies from Lamb's praise
      to Archer's intense antipathy. Although he is usually compared,
      in tragedy, to Shakespeare, Bogard (1955.4) sees him with others,
      especially Marston and Chapman.

25   SALINGAR, L.G. "Tourneur and the Tragedy of Revenge." In A
      Guide to English Literature. Edited by Boris Ford. Vol. 2,
      The Age of Shakespeare. London: Penguin Books, pp. 334-54.
           Finds that in later revenge plays, the accent is on defiance,
      not resignation, on restless individualism in an Italianate atmos-
      phere of lust and moral corruption. Believes Webster aims less
      at allegory than at a realistic depiction of the corruption of
      greatness. The emotions of his works are sharp but chaotic. His
      world is corrupt but unchangeable. The kernel of the Elizabethan
      popular tradition is gone--only the husk remains.

26   SEIDEN, MELVIN. "The Revenge Motive in Websterean Tragedy."
      Ph.D. dissertation, University of Minnesota, 238 pp. [Appears
      in book form: 1973.29.]
           Finds modern criticism reluctant to place Webster in any
      school or genre. The tendency is to attribute what is new in his
      works to the poet, what is commonplace to the dramatist, e.g., the
      "revenge motif." Actually, believes Webster uses revenge uniquely
      --his plays belong to that species of revenge tragedy called
      "Punitive Tragedies."

27   _____. "Two Notes on Webster's Appius and Virginia."
      Philological Quarterly 35:408-17.
           1. Suggests some confusing speeches in act 5 can be un-
      raveled by reassigning them from Icilius to Virginius.
           2. Argues, contrary to the thesis of Rupert Brooke (1913.3),
      that Appius and Virginia is not unlike Webster's other works.

While details differ, the point of view is similar--a world of
evil, in which "moral goodness" triumphs over evil through a puni-
tive structure.

28   SMITH, GROVER. T.S. Eliot's Poetry and Plays: A Study in
      Sources and Meanings. Chicago: University of Chicago Press,
      338 pp., passim.
           Cites Webster throughout this study of Eliot's sources.

29   THOMAS, SIDNEY. "Webster and Nashe." Notes and Queries, n.s.
      3, no. 1:13.
           Suggests that the image in the dying words of Ferdinand in
      The Duchess of Malfi (diamonds cut by their own dust) comes from
      Nashe's Christs Teares Over Jerusalem (1593).

30   TODD, F.M. "Webster and Cervantes." Modern Language Review
      51, no. 3:321-23.
           Suggests that a passage (5.5) in The Duchess of Malfi quarto
      of 1623 seems an echo of Don Quixote. This passage could not have
      been in the version acted in 1614, since it was from the 1615 edi-
      tion of Cervantes' work. Webster seems to have had access to the
      original Spanish version, not the 1620 English translation.

31   WADSWORTH, FRANK W. "Webster's Duchess of Malfi in the Light
      of Some Contemporary Ideas on Marriage and Remarriage."
      Philological Quarterly 35:394-407. [Excerpted: 1968.23.]
           Contends that there were some defenders of remarriage in
      Webster's time, contrary to the theories of Clifford Leech (1958.15).
      The Duchess seems, in Webster, less lustful that in Painter. Some
      Renaissance writers did defend marriages that violated "degree,"
      and Webster tried to make Antonio a "man of worth"--an ideal type,
      in fact.

*32   WHITMAN, ROBERT F. "The Opinion of Wisdom: Montaigne and John
      Webster." Ph.D. dissertation, Harvard University.
           Source: Mahaney, 1973.23. See 1973.31 for a revised version.

                              1957

1   BARBER, CHARLES LAWRENCE. The Idea of Honour in the English
      Drama 1591-1700. Gothenburg Studies in English, 6. Gothenburg,
      Sweden: Elanders, 362 pp., passim.
           Recounts the ways in which the world "honour" was used in
      the seventeenth century, as revealed by the drama. Includes tables
      of usage citing Webster.

2   _____ . "A Rare Use of the Word Honour as a Criterion of
      Middleton's Authorship." English Studies 38:161-68.
           Finds a peculiar use of the word occurs only a few times in
      Renaissance drama, mostly (eight of twelve times) in Middleton,
      never at all in Webster.

3   BLAU, HERBERT. "Language and Structure in Poetic Drama."
     Modern Language Quarterly 18:27-34.
          Comments upon The White Devil: the opening "banished" sug-
     gests immediacy without an excessively premature release of emotion.
     The rest of the first scene gives the first line perceptual meaning
     and establishes the conventions of the play.

4   BODTKE, RICHARD A. "Tragedy and the Jacobean Temper: A
     Critical Study of John Webster." Ph.D. dissertation, Columbia
     University, 454 pp. [Published as 1972.6.]
          Sees The White Devil and The Duchess of Malfi as products
     of Renaissance pessimism. Like Montaigne, Webster is skeptical
     and sees mankind as degenerate. He is self-consciously morally
     ambivalent, seeing man as an animal and reason as useless, and
     accepting Machiavelli's view of man's inherent evil. He utilizes
     the Senecan theme of the personality as the last value in a dis-
     integrating world. Believes Webster uses revenge as an ironic
     version of the search for justice. Like Marston and Jonson, he
     fuses satire and tragedy. Thus, Flamineo and Bosola undercut more
     heroic characters. See Dissertation Abstracts 17 (1957):1550.

5   BOKLUND, GUNNAR. The Sources of "The White Devil." Essays and
     Studies on English Language and Literature, no. 17. Uppsala:
     Lundequistska Bokhandeln; Cambridge, Mass.: Harvard University
     Press, 226 pp.
          Begins with a factual chronology of the real life of Vittoria
     Accoramboni, and a discussion of early papers presenting those
     facts. This suggests which features of the play must come from
     sources other than reports of the true Vittoria. Surveys various
     early versions and accounts. Suggests the "Fugger" papers and "A
     Letter Lately Written from Rome" are the origins of special fea-
     tures, such as Vittoria's death. Concludes the "Fugger Newsletter"
     must be a main source, supplemented by other material, making
     possible the reconstruction of the "historical" story as Webster
     knew it. Discusses Webster's alterations as they reveal the major
     themes of the play. Finds Flamineo presents a view of life from
     which we may view the play's action--a completely amoral view,
     which yet achieves a "victory" over death through wit and bravery.
     This becomes a moral pattern, not just a case of evil against evil.
     Thus, the play presents various degrees of evil at war, countered
     by the futile virtues of Cornelia, Marcello, and Isabella. The
     defiance with which Vittoria and Flamineo face death is at once
     a tribute to human courage and an ironic comment on human perversity.
     The play presents, realistically, views of moral and amoral lives.
     Finds The White Devil does have limitations--no moral center, a
     somewhat petty setting, and insufficient timelessness--yet it is
     a work of great scope and daring. An appendix deals with Vittoria
     in life and literature. Reviewed: 1958.4, 10, 13, 16; 1959.5. 9.

6   BRIDGES, ADAMS W. Irresistible Theater. New York: World
     Publishing, pp. 300-321.

Finds The White Devil is a "congested and ill-proportioned work" but full of "beauty for the ear." Sees Webster's art as ghostly and dream-like: "Bosola disguised as a sexton is on one plane absurd; on another he is an appropriate emblem of mortality."

7   BROWN, JOHN RUSSELL. "The Papal Election in John Webster's The White Devil (1612)." Notes and Queries, n.s. 4 (November): 490-94.
     Notes that the scene of the papal election has many exact details but few stage directions. Finds a parallel in an English translation of Jerome Bibnon's Traicte [Treatise of the Election of Popes]. Thus, the descriptions in the Treatise might be helpful in staging the play.

8   CIARAMELLA, MICHELE. The Heritage of English Literature. Rome: Edizione Cremonese. [Published in the U.S. as A Short History of English Literature (New York: Crowell, 1967), p. 56.]
     Comments that Webster took up the tradition of Gorbuduc in his tragedies of blood, which are full of physical horrors but include some passages of lyrical beauty.

9   EKEBLAD, INGA-STINA. "Webster's Constructional Rhythm." English Literary History 24, no. 3:165-76.
     Shows that A Cure for a Cuckold has been attributed to Webster, Rowley, and Heywood variously, largely on the basis of parallel passages, which is never a good method and especially bad here. Suggests we should instead examine the structure and rhythm of the scenes. In the tragedies, scenes begin with pointed, brief dialogue, become complicated and lead to long speeches. The same pattern is seen in A Cure for a Cuckold, in the scenes usually ascribed to Webster (3.4 and 4.2). Long speeches tend towards metaphoric self-analysis in both, often in a deliberate series of images. At their peaks, the scenes become very simple and lucid. This pattern--swift dialog followed by monologues beginning highly imagistically and ending simply and lucidly--parallels the construction of entire Webster plays. See 1959.4 for a related discussion.

10   FRYE, NORTHROP. Anatomy of Criticism. Princeton: Princeton University Press, pp. 206-33. [Excerpted: 1968.23; 1975.18.]
     Uses The Duchess of Malfi as an example of the first phase of tragedy, in which the sources of dignity are courage and innocence. Heroes of this type are often women. Finds the Duchess is innocent in a sick and melancholy society. The White Devil is an ironic parody of the same pattern.

*11 GILCH, FRITZ. "Untersuchungen zu Schicksalsauffassung und Weltbild in der elizabethanischen und jakobäischen Literatur mit besonderer Berücksichtigung von John Webster." Ph.D. dissertation, Tubingen.
     Source: Mahaney, 1973.23.

12   GLIER, INGEBORG. "Struktur und Gestaltungsprinzipien in den
      Dramen John Websters." Ph.D. dissertation, Munich, 171 pp.
          Analyzes Webster's structural techniques. Makes an especial-
      ly noteworthy case for The Devil's Law Case as a careful and or-
      dered production. Concentrates upon the formal aspects of struc-
      ture--acts, scenes, etc. The White Devil is not a five act play,
      but consists of four "szenenkomplexe" including today's acts 1 and
      2, then 3, 4, and 5. The first and last of these units are dy-
      namic, the middle two are more static. Reviewed: 1961.6.

13   GRIVELET, MICHEL. Thomas Heywood et le drama domestique
      élizabéthain. Etudes anglaises. Paris: Didier, 408 pp.,
      passim.
          Cites Webster often in passing for his association with
      Henslowe and Henslow'e employees; his remarks about theater and
      the audience at the Red Bull; his Lord Mayor's show; etc. Also
      considers the question of the attribution of Appius and Virginia
      and A Cure for a Cuckold.

14   GROSS, SEYMOUR L. "A Note on Webster's Tragic Attitude."
      Notes and Queries, n.s. 4:374-75. [Excerpted: 1968.23.]
          Suggests Webster's moral point of view is much misunderstood,
      for example by Brooke (1916.1), as the nonmoral struggle between
      evils. Argues that "integrity" is bound up with virtues such as
      humility, courage, and the like. Also, suggests Bosola's dying
      speech shows he knows what is just and that he laments the in-
      justice of his acts.

15   HIBBARD, GEORGE R. "The Tragedies of Thomas Middleton and the
      Decadence of the Drama." Renaissance and Modern Studies 1:35-64.
          Argues the drama declined after 1612-13 as the audience be-
      came less interested and playwrights trusted it less. The White
      Devil and The Duchess of Malfi show signs of decadence in the re-
      venge play tradition in their focus, not on revenge nor its morali-
      ty, but on the sensational possibilities of the situation it creates.

16   HOOK, F.S. "Marlowe, Massinger, and Webster Quartos." Notes
      and Queries, n.s. 4:64-65.
          Describes recent additions to the Lehigh University Library,
      including three Webster quartos.

17   HUNTER, G.K. "Notes on Webster's Tragedies." Notes and Queries,
      n.s. 4:53-55.
          Fifteen notes, mostly on sources of lines.

*18   JHA, R. "The Influence of Philosophical Skepticism on Some
      Elizabethan Dramatists." Ph.D. dissertation, University of
      Manchester.
          Source: Index to Theses Accepted for Higher Degrees by the
      Universities of Great Britain and Ireland and the Council for
      National Academic Awards 8:item 153.

19   LEECH, CLIFFORD. John Ford and the Drama of His Time. London: Chatto & Windus, pp. 43-48, 79-80, 95-96.
      Suggests Webster's tragedies depend upon anthropomorphic conceptions of the universe for their sense of injustice in the world, i.e., the Duchess has to curse the stars, and Vittoria wins us in part because of her blasphemous attitude. Also, finds echoes of Webster in Loves Sacrifice and Perkin Warbeck.

20   MANDER, R., and MITCHENSON, J. A Picture History of the British Theatre. New York: Macmillan, p. 155.
      Plate 519 is of Robert Helpman and Margaret Rawlings in the 1947 production of The White Devil.

21   McCOLLOM, WILLIAM GILMAN. Tragedy. New York: Macmillan, 254 pp., passim.
      Cites Webster frequently. His characters glorify individuality; they are tough minded, disillusioned, full of bitter humor. His villains are honestly cynical. He tried to merge dramatic illusion with sententiousness, and his scenes can't always absorb all this.

22   MOUSSINAC, LEON. Le Théâtre: Des origines à nos jours. Paris: Amiot-Dumont, p. 139.
      Notes especially the language and imagery of The Duchess of Malfi.

*23   PADGETT, LAWRENCE E. "An Entry from Guevara in Webster's Commonplace-Book?" Notes and Queries, n.s. 4:145-46.
      Source: PMLA Bibliography, 1957, item 2763.

24   PEACOCK, RONALD. The Art of the Drama. London: Routledge & Kegan Paul, pp. 183, 217.
      Comments on The Duchess of Malfi's fifth act as an illustration of vigorous dramatic moralizing. Sees Ferdinand as too ugly himself to be poetic, but the tragic action of which he is an aspect does as a whole achieve poetry.

25   RIBNER, IRVING. The English History Play in the Age of Shakespeare. Princeton: Princeton University Press, pp. 215-19. [Rev. ed. London: Methuen, 1965.]
      Gives The White Devil and The Duchess of Malfi as examples of plays that use history, but that Elizabethans would say do not serve the ends of history plays. Mentions Sir Thomas Wyat as a careless production of little merit that does fit the formal requirements of the history play: it has strong political implications that deal, at the end of Elizabeth's reign, with the succession question.

26   SHARPE, ROBERT B. "Nine Steps to the Tragic Triumph." University of North Carolina Extension Bulletin 36, no. 3:22-40.
      Includes the same material as 1959.14 presented as a "lecture in the Humanities."

27   TAYLOR, WILLIAM EDWARDS. "The Villainess in Elizabethan Drama."
      Ph.D. dissertation, Vanderbilt University, 402 pp.
          Argues that three major influences shape the Elizabethan
      dramatic villainess: domestic ecclesiastical prejudice, Senecan
      dramatic types, and Italian novella. The Italian version is at
      her highest artistic development in The White Devil. See
      Dissertation Abstracts 17 (1957):1756-57.

28   THAYER, CALVIN G. "The Ambiguity of Bosola." Studies in
      Philology 54:162-71. [Excerpted: 1968.23.]
          Depicts Bosola as a complex and elusive character and a major
      tragic protagonist. Early in the play, he is both a villainous
      malcontent and a poisoned good man. He is an actor, a counter-
      feiter when in the service of the Aragonian brothers. He emerges
      at the play's end to become himself and face his tragic fate.

29   WEST, MURIEL. "The Devil and John Webster: A Study of the
      Characters in The White Devil and The Duchess of Malfi Based on
      Imagery in the Plays Related to Ideas Current in the Jacobean
      Period Concerning Demonology and Witchcraft." Ph.D. disserta-
      tion, University of Arkansas, 411 pp. [Published as 1974.27.]
          Finds Webster uses the imagery of demonology to give his
      characters an extra dimension as devils of air, fire, and water,
      and as witches and magicians. See Dissertation Abstracts 17 (1957):
      1077-78.

                              1958

1   BARKER, RICHARD H. Thomas Middleton. New York: Columbia
      University Press, pp. 90, 98, 140, 151-52.
          Suggests Middleton and Webster collaborated on Anything for
      a Quiet Life. Observes Middleton's main theme, like Webster's,
      is sin, but he has less grandeur than Webster because he does not
      compromise with sin--he creates no ambiguous characters like
      Flamineo or Vittoria (heroic sinners).

*2   BRENNAN, ELIZABETH M. "The Concept of Revenge for Honour in
      English Fiction and Drama between 1580 and 1640." Ph.D. dis-
      sertation, University of London.
          Source: Index to Theses Accepted for Higher Degrees in the
      Universities of Great Britain and Ireland 8:8.

3   BROWN, JOHN RUSSELL. "The Date of John Webster's The Devil's
      Law Case." Notes and Queries, n.s. 5:100-101.
          Believes Bentley's date of 1610 (1956.1) is "rash" since it
      is based on the trial scene. Actual borrowings suggest a much
      later composition--1616-19.

4   _____. Review of The Sources of "The White Devil," by Gunnar
      Boklund. Modern Language Review 53, no. 4:564-66.

Finds Boklund (1957.5) shows how rumors and half-truths, as well as historical fact, influenced Webster's treatment of Vittoria's story. Judges the book a necessary piece of research, presented with a bit too much suspense.

5   BROWNING, D.C. Everyman's Dictionary of Literary Biography.
    London: Dent, p. 709.
        Comments that little is known of Webster's life: it appears he was a freeman of the Merchant Taylors' Company and a parish clerk at St. Andrews. Although not much regarded in his own day-he was appreciated by Lamb and Swinburne. Webster revels in the horrible, but a touch of genius saves his work from mere brutality. (Supersedes an earlier edition by John W. Cousin.)

6   CAUTHEN, I.B., Jr. "Another Webster Allusion in 'The Wasteland.'"
    Modern Language Notes 73, no. 7 (November):498-99.
        Argues The Wasteland, 2.117-26, is an echo of The White Devil, 5.6.223-27. Several other allusions to Webster were noted by Eliot himself.

7   COOKMAN, A.V. "Shakespeare's Contemporaries on the Modern
    English Stage." Shakespeare-Jahrbuch 94:29-41.
        Describes how the 1919 revival of The Duchess of Malfi was poorly received (see 1921.9), but a World War II era production was greeted with enthusiasm. Notes The White Devil also had a gratifying long run at the Duchess theater.

8   DAVIES, CECIL W. "The Structure of The Duchess of Malfi: An
    Approach." English 12:89-93.
        Finds The Duchess of Malfi makes a single and strong impact, yet seems to have a sprawling and chaotic structure. A consistent linguistic pattern of recurring images exemplifies themes from the plot, thus producing a kind of unity. The scene of the madmen is the clearest example. The scene is grotesque, and the lunatics' imagery is grotesque, all of which highlights the horror of the Duchess' torture.

9   EKEBLAD, INGA-STINA. "The 'Impure Art' of John Webster."
    Review of English Studies, n.s. 9:253-67. [Excerpted: 1961.11;
    1968.23; 1969.17.]
        Finds that Webster's work, as Eliot suggests, runs from real-ism to convention. He fuses these elements especially in scenes like The Duchess of Malfi 4.2, the Duchess' death scene. The pene-trating and realistic character analysis of the Duchess is coupled with the masque of madmen, whose imagery (hell, animals) links the masque to the themes of the play. The masque presents disunity. It is also related to the Duchess' "double crime" (second marriage below her station) in that it is like a charivari--mock music for an over hasty second marriage. The masque is related to the scene as a whole by poetic means, as a kind of analogy.

10   GUILLEN, CLAUDIO. Review of The Sources of "The White Devil,"
        by Gunnar Boklund. Comparative Literature 10, no. 3:261-63.
            Finds that while Boklund's book (1957.5) shows scholarship,
    precision, and care, its method is wrong and the results therefore
    unconvincing. Boklund is interested in historical, not literary,
    sources. Actually, "the only unshakable evidence which we possess
    is that John Webster was a splendid poet and that The White Devil
    is a work of great inner coherence and self-imposed necessity."
    Boklund also discounts the possibilities of oral sources, many of
    whom were available. However, the criticism in the final chapters
    is illuminating.

11   HARRISON, G.B. Elizabethan Plays and Players. Ann Arbor:
        University of Michigan Press, p. 282.
            Mentions Webster in the chapter on "The End of an Era," as
    a new face in 1602, about whom, in spite of two masterpieces,
    nothing is known.

12   JONES-DAVIES, MARIE-THERESE. Un Peintre de la vie londonienne:
        Thomas Dekker. 2 vols. Etudes anglaises, 6. Paris: Didier,
        893 pp., passim.
            Cites Webster repeatedly as Dekker's collaborator on the
    London Citizen comedies.

13   LAGARDE, FERNAND. "Les Sources de The White Devil." Etudes
        Anglaises 11:303-9.
            In a review of 1957.5, finds Boklund has examined all the
    relevant texts to uncover Webster's sources. Reviews the case for
    the "Fugger Newsletter," John Florio, and others. Concludes
    Boklund is generally cautious and careful.

14   LARKIN, DANIEL I. "Hooker and Webster." Notes and Queries,
        n.s. 5 (October):437.
            Shows Webster borrows from Laws of Ecclesiastical Polity in
    The Devil's Law Case. There is an interesting relationship between
    the source and the borrower in their treatments of violations of
    law and order.

15   LEECH, CLIFFORD. "An Addendum to Webster's Duchess."
        Philological Quarterly 37 (April):253-56.
            Argues contrary to Wadsworth's thesis that the Duchess is
    wholly virtuous and not punished for marrying below herself
    (1956.31). Leech finds she does contribute to--if not "deserve"
    --her fate. A second marriage, and one below her rank, was doubt-
    ful behavior--below the ideal. She also seems to neglect her pub-
    lic duties. Webster imperfectly resolves the tension between our
    sympathy and the Duchess' imperfections.

16   LILJEGREN, S.B. Review of The Sources of "The White Devil," by
        Gunnar Boklund. Revue de Littérature Comparée 32:586-88.
            Finds Boklund's (1957.5) care in not trying to prove too

much is admirable and his judgment is sound. Notes the book is really more on the historical tradition of The White Devil than on Webster's sources. Claims that Webster saw Italy in terms of the Catholic-Protestant conflict.

17 LUCAS, F.L., ed. The Duchess of Malfi. London: Chatto & Windus, 223 pp.
   Reprints, with revisions and additions, the text from 1927.11.
   Reviewed: 1959.3.

18 _____, ed. The White Devil. London: Chatto & Windus, 224 pp.
   Reprints, with revisions and additions, the text from 1927.11.
   Reviewed: 1959.3.

19 MAGILL, FRANK N. Cyclopedia of World Authors. New York: Harper, pp. 1134-35.
   States that "the important fact in the life of John Webster is that he wrote The White Devil and The Duchess of Malfi." Finds Webster a remarkable writer whose tragedies are powerful and moving as poetry and theater.

20 MARTIN, MARY FOSTER. "Stowe's Annals and The Famous Historie of Sir Thomas Wyat." Modern Language Review 53, no. 1:75-77.
   Argues that this history play is based on Stowe's Annals, which is also a source for Holinshed. Finds Webster does take some material from Foxe's Acts and Monuments and possibly Grafton's Chronicles.

*21 MAUGERI, ALDO. Studi su Thomas Dekker. Messina: Grafiche La Sicilia, 117 pp.
   Source: Mahaney, 1973.23.

22 SCHOENBAUM, SAMUEL. "'Decadence' in Jacobean Drama." History of Ideas Newsletter 4:50-55; 5(1959-60):3-11.
   In the second section compares Massinger and Shirley to Webster and the authors of his decade. The later writers were quite craftsmanlike, but uninspired. Thus, "decadence" means the diminution of creative energy, not moral degeneracy.

23 VILLAREJO, OSCAR M. "Lope de Vega and the Jacobean Drama: A Note on Points of Contract." Research Opportunities in Renaissance Drama 1:18-23.
   Argues La Duquesa de Almalfi pre-dates The Duchess of Malfi and thus could be a source for Webster's work.

24 WOOD, GLENA DECKER. "Retributive Justice: A Study of the Theme of Elizabethan Revenge Tragedy." Ph.D. dissertation, University of Kentucky, 308 pp.
   Discusses three periods in the Elizabethan literary treatment of the theme of universal retribution, intermittently citing Webster's use of revenge in his tragedies. In the first period,

revenge is justified, in the second it was frowned upon, in the third there was no divine duty to revenge. See <u>Dissertation Abstracts</u> 24 (1963):2466-67.

1959

1   AKRIGG, G.P.V. "John Webster and <u>The Book of Homilies</u>." <u>Notes and Queries</u>, n.s. 6:217-18.
          Suggests <u>Certain Sermons or Homilies</u> was a source for Webster.

2   ARMSTRONG, WILLIAM. "The Audience of the Elizabethan Private Theaters." <u>Review of English Studies</u>, n.s. 10:234-49.
          Cites the induction to <u>The Malcontent</u> as evidence that the country gentry were among those who attended the theater.

3   EMSLIE, MCDONALD. "Motives in Malfi." <u>Essays in Criticism</u> 9, no. 4 (October):391-405.
          Reviews Lucas's revised editions (1958.17, 18). Argues that the Duchess is guilty of "crimes of blood," but Ferdinand's revenge is disproportionate.

4   ERDMAN, DAVID V. "The Signature of Style." <u>Bulletin of the New York Public Library</u> 63:88-109. [Reprinted: 1966.8.]
          In a general discussion of internal stylistic evidence as used in attributions of authorship, cites the case of <u>The Cure for a Cuckold</u> and considers question of parallel passages and structural similarities. See 1957.9 for a related discussion.

5   EVANS, G. BLAKEMORE. Review of <u>The Sources of "The White Devil</u>," by Gunnar Bokland. <u>Journal of English and Germanic Philology</u> 58:124.
          Suggests it is important that Boklund established what parts of the Vittoria story Webster did <u>not</u> know. See 1957.5.

6   GIBBS, LLOYD GRAHAM. "A History of the Development of the Dumb Show as a Dramatic Convention." Ph.D. dissertation, University of South Carolina, 351 pp.
          Chronicles the dumb shows of <u>Gorboduc</u> and early academic and courtly drama. Later, the shows often combined allegorical and synoptic material. Still later, the synoptic came to dominate, frequently to convey death, e.g., as in <u>The White Devil</u>. See <u>Dissertation Abstracts</u> 20 (1960):3282-83.

7   KERNAN, ALVIN B. <u>The Cankered Muse</u>. New Haven: Yale University Press, pp. 232-42.
          Discusses Webster in the chapter on tragical satire. His Duchess and Antonio lived in a depraved and decaying world, surrounded by men and women striving for power, gold, and the gratification of lust. "The metaphors which the satirist traditionally uses to describe the filthiness and idiocy of mankind now become

literal realities before our eyes." Presents Bosola as a satirist, who sometimes sees his own deformation; contrasts him to the Duchess, a figure of love, life, joy, and society.

8   LAYMAN, B.J. "The Equilibrium of Opposites in The White Devil:
     A Reinterpretation." PMLA 74, no. 4:336-47.
          Suggests Webster's works emphasize deceptive appearance as
     a reaction to the Machiavellianism he saw around him. Sees
     Flamineo as cynical and free from cant, opposed to and by Vittoria:
     they are "brilliantly" brother and sister. He confronts the
     Machiavellian "real" world; she imposes the shield of imagination
     between it and her. Flamineo tries to disintegrate his family in
     order to affirm his own world view and is cursed by his honesty.
     Vittoria at first appears a pure whore, but in the trial scene
     she shows increasing radiance and vitality and an ability to im-
     agine herself in a variety of roles. Vittoria and Flamineo are,
     respectively, a mask wearer and a mask destroyer. At the conclu-
     sion Flamineo is forced to confront his own sardonic views in
     several scenes, culminating in his true death. He discovers his
     sister's true nobility and therefore dies freed from his total
     cynicism.

9   LEECH, CLIFFORD. Review of The Sources of "The White Devil,"
     by Gunnar Boklund. Review of English Studies, m.s. 10:89-91.
          Finds this is a valuable book, which accomplishes more than
     the title indicates. By showing how Webster used his sources,
     Boklund makes a contribution to criticism, but his method of pre-
     senting all possible alternatives is a bit hard to follow.

10   MILLER, EDWIN H. The Professional Writer in Elizabethan England:
     A Study of Nondramatic Literature. Cambridge, Mass.: Harvard
     University Press, pp. 7, 28.
          Observes that Webster's father was a merchant-taylor, and
     this makes him a typical Renaissance author in that he comes from
     a family of modest means.

11   NICOLL, ALLARDYCE. "Passing Over the Stage." Shakespeare
     Studies 12:47-55.
          Discusses the meaning of the stage direction "passing over
     the stage," which is used to describe the parade of ambassadors
     in The White Devil.

12   POWER, WILLIAM. "Double, Double." Notes and Queries, n.s. 6:
     4-8.
          Finds two characters with the same name in Anything for a
     Quiet Life and Middleton and Dekker's The Roaring Girl. These are
     examples of unintended duplication indicating problems of hasty
     collaboration.

13   SEWALL, RICHARD B. The Vision of Tragedy. New Haven: Yale
     University Press, p. 81.

Argues Webster is a "good moralist." But in the Jacobean era the tragic tension in the drama slacked off generally, as in The Duchess of Malfi, where the vision becomes clouded, and the characters are "in a mist."

14   SHARPE, ROBERT B. Irony in the Drama. Chapel Hill: University of North Carolina Press, 222 pp., passim.
      Comments that the splendid psychological horrors of The Duchess of Malfi are much more than unmotivated sensationalism-- they test the Duchess and she chooses Christian humility and hope over despair. (1957.26 is an earlier version of much of the same material.)

15   SLOMAN, ALBERT E. "The Spanish Sources of The Fair Maid of the Inn." In Hispanic Studies in Honour of I. González Llubera. Edited by Frank Pierce. Oxford: Dolphin, pp. 331-41.
      Finds The Fair Maid of the Inn derives from Lope de Vega's Ventiquartro parte perfecta that was based in turn on La ilustre fregona of Cervantes.

16   WHITMAN, ROBERT F. "Webster's Duchess of Malfi." Notes and Queries, n.s. 6:174-75.
      Describes Webster's borrowings from Montaigne's Essays (translated by Florio) and from Sidney's Arcadia.

1960

1   AVERY, EMMETT L., ed. The London Stage, 1660-1800. Part 2, 1700-1729. 2 vols. Carbondale: Southern Illinois University Press, 1044 pp., passim.
     Chronicles season by season all stage performances in London, including Webster revivals.

2   BOULTON, MARJORIE. The Anatomy of Drama. London: Routledge & Paul, 212 pp., passim.
     Mentions Webster frequently. The Duchess of Malfi is an example of a complicated plot ("an improbable and melodramatic plot is given most of the quality of great tragedy by the magnificent poetry and the force of the characterization"); the Duchess is a woman of "revolutionary moral courage."

3   BROWN, ARTHUR. "Citizen Comedy and Domestic Drama." In Jacobean Theater. Stratford-upon-Avon Studies, 1, edited by Bernard Harris and John R. Brown. London: Edward Arnold, pp. 63-84.
     Observes Northward Ho, under the influence of Webster's collaboration, deals with the theme of conjugal relations, but the satire of citizens as frequenters of brothels is not pushed to its bitter end.

4   _____. "The Rationale of Old-Spelling Editions of the Plays
     of Shakespeare and His Contemporaries: A Rejoinder." Studies
     in Bibliography 13:69-76.
          A reply to 1960.6. Argues photographic editions have limi-
     tations--they can't substitute for original copies. Some old
     spelling editions actually help readers get closer to texts than
     do photocopies of the originals.

5   BROWN, IVOR. Shakespeare in His Time. Edinburgh: Nelson,
     pp. 179-80.
          Somewhat belletristically observes that The Duchess of Malfi
     and The White Devil loom out with a sinister glow of sulphurous
     fire, displaying the best of poetry, the worst of human behavior.
     Webster's high points are such that even Shakespeare would have
     envied, but they are few.

6   BROWN, JOHN RUSSELL. "The Rationale of Old-Spelling Editions
     of the Plays of Shakespeare and His Contemporaries." Studies
     in Bibliography 13:49-67.
          Suggests there are two models of modern scholarly editions
     of old works: facsimile reprints and old spelling critical edi-
     tions. Cites both The White Devil and The Duchess of Malfi as
     examples. Two more extreme versions of these possibilities are
     photographic and modernized editions. See the "rejoinder," 1960.4.

7   _____, ed. The White Devil. Revels Plays. London: Methuen,
     205 pp. [Excerpted: 1969.17; 1975.18.]
          In the introduction describes Webster's early collaborative
     career; the date of the first performance of The White Devil
     (Winter, 1612) at the Red Bull theater by the Queen's Men; and his
     career after The White Devil. Outlines Webster's sources. The
     tragedy itself is conventionally Italianate, and utilizes the
     chronicle play tradition combined with the medieval tragedy of
     Fortune. It also incorporates the sensationalism of Beaumont and
     Fletcher, and Marston's satiric vision: it is a "mongrel drama."
     The White Devil's title shows a concern with deceptive appearances,
     and it implies an ironic perspective. Even "good" characters (e.g.,
     Isabella) are not what they seem. On the other hand, Vittoria is
     at times susceptible to conventional morality. Reviews theatrical
     productions, including the 1925 and 1935 London performances, dis-
     cusses the texts, and describes and analyzes the quarto of 1612.

8   BURTON, E.J. The British Theatre, Its Repertory and Practice.
     London: Herbert Jenkins, p. 137.
          Finds The White Devil suggests the skulker behind the arras:
     its violence is always ready to burst forth. In the play, decay
     lurks behind outward luxury.

9   CROSS, GUSTAV. "The Date of The Malcontent Once More."
     Philological Quarterly 39, no. 1:104-13.
          The emphasis in this piece is on the date of the pre-augmented
     version (c. 1600).

10   _____. "Webster and Marston: A Note on The White Devil 5.3.
        106." Notes and Queries, n.s. 7:337.
             Suggests that the image of the devil in Brachiano's dying
        speech was taken by Webster from the description of the devil as
        a linguist in The Malcontent.

11   DAICHES, DAVID. A Critical History of English Literature.
        Vol. 1. New York: Ronald Press, pp. 329-32. [2d. ed. 1970.]
             Observes that Webster is a greater poet than Tourneur, but
        with less control of dramatic structure. We are interested in the
        cunning of his cruel characters and the nobility with which they
        face doom. In The White Devil Vittoria is both hero and villain.
        She and Flamineo achieve dignity in their deaths. The play's con-
        ventions include the revenge play motif, satire of the court and
        the Machiavellian man, Italianate cruelty, and stoic dignity. The
        Duchess of Malfi is structurally simpler, but the motives of its
        characters are sometimes obscure. Concludes that Webster's art is
        one of brilliant sensationalism.

12   DENT, ROBERT W. John Webster's Borrowing. Berkeley: University
        of California Press, 323 pp. [Excerpted: 1969.17.]
             An introduction and appendix, plus commentary on The White
        Devil, The Duchess of Malfi, A Monumental Column, Characters and
        The Devil's Law Case, with a line-by-line citation of sources.
        Describes Webster's borrowing as very extensive and somewhat ex-
        otic. It is also very careful and labored. He probably took al-
        most every line from somewhere, and this is a density of borrowing
        unrivaled in English literature. Asks how much of his sources
        Webster had actually read carefully, and what is a direct source,
        and what is intermediate? He did not draw very much on the bible
        or the classics, or on much material in foreign languages, although
        he did have a strong attraction to continental literature in trans-
        lation. Compares Webster to other Renaissance dramatists in terms
        of borrowing, e.g., Shakespeare did not use a commonplace book.
             The appendix focuses upon dating and ascription. Sources
        and other evidence suggest these dates: The White Devil--1610,
        The Duchess of Malfi--1612, A Monumental Column--1612, The Devil's
        Law Case--1617.
             Reviewed: 1962.2, 19, 22. See 1953.3 for an earlier work
        by Dent; 1966.11, 18; 1981.7 for additions to this effort.

13   FREEMAN, ARTHUR. "A Note on The White Devil." Notes and
        Queries, n.s. 7:421.
             Suggests 3.3. 72-77 involve a joke that invokes taffeta as
        a louse-proof cloth.

14   HENINGER, S.K., Jr. "French Scholarship in Elizabethan Drama:
        A Survey." Etudes Anglaises 13:283-92.
             Surveys specific, general, and Shakespearean studies from
        the end of the nineteenth century to 1960. Notes several studies
        in which Webster is mentioned.

15   _____. A Handbook of Renaissance Meteorology, with Particular
Reference to Elizabethan and Jacobean Literature. Durham:
Duke University Press, 269 pp., passim. [Reprint. New York:
Greenwood Press, 1968.]
        Cites Webster intermittently for some storm imagery and lore
regarding weather prognostication.

16   HOOPER, VINCENT F., and FAHEY, G.B., eds. The Duchess of Malfi.
With "A Note on the Staging" by George L. Hersey. Great Neck,
N.Y.: Barron's Educational Series, 211 pp.
        An inexpensive edition, intended for student use, with in-
troductory material describing the theatrical possibilities of
the work.

17   HUNTER, G.K. "English Folly and Italian Vice: The Moral
Landscape of John Marston." In Jacobean Theater. Stratford-
upon-Avon Studies, 1, edited by Bernard Harris and John R.
Brown. London: Edward Arnold, pp. 85-112.
        Relates Webster's two great Italian plays to the traditional
portrait of Italy by Marston, Jonson, and others. Finds Webster
is not historically accurate. He uses the maze of Guicciardini's
Italy to provide a setting for scholar-malcontent satirists who
keep before us an ideal of virtue with which they themselves cannot comply.

18   LITTLETON, TAYLOR D. "The Moral Environment of Jacobean Tragedy
Ph.D. dissertation, University of Florida, 247 pp.
        Finds various causes for early seventeenth-century intellec-
tual pessimism: the new science, schisms within Protestantism,
and James's inept religious policies, plus a deepening Calvinism.
Two specific dramatic themes derive from this pessimism: (1) the
surrender of men to sin and the incapability of regeneration, seen
partially in The White Devil; (2) conflict with "natural reason"
that leads often to atheism and revelation. The Duchess is the
only hero who fuses a Christian humanist faith in both God and
human reason. Yet humanity as a whole is viewed pessimistically
in The Duchess of Malfi, which shows Jacobean pessimism blotting
out the optimistic spirit of Renaissance humanism. See
Dissertation Abstracts 20 (1960):4409.

19   MULRYNE, J.R. "The White Devil and The Duchess of Malfi." In
Jacobean Theater. Stratford-upon-Avon Studies, 1, edited by
Bernard Harris and John R. Brown. London: Edward Arnold, pp.
200-225.
        Contends that The White Devil evokes a strong, yet ill-
defined reaction through language and setting. Webster's use of
metaphoric language is like the metaphysical poets' in that it is
based on ingenious comparisons. Like Flamineo, Webster sees things
in a complex texture of mockery. The play simultaneously disturbs
and exalts.
        Presents The Duchess of Malfi as less challenging and less

exuberant, yet more satisfying since it represents an identifiable
moral viewpoint. It values a well-run state. The play sets the
ideal security of the Antonio/Duchess relationship against the
stealthy unreality of the evil forces in its world (an example of
which is Ferdinand's lack of explicit motivation).

20   ORAS, ANTS. Pause Patterns in Elizabethan and Jacobean Drama:
      An Experiment in Prosody. University of Florida Monographs,
      Humanities, no. 3. Gainesville: University of Florida Press,
      90 pp., passim.
           Studies the incidence of internal pauses within the iambic
      pentameter line. Webster's patterns show "no clear physiognomy
      of their own." Includes graphs for The White Devil, The Duchess
      of Malfi, The Devil's Law Case, and several collaborations.

21   ORNSTEIN, ROBERT. The Moral Vision of Jacobean Tragedy.
      Madison: University of Wisconsin Press, pp. 128-50. [Excerpted:
      1968.23.]
           Finds The Duchess of Malfi a more profound interpretation of
      experience than The White Devil. In neither are conventional mor-
      als confused: murder is called murder and the wages of sin are
      paid. But Webster's aphorisms seem like Christian commentary in
      a pagan epic: innocence and guilt seem irrelevant in The White
      Devil. Virtue is real, but impotent. Webster's heroes are glori-
      ous villains ruined by their own desires. Surveys the characters
      in The Duchess of Malfi: The Duchess scores a spiritual victory,
      not a glorious defeat; Bosola and Antonio both seek the illusion
      of safety; Ferdinand and the Cardinal are slaves of egotism. In
      a cloudy world, the Duchess alone has the courage to be good.
      Thus, the play is an affirmation of the human spirit.

22   POWER, WILLIAM. "Middleton's Way with Names." Notes and
      Queries, n.s. 7:26-29; 56-60; 95-98; 136-40; 175-79.
           Finds the use of names in Anything for a Quiet Life typical
      of Middleton's practice.

23   ROSENBERG, EDGAR. From Shylock to Svengali: Jewish Stereotypes
      in English Fiction. Stanford: Stanford University Press, p. 26.
           Discusses Romelio's disguise as a Jew in The Devil's Law Case,
      a matter of general villainy, with no theological import at all.

24   SEHRT, ERNST THEODOR. Der dramatische Auftakt in der
      elisabethanischen Tragödie: Interpretationen zum englischen
      Drama der Shakespearezeit. Gottingen: Vandenhoeck & Ruprecht,
      pp. 21, 26, 196-99.
           Cites Webster for the pantomimic dumb shows in The White
      Devil. Compares the opening scenes of The White Devil and The
      Duchess of Malfi to The Atheist's Tragedy and The Revenger's
      Tragedy.

<u>1961</u>

1   No entry.

*2   BEMBOSE, J.M.J. "The Influence of William Shakespeare upon His
     Contemporaries." Ph.D. dissertation, University of Birmingham.
          Source: <u>Index to Theses Accepted for Higher Degrees by the</u>
     <u>Universities of Great Britain and Ireland and the Council for</u>
     <u>National Academic Awards</u> 12:item 151.

3   BLUESTONE, MAX, and RABKIN, NORMAN, eds. <u>Shakespeare's</u>
     <u>Contemporaries: Modern Studies in English Renaissance Drama</u>.
     Englewood Cliffs, N.J.: Prentice-Hall, 300 pp. [Pp. 271-77
     is reprint of 1955.4 (pp. 119-28).]
          Includes Travis Bogard, "'Courtly Reward and Punishment':
     An Interpretation of <u>The White Devil</u>," pp. 271-77, 1962.7, and
     part 1 of 1947.2.

4   BOGARD, TRAVIS, ed. <u>John Webster, "The White Devil</u>." San
     Francisco: Chandler Printing Co., 101 pp.
          In a short introduction, notes the play captures the dark,
     lustrous world of the Englishman's conception of Renaissance Italy,
     a world of evil and desire. But it is also concerned with Webster's
     English world, commenting on the evils of the British court, espe-
     cially its system of preferment. There are two protagonists,
     Vittoria and Flamineo. She is evil, yet claims our sympathy.
     Where she is tragic, Flamineo is satiric. Where she is passionate,
     he is intellectual. His commentary keeps the play's perspective
     firm.

5   BROWN, ARTHUR. "Studies in Elizabethan and Jacobean Drama since
     1900." <u>Shakespeare Survey</u> 14:1-14.
          A survey of criticism arranged topically (e.g., general works,
     dramatic forms, etc.) including editions of Webster and criticism
     (p. 11).

6   BROWN, JOHN RUSSELL. Review of <u>Sturktur und Gestaltung-</u>
     <u>sprinzipien . . .</u> , by Ingeborg Glier. <u>Shakespeare Quarterly</u>
     12:338.
          Notes Glier's work (1957.12) considers techniques of dramatic
     presentation, then analyzes themes, characterization, and poetic
     utterance in Webster's works. Glier contends justice and integrity
     rule the beginning and end of each tragedy, and Webster is a master
     user of contrasts.

7   CAPUTI, ANTHONY. <u>John Marston, Satirist</u>. Ithaca: Cornell
     University Press, pp. 264-65.
          Includes a brief discussion of the authorship of <u>The</u>
     <u>Malcontent</u>, in light of the title page attribution of the "addi-
     tions" to Webster, as well as the induction. Finds Webster's
     authorship unlikely.

8   FRANKLIN, H. BRUCE. "The Trial Scene of Webster's The White
     Devil Examined in Terms of Renaissance Rhetoric." Studies in
     English Literature 1, no. 2:35-51.
         Argues deceit and diabolism are the basis of this play's
     dramatic structure. Vittoria is not the only "white devil"--all
     the characters are deceitful. Analyzes the rhetorical tactics
     and effectiveness of the various participants in the trial scene,
     showing Vittoria's superior oratorical skills. At the conclusion,
     her eloquence makes a shambles of the trial. Her performance does
     not convince us that she is innocent, but she does appear less
     guilty than her accusers. As Webster suggests, there are "degrees
     of devils."

9   HIBBARD, GEORGE R. "The Early Seventeenth Century and the
     Tragic View of Life." Renaissance and Modern Studies 5:5-28.
         Argues that Webster held the conviction that "the play of
     life" had neither significance nor author. All his main characters
     die in a mist of uncertainty, and he viewed man as the random play-
     thing of the gods. The dramatist considered greatness more allied
     to courage than to conventional morality.

10   JENKINS, HAROLD. "The Tragedy of Revenge in Shakespeare and
     Webster." Shakespeare Survey 14:45-55. [Reprinted: 1969.17.]
         Considers Webster's variations on the revenge plot convention.
     His protagonists do not pursue, but suffer, revenge. The diffi-
     culty is that they must still commit the crime, yet we must sympa-
     thize with the criminals, not the victims. Thus, the crimes are
     diminished, as, for example, by presentation in dumb show in The
     White Devil. Vittoria and Brachiano suffer as a consequence of
     their sin, but the cause of their evil also is responsible for
     their love. It is that vitality that interests Webster. The
     Duchess of Malfi is another twist in a revenge play without a
     crime. (The Duchess' remarriage is not presented in the play as
     a crime.) The fundamental contest in Webster's plays is not good
     vs. evil, but life vs. death--the grave must win.

11   KAUFMANN, RALPH J., ed. Elizabethan Drama: Modern Essays in
     Criticism. New York: Oxford University Press, pp. 225-67.
         Reprints of 1955.22; 1958.9.

12   KAUL, R.K. "What Theobald Did to Webster." Indian Journal of
     English Studies (Calcutta) 2:138-44.
         Compares the verse of The Fatal Secret to that of The Duchess
     of Malfi, finding Theobald deserves most of the ridicule critics
     have heaped upon him. But his verse is appropriate to a Restoration
     tragedy, if not a Jacobean one. He writes mostly in blank verse,
     while Webster shfits from prose to rhyme. Theobald is more bombas-
     tic. He does achieve some clarity and cohesion: his version is
     neater, with characters and action, as well as language, less wild
     and more regular. He removes macabre effects like the wax figures
     and the disgusting imagery.

13   LEWIS, GEORGE L.   "Elements of Medieval Horror Tragedy in The
     Duchess of Malfi."   Central States Speech Journal 12:106-11.
         Discusses terror and horror as essential within The Duchess
     of Malfi and a sharp contrast with the love story. Webster in-
     corporates the mediveal gothic outlook that associated death and
     tragedy. Torture points to the weakness of man's physical nature
     --and the strength of his spirit. This use of terror helps achieve
     majesty for his plays.

14   MANDEL, OSCAR. A Definition of Tragedy. New York: New York
     University Press, pp. 27, 32, 94, 106.
         Argues The White Devil and The Duchess of Malfi are not
     tragedies, due to a lack of single purpose carrying from the begin-
     ning the necessity of the hero's end. Thus, the Duchess is just
     a victim.

15   RIBNER, IRVING. "Webster's Italian Tragedies."   Tulane Drama
     Review 5, no. 3:106-18. [Reprinted: 1962.18.]
         Views Webster's tragedies as a flash of greatness in the
     midst of an otherwise mediocre career. They search for moral order
     in the chaotic world of Jacobean skepticism. The White Devil sug-
     gests that the only value to be found in such a world lies in a
     brave death. The Duchess of Malfi asserts that nobility may be a
     basis for moral order.
         In The White Devil, "evil wears the mask of good, and good
     disguises itself as evil, so that at last the two are indistinguish-
     able." This moral ambivalence is at its height in Vittoria, whose
     heroic death shows how integrity can bring nobility out of evil.
     Flamineo does not speak for Webster but for the view he wishes to
     escape--unredeemed cynicism.
         The Duchess of Malfi moves out of the moral mist of its
     predecessor and asserts that the inherent dignity of man is stronger
     than the evil of the world. Bosola unifies the play in his several
     symbolic roles, moving from evil to faith, penance, and hope of
     heaven. In the final act, through Bosola, the spirit of the Duchess
     enters the world, while evil is shown to lead to madness and dam-
     nation. The Duchess is life; her brothers represent its destruc-
     tion. Bosola is converted from the latter position to the former.
     The good in life comes from accepting life and death with integrity
     and dignity.

16   SHARPE, ROBERT B. "Metaphysical Paradox in Jacobean Drama."
     Renaissance Papers, 1961, pp. 19-23.
         Finds Webster's tragedies incline to stoic types of epigram-
     matic paradoxes, for example the conclusion of The Duchess of Malfi,
     but also religious and ambiguous ones, as in Flamineo's dying coup-
     lets.

17   STEINER, GEORGE. The Death of Tragedy. New York: Knopf,
     354 pp., esp. pp. 145-48.
         Cites Webster throughout this large theoretical study, for

example for his prefatory defense of The White Devil that apologizes for digressing from a critical, classical ideal. Webster and his fellows were later important to the romantics, especially Shelley.

1962

1 BOKLUND, GUNNAR. "The Duchess of Malfi": Sources, Themes, Characters. Cambridge, Mass.: Harvard University Press, 189 pp.
Intended as a sequel to his study of the sources of The White Devil (1957.5), but also an analysis of both tragedies.
Discusses the actual facts of the Duchess' life, and the sources of Webster's version including Bandello, Belleforest, Painter, and Lope de Vega. Sidney's Arcadia, Herodotus, and Cinthio are potential secondary sources. Webster may also have borrowed themes from some of these, and other, works. Belleforest is probably the main source of the plot, but not of the play's moral dimension. Webster's use of these sources emphasizes the themes of sexual depravity and evil disguised as beauty. Unlike his sources, Webster makes the Aragonian brethren outright villains, while the character of the Duchess is more varied than elsewhere and Antonio becomes more hesitant, less heroic.
Finds The White Devil gives no example of the virtuous life, but The Duchess of Malfi does in the Duchess. The world is still futile, but the good can exist, if not thrive. Reviewed: 1962.26; 1963.6, 7, 15; 1964.3, 13, 22.

2 _____. Review of John Webster's Borrowing, by Robert W. Dent. Shakespeare Quarterly 13, no. 1:97-98.
Finds Dent's work (1960.12) sound and valuable scholarship, and his judiciousness admirable. Unlike Boklund's studies, Dent limits himself to verbal borrowings, not thematic ones. It is interesting to note how different the compositional methods of Shakespeare and Webster were.

3 BRADBROOK, MURIEL C. The Rise of the Common Player. London: Chatto & Windus, pp. 90, 130, 292.
Comments on Webster's use of the figure of the revenger as created by Kyd and Alleyn; his relationship with Heywood's Apology for Actors; and his connection with the merchant-taylors.

4 BRIGGS, KATHERINE MARY. Pale Hecate's Team: An Examination of the Beliefs on Witchcraft and Magic among Shakespeare's Contemporaries and His Immediate Successors. London: Routledge & Kegan Paul, pp. 108-65.
Studies the darker side of folk magical belief. Notes the verbal references to various beliefs concerning magic and witchcraft in Webster's tragedies. (Another John Webster, who wrote "Displaying of Supposed Witchcraft" (1677), is cited and misindexed with The Duchess of Malfi and The White Devil.)

*5   BRISSENDEN, ALAN J. "Sexual Themes in Jacobean Drama." Ph.D.
      dissertation, University of London.
          Source: Index to Theses Accepted for Higher Degrees by the
      Universities of Great Britain and Ireland and the Council for
      National Academic Awards 13:9.

6   BROWN, JOHN RUSSELL. "The Printing of John Webster's Plays
      (III): The Duchess of Malfi." Studies in Bibliography 15:
      57-69. [Continuation of 1954.2; 1956.4.]
          Describes some of the processes that must have been used for
      editing The Duchess of Malfi in the 1623 printing by Nicholas Okes.
      There appear to have been two compositors and a scribe named Ralph
      Crane. Discusses the relationship of printing house practices to
      Webster's original versification.

7   CALDERWOOD, JAMES L. "The Duchess of Malfi: Styles of Ceremony."
      Essays in Criticism 12:133-47. [Excerpted: 1968.23; 1969.17;
      1975.18.]
          Notes that previous critics have objected to Webster's lack
      of a governing moral perspective. Actually, The Duchess of Malfi
      investigates the theme of individual and social norms, especially
      the doctrine of degree. Webster utilizes ceremony and ritual to
      evaluate the ethicality of private action. Thus, the wooing scene
      is the Duchess' ceremonially absolving herself of degree, and
      Ferdinand attempts to turn his private, incestuous, passion into
      a public sacrificial ritual.

8   DAIJI, JORI. "The White Devil and the Boy Ambassadors."
      Studies in English Literature (Tokyo), English Number:1-97.
          Attempts an imaginative description of J.A. Symonds's intro-
      duction to the Italian Renaissance and a creative reconstruction
      of the history behind The White Devil.

9   ELIOT, T.S. "Seneca in Elizabethan Translation." In Essays
      on Elizabethan Drama. New York: Harcourt, Brace, pp. 3-56.
      [Published in England as Elizabethan Dramatists (London: Faber
      & Faber). First published as an introduction to Seneca His
      Tenne Tragedies Translated into English, vol. 1, Tudor Trans-
      lations, 2d ser., 11 (London: Constable; New York: Knopf,
      1927), pp. x-liv.]
          Briefly mentions Senecan influence on Webster.

10   HARBARGE, ALFRED B. "Intrigue in Elizabethan Tragedy." In
      Essays on Shakespeare and Elizabethan Drama in Honor of Hardin
      Craig. Edited by Richard Hosley. Columbia: University of
      Missouri Press, pp. 37-44.
          Finds that The Spanish Tragedy gave to Renaissance dramatic
      tragedy a plot element of intrigue wherein complications due to
      comic-like trickery lead to tragic ends. The Duchess of Malfi
      concludes in a welter of such tricks. The danger is that this
      device may produce a comic effect.

11   HOWARTH, ROBERT GUY. "Two Notes on Webster." <u>Notes and Queries</u>,
      n.s. 9:334-36.
           1. "John Webster Not a Parish Clerk." In spite of the opin-
      ions of Gildon and Lamb, affirms that Webster was neither buried
      as a Parish Clerk nor cited as such in any contemporary documents.
           2. "A Deed of Gift (1624) and John Webster." Shows that
      this deed, which includes a signature of a John Webster, probably
      does not involve the dramatist.

12   HURT, JAMES R. "Inverted Rituals in Webster's <u>The White Devil</u>."
      <u>Journal of English and Germanic Philology</u> 61:41-47.
           Finds three inverted religious rituals in <u>The White Devil</u>:
      Act 2, scene 1 is a parody of the wedding service, as Brachiano
      divorces Isabella; 4.3 is a false confession of Lodovico to
      Monticelso; 5.3 presents the killing of Brachiano in a parody of
      extreme unction. These ritual parodies are like Price's "figures-
      in-action" (1955.22) in showing the contrast between fair show
      ("white") and foul truth ("devil"). The play is linked to hell
      and the characters to devils and witches; thus, it is appropriate
      to reverse religious rituals.

13   KNIGHT, G. WILSON. <u>The Golden Labyrinth</u>. New York: Norton,
      pp. 104-12.
           Surveys the drama from the Greeks through the Georgians, dis-
      cussing Webster in the chapter on Jacobeans. His world is grim
      and peopled by villains of complex fascination and heroines of in-
      domitable courage. Offers comments on specific works. <u>The White
      Devil</u> depicts events not always clearly motivated; thus, Vittoria's
      degree of guilt is unresolved. The play's characters are driven
      by powerful passions, its poetry is both extravagant and condensed,
      and the plot is unruly, but of great force. <u>The Duchess of Malfi</u>
      is less energetic. Good and evil are more clear, but the play
      offers no easy solutions. <u>The Devil's Law Case</u> also has a strong
      heroine and two "remarkable" plot devices.

14   LEECH, CLIFFORD. "Le Dénouement par le suicide dan la tragédie
      élizabéthaine et jacobéene." In <u>Le Théâtre tragique</u>. Edited
      by Jean Jacquot. Paris: Editions du Centre National de la
      Recherche Scientifique, pp. 179-89.
           Finds that the attitude of Renaissance dramatists towards
      suicidal heroes varied. In some plays such behavior is considered
      valiant, while in others (including some of the doubtful Webster
      attributions) it is considered cowardice.

15   _____. <u>The John Fletcher Plays</u>. London and Cambridge, Mass.:
      Harvard University Press, 179 pp., passim.
           Cites Webster frequently, e.g., when Webster collaborates
      with Fletcher, it is Fletcher who gives the works unifying quali-
      ties, yet he is less a major force than Webster; in Webster's
      tragedies, conclusions arise from barbarities of beginnings;
      Webster's tragic vision can be compared to Fletcher's--Webster
      shows more of a sense of darkness surrounding the hero.

16   MURRAY, PETER B. "The Collaboration of Dekker and Webster in
      Northward Ho and Westward Ho." Papers of the Bibliographical
      Society of America 56:482-86.
            Claims that the "colloquial contraction test" proves Webster
      wrote more of the "Ho" plays than has been assumed (about 40% of
      both).

17   NICOLL, ALARDYCE. "The Dramatic Portrait of George Chapman."
      Philological Quarterly 41, no. 1:215-28.
            Thinks a biography of Chapman can be constructed from the
      satiric portrait of Bellamont in Dekker and Webster's Northward Ho.

18   RIBNER, IRVING. Jacobean Tragedy: The Quest for Moral Order.
      New York: Barnes & Noble, 179 pp. [Includes 1961.15.]
      Reviewed: 1963.15.

19   RICKS, CHRISTOPHER. Review of John Webster's Borrowing, by
      Robert W. Dent. Review of English Studies, n.s. 13, no. 52:
      410-11.
            Notes Dent's work (1960.12) suggests the importance as well
      as the manner and extent of Webster's borrowing, but finds it weak
      on the literary implications of Webster's compositional habits.

20   SASTRI, J.S. "The Latent Motive for Ferdinand's Conduct in
      The Duchess of Malfi." Osmania Journal of English Studies 2:
      13-27.
            Agrees with Leech (1951.12) that incest is Ferdinand's moti-
      vation. The play's imagery, especially horse images, support the
      reading of the incestuous motivation.

21   _____. "Webster's Masque of Madmen: An Examination." Indian
      Journal of English Studies 3:33-34.
            Finds the madman scene the crux of the play; it projects
      the ferment within the mind of Ferdinand and his own madness.

22   SCHOENBAUM, SAMUEL. Review of John Webster's Borrowing, by
      Robert W. Dent. Modern Language Review 57, no. 2:247-49.
            Believes Webster is the second ranked tragic dramatist of
      his age, and the strange nature of his work habits justifies this
      study of his sources. Although Dent does not explain how Webster
      transmuted borrowings into an individual and unique voice, his
      work on the actual sources is judicious and diligent. See 1960.12.

*22a SHANKER, SAVITHRIK. "The Supernatural in the Tragedies of
      Shakespeare and Webster." Ph.D. dissertation, McMaster
      University.
            Source: Canadian Theses 1962/63, p. 56.

23   STACTON, DAVID. A Dancer in Darkness. New York: Pantheon
      Books, 247 pp.
            A novelization of Webster's The Duchess of Malfi that

reveals some of the many differences between novels and plays
(e.g., Stacton adds characters such as a troop of dwarfs and
Bosola's sister) and the twentieth and seventeenth centuries (e.g.,
a more overt incestuous drive for Ferdinand). There are also some
alterations in plot (such as the death of the Duchess and Antonio's
first child) and character (especially Cariola, who is a more important and sympathetic character).

24   STEIN, WILLIAM BYSSHE. "Melville's Poetry: Two Rising Notes."
      Emerson Society Quarterly, no. 27, pp. 10-13.
            In the second note ("Melville's Poetic Art") compares the
      dirge from The White Devil to Melville's "The Little Good Fellows,"
      which is based on Webster, and finds Melville is poetically su-
      perior to his model. See 1963.3 for an additional note on this
      subject.

25   WAITH, EUGENE M. The Herculean Hero. New York: Columbia
      University Press, pp. 144-45.
            Admires the extraordinary dramatic life of Webster's female
      characters. The Duchess and Vittoria stand up courageously against
      a corrupt society. Both are heroic, and neither are "herculean":
      the Duchess is too virtuous, while Vittoria is too evil.

26   WILSON, R.M. Review of "The Duchess of Malfi" . . . , by
      Gunnar Boklund. English 14:199-200.
            Finds Boklund (1962.1) provides an excellent account of
      probable and possible sources, together with a balanced assessment
      of the play. He is judicious and shrewd.

27   YARRINGTON, EUGENE NEWCOMB, Jr. "The Metaphysical Drama: A
      Study of the Similarities between the Poems of John Donne and
      Certain Jacobean Plays Particularly Those of John Webster."
      Ph.D. dissertation, University of Illinois, 598 pp.
            Compares Webster's three independent dramas to Donne's works
      in order to justify the description "metaphysical drama." The
      plays deal with current religious, social, and moral problems,
      especially that of corruption in high places. Finds Webster main-
      tains a witty tension between tragedy and satire, creating "the
      tragedy of individual assertion." See Dissertation Abstracts 23
      (1963):2906-7.

1963

*1   BERRY, RALPH T. "Language and Thought in Webster's Plays."
      Ph.D. dissertation, University of London.
            Source: Index to Theses Accepted for Higher Degrees by the
      Universities of Great Britain and Ireland and the Council for
      National Academic Awards 14:10.

2   BRENNAN, ELIZABETH M.   "The Relationship between Brother and
    Sister in the Plays of John Webster." Modern Language Review
    58, no. 4:488-94. [Included in 1969.17.]
        Believes Webster is interested in how dishonor of a sister
    affects a brother, although Flamineo and Romelio seem interested
    in honor only as an excuse. In The Duchess of Malfi, the same ex-
    cuse is used for Ferdinand's incestuous passions.

3   COHEN, HENNIG.   "Melville and Webster's The White Devil."
    Emerson Society Quarterly, no. 33, p. 33.
        Adds to 1962.24 that Melville uses the dirge from The White
    Devil in the lyric "The Two Little Goodfellows" as well as in "The
    Armies of the Wilderness."

4   DAY, MARTIN S.   A History of English Literature to 1660.
    Garden City, N.Y.: Doubleday, pp. 327-29.
        Discusses Webster in the section entitled "Shakespeare's
    Contemporaries and Post-Shakespearean Dramatists (1595-1642)."
    Surveys the works individually. The "Ho" plays affirm the bour-
    geois morality of London wives, with no characters coming to harm.
    The White Devil is a sensational tragedy, dominated by sadistic
    frenzy and bizarre ingenuity in violence of word and deed. Sees
    The Duchess of Malfi primarily in terms of its two central charac-
    ters: The Duchess (guilty, but not meriting the treatment she
    receives) and Bosola (Webster's greatest character).

5   DICKENS, LOUIS GEORGE.   "The Story of Appius and Virginia in
    English Literature." Ph.D. dissertation, University of
    Rochester, 328 pp.
        Traces the Appius and Virginia story in its early versions;
    Italian and French variations; Chaucer, Gower and Lydgate; and
    considers dramatic retellings by Webster and later authors. Finds
    that each age tells the story in a way that reflects the theatrical
    conventions and tastes of its day. See Dissertation Abstracts 24
    (1963):2011-12.

6   ENCK, JOHN S.   Review of "The Duchess of Malfi" . . . , by
    Gunnar Boklund. English Language Notes 1, no. 2:144-46.
        Finds Boklund (1962.1) succeeds in discovering whatever re-
    sults historical probings and scholarly acumen can wring from
    Webster's sources, but he fails to demonstrate a firm grasp of
    Jacobean dramatic conventions.

7   EVANS, G. BLAKEMORE.   Review of "The Duchess of Malfi" . . . ,
    by Gunnar Boklund. Renaissance News 16:239-41.
        Finds that the first part of Boklund's book (1962.1) is
    painstaking and helpful. In it, the Duchess is presented as op-
    posed to the rules of social decorum but becomes the victim of
    lust.

8   FELVER, CHARLES S.   "The Commedia dell'arte and English Drama
     in the Sixteenth and Early Seventeenth Centuries." Renaissance
     Drama 6:24-34.
          Discusses Italian popular comedy and English comic drama,
     especially Shakespeare's, finding traces of the commedia in The
     White Devil.

9   FREEMAN, ARTHUR.   "The White Devil, I. ii. 295: An Emendation."
     Notes and Queries, n.s. 10:101-2.
          Argues Flamineo's line "Are you out of your wits, My Lord?"
     (after Cornelia interrupts Brachiano and Vittoria) should read
     "Are you out of your wits [to Cornelia]. My Lord . . . [to
     Brachiano]," i.e., it is an angry aside to his mother.

10   HORN-MONVAL, MADELEINE.   Répertoire bibliographiques des
     traductions et adaptations françaises du théâtre étranger.
     Vol. 5.   Paris: Centre National de la Recherche Scientifique,
     p. 39.
          Records one manuscript and four printed versions of The
     Duchess of Malfi and ten printed versions of The White Devil, from
     the 1865 translations of E. Lafond to the 1955 The White Devil of
     Robert de Smet.

11   HOWARTH, ROBERT GUY.   "Webster Not a Parish Clerk." Notes and
     Queries, n.s. 10:193.
          Argues that the stories that Webster served as a parish
     clerk are proven inaccurate by an extensive list of such clerks
     that does not mention Webster.

12   _____ .   "Who Held Those Horses' Heads?" Lion and the Impala
     (University of Cape Town Dramatic Society) 2, no. 1:3-7.
          Suggests it was not Shakespeare, but Webster, who was the
     horse holder.

13   KLEIN, DAVID.   The Elizabethan Dramatists as Critics. New
     York: Philosophical Library, pp. 144-73. [Originally pub-
     lished as Literary Criticism from the Elizabethan Dramatists
     (New York: Philosophical Library, 1910).]
          Cites Webster often in the section on Shakespeare and Jonson,
     e.g., for his appraisal of his contemporaries in the preface to
     The White Devil; his citation of the difficulty of composition in
     the same piece; the superiority of stage presentation cited in the
     preface to The Devil's Law Case; and the use of stage directions
     to control the presentation of his plays.

14   LAGARDE, FERNAND.   "Les Emprunts de John Webster." Etudes
     Anglaises 16:243-50.
          Reviews Dent, 1960.12, finding it valuable in the study of
     Webster's sources and borrowing habits.

15   LEECH, CLIFFORD. "Recent Studies in the Elizabethan and
     Jacobean Drama." Studies in English Literature 3, no. 2:
     269-85.
          Reviews Boklund, 1962.1 as an excellent study of Webster's
     sources. As in his book on The White Devil (1957.5), Boklund tends
     to underemphasize Webster's tragic effect and feature a bit too
     much Brooke's emphasis (1916.1) on morbidity of character. Also
     considers Ribner (1962.18), finding the optimism with which he
     views the conclusion of The White Devil probably unjustified.

16   _____. Webster: "The Duchess of Malfi." Studies in English
     Literature, 8. London: E. Arnold, 63 pp. [Excerpted:
     1968.23; 1967.17.]
          Introduces The Duchess of Malfi, beginning with a look at
     how it would appear in its time and what a Jacobean audience would
     already know (the conventions of tragedy, tragi-comedy, and rail-
     ing comedy). Describes the action with comments, then focuses
     upon the construction of the play, especially its divisions into
     acts. Finds the subplot is somewhat laborious and used mainly
     to contrast the Duchess and Julia. Webster creates distance
     through interposed fables, sententiae, theater imagery, extensive
     borrowing, complex imagery, and elaborate and macabre comparisons
     that show a world of cosmic anarchy. There are some inconsistencies
     within the play, but they are few and not noticed in performance.
     Considers the play's themes and implications. Contends Jacobeans
     would have found unequal marriages not acceptable. Secret mar-
     riages, especially those disregarding the church, and second mar-
     riages were also disapproved. Therefore, although Webster does
     not condemn the Duchess, he does show her goodness springing from
     questionable actions. Reviewed: 1964.10, 17, 19, 21, 38.

17   RIBNER, IRVING. "Criticism of Elizabethan and Jacobean Drama."
     Renaissance Drama 6:7-13.
          In this large, general review article, describes numerous
     works on Elizabethan and Jacobean Drama, including several partial-
     ly on Webster.

18   ROSS, LAWRENCE J. "Art and the Study of the Early English
     Renaissance Drama." Renaissance Drama 6:35-46.
          Cites the carpet and cushions that Zanche brings to the
     assignation of Vittoria and Brachiano in The White Devil as emblem-
     atic of luxury and idleness.

19   STAGG, LOUIS CHARLES. "An Analysis and Comparison of the
     Imagery in the Tragedies of Chapman, Heywood, Jonson, Marston,
     Webster, Tourneur, Middleton." Ph.D. dissertation, University
     of Arkansas, 404 pp.
          Examines the figurative imagery of seven tragedians accord-
     ing to Caroline Spurgeon's categories, finding that Webster uses
     much imagery of wild animals and demons, and, in The White Devil
     particularly, many images of food and drink. See Dissertation
     Abstracts 24 (1963):1163-64.

20   STERNFELD, FREDRICK W. Music in Shakespearean Tragedy. London
     and New York: Routledge & Kegan Paul, pp. 12-14.
         Finds Webster's major tragedies are representative and suc-
     cessful in their use of music. Cornelia's song reminds us of
     Ophelia, but it is not particularly successful. There are three
     songs in The Duchess of Malfi, and the two in the masque of madmen
     are very effective.

21   STERNLICHT, SANFORD V. "John Webster's Imagery." Ph.D. dis-
     sertation, Syracuse University, 283 pp. [Published as 1972.39.]
         Analyzes the architectonic imagery of The White Devil, The
     Duchess of Malfi and The Devil's Law Case. Webster's iterative
     imagery includes death, war, disease, sex, degeneration, and the
     devil, used to establish character, mood, theme, etc. These images
     occur in clusters, e.g., death/war/sex. Examines Appius and
     Virginia's imagery to determine authorship: several scenes seem
     Websterian in their figures. See Dissertation Abstracts 23 (1963):
     2905-06.

22   STROUP, THOMAS B. "The Testing Pattern in Elizabethan Tragedy."
     Studies in English Literature 3, no. 2:175-90.
         Suggests that in The Duchess of Malfi, the Duchess is tested
     by her brothers and destroys them, and in The White Devil Vittoria
     and Flamineo become similarly "lost."

23   THAYER, CALVIN G. Ben Jonson, Studies in the Plays. Norman:
     University of Oklahoma Press, 280 pp., passim.
         Cites Webster often, e.g., as an illustration of Jacobean
     cosmological confusion. He was a "tortured Manichean ironist,
     raging and intense, raising great ontological questions without
     answering them."

24   UMPHREY, ROBERT ELLIS. "John Webster: The Devil's Advocate."
     Ph.D. dissertation, University of Washington, 299 pp.
         Finds Webster's major tragedies are based on the spiritual
     values of the English Renaissance and their disintegration, espe-
     cially the willful departure from order. In The White Devil, sex
     becomes demonic, leading to social disintegration. The Duchess of
     Malfi concerns the fall not of individuals but of order itself.
     The Duchess chooses individuality over sovereignty and thus un-
     leashes chaos. See Dissertation Abstracts 24 (1964):2896.

25   VERNON, P.F. "The Duchess of Malfi's Guilt." Notes and Queries,
     n.s. 10:335-38.
         Raises the question of the Duchess' guilt. Webster seems to
     have altered his sources so as to avoid implying she is a sinner.
     Yet she is not entirely blameless. Like the villains, she and
     Antonio are secret and disguised. The lovers condemn themselves
     in aphorisms, asides, and soliloquies.

*26   WARREN, MICHAEL J. "The Rhetorical Foundation of the Dramas
       of John Webster." Ph.D. dissertation, Dalhousie University.
       Source: Canadian Theses 1963/64, p. 57.

                              1964

 1   ALLISON, ALEXANDER. "Ethical Themes in The Duchess of Malfi."
      Studies in English Literature 4, no. 2 (Spring):263-73.
          Finds there are ethical similarities and differences between
      the Duchess and her brothers. Like Ferdinand, she is impulsive
      and willful. The Cardinal is an opposite type--cold and Machia-
      vellian. The primary ethical design of the play is a polar con-
      trast: The Duchess is good and her antagonists are evil. Since
      evil seems to win, Bosola concludes it is stronger, but the
      Duchess, through her freedom and the integrity of her soul, af-
      firms a virtue that transcends evil and death.

 2   BARRANGER, MILLY SLATER. "Women as a Tragic Focus in
      Elizabethan and Jacobean Drama." Ph.D. dissertation, Tulane
      University, 208 pp.
          Traces the development of distinctive qualities in heroines
      of non-Shakespearean tragic drama of the sixteenth and seventeenth
      centuries. Themes of plays featuring such characters generally
      have to do with unlicensed or abortive love relationships.
      Webster's heroines, framed against a dark background, affirm a
      traditional morality. See Dissertation Abstracts 25 (1965):4296.

 3   BAWCUTT, N.W. Review of "The Duchess of Malfi" . . . , by
      Gunnar Boklund. Notes and Queries, n.s. 11:159-60.
          Finds the critical scope of this book (1962.1) is wider than
      that of Boklund's earlier study of The White Devil (1957.5).
      Boklund keeps several threads going as the study moves through
      the play. At times, though, the work is confusing, repetitive
      and inconsistent.

*4   BEJBLÍK, ALOIS. "Shakespeare a Webster." Slovenské Divadlo
      12:515-33.
          Source: Mahaney, 1973.23. In Czech.

 5   BENNETT, FORDYCE JUDSON. "The Use of the Bible in the Works
      of George Chapman, Thomas Dekker, and John Webster." Ph.D.
      dissertation, University of Illinois, 448 pp.
          Finds many biblical quotations, paraphrases, echoes, ana-
      logues, and themes in the works of Chapman, Dekker, Marston,
      Tourneur and Webster. Webster preferred the King James version.
      Some of his best figurative language is biblical. See
      Dissertation Abstracts 25 (1964):1187-88.

 6   BENTLEY, ERIC. The Life of the Drama. New York: Atheneum,
      371 pp., passim.

Mentions Webster often in passing in a broad general study
of the aspects of a play. Webster's plays are not fully poetic
drama but are dramas with highly colored language. He wrote
"ostentatiously morbid" tragedies.

7	BÖHM, RUDOLF. <u>Wesen und Funktion der Sterberede im elisabethan-</u>
	<u>ischen Drama</u>. Britannica et Americana, 13. Hamburg: De
	Gruyter, 182 pp., passim.
		Discusses death in several Elizabethan dramas. Webster is
cited intermittently but is not an object of major consideration.

8	BRENNAN, ELIZABETH M., ed. <u>The Duchess of Malfi</u>. New Mermaid
	Series. London: Benn, 129 pp.
		In the introduction considers Webster's life, the chronology
of his works, the historical and literary sources of <u>The Duchess</u>
<u>of Malfi</u>, then moves to a discussion of the play itself. Finds
that Webster favors the Duchess, stressing her purity and integrity
set against the corruption of the court and her brothers. Also of
thematic importance are the revenge play and madness conventions,
as well as the satire of courtly reward. Stresses images and
characterization, and the thematic conflict between reality and
appearance.

9	BROWN, JOHN RUSSELL, ed. <u>The Duchess of Malfi</u>. Revels Plays.
	London: Methuen, 220 pp. [Introduction excerpted: 1969.17.]
		In the introduction surveys the date, early performances,
revivals, publication, and sources of the drama. Concentrates on
Webster's alteration of his sources that stress Bosola and the
brothers' roles. Finds a relationship between Webster's dramatic
vision of political corruption and the actual conditions of the
England of his time. Also discusses imagery, parallel structure
of characterization, and poetry. Finds Webster's characterization
complex, but effective on stage. Appendices present musical possibilities for the play, an index of passages from other authors, and
selections from Painter.

10	EMPSON, WILLIAM. "'Mine Eyes Dazzle.'" <u>Essays in Criticism</u>
	14, no. 1:80-86. [Excerpted: 1969.17; 1968.23.]
		Feels Leech's work on <u>The Duchess of Malfi</u> (1963.16) is
scholarly and up to date and reveals certain difficulties of modern
criticism. For example, Leech assumes that the Duchess is somehow
guilty, but this interpretation is unstageworthy. Notes Webster's
audience did not understand the "Italianate convention" and did
not confuse Italian villains for Englishmen. Finds that the point
of the play is not that the Duchess is wanton but that her brothers
are sinfully proud--with a pride that seems to include incestuous
implications. Webster's audience of artisans admired aristocratic
courage but disliked family pride, Catholics, and Italians.

11	EVERITT, E.B., and ARMSTRONG, R.L., eds. <u>Six Early Plays</u>
	<u>Related to the Shakespeare Canon</u>. Anglistica, 14. Copenhagen:

Rosenkilde & Bagger, pp. 61-63.
Finds The Weakest Goeth to the Wall a play embracing romantic comedy and chronicle history, well built, but with no great passages. It may be ascribed to Dekker and/or Webster, with no compelling arguments for either.

12   FORKER, CHARLES R., ed. The Cardinal. By James Shirley. Bloomington: Indiana University Press, pp. xvi-lxxii.
Notes Webster's influence on the style of the play, observed earlier by Collier and Dyce. Also finds similarities of character, plot, imagery, and thought.

13   _____. Review of "The Duchess of Malfi" . . . , by Gunnar Boklund. Journal of English and Germanic Philology 63:353-56.
Finds Boklund (1962.1) has presented and rethought most of the material on Webster's sources in a painstaking and restrained manner. Occasionally his discussion is a bit hard to follow. His criticism of the play itself is unified and sensitive. Notes Boklund's thesis that Webster expanded his sources and achieved unity through tone and thematic contrasts.

14   GOLDBERG, DENA SAMBERG. "Crime and Law in the Plays of John Webster." Ph.D. dissertation, University of Wisconsin, 202 pp.
Argues that Webster's sympathy with criminal characters indicates his objections to a corrupt legal system. Further, he sees the legal system as often oppressive of the passionate nature of most human beings. In The Duchess of Malfi, Webster depicts the brothers as immoral law-makers, opposed to the natural goodness of the Duchess. Finds Webster denies such natural goodness entirely in The Devil's Law Case and Appius and Virginia. In the latter play, the law is good, triumphing over a corrupt law giver. Thus, at the end of his career, Webster comes to accept reason and social instinct as grounds for a satisfactory rationale for law. See Dissertation Abstracts 25 (1964):2465-66.

15   HARBAGE, ALFRED B. Annals of English Drama, 975-1700. Revised by Samuel Schoenbaum. London: Methuen, 321 pp. [Revision of an earlier, less useful version (London: Oxford University Press, 1940).]
A playlist, chronologically ordered, listing auspices, play type, date limits, most recent editions, and the like.

16   HOWARTH, ROBERT GUY. A Pot of Gillyflowers. Cape Town: Published by the author, 107 pp., passim.
Includes several notes on Webster, dealing with sources of lines in the tragedies and similar items.

17   _____. Review of Webster: "The Duchess of Malfi," by Clifford Leech. Modern Language Review 59, no. 4:633.
Argues that Webster obviously preferred worth to birth, although Leech thinks it clear the Duchess should not have married

below herself. Otherwise, finds this a deep and profitable study.
See 1963.16.

18   HOY, CYRUS. The Hyacinth Room. New York: Knopf, 317 pp.,
     passim.
        Cites Webster throughout. Finds his grotesque and burlesque
tragedies prefigure tragicomedy, creating a world of evil in which
reason only serves lust and greed. Webster's tragic satire depicts
life and death as equally absurd.

19   JACKSON, B.A.W. Review of Webster: "The Duchess of Malfi," by
     Clifford Leech. University of Toronto Quarterly 33:419-20.
        Describes Leech's three-part study (1963.16) as a thoughtful
delineation of Webster's tragic vision showing tact, good judgment,
and sophistication.

20   KLEINMAN, NEIL JAY. "The Shape of Ideas and the Form of Art."
     Ph.D. dissertation, University of Connecticut, 199 pp.
        Presents the Renaissance drama generally as a theater of
illusions. In The White Devil, specifically, actions end in confusion, and language becomes the rhetoric of illusion and convention. Argues Webster creates a universe of chaos, in which man
is his own only judge. See Dissertation Abstracts 26 (1966):
6697-98.

21   LAGARDE, FERNAND. Review of Webster: "The Duchess of Malfi,"
     by Clifford Leech. Etudes Anglaises 17:190-91.
        Notes the importance of rising above critical partisanship
in a work intended for students. Finds Leech does an excellent
job in this clear and rich presentation (1963.16).

22   LEECH, CLIFFORD. Review of "The Duchess of Malfi" . . . , by
     Gunnar Boklund. Review of English Studies, n.s. 15:317-18.
        Observes that, since Dent's work (1960.12), Webster has
sometimes been seen as a mere assembler of plays. Boklund (1962.1),
however, presents him as a craftsman. Observes that Boklund denies
Ferdinand's motivation is incestuous, and that while he sees a morbid appeal in act 4, he finds possible an optimistic reading of the
play as a whole.

23   LUECKE, JAMES MARIE, O.S.B. "The Duchess of Malfi: Comic and
     Satiric Confusion in a Tragedy." Studies in English Literature
     4, no. 2:275-90.
        Sees the mixture of satiric and comic elements in the play
as a source of confusion. The death of the Duchess is caused by
a social gaffe, not a tragic blunder, and thus fits the pattern
of comedy. Her opposition to the social order is a comic flaw for
which she is made to pay the tragic price. Argues that tragedy
and satire are hard to mix since the former concentrates on the
inner life of the hero, the latter on the external world. The
Duchess of Malfi, suffering from this confusion, does not fail but
succeeds only as satire and comedy, not as tragedy.

24 MEHL, DIETER. <u>Die Pantomime im Drama der Shakespearezeit</u>.
    Schriftenreihe der Deutschen Shakespeare-Gesellschaft-West,
    n.s. 10. Heidelberg: Quelle & Meyer, 160 pp. [Translated as
    <u>The Elizabethan Dumb Show</u> (Cambridge, Mass.: Harvard University
    Press, 1966), pp. 138-45. Annotation based upon English ver-
    sion.]
        Argues that in Webster's drama, realism and convention il-
    luminate each other. Thus, the dumb shows achieve novel effects
    while illuminating the main action. In both tragedies, dumb shows
    provide opportunities for the major characters to comment upon
    actions. Also finds, in both plays, that pantomimic shows occur
    at a turning point in the plot, as the actual revenge begins.

25 MERCHANT, W.M. "Lawyer and Actor: Process of Law in Elizabethan
    Drama." In <u>English Studies Today--Third Series</u>. Edited by G.I.
    Duthie. Edinburgh: University Press, pp. 107-24.
        Notes Webster's use of Hooker's <u>Laws of Ecclesiastical Polity</u>
    in The Devil's Law Case, a play that raises issues of justice and
    mercy (like <u>The Merchant of Venice</u>) in its trial scene. Argues
    that this trial scene points to an essential ambiguity at the cen-
    ter of the process of human justice wherein human law opposes na-
    tural law.

25a MOORE, DON D. "John Webster and His Critics." Ph.D. disserta-
    tion, Tulane University, 199 pp. [Published as 1966.19.]
        Begins with contemporary commendatory verses and notices.
    Webster's plays were revived and commented upon in the Restoration,
    then slipped in popularity in the eighteenth century. Plays were
    revised (by Tate and Theobald) to conform to classical standards.
    Traces the revival of interest in Elizabethans, wherein the later
    eighteenth and early nineteenth centuries glorified the imagina-
    tion, and renewed interest in Webster. At the end of the century,
    Archer's attacks (1893.1) provoked continuing controversy. This
    century began with Eliot (1924.4), the <u>Scrutiny</u> critics, and sev-
    eral historical studies of the 1900-1920 era. Some contemporary
    critics see Webster as presenting a morally gray world. Others
    stress his medieval heritage. Discusses Webster performances on
    the modern stage. (The last chapter published as an article
    1965.15.)

26 MURRAY, PETER B. <u>A Study of Cyril Tourneur</u>. Philadelphia:
    University of Pennsylvania Press, pp. 159-64.
        Compares Webster's dramatic language to that of <u>The Revenger's</u>
    <u>Tragedy</u>.

27 ORRELL, JOHN OVERTON. "The Repeated Scene: A Study of Formal
    Parallelism in Elizabethan Tragedy." Ph.D. dissertation,
    University of Toronto, 284 pp.
        Suggests that in <u>The White Devil</u> repeated patterns of action
    help to mold our perceptions of the whole work. See <u>Dissertation</u>
    <u>Abstracts International</u> 31 (1970):2933A.

*28   PARK, H.Y. "The Evolution of John Webster's Bosola." In <u>A
      Collection of Themes and Essays in Commemoration of the Tenth
      Anniversary of the Founding</u>. Haukuk University of Foreign
      Study (Korea), pp. 135-90.
         Source: Mahaney, 1973.23.

 29   PARTRIDGE, A.C. <u>Orthography in Shakespeare and Elizabethan
      Drama: A Study of Colloquial Contractions, Elision, Prosody
      and Punctuation</u>. Lincoln: University of Nebraska Press, 200
      pp., passim.
         Cites Webster frequently, e.g., for the use of "us" for "we"
      in <u>Sir Thomas Wyat</u> and <u>The Duchess of Malfi</u> and compares his prosody
      to that of Donne.

*30   RICHARDSON, MAURICE. "Back To The Bad Old Days." <u>Observer
      Weekend Review</u>, 3 May, p. 25.
         Source: Mahaney, 1973.23.

 31   RIEWALD, R.G. "Shakespeare Burlesque in John Webster's <u>The
      Duchess of Malfi</u>." English Studies 45 (Supplement):177-89.
         Finds that in <u>The White Devil</u> Webster borrowed frequently
      from Shakespeare; in <u>The Duchess of Malfi</u>, much less. Suggests
      his attitude toward Shakespeare changed between the two--that
      Shakespeare's major tragedies had less appeal to the later Webster.
      There are some striking echoes of <u>Macbeth</u> in the latter Webster
      tragedy, though, in imagery, character, etc., but these seem un-
      conscious imitations. The sleepwalking scene is parodied when
      Ferdinand beats the doctor in the Lycanthropia episode--a touch
      that heightens the charivari-like effect of the play.

 32   SASTRI, J.S. "Two Machiavellians of Shakespeare and Webster."
      <u>Osmania Journal of English Studies</u> 4:19-34.
         Notes Webster's reversal of the revenge play convention:
      his heroes suffer, rather than commit, revenge. His villains are,
      like Shakespeare's, Machiavellians. Finds many parallels between
      Iago and Bosola, yet they produce different impressions--Iago seems
      fathomless but real, Bosola is more wraith-like. Iago is a demonic
      disruptive fiend; Bosola is not integrated into any sort of notion
      of cosmic order at all.

 33   SCOTT-KILVERT, IAN. <u>John Webster</u>. Writers and Their Work
      Series, no. 175. London: Longmans, Green, 51 pp.
         Argues that the dominant theme of Webster (and the mature
      seventeenth-century tragedy) is the misdirection of human attri-
      butes. Writing in a period of national disillusionment, Webster
      creates tragedies that produce effects opposite to those claimed:
      for example, in <u>The White Devil</u>, our sympathies are with the
      guilty lovers. Sees Webster as admiring integrity more than any
      conventional notions of good and evil. Comments on specific plays:
      <u>The White Devil</u> combines many theatrical sources, most of which it
      alters. It is filled with contradictory and ambiguous values and

is without a moral center. Finds that while the drama has great
scenes, it is weak in overall construction. In The Duchess of
Malfi, Webster again shows a woman's passion pursued in defiance
of social order, but in this play, the mood is more melancholy and
somber, just as mankind is less magnificent. Although the Duchess
violates degree, her death is one of spiritual exaltation. Concludes that Webster's wrold is a pit of darkness through which men
grope in an effort not to be annihilated by evil.

34   No entry

35   SJÖGREN, GUNNAR. "John Webster--en forbisedd dramatiker."
     Samtid och Framtid 21:34-37.
          Briefly discusses Webster's tragedies and their source mate-
     rial in the context of other Jacobean drama. In Swedish.

36   STODDER, JOSEPH HENRY. "Satire in Jacobean Tragedy." Ph.D.
     dissertation, University of Southern California. [Published
     as 1974.23.]
          Finds Webster's villain Appius a typical Machiavellian in a
     plot of political corruption with much satire. Argues that Appius
     and Virginia is more technically competent, but without the power
     of the tragedies. In The White Devil, Flamineo is the satirist--
     objective and cynical. The play is filled with sardonic writing,
     especially the ironic use of moral epigrams. Finds Bosola plays
     a similar role in The Duchess of Malfi, but, unlike Flamineo, he
     is bothered by his conscience. This play depicts a corrupt and
     corrupting universe, and Bosola's satiric view of man contrasts
     with the Duchess' tragic stature. Argues that The Duchess of
     Malfi is the best blend of satire and tragedy in Jacobean drama.

37   TOMLINSON, T.B. A Study of Elizabethan and Jacobean Tragedy.
     Cambridge: Cambridge University Press, pp. 132-57, 223-37.
          Discusses the two tragedies separately. In The Duchess of
     Malfi, what holds the play together is an intense moral effort,
     involving great vitality and will, to resist chaos. In particular,
     act 4 shows the Duchess and her integrity surrounded by disorder.
     This image dominates the rest of the play. The work is unique in
     its relating of the forces of greatness and anarchy/violence.
          Presents The White Devil as the most powerful Jacobean fail-
     ure of all. It is fragmented and comic-like, touched with cynicism,
     and full of power and energy. Webster's attitude toward Vittoria
     seems uncertain and is never fully integrated. Overall, finds the
     play less humane than The Duchess of Malfi.

38   WAITH, EUGENE M. "Recent Studies in the Elizabethan and Jacobean
     Drama." Studies in English Literature 4:325-49.
          Includes a review of Leech, 1963.13. Finds it to be an ad-
     mirable short study, with a rational discussion of Webster's sources
     and the issue of the Duchess' remarriage. Waith, however, rejects
     Leech's belief in Ferdinand's incestuous motivation.

<u>1965</u>

1   BATESON, F.W. <u>A Guide to English Literature</u>. Garden City,
    N.Y.: Anchor, pp. 88-89. [The 3d ed. is retitled <u>A Guide to</u>
    <u>English and American Literature</u>, Harrison J. Meserole, coauthor
    (New York: Longman, 1976).]
        A series of "approaches" followed by reading lists. The
    reading lists include general works, works on drama, anthologies,
    background studies, and a section on "the principal writers" that
    includes Webster.

2   BENJAMIN, EDWIN. "Patterns of Morality in <u>The White Devil</u>."
    <u>English Studies</u> 46:1-15.
        Argues that Webster is not as pessimistic and nihilistic as
    many critics (e.g., Bogard, Leech, Ornstein) assert, nor is <u>The</u>
    <u>White Devil</u> amoral. This can be seen in an examination of the
    major characters, including Lodovico, Vittoria, Flamineo, and
    Brachiano. Often flashes of a better nature are seen beneath their
    cynicism and evil. One important moral theme of the play is to
    avoid courts and great men. Webster's evil characters tend to
    destroy themselves. Their paths are strewn with moral signposts,
    warnings, and recognitions of different possibilities, and thus
    they become moral agents.

3   BRADBROOK, MURIEL C. <u>English Dramatic Form: A History of Its</u>
    <u>Development</u>. London: Chatto & Windus, pp. 103-6. [Reprint.
    <u>English Dramatic Form: In the Old Drama and the New</u>. 1970.]
        Finds Webster's works reveal a questioning, skeptical temper.
    In <u>The Duchess of Malfi</u> there is a detached curiosity in both vic-
    tim and torturer. The Duchess sees herself as an icon. Asks if
    the Duchess or Bosola provides the tragic center of the drama.
    In performance, Bosola can dominate the play.

4   BRUCKL, O. "Sir Philip Sidney's <u>Arcadia</u> as a Source for John
    Webster's <u>The Duchess of Malfi</u>." <u>English Studies in Africa</u> 8:
    31-35.
        Finds Webster makes ironic use of the contrast in moods be-
    tween his play and its source. This is seen in a review of some
    borrowed passages and how Webster employs them. Discusses the
    references to the <u>Arcadia</u>, one by one, noting Webster's alterations
    and their reasons and effects.

5   CUNNINGHAM, JOHN E. <u>Elizabethan and Early Stuart Drama</u>.
    London: Evans Brothers, pp. 89-101.
        Presents Webster as a unique writer of hard and bitter plays
    that feature women as heroes. Outlines the plots of both tragedies
    and notes they are not good theater--they must be read. Webster
    creates a world where our values don't work: characters face the
    consequences of their actions--usually death--resolutely.

6   FORKER, CHARLES R.   "Robert Baron's Use of Webster, Shakespeare,
     and Other Elizabethans." Anglia 83:176-98.
          Shows Baron's youthful and affected Cyprian Academy (1647)
     uses much from The Duchess of Malfi and thus tells us of the appeal
     of Webster to young intellectuals of the next generation. Baron
     also used Webster in his later works. As Webster improved what
     he borrowed, Baron "very often did the opposite" to Webster.

7   HERNDL, GEORGE C.   "Changing Conceptions of Natural Law in the
     Jacobean Period: The Philosophical Origin of the Decline of
     Tragedy." Ph.D. dissertation, University of North Carolina,
     pp. 147-82.
          Argues that in Webster's world the only redeeming aspect is
     the spirit and courage of exceptional persons (Vittoria and
     Brachiano) who defend the claims of nature against conventional
     systems. Life is vindicated by the spirit's defiance of an alien
     and inhuman world.

8   HOWARD-HILL, T.H.   "Ralph Crane's Parenthesis." Notes and
     Queries, n.s. 12:334-40.
          Studies the use of parenthesis by the Renaissance scribe in
     order to identify him with the production of the first quarto of
     The Duchess of Malfi.

9   HOWARTH, ROBERT GUY. "John Webster, Property Owner?" Notes
     and Queries, n.s. 12:236-37.
          Observes that a "Webster," perhaps the dramatist, is recorded
     in the Dorset Papers in the Sackville Collection as a householder,
     and could have been a property-owner as well.

10   _____. "Worms in Libraries." Notes and Queries, n.s. 12:154-55.
          Attributes A Speedie Post, With Certaine New Letters by "I.W.
     Gent." (1625) to Webster on the basis of the repetition of the
     phrase "worms in libraries" from the dedication to The Duchess of
     Malfi.

11   JONES, ELDRED. Othello's Countrymen: The African in English
     Renaissance Drama.   London: Oxford University Press, pp. 71,
     78-80.
          Discusses the image and portrayal of Africa and Africans
     in Elizabethan drama, masque, and pageantry. Notes The White Devil
     makes much use of white/black imagery, including the title, which
     becomes a symbol made flesh in Zanche and Francisco's disguise.
     Zanche is the black parallel to Vittoria's white devil.

12   KEYISHIAN, HARRY.   "Thomas Dekker and the Rival Tradition."
     Ph.D. dissertation, New York University, 241 pp.
          Compares the "Ho" plays to Dekker's other popular stage work,
     finding their tone is quite different, in part due to the influence
     of Webster. See Dissertation Abstracts 27 (1967):2104-11A.

13   LAGARDE, FERNAND. "Wycherley et Webster." Caliban, n.s. 1,
      no. 1:33-45.
          Finds Wycherley indebted to the Renaissance English drama,
      including Webster. The White Devil is especially important for
      its intrigue, irony, jealousy and other thematic and linguistic
      borrowings.

14   LEECH, CLIFFORD. "Shakespeare, Elizabethan and Jacobean."
      Queen's Quarterly 72:5-25.
          Argues there was verse satire, of the kind favored by
      Flamineo, before 1600, and also that Marlowe's tragedy of vanity,
      cruelty, and damnation prefigured the Jacobeans. The Duchess'
      dying speech illustrates the linking of tragic and satiric impulses,
      the fusion of the general with the particularized.

15   MOORE, DON D. "John Webster in the Modern Theater." Educational
      Theater Journal 17:314-21.
          Reports most twentieth-century productions of Webster have
      failed, critically and in audience reactions. For example, a 1919
      production provoked titters from the audience and mixed notices.
      Surveys important productions of both tragedies in England and
      America. Webster seems more successful in the study than on stage
      because he has too much of everything. On stage, Webster's Grand
      Guignol often surpasses his grandeur. See 1966.19 for a larger
      work that incorporates this material.

16   REED, ROBERT R. The Occult on the Tudor and Stuart Stage.
      Boston: Christopher, 284 pp., passim.
          Cites Webster briefly and intermittently as an example of
      Jacobean skepticism about the potential grandeur of human nature.
      In The White Devil, the demonic energy of real men and women could
      exceed in evil that of real demons. Also comments upon The Fair
      Maid of the Inn and The Honest Man's Fortune.

17   RIDLEY, M.R. Second Thoughts: More Studies in Literature.
      London: Dent, pp. 74-132.
          Remarks on the diversity of critical reactions to Webster--
      ranging from Lamb to Archer. This may be due to Webster's effort
      to construct plays for emotive effects, not structural neatness.
      Examines the two tragedies:
          1. The White Devil is a play of complex character relations.
      The plot does not run smoothly; indeed, it is constructed incom-
      petently. But individual scenes, e.g., the trial scene, are
      brilliant.
          2. The Duchess of Malfi is a succession of brilliant scenes
      following dull ones.
          In general, finds Webster's characterization goes beyond
      stereotypes into genuine human portraits, especially with Bosola
      and Flamineo. The plays are vibrant and in them good remains good
      although it is defeated often by evil. Both end with hope for the
      future.

18   SENSABAUGH, GEORGE F.   "Tragic Effect in Webster's The White
      Devil." Studies in English Literature 5, no. 2:345-61.
           Presents The White Devil as a mix of satiric detachment and
      tragic involvement.   Scenes tend to alternate from one to the
      other.   The conclusion inclines towards the satiric, unelevated
      view of man held by Vittoria and Flamineo.   Thus, the play presents
      no great and suffering hero, and no insight into the relationship
      of man and the universe.

*19   SINGHA, M.P.   "Shakespeare and Webster as Tragic Writers."   In
      A Tribute to Shakespeare.   Edited by H. Dutta.   Assam: n.p.,
      pp. 63-66.
           Source: Mahaney, 1973.23.

20   SORELIUS, GUNNAR.   "The Rights of the Restoration Theatrical
      Companies in the Older Drama." Studia Neophilologica 37:174-89.
           Deals with the division of ownership, at the Restoration,
      of older plays by the reformed companies.   Davenant claimed The
      Duchess of Malfi in 1660.

21   STERNLICHT, SANFORD V.   "Brachiano in The White Devil."
      American Notes and Queries 3:84.
           Believes Vittoria's image of having a limb "corrupted to an
      ulcer" shows Webster knew what the historical Brachiano was like,
      even though his dramatic character is a handsome, youthful and
      energetic man.

22   STROUP, THOMAS BRADLEY.   "Flamineo and the 'Comfortable Words.'"
      Renaissance Papers 1964, pp. 12-16.
           Suggests Flamineo's expression "comfortable words" refers to
      a section of readings on penitence in the Book of Common Prayer.
      But Flamineo cannot repent; he remains a self-knowing humanist and
      cynically scorns Christianity.

23   _____. Microcosmos: The Shape of the Elizabethan Play.
      Lexington: University of Kentucky Press, pp. 75-76, 108-9,
      140, 199.
           Sees Webster's plays as dealing with microcosmic drama within
      the individual soul, especially in the case of the Duchess.

24   STRZETELSKI, JERZY.   "A Common Fountain: John Webster's
      Iterative Imagery Re-interpreted." Prace Historycznolterackie
      (Cracovic) Zeszyr 8:103-25.
           Examines Webster's iterated imagery in its dramatic context
      --as it is said on stage.   Finds that in both tragedies, the meta-
      phoric language illuminates the moral theme of the plays more than
      it defines character.   Specifically, there are image patterns re-
      volving around holiness, evil, and the state.   Concludes that both
      plays focus upon a character (Brachiano and the Duchess) at first
      active, then the passive object of revenge.

1966

1   BRENNAN, ELIZABETH M., ed. The Duchess of Malfi. John Webster.
     New Mermaid. New York: Hill & Wang, 159 pp.
        Contains the usual editorial apparatus. The introduction
     (pp. vii-xxvi) includes a brief survey of Webster's life and
     career, early performances, and the sources of the play. Finds
     Webster stresses the Duchess' purity and integrity in a world of
     evil. This work has fewer trappings of a revenge play than The
     White Devil. Its themes include madness, courtly reward and
     punishment, and others, often expressed in sententiae. The con-
     flict between reality and appearance is at the heart of the play.

2   ____. The White Devil. John Webster. New Mermaid Series.
     New York: Hill & Wang, 208 pp.
        Includes the usual editorial material. The introduction
     (pp. vii-xxxi) outlines Webster's life and career, surveys early
     performances of his works, and discusses the sources of The White
     Devil. Compares Webster's actual play with its sources to show
     how he stresses the contradictions in Vittoria's character. It
     is in the attempted murder of Flamineo that Vittoria is most devil-
     ish, her soul least white; but within a matter of minutes she is
     brought face to face with her devilish murderers, in comparison
     to which she again appears virtuous. The play's revenge tragedy
     structure presents humanity as diabolic, the world as hell.
     Webster shows what order lies behind a world of evil, through the
     play's commentary on life in court and more generalized moral com-
     ments.

*3   BUCHAN, MOYRA J. "The Hired Villains in the Plays of John
     Webster." Ph.D. dissertation, University of Alberta.
        Source: Canadian Theses 1966/67, p. 106.

4   COLE, DOUGLAS. "The Comic Accomplice in the Elizabethan Revenge
     Tragedy." Renaissance Drama 9:125-36.
        Shows Webster's Flamineo with his "dark cynicism" is a de-
     velopment of the "comic accomplice" figure.

5   COLEMAN, ARTHUR, and TYLER, GARY R. Drama Criticism: A
     Checklist of Interpretation since 1940 of English and American
     Plays. Vol. 1. Denver: Swallow, pp. 214-18.
        Includes a selective bibliography of post-World War II
     Webster criticism.

6   DENT, ROBERT W. "The White Devil, or Vittoria Corombona?"
     Renaissance Drama 9:179-203.
        Considers the roles of Vittoria and Flamineo in relation to
     the structure, characterization, and theme of The White Devil.
     Flamineo is the center of a subplot. He is also the center of
     the third main segment of the play, act 5. Vittoria actually ap-
     pears less in the play than the stress she has received would

suggest. Early critics saw her as evil; moderns stress her courage
and love as paramount. This is an over-romantic view, since she
does not "love" Brachiano.

7   EATON, WINIFRED KITTRIDGE. "Contrasts in the Representation of
     Death by Sophocles, Webster, and Strindberg." Ph.D. disserta-
     tion, Syracuse University, 363 pp. [Published as 1975.10.
          Argues that the attitude of the dying is an important clue
     to the cultures that produced dramas. Webster's death scenes re-
     flect the unresolved conflicts of the Elizabethans. His two hero-
     ines, against a dark, chaotic, and pessimistic background, are
     valiant, witty, and steadfast. Their courage and personalities
     have a value, regardless of conventional virtue. See Dissertation
     Abstracts 26 (1966):6020-21A.

8   ERDMAN, DAVID, and FOGEL, EPHIM, eds. Evidence for Authorship:
     Essays on Problems of Attribution. Ithaca: Cornell University
     Press, 559 pp.
          Reprint of 1943.7; 1951.17; portions of 1956.16; 1959.4.

9   GILL, ROMA. "'Quaintly Done': A Reading of The White Devil."
     Essays and Studies 19:41-59. [Included in 1975.18.]
          Argues The White Devil is less perfect but has more energy
     than The Duchess of Malfi. It blends revenge tragedy, psycho-
     logical probing and moral ambiguity. Webster tends to concentrate
     more on the small unit than the large structure, relying upon the
     conventions of the revenge drama to hold the play together. This
     does not always work. He does not depend on any conventions when
     drawing characters. Vittoria is seen from many angles--bold mascu-
     line virtue, female frailty, artful adulteress, coldly poised,
     tearful, etc. She is a "new woman," whose suffragette eloquence
     is blended with the agonies of sexual and social ambition. Finds
     none of Webster's characters provides a sure moral guide; there-
     fore, the audience is forced to judge for itself. An example is
     the trial scene, where our morals and our sympathies clash. Over-
     all, our response is never permitted to be simple or single.

10   GRIFFIN, ROBERT P. "John Webster: Politics and Italianate
     Tragedy." Ph.D. dissertation, University of Connecticut,
     151 pp. [Published as 1972.14.]
          Argues tragedies discover and give shape to cultural con-
     flicts--for Webster, between the ideal of order and anarchic will.
     This is a Jacobean political question, a reflection of the politi-
     cal crisis of the fall of James I and the collapse of the Tudor
     myth of divine right. The White Devil and The Duchess of Malfi
     depict a tragic sense of inevitability. Characters chose either
     to flee the court and avoid glory, or to participate in corruption.
     Neither play proposes a solution, although The Duchess of Malfi
     shows the insufficiency of the Machiavellian model. Finds Appius
     and Virginia celebrates the pieties of post-Jacobean politics with-
     out tragic inevitability and demonstrates the passing of the
     Jacobean crisis. See Dissertation Abstracts 26 (1966):5412A.

11 GUNBY, D.C. "Further Borrowings by Webster?" Notes and
    Queries, n.s. 12:296-97.
        Adds to Dent, 1960.12, two borrowings from The Insatiate
    Countess in The Duchess of Malfi.

12 HOWARTH, ROBERT GUY. "A Commendatory Sonnet by John Webster."
    English Studies in Africa 9:109-16.
        Believes Webster is the author of the first of four commenda-
    tory poems (signed "I.W.") prefixed to Mirrha, the Mother of Adonis
    by William Barksted. Adds that the poem shows a warm heart and
    not much skill.

13 _____. "Webster's Guise." Notes and Queries, n.s. 13:294-96.
        Presents miscellaneous information about the lost play. On
    the basis of the dedication to The Devil's Law Case, Guise must
    have been in print before 1623. Earliest records (playlists of
    Archer, Kirkman, etc.) suggest it was a comedy. It could be re-
    lated to a visit by a member of the Guise family to London in 1607.
    It could also be "Guise" in the sense of "custom, habit, or fashion."

14 JUMP, JOHN D. "The White Devil" and "The Duchess of Malfi."
    Notes on English Literature. Oxford: B. Blackwell, 69 pp.
        Explains Webster's Italian setting for both plays. Ambition,
    lust, and revenge motivate deeds of sensational violence, an image
    derived from Machiavelli and his myth.
        Sketches the main characters, language, and imagery of The
    White Devil, which depicts a "morally ambiguous world." Describes
    the action in an act-by-act commentary.
        Suggests that in The Duchess of Malfi the heroine is as virtu-
    ous as Vittoria is evil. Her brave death is the heart of the play.
    The language mixes prose and verse, with much of the prose spoken
    by Bosola, including many brief, memorable, lines. Traces, with
    commentary, the action of the play. Suggests the play adds to the
    evils of the court those of natural decay and death. It is less
    fierce and more melancholy than The White Devil.
        Overall, finds Webster's major flaws are a lack of verbal
    and plot coherence, and lapses into sensationalism.

15 KORNINGER, SIEGFRIED. "Die Geisterszene im elisabethanischen
    Drama." Shakespeare-Jahrbuch 102:124-45.
        Studies ghost scenes in Renaissance drama, beginning with
    The Spanish Tragedy, and with a heavy emphasis on Hamlet. Notes
    the scene in The White Devil between Flamineo and Brachiano's
    ghost.

16 KOSKENNIEMI, INNA. John Webster's "The White Devil" and Ludwig
    Tieck's "Vittoria Accorambona": A Study of Two Related Works.
    Turan Yliopiston julkaisuja, ser. B., 97. Turku: Turan
    Yliopisto, 51 pp.
        Shows Tieck knew Webster's work forty years before he wrote
    his novel of 1840. He thought that Webster misinterpreted Vittoria.

He read much non-Webster source material and in the novel tries
to revise the heroine and the events leading to her death. Tieck
keeps the trial scene at the center of the work, however. He also
borrows from Webster the scenes of Cornelia's madness and
Brachiano's death. There are, however, considerable alterations
in character. The White Devil emphasizes the theme of appearance
and reality, questions of death and guilt, and is socially satiri-
cal. Tieck, with an innocent Vittoria, makes the love theme more
central. Finds both works show a lack of unity.

17   McDONALD, CHARLES O. The Rhetoric of Tragedy: Form in Stuart
     Drama. Amherst: University of Massachusetts Press, pp. 269-313.
           Presents The White Devil as an example of the decline of
     Stuart drama into amoral sensationalism and verbal pyrotechnics.
     It is fragmentary in rhetorical design because Webster could not
     integrate the world around him into a vision of his own. He has
     been subject to "amazingly extravagant over-estimation." Webster
     was hysterical and produced only counterfeit versions of true dra-
     matic rhetorical coins. Reviewed: 1967.20.

18   MOONSCHEIN, HENRY. "A Note on The White Devil V. i. 230."
     Notes and Queries, n.s. 13:296.
           Contrary to Dent (1960.12) a line in The White Devil (5.1.
     230) is not from a proverb but, like several other borrowings,
     from Guazzo's The Civile Conversation.

19   MOORE, DON D. John Webster and His Critics 1617-1964.
     Louisiana State University Studies, Humanistic Series, 17.
     Baton Rouge: Louisiana State University Press, 199 pp.
           See 1964.25a. Reviewed: 1967.10.

20   PROUDFOOT, RICHARD. "Shakespeare and the New Dramatists of the
     King's Men, 1606-1613." In Later Shakespeare. Edited by
     Bernard Harris and John R. Brown. Stratford-upon-Avon Studies,
     8. London: E. Arnold, pp. 236-61.
           Discusses Webster as one of a group of dramatists influenced
     by Shakespeare. His major tragedies are in the revenge tradition
     of Hamlet. Finds Shakespearean echoes in Cornelia's reactions to
     Flamineo's murder of his brother.

21   RIBNER, IRVING, comp. Tudor and Stuart Drama. Goldentree
     Bibliographies. New York: Appleton-Century-Crofts, pp. 51-53.
     [Supplemented by 1972.21.]
           Includes several general sections (e.g., Basic Works of
     Refer nce, The Printing and Publication of Plays, etc.) and a
     selective bibliography of Webster.

22   SCHOENBAUM, SAMUEL. Internal Evidence and Elizabethan Dramatic
     Authorship. Evanston: Northwestern University Press, 281 pp.,
     passim. [An expansion of 1951.17, which is reprinted in 1966.8.]
           Surveys the history of attribution studies and investigates

the methodologies of such efforts. Includes an appendix on dramatic collaboration. Cites Webster often throughout, e.g., in the
context of Brooke's work (1916.1) and its concern with canonical
problems, the attribution studies of Sykes, and the like. Notes
that among the works subject to attributors and textual disinte-
grators were Appius and Virginia, A Cure for a Cuckold, Anything
for a Quiet Life, The Fair Maid of the Inn, and The Thracian
Wonder, and tells "the story of how these drift in and out of the
Webster canon."

*23   SERPIERI, ALESSANDRO. John Webster. Bari: n.p.
         Source: Mahaney, 1973.23.

24   STRATMAN, CARL J., comp. A Bibliography of English Printed
         Tragedy, 1565-1900. Carbondale: Southern Illinois University
         Press, pp. 675-82.
             Lists plays alphabetically, including title page data, and
       libraries where early editions of the works may be found. Includes
       several Webster items.

25   TROTT, ANTHONY, ed. Webster: "The White Devil." London:
         Macmillan, 168 pp.
             Includes an introduction, text (modernized spelling), notes
       and appendices. The introduction surveys Jacobean theater, Webster's
       life and writing career, the dates of his plays, the sources of The
       White Devil, and the play itself. Stresses the thematic importance
       of the aristocratic moral code and of court satire. The appendices
       focus upon the conventions of revenge and Italianate drama.

26   URE, PETER. "The Duchess of Malfi: Another Debt to Sir William
         Alexander." Notes and Queries, n.s. 13:296.
             Suggests Webster's line about the "star's tennis balls"
       (5.4. 54) may come from Alexander's The Alexandrine Tragedy.

                                    1967

1   AGGELER, GEOFFREY. "Irony and Honour in Jacobean Tragedy."
         Humanities Association Bulletin 18, no. 2:8-19.
             Suggests that in The White Devil a devotion to false "honour"
       is a major cause of suffering. What is false is an equation of
       honor and reputation that ignores morality. Finds that it is this
       confusion of repute with virtue that causes the drama's ironies of
       appearance vs. reality.

*2   BUCKLE, REGINALD W. "Webster and the Theatre of Cruelty: A
         Theatrical Context for The Duchess of Malfi." Ph.D. disserta-
       tion, University of British Columbia.
         Source: Canadian Theses 1966/67, p. 106.

3   CLEAVER, JAMES. <u>Theatre Through the Ages</u>. New York: Hart,
     pp. 80-85.
         Cites Webster as a contemporary of Shakespeare and notes
     that Burbage appeared in his "popular tragedy <u>The Duchess of Malfi</u>."

4   DAVISON, RICHARD A. "A Websterian Echo in <u>The Cenci</u>." <u>American</u>
     <u>Notes and Queries</u> 6:53-54.
         Points to a specific Elizabethan influence on Shelley's play:
     the parallel between Bosola and Cardinal Camillo as they react to
     the murder of innocent women.

5   DONOVAN, DENNIS, comp. <u>Elizabethan Bibliographies Supplements</u>
     <u>I: Thomas Middleton, 1939-1965; John Webster, 1940-1965</u>.
     London: Nether Press, pp. 37-61.
         Supplements 1941.16 with an additional twenty-five years of
     secondary material.

6   DRABECK, BERNARD A. "The Brother-Sister Relationship as a
     Thematic and Emotive Device in Revenge Tragedy." Ph.D. disser-
     tation, University of Massachusetts, 278 pp.
         Discusses several Elizabethan-Jacobean plays in which a
     brother manipulates his sister for his own benefit, especially
     revenge plays in which the brother commonly adopts an ethic of
     Machiavellian self-service in opposition to blood bonds. Comments
     on this type of villainy in both of Webster's major tragedies.
     See <u>Dissertation Abstracts</u> 28 (1968):3636A.

7   DRISCOLL, JAMES P. "Integrity of Life in <u>The Duchess of Malfi</u>."
     <u>Drama Survey</u> 6, no. 1:42-53.
         Argues that the struggle to maintain integrity of life in a
     universe bent upon its obliteration is the unifying idea of <u>The</u>
     <u>Duchess of Malfi</u>. Arrayed against integrity are appearance, con-
     vention, corruption, decay, death, madness, and sex. Suggests
     that the Duchess' murder was motivated not by her brothers's in-
     cestuous lust, but because her integrity forces them to question
     themselves, which in turn forces them to try to destroy her. Al-
     though she dies in act 4, her integrity survives throughout the
     remainder of the play.

8   DUNFEY, Sister FRANCESCA, S.N.C. "'Might Showes': Masque
     Elements in Jacobean and Caroline Drama." <u>Shakespeare Studies</u>
     (Tokyo) 6:122-46.
         Examines the masque of madmen in <u>The Duchess of Malfi</u>, which
     emphasizes the contrast between the grotesques of the anti-masque
     and the dignity of the Duchess, creating a mood and tension typi-
     cal of Webster.

9   FIELER, FRANK B. "The Eight Madmen in <u>The Duchess of Malfi</u>."
     <u>Studies in English Literature</u> 7:343-50.
         Notes that the text of the masque of madmen in <u>The Duchess</u>
     <u>of Malfi</u> is not clear about who speaks which lines. Attributes
     the lines to eight speakers, on the basis of internal references.

10   FORKER, CHARLES R. Review of John Webster and His Critics . . . ,
     by Don D. Moore. Shakespeare Studies 3:298-302.
         Describes Moore's book (1966.19) as an especially useful con-
     tribution because of the variety of responses to Webster. Finds
     the treatment of Webster's influence on seventeenth-century authors
     somewhat slight, but praises Moore's separation of reactions to
     Webster on the stage and in the study.

11   HOWARTH, ROBERT GUY. "Webster's Appius and Virginia."
     Philological Quarterly 46, no. 1:135-37.
         Attributes Appius and Virginia largely to Webster, not
     Heywood. It was probably written late in Webster's career, under
     the influence of Heywood, especially in word usage.

12   HUNTER, G.K. "Seneca and the Elizabethans: A Case-Study in
     'Influence.'" Shakespeare Survey 20:17-26.
         Denies the simple insistence on the importance of Seneca in
     all Elizabethan tragedy. Argues that genres are not airtight,
     other classical traditions also exist, and the vernacular tradi-
     tion is important. Cites Webster often to illustrate this thesis.

13   KNIGHT, G. WILSON. "The Duchess of Malfi." Malahat Review
     4:88-113.
         Finds the play has a somber, dun tone, shaped by an alterna-
     tion of drab and rich imagery. It is weighty with death. Argues
     that The Duchess of Malfi has as perfect an organic life as any
     work in our literature. Comments upon Webster's satire of the
     professions, and his characters (especially women characters and
     Bosola). The work seeks to express the quality of death--to make
     "not-being" vivid. Although it has flaws, it is the most profound
     creation of mood in our literature.

14   MAHANEY, WILLIAM E. "The John Webster Plays: An Analytical
     Study and a Preliminary Bibliography." 2 vols. Ph.D. disser-
     tation, Ohio State University, 421 pp. [Pt. 2 is a bibliography,
     published as 1973.23. Pt. 1 published as 1973.22.]
         Analyzes four kinds of deception (intentional; unintentional;
     self; and unintended self-deception) from which all of Webster's
     plots arise, to be complicated by further deceptions and resolved
     by undeception. Argues that this motif colors our perceptions of
     Webster's characters as well and creates the tone of the dramas.
     See Dissertation Abstracts 28 (1968):3677A.

15   MARGESON, JOHN M.R. The Origin of English Tragedy. Oxford:
     Clarendon Press, pp. 145-46, 150-56.
         Presents The White Devil as a "villain tragedy" but with a
     difference: the major figures are involved in a web of evil but
     are not themselves cruel and cunning. Finds an immense amount of
     deception in the play: "nothing is ever what it seems on the sur-
     face." Notes that, although Webster may make us sympathize with
     evil people, he does not confuse good with vice. Concludes the

play is tragic in its final affirmation of the vanity of earthly striving.

16   NESS, VERNA M. "Some Aspects of Renaissance English Tragedy."
      Ph.D. dissertation, University of Washington, 206 pp.
          Notes that Bosola's conversion in The Duchess of Malfi is a
      type of Aristotelian "recognition" scene. See Dissertation
      Abstracts 29 (1968):235A.

17   REXROTH, KENNETH. "The Duchess of Malfi." Saturday Review,
      4 March, p. 21. [Reprinted in his Classics Revisited (Chicago:
      Quandrangle Books, 1968).]
          Suggests that Webster, who was interested in the collective
      nervous system of his audience, revived the revenge play conven-
      tion in The Duchess of Malfi and did so in conscious imitation of
      Shakespeare. He utilized the form to try to hypnotize the spec-
      tators, presenting them with a stage littered with decay. Thus,
      although the play does not "mean" much, it rubs nerves raw and is
      its own excuse for being.

18   SAVAGE, JAMES E. "An Unpublished Epigram, Possibly by John
      Webster." University of Mississippi Studies in English 8:13-18.
          Suggests that a short, hand-written, anti-feminist poem found
      in the manuscript of Overbury's character of "A Wife" may be by
      Webster, based on the nature of the accretions to Overbury's work
      and some similarities with Webster's plays.

19   SCOLNICOV, ANN. "Dramatic Unity in Webster's The White Devil
      and The Duchess of Malfi." Scripta Hierosolymitana 19:209-18.
          Suggests three means by which Webster created dramatic unity
      out of Italian novella-type materials: foreshadowing of scenes;
      patterning of characters; a binding philosophy of life. That
      philosophy is one in which man is seen as the victim of a godless
      world of his own creation.

20   SHAABER, M.A. "Recent Studies in Elizabethan and Jacobean
      Drama." Studies in English Literature 7:351-76.
          In reviewing 1966.17, argues that while Webster's talents
      are limited and he has been extravagantly praised, McDonald's
      hostility seems equally extravagant deflation.

21   SHAW, CATHERINE M. "The Dramatic Function of the Masque in
      English Drama: 1592-1642." Ph.D. dissertation, University of
      Texas, 374 pp.
          Studies masques in seventy plays, with special attention to
      their functions. In tragedies, such as Webster's, masques often
      provide an ironic view of the ideal to contrast with the reality
      of the play. See Dissertation Abstracts 28 (1968):4144A-45A.

22   SIBLY, JOHN. "The Duty of Revenge in Tudor and Stuart Drama."
      Review of English Literature 8, no. 3:46-54.

Suggests a Jacobean orthodoxy wherein a weak or bad king
must be suffered but a regicide could be revenged. Thus, Bosola
could legitimately enact revenge upon a Duke and a Cardinal for
the unjust murder of a Duchess.

23   SILVETTE, HERBERT. The Doctor on Stage. Edited by F. Butler.
     Knoxville: University of Tennessee Press, 291 pp.
     Incorporates 1936.6.

24   STAGG, LOUIS C. An Index to the Figurative Language of John
     Webster's Tragedies. Charlottesville: Bibliographical Society
     of the University of Virginia, 58 pp.
     Alphabetically lists images, with no criticism or comment.
     See 1977.21 for an expanded version.

*25   TSOW, FAU M. "A Study of John Webster's Dramatic Technique."
     Ph.D. dissertation, University of Toronto.
     Source: Canadian Theses 1966/67, p. 114.

26   WADSWORTH, FRANK W. "Some Nineteenth Century Revivals of The
     Duchess of Malfi." Theatre Survey 8:67-83.
     Comments upon the very popular Phelps revival at Sadler
     Wells in 1850 featuring Miss Glyn in the leading role--a part she
     revived through 1868. Also discusses the Wallers' American produc-
     tion. The Duchess was an important role for many actresses, and
     the play afforded ample opportunity for dramatic pictorial effects.

27   WILSON, EDMUND. "The Duchess of Malfi in London, 1947," in
     "Notes on London at the End of the War." In Europe Without
     Baedecker. London: Hart-Davis, pp. 3-37. [Excerpted: 1969.17.]
     Reports that George Rylands's production was skillful and
     imaginative, not at all boring or comic as predicted. The play
     has a relation to the horrors of a world at war, for example there
     is a tie between the lunacy of the masque of madmen and the concen-
     tration camps.

1968

1   AXELRAD, ALBERT JOSÉ, and WILLEMS, MICHÈLE. Shakespeare et le
     théâtre élizabéthain. Paris: Presses Universitaries de France,
     pp. 53-58.
     Includes Webster among portraits of a number of Elizabethan
     dramatists, observing that we know little beyond his works and
     collaborations. Notes his borrowing and careful compositional
     habits. Cites briefly the minor works, then discussses the major
     tragedies. The White Devil shows Webster altering his sources in
     order to make life fit his artistic goals. The play is especially
     memorable for its characters. In The Duchess of Malfi, the heroine
     has all our sympathy. This play shows two kinds of passion: love
     and hate. Notes that Vittoria and the Duchess are entirely differ-
     ent types of heroines.

2   BANK, WILBERT. "Webster=Artaud + Brecht." De Gids 131, no.
    4:252-55.
        Webster, like Marlowe in Edward II, manipulates response to
    his works in ways similar to the modern dramatists of alienation.

3   BERGERON, DAVID M. "Prince Henry and English Civic Pageantry."
    Tennessee Studies in Literature 13:109-16.
        Notes how Prince Henry, who was for many Englishmen an ideal
    prince, provided the subject and occasion of much literature, in-
    cluding civic pageantry such as Webster's Lord Mayor's show
    Monuments of Honour. Notes that while Webster's poetic elegy for
    the Prince (A Monumental Column) was written in 1613, the show is
    later, appearing in 1624.

4   BERLIN, NORMAND. The Base String: The Underworld in Elizabethan
    Drama. Rutherford, N.J.: Fairleigh Dickinson University Press,
    pp. 96, 110-12.
        Shows how the Elizabethan underworld figures in many of the
    period's plays, including the "Ho" dramas, where it provides a
    norm for a satiric look at the middle class.

5   BEVINGTON, DAVID. Tudor Drama and Politics. Cambridge, Mass.:
    Harvard University Press, p. 292.
        Very briefly discusses Sir Thomas Wyat and its relation to
    the Essex faction, and the play's anti-Spanish motif.

6   BROCKETT, OSCAR G. History of the Theatre. Boston: Allyn &
    Bacon, pp. 165-66. [An essentially similar revised edition
    appeared in 1974. The same author's The Theatre, an Introduction
    (New York: Holt, Rinehart & Winston, 1964) simply mentions
    Webster among other noteworthy writers of Shakespeare's day.]
        Notes that Webster collaborated, but is remembered chiefly
    for his tragedies, which rank closest to Shakespeare in modern
    estimation. Finds his works flawed by obscurity and by action
    always taking a second place to characterization. Furthermore,
    the plays lack an affirmation and raise questions without offering
    answers. Poetry and characterization are Webster's virtues.

7   CAMOIN, FRANÇOIS ANDRE. "The Revenge Convention in Tourneur,
    Webster and Middleton." Ph.D. dissertation, University of
    Massachusetts, 145 pp. [Published as 1972.8.]
        Shows that revenge unifies Jacobean plays by providing a
    causal link of actions of violence. Also, the isolation and stress
    demanded of the revenger reveal character. Finds that for Webster
    the major use of revenge is the exploration of the relationship
    between man and his universe: Webster focuses not upon good vs.
    evil, but the prior question of the existence of good and evil.
    See Dissertation Abstracts 28 (1968):2643A.

8   CORNELIA, Sister MARIE BONAVENTURE, S.S.T. "The Function of
    the Masque in Jacobean Tragedy and Tragicomedy." Ph.D.

dissertation, Fordham University, 196 pp. [Published as
1978.10.]
    Finds the function of the masque in The Duchess of Malfi is
to mirror, not contrast, the main action of the play. See
Dissertation Abstracts 29 (1969):2705A.

9   FISK, VIVA K. "Court Satire in the Dramas of John Webster,
     Thomas Middleton, and John Marston." Ph.D. dissertation,
     University of New Mexico, 259 pp.
         Sees Webster's tragedies as akin to "absurdist" drama yet
     gounded in Jacobean political realities. Webster utilized the
     "Misery-of-Court" convention that showed the gulf between an ideal
     and a depraved prince, to reflect his fear of Machiavellian rulers.
     See Dissertation Abstracts 29 (1969):4454A.

10   FORKER, CHARLES R. "Two Notes on John Webster and Anthony
     Munday: Unpublished Entries in the Records of the Merchant
     Taylors." English Language Notes 6:26-34.
         Examines the records to show that Webster was admitted to
     the Company in 1615, on the basis of patrimony, and that his
     father's name was also "John."

11   FRASER, RUSSELL. "Elizabethan Drama and the Art of Abstractions."
     Comparative Drama 2:73-82.
         Studies the tendency of the language of Elizabethan drama to
     be abstract, e.g., so that young men are called "courages." Webster
     sees the murders in The Duchess of Malfi as "Murther."

12   FROST, DAVID L. The School of Shakespeare: The Influence of
     Shakespeare on English Drama 1600-1642. Cambridge and London:
     Cambridge University Press, pp. 119-56.
         Finds that Webster utilizes Shakespearean elements but re-
     jects his world view and achieves a tragic effect by opposite means.
     Argues that Webster uses ideas, such as the idea of second marriage
     as a moral issue, but does not entertain them. Therefore, the ac-
     tion of his plays tends to contradict their moral tags. Suggests
     that Webster's borrowings from Shakespeare led to disjointed and
     ambiguous characterization. Concludes that Webster borrowed much
     from Shakespeare--words, emotional effects, stage traditions, lin-
     guistic patterns, and images--but that he forces what came natural-
     ly to Shakespeare.

*13 GAMMER, ROTRAUD. Die Bildersprache in den Dramen John Websters.
     Ph.D. dissertation, University of Vienna. Vienna: Notring.
         Source: MLA International Bibliography for 1969 1:Item 3450.

14   GIBBONS, BRIAN. Jacobean City Comedy. Cambridge, Mass.:
     Harvard University Press, pp. 135-41.
         Includes a discussion of the "Ho" plays, which do not articu-
     late a satiric theme but are merely conventional set-pieces, with
     standard metaphors, similes, characters, actions, etc.

*15   GUNBY, D.C. "Anglicanism and the Jacobean Drama." Ph.D. dis-
       sertation, Cambridge University.
          Source: Index to Theses Accepted for Higher Degrees by the
       Universities of Great Britain and Ireland and the Council for
       National Academic Awards 19:15.

16   . "The Devil's Law Case: An Interpretation." Modern
       Language Review 63, no. 3:545-58.
          Begins by noting many misconceptions about the play and its
       genre: actually, it is a didactic thesis play, related to the
       preceding two tragedies. Its plot and characters are devised to
       air social attitudes; in particular, the work attacks the abuse
       of law. Finds Romelio a hero villain who has his pride tamed and
       is redeemed. At the start of the drama he is diabolically anti-
       religion, but he is brought down by God in the course of the ac-
       tion. Concludes by noting parallels with The Duchess of Malfi,
       especially the masque-like treatment of death.

17   HART, CLIVE. "Wild-Fire, St. Anthony's Fire, and The White
       Devil." Notes and Queries, n.s. 15:375-76.
          Suggests that Webster's use of "St. Anthony's Fire" in The
       White Devil (2.1. 298-301) refers to a skin eruption.

18   HEILMAN, ROBERT B. Tragedy and Melodrama: Versions of
       Experience. Seattle and London: University of Washington
       Press, pp. 61-72, 197-98.
          Claims The Duchess of Malfi is, like The Diary of Anne Frank,
       a drama of disaster, featuring the victims of evil men. The
       Duchess, thus, is charming but not a tragic heroine, since her
       marriage just happens to run afoul of her brothers' passions.
       She does not "earn" her fate, and she has no responsibility for
       the action, which creates disaster, not tragedy. Discusses the
       play's treatment of motivation: although Ferdinand's motives are
       obviously insufficient, the very unconvincingness with which they
       are presented makes us suspect other, unstated, motives, specifi-
       cally, incest. With its emphasis on the evil brothers and the
       suffering Duchess, The Duchess of Malfi is like a horror show,
       redeemed only by its great language, imagery, and creation of mood.
          Sees The White Devil as an innovation in melodrama, featur-
       ing unappetizing revengers and thus creating sympathy for the
       original "criminals," who seem great, suffering lovers.

19   HOWARTH, ROBERT GUY. "The Model-Source of John Webster's A
       Monumental Columne." English Studies in Africa 11:127-34.
          Finds the ideas and language of Webster's elegy based on "A
       Funeral Poem Upon . . . The Earl of Devonshire," (1606) by Samuel
       Daniel. Suggests that other sources include Sidney and Matthieu.

20   . "Two Notes on John Webster." Modern Language Review
       63, no. 4:785-89.
          1. Finds Webster the dramatist was the son of another John

Webster, merchant-taylor. John Webster the dramatist did not
practice the trade, nor did he attend their school, but he was
still entitled to write the Lord Mayor's show when a merchant-
taylor held that office.

2. Suggests that the poet had a brother, Edward, who could
have been an undertaker as well as a tailor. Suggests this may
have something to do with Webster's interest in death.

21   LAGARDE, FERNAND. John Webster. Toulouse: Association des
     Publications de la Faculté des Lettres et Sciences Humaines,
     1420 pp.

         Considers Webster's place within the Elizabethan theater,
then surveys his life and career. Discusses the collaborative
period in two segments, dealing with dramatic works and nondramatic
Considers the sources, text, and date of The White Devil and The
Duchess of Malfi. Discusses Webster's use of Machiavelli and
Machiavellians, and that of his contemporaries. Analyzes specific
characters who are especially important in this regard, then considers the victims of the Machiavellians, Brachiano and Vittoria,
and the Duchess and Antonio. Finds Webster's world Italianate but
with a strong relation to contemporary England. Considers
Webster's dramatic technique, and his critical statements in pre-
faces and elsewhere. Also discusses metrics, character development, point of view, language, etc. Concludes with a survey of
Webster's reputation and a history of criticism and productions.
Reviewed: 1972.11.

*22 ONO, KYOICHI. "Malfi Koshaku Fujin no Higeki" [The tragedy of
     the women of The Duchess of Malfi]. Eigo Seinen (Tokyo) 114:
     584-85.
         Source: MLA International Bibliography for 1970 1:Item 3268.

23   RABKIN, NORMAN, ed. Twentieth Century Interpretations of "The
     Duchess of Malif": A Collection of Critical Essays. Englewood
     Cliffs, N.J.: Prentice-Hall, 120 pp.
         A collection of previously published material, with an in-
troduction, chronology, and brief bibliography. Includes in part
1 ten essays or excerpts, and in part 2 briefer quotations from
fourteen more works. All are included elsewhere in this text and
cross referenced to this volume. The introduction consists of a
brief biography, presenting Webster as a professional playwright
who worked in several forms. His career comes at the end of
England's period of great tragic drama. Notes that his victim/
heroes are women. Finds The Duchess of Malfi quirky, full of ex-
aggerated conventions, and in many ways like opera. The play features an improbable plot, with complete integrity of moral vision
emerging from the characterizations of the villains, Bosola, and
the Duchess, a figure of gallantry in a world of utter depravity
who wants only to find a life of bourgeois comfort with Antonio.

24   ROSENTHAL, LEWIS S. "John Webster's Dramaturgy." Ph.D. dis-
      sertation, Louisiana State University, 233 pp.
          Argues that Webster's plays are not slovenly but, by
      Renaissance standards, sound. Critics have often complained about
      Webster's dramaturgy, e.g., the last act of The Duchess of Malfi,
      and that play's lack of motivation, etc. Affirms Renaissance
      dramatic technique was not classical, but generally "pyramidal:
      an exposition, rising action, turning, fall and denouement."
      Examines all three tragedies to find this pattern, scene by scene.
      Within this structure, Webster's characters seem psychologically
      well motivated. Admits that Webster did tend to concentrate on
      the big scene, which weakens his overall structure and effect.
      See Dissertation Abstracts 29 (1968):1518A-19A.

25   SAAGPAKK, PAUL F. "A Survey of Psychopathology in British
      Literature from Shakespeare to Hardy." Literature and
      Psychology 18, no. 2-3:135-65.
          Surveys physical and psychological theories of madness,
      especially as manifested in melancholy and malcontent types in
      the drama. Finds Bosola one of the melancholy villain types: he
      furthers the criminal action of the play, but his melancholy turns
      to remorse. Also notes the presentation of madness in The Duchess
      of Malfi in Ferdinand's lycanthropia.

26   SCHUMACHER, PAUL J. "Virtue and Vice: A Study of the Charac-
      ters of Hall, the Overburians, and Earle." Ph.D. dissertation,
      St. Louis University, 202 pp.
          Shows that the Overburians, including Webster, gave the
      "virtue/vice" tradition of the "Character" a new twist by adding
      wit and converting the moralizing tradition to satire--yet the
      concepts of virtue and vice still remained as ordering principles.
      Thus, the character-writers tend to polarize their portraits into
      praise and blame. See Dissertation Abstracts 29 (1968):1214A.

27   SCHWARTZ, PAULA. "Images of the Will in Jacobean Tragedy:
      Assertion and Control in the Plays of Webster, Middleton, and
      Ford." Ph.D. dissertation, Yale University, 393 pp.
          Finds Webster's work is not "decadent," in spite of its
      focus on domestic and psychological issues at the expense of so-
      cial themes. Characters are impelled by the same drives for in-
      dividual rights that underlie the Stuart revolutionary spirit.
      The Duchess of Malfi shows a faith in the power of the creative
      will through its imagery of spatial expansion. See Dissertation
      Abstracts 29 (1968):878A.

28   STEVENSON, WARREN. "Shakespeare's Hand in The Spanish Tragedy,
      1602." Studies in English Literature 8:307-21.
          Asks who wrote the additions to The Spanish Tragedy. Rejects
      Webster, because it was too early in his career, and the style of
      the additions is too fluid, even for the later, mature Webster.

1969

1   ALLEN, RICHARD O.   "Jacobean Drama and the Literature of Decay:
    A Study of Conservative Reaction in Literature." Ph.D. disser-
    tation, University of Michigan, 331 pp.
        Presents "decay literature" as a two-fold reaction to social
    change, distorting the change itself or depicting the disintegra-
    tion of character in the face of such change. This accounts for
    the defining features of Webster's drama, its apocalyptic scene,
    its disassociated, self-dramatizing heroes, and its blend of tragic
    and comic effects. See Dissertation Abstracts International 30
    (1970):3899A-3900A.

2   ANSARI, K.H.   John Webster: Image Patterns and Canon. Delhi:
    Sterling; Mystic, Conn.: Verry, 296 pp.
        Finds in Webster's works a gloomy atmosphere and a morbid
    preoccupation with death, satire, occasionally superb scenes, and
    vital characters. Discusses imagery (symbolic or iterative) in
    three parts: subject matter of images (hunting, sport, war, sex,
    etc.); the dramatic functions of imagery (creation of character,
    atmosphere, and mood); and the use of imagery to determine the
    authorship of Appius and Virginia (here assigned to Webster on the
    basis of image clusters). Concludes with a useful appendix on
    emblems. Reviewed: 1972.2.

*3 BEGLEY, P.J.   "The Characters of John Webster's Tragedy." Ph.D.
    dissertation, National University of Ireland.
        Source: Index to Theses Accepted for Higher Degrees at the
    Universities of Great Britain and Ireland and the Council for
    National Academic Awards 19:Item 371.

4   BENTLEY, G.E., ed.   The Seventeenth-Century Stage. Chicago:
    University of Chicago Press, 287 pp., passim.
        Cites Webster in several of the fifteen previously published
    essays in this collection focusing upon general matters related to
    seventeenth-century play production.

5   COOK, DAVID.   "The Extreme Situation: A Study of Webster's
    Tragedies." Komos 2:9-15.
        Sees Webster's plays as arising out of a world of doubt
    wherein morality and reality collide. Webster seeks to know if
    humanity has any importance when stripped down to its true condi-
    tion. He knows his main characters are guilty, but that seems
    irrelevant. Argues that Webster seeks meaning in the manner of
    life and death: there is comfort to be found in facing despair
    with resolution.

6   DAVISON, RICHARD A.   "John Webster's Moral View Reexamined."
    Moderna Språk 63:213-23.
        Finds a strong current of moral affirmation in Webster's
    works, making them fully tragic. The Duchess of Malfi suggests

four areas of hope or redemption: harmony in nature; unselfish friendship or love; integrity of life; and temperance or moderation. Shows that, while the major characters are devoted to extremes, the dramatist advocates a moderate life.

7   DUVALL, ROBERT F. "The Theater of Judgment." Ph.D. dissertation, Claremont, 220 pp.
      Argues that Jacobean tragedy, unlike medieval plays, shows individuals confronting death without apparent divine intervention. But the secular judgments they face reflect religious language and concepts and thus present a moral ordering. Finds that playwrights like Webster create, in this fashion, a secular drama with a religious cast. See <u>Dissertation Abstracts International</u> 31 (1970): 354A.

8   FORKER, CHARLES R. "A Possible Source for the Ceremony of the Cardinal's Arming in <u>The Duchess of Malfi</u>." <u>Anglia</u> 86:398-403.
      Suggests a previously unnoted source of 3.4. 2-23, in a scene from <u>Lust's Dominion</u>, wherein a Cardinal dedicates himself to revenge. This play is also a possible source of <u>The Devil's Law Case</u>.

9   ____. "'Wit's descant on any plain song': The Prose Characters of John Webster." <u>Modern Language Quarterly</u> 30, no. 1:33-52.
      Notes that despite the interest in characterization in Webster's dramas, there is little real "character" in his "Characters." Surveys the rather complex bibliographical facts surrounding Webster's work in the genre. His "characters" show quite a wide range and include some social history and satire. They also involve rather feeble and baroque experiments with language, and some nice imagery. Finds that all of Webster's "characters" are based on organized distortion, stressing either ideals or flaws and thus depicting mankind as caught between angel and beast.

10 GASSNER, JOHN, and QUINN, EDWARD, eds. <u>The Reader's Encyclopedia of World Drama</u>. New York: Crowell, pp. 908-9.
      In the entry on "John Webster" Quinn notes the dark brooding pessimism of the tragedies and his morbidity, yet finds that, for all its darkness, his work is not to be denied. Also includes specific articles on <u>The White Devil</u> (presented as a brilliant evocation of passion, pride, and death) and <u>The Duchess of Malfi</u> (one of the most moving tragedies in English, which questions the meaning of suffering, death, and evil).

11 GENTILI, VANNA. <u>Le Figure della pazzia nel teatro elisabettiano</u>. Studi e Testi, 11. Lecce: Edizione Milella, 276 pp., passim.
      Studies the lunatic on the Elizabethan stage, citing Webster's characters Cornelia (who can not adjust to a Machiavellian society), the malcontents Flamineo and Bosola, the bedlamites in <u>The Duchess of Malfi</u>, and that play's lycanthropia motif.

12 GENTRY, THOMAS B. "The Dramatic Functions of Rhetorical
    Devices in the Plays of John Webster." Ph.D. dissertation,
    University of Kentucky, 257 pp.
        Discusses Webster's use of rhetorical devices for characteri-
    zation, mood, continuity, satire, argument, wit, and irony, and
    includes tables showing the uses of various rhetorical techniques
    by specific characters. Finds that speeches in The White Devil
    follow the form of the oration, in The Duchess of Malfi, of the
    sermon, epithalamium, meditation, character, and dirge. The
    Devil's Law Case, like the earlier tragedy, is more formal. See
    Dissertation Abstracts International 30 (1969):1980A-81A.

13 GIANNETTI, LOUIS D. "A Contemporary View of The Duchess of
    Malfi." Comparative Drama 3, no. 4:297-307.
        Argues that although the new criticism emphasized the liter-
    ary values of plays, The Duchess of Malfi achieves much of its ef-
    fect through nonverbal means, for example the opening tableau,
    which defines character and relationships. Finds the horrors of
    act 4 a theatricalization of Ferdinand's soul--an illustration of
    Webster's ability to use spectacle to convey complex ideas.

14 GREENFIELD, THELMA N. The Induction in Elizabethan Drama.
    Eugene: University of Oregon Books, 173 pp., passim.
        Cites Webster often, noting his uses of inductions and re-
    lated pageantry. For example, the opening of The Duchess of Malfi
    turns Antonio and Delio into spectators at a processional dumb
    show, while the induction to The Malcontent is a frank and comic
    discussion of the actual circumstances of the production for which
    it was written. See 1952.9 for an earlier version.

15 HART, CLIVE. "Press Variants in The Duchess of Malfi and The
    White Devil." Notes and Queries, n.s. 16:292-93.
        A supplementary table to J.R. Brown's list of press variants
    in the first quarto of The Duchess of Malfi plus two variants based
    upon a collation of The White Devil quartos. See 1954.2, 1956.4,
    and 1962.6 for Brown's original study.

*16 HOWARTH, ROBERT GUY. "The Valiant Scot as a Play by John
    Webster." Bulletin of the English Association, South African
    Branch 9/10:3-8.
        · Source: Mahaney, 1973.23. See 1973.4 for a discussion of
    this thesis.

17 HUNTER, G.K., and HUNTER, S.K., eds. John Webster: A Critical
    Anthology. Baltimore: Penguin, 328 pp.
        Includes only material previously published, often in very
    short excerpts. Fifty-two items are included--all cited elsewhere
    in this work and cross-referenced to this entry--under three head-
    ings: Contemporaneous Criticism; the Developing Debate; and Modern
    Views. Each of these sections has a short introduction, explaining
    critical movements and surveying reactions to Webster's works at
    various periods.

18   KIRSCH, ARTHUR C. "A Caroline Commentary on the Drama."
      Modern Philology 66, no. 3:256-61.
            Reproduces a manuscript (c. 1640) by Abraham Wright contain-
      ing his comments on twenty-eight plays including The Devil's Law
      Case (an indifferent play, with an intricate and faulty plot),
      The Duchess of Malfi (a good work, especially at the conclusion),
      and The White Devil (an indifferent piece to read, "but for ye
      presentments I beeleeve good").

19   KROOK, DOROTHEA. Elements of Tragedy. New Haven: Yale
      University Press, 279 pp., passim.
            Webster is not a major focus of this study, but is cited
      often, e.g., for his creation of heroines capable of "charm" and
      for the development of Bosola as a malcontent.

20   LEECH, CLIFFORD. "The Function of Locality in the Plays of
      Shakespeare and His Contemporaries." In The Elizabethan Theatre
      I. Edited by David Galloway. Toronto: Macmillan, pp. 103-16.
            Notes that in The Duchess of Malfi, all of act 1 is set in
      the Duchess' home territory of Malfi, act 2 alternates between
      Rome and Malfi, 3 and 4 move back to Malfi, where the Duchess is
      imprisoned in her own palace, and act 5 is set in Milan, where no
      character is at home. The White Devil moves from Rome to Padua.
      Both plays move away from a geographical "center."

21   LEVIN, HARRY. "The End of English Drama." Comparative Drama
      3, no. 4:275-81.
            Considers the periods of the development of English drama
      until 1642, and notes that by 1612, Webster felt himself to be
      somewhat old fashioned.

22   LOFTIS, JOHN. "The Duchess of Malfi on the Spanish and English
      Stages." Research Opportunities in Renaissance Drama 12:25-31.
            Compares Lope de Vega's and Webster's versions of the Duchess'
      story. Finds that both require fluid action and involve the pas-
      sage of much time and space. Also, both works exploit the pathos
      of family emotions. But they differ in emotional structure, with
      the Spanish drama seeming a lyrical celebration of love, while
      Webster deals in corruption, sin, and depravity. Also finds much
      rhetorical difference: the Spanish is in the form of set speeches,
      while Webster's language is clipped, cryptic, and colloquial.

23   MAIR, GEORGE H. Modern English Literature, 1450-1900. 3d ed.
      London and New York: Oxford University Press, p. 98.
            Depicts Webster as the most powerful exponent of the melan-
      choly spirit of Jacobean drama, creating tragedies full of lust
      and crime, hate and bitterness. Finds his characters gloomy--
      philosophical murderers, cynics, loving and bad women, and the
      like.

24   MAXWELL, J.C.   "Lodowick Carlell: An Echo of Webster." Notes
     and Queries, n.s. 16:288.
        Observes that Carlell's Osmond The Great Turk echoes The
     White Devil 5.6. 240-41.

25   McPEEK, JAMES A.S.   The Black Book of Knaves and Unthrifts.
     Storrs: University of Connecticut Press, 298 pp., passim.
        Cites Webster, intermittently, e.g., for his use of Robert
     Copland's The Hyeway to the Spyttell Hous (1536-37), which influ-
     ences Monticelso's "Black Book" in The White Devil and also the
     depiction of the house of convertites in that play and the lunatic
     scenes of The Duchess of Malfi.

26   MEHL, DIETER.   "Emblems in English Renaissance Drama."
     Renaissance Drama, n.s. 2:39-57.
        Studies the historical and theoretical links between emblem
     books and plays as verbal and visual mixed presentations. Cites
     Webster for the scene in The White Devil in which Camillo is in-
     formed of his cuckoldry by means of an emblem, and for Flamineo's
     "emblematic" manner of speech. See 1969.29 and 1977.14 for related
     studies of Webster and the emblems.

27   MURRAY, PETER B.   A Study of John Webster.   Studies in English
     Literature, 50. The Hague: Mouton, 274 pp. [Excerpted:
     1975.18.]
        Reviews Webster's obscure life and his amply documented
     literary career. Finds his output slight, but dense. Surveys
     the early, collaborative efforts as prefigurations of larger great
     themes, especially the stoic, Christian strength of the heroine of
     Sir Thomas Wyat. The White Devil depicts the hell men create when
     they isolate themselves--the play presents an entire world of evil,
     often disguised as good. Finds its title based on biblical "white
     devils" as disguised evils. Monticelso is the source of the play's
     diabolical evil, and from him emanate the play's perverse rituals.
     Brachiano and Vittoria, while still evil, are vital. Notes that
     while the play has some morality play features, it is complex,
     especially in the mixed figure of Vittoria, who is both glorious
     and evil. Argues that another important theme of the play is ban-
     ishment--the spiritual result of evil and, in a Christian sense,
     the cause of despair.
        The Duchess of Malfi explores the possibility of goodness in
     life. Finds that while there are many ways in which the worlds of
     the two plays coincide, the Duchess strongly contrasts with
     Vittoria. The latter is presented as embodying the spirit of life
     and love. Her integrity reaps spiritual reward, as demonstrated
     by her great impact on other characters in act 5, after she has
     been killed. The unifying idea of the play is that suffering
     tests good and evil alike. Considers Bosola as a moral commentator,
     with doubts about morality.
        Discusses, more briefly, The Devil's Law Case (which exhibits
     the hand of heaven in this world), A Cure for a Cuckold (which

explores the basis of healthy human relationships), and <u>Appius and
Virginia</u> (a possible collaborative effort with Heywood).

Concludes with a discussion of Webster's overall theme: How
is man to behave in an evil world? Finds Webster's answer suggests
a Christian stoicism in which virtue will be rewarded but probably
not in this world.

Appendices deal with authorship issues.

28   ROWAN, D.F. "The Cockpit-in-Court." In <u>The Elizabethan
     Theatre I</u>. Edited by David Galloway. Toronto: Macmillan,
     pp. 89-102.
     Suggests that Inigo Jones's drawings of "The Cockpit at
Court" Theater probably represent the building in which the King's
Men staged, among other works, <u>The Duchess of Malfi</u>.

29   SCHUMAN, SAMUEL. "The Theater of Fine Devices: Emblems and
     the Emblematic in the Plays of John Webster." Ph.D. disserta-
     tion, Northwestern University, 211 pp.
     Surveys the history of the emblem books and defines the
"emblematic" as an allegorical mixture of the verbal and visual.
Considers the use of verbal imagery of an emblematic nature in
the tragedies, then the use of physical elements of the stage--
props, masks, disguises, etc. Emblematic dumb shows, masques and
stage pictures are also found in the tragedies. Discusses the use
of emblematic materials in <u>The Devil's Law Case</u> and other lesser
works. Concludes that Webster uses the hackneyed morality of the
emblems to reveal and clarify his rejection of conventional ethics.
See 1972.34; 1980.34. See also <u>Dissertation Abstracts International</u>
30 (1970):4425A.

30   THORNTON, R.K. "The Cardinal's Rake in <u>The Duchess of Malfi</u>."
     <u>Notes and Queries</u>, n.s. 16:295-96.
     Shows how Webster altered his source from "sword" to "rake"
to emphasize the concept of sin over that of direct threat.

31   TRAUX, ELIZABETH. "Preview of the Vanishing Hero: A Study of
     the Protagonists in Jacobean Drama." Ph.D. dissertation,
     University of Southern California, 216 pp.
     Considers five plays, inlcuding <u>The Duchess of Malfi</u>, to show
that between 1600 and 1630 heroes diminished in social station.
They also tended to surrender to sexual emotions and were usually
punished, but unrepentant, at the dramas' conclusions. Argues the
Duchess has a heroic spirit but does no acts of glory. See
<u>Dissertation Abstracts International</u> 29 (1969):3159A-60A.

32   WADSWORTH, FRANK W. "'Shorn and Abated'--British Performances
     of <u>The Duchess of Malfi</u>." <u>Theater Survey</u> 10, no. 2:89-104.
     Describes Horne's acting version--he was a serious literary
man and an admirer of the Elizabethans, but his revision is very
weak. Finds Horne changed characters, altered structure, and
neatened language, all with a heavy hand, creating a Victorian,

not a Jacobean, play. Notes that Mrs. Glyn's portrayal of the
Duchess was very popular, creating a heroic, but human, character.

33 WICKHAM, GLYNNE. Shakespeare's Dramatic Heritage. New York:
    Barnes & Noble, pp. 46-48, 50-52, 60-63.
        Suggests that the verbal context in which Flamineo, Brachiano,
    and Vittoria are placed is Rome--and the Garden of Eden. The play,
    thus, is seen as about the collapse of society brought about by
    original sin: all men are guilty, and if governors sin, society
    disintegrates.

                                  1970

1   ALEXANDER, NIGEL. "Intelligence in The Duchess of Malfi." In
    John Webster. Edited by Brian Morris. London: Benn, pp.
    93-112.
        Argues that a central feature of The Duchess of Malfi--and
    of tragedy--is human consciousness of the unique self confronting
    the inevitability of human mortality. The action of the play con-
    cerns two secrets--the marriage of the Duchess, then her murder.
    Although she is, thus, at the center of the plot of the play, it
    is Bosola who interprets the action to the audience. But he fails
    to grasp the Duchess' nobility. Finds Ferdinand's motivation more
    complex than simple sensuality; he needs to destroy the whole world
    of love. Act 5 shows a world of policy from which love, in the
    shape of the Duchess, has been removed.

2   BAKER-SMITH, DOMINIC. "Religion and John Webster." In John
    Webster. Edited by Brian Morris. London: Benn, pp. 205-28.
        Notes that the Reformation brought with it a rise in spiri-
    tual insecurity and an increased concentration on death and damna-
    tion. Webster touches this raw nerve and plays upon this pessimism.
    The White Devil presents the destructive consequences of sin, while
    The Duchess of Malfi concentrates on the virtues of suffering.
    Shows that to Webster the world of human activity or "policy" is
    an arena of diabolic guilt. Religion itself is corrupted, and
    only the Duchess escapes general damnation, through her suffering.

3   BARBOUR, CHARLES MANSON, III. "Pathos and Satire in Jacobean
    Tragedy." Ph.D. dissertation, University of Virginia, 228 pp.
        Discusses the dramatic history of satiric comedy and domestic
    drama as antecedents of Jacobean tragedy, then focuses upon Webster,
    Tourneur, and Middleton. The Duchess of Malfi is an ordeal for the
    audience, as well as the Duchess. The last act is a satiric counter-
    point to the earlier portions.

4   BERLIN, NORMAND. "The Duchess of Malfi: Act V and Genre."
    Genre 3:351-63.
        Finds that act 5 of The Duchess of Malfi combines elements
    of irony and horror comedy with dark seriousness, suggesting that

Webster was not aiming for pure tragedy. Rather, he creates a
distance between us and the act's deaths in keeping with the tragic
satire of the entire work. Webster's play creates a world which is
more absurd than tragic: it is, as a genre, a "comitragedy."

5   BOKLUND, GUNNAR. "The Devil's Law Case--An End or a Beginning?"
    In John Webster. Edited by Brian Morris. London: Benn, pp.
    113-30.
        Finds The Devil's Law Case less imitative than the tragedies,
and unlike them its plot comes from several sources. Asks if The
Devil's Law Case is more Websterian (tragic) or Fletcherian (tragi-
comic)? It can be seen as a more everyday sized--and less perfect
--version of the tragedies.

6   BRENNAN, ELIZABETH M. "'An Understanding Auditory': An Audi-
    ence for John Webster." In John Webster. Edited by Brian Morris.
    London: Benn, pp. 3-19.
        Comments upon the attack on the audience in Webster's address
"To The Reader" in The White Devil. Asks if Webster was dependent
upon the successes of his plays and, if so, did he write to please
the audience? Notes that The White Devil when written was outdated
in its use of the revenge convention. Like the plays of Jonson,
its moral didacticism makes an audience uncomfortable.

7   CAREY, ROBIN. "A Critical Edition of John Webster's The Duchess
    of Malfi." Ph.D. dissertation, University of Washington, 254 pp.
        A modern spelling edition of the 1623 quarto, with critical
notes that focus on meaning, not borrowings. The introduction
focuses upon the play in relation to Renaissance dower and inheritance laws and contemporary concepts of rank. Finds that the play's
thematic structure is based upon a moral vision that is traditional,
but with an emphasis on integrity. See Dissertation Abstracts
International 30 (1970):4937-38A.

8   EWBANK, INGA-STINA. "Webster's Realism, or 'A Cunning Piece
    Wrought Perspective.'" In John Webster. Edited by Brian Morris.
    London: Benn, pp. 157-78.
        "Perspectives" were pictures that only made sense if viewed
from a certain angle. Argues that The Duchess of Malfi is organized
in this fashion, as are the character relationships and plot line
of The White Devil, but the earlier work never snaps into the right
view--we are simply left "in a mist." In the second tragedy,
though, jerks of plot produce a final clear vision. We see the
play most clearly at the moment when Ferdinand sees the dead
Duchess as his sister. Finds that Bosola's verbal contortions
and the simple language of the Duchess reinforce this "perspective"
effect.

9   FEATHER, JOHN, introd. John Webster. "The White Devil"--1612.
    Menston: Scolar Press, 92 pp.
        A facsimile reprint of a Bodleian library copy of the play.
The brief introduction describes the text and printer.

10   FOAKES, R.A. "Tragedy at the Children's Theatres after 1600:
      A Challenge to the Adult Stage." In Elizabethan Theater II.
      Edited by David Galloway. Toronto: Macmillan, pp. 37-59.
          Notes that Webster's additions to The Malcontent were de-
      signed for that play's reintroduction at the Globe by an adult
      acting troupe.

11   GLIER, INGEBORG. "The White Devil." In Das englische Drama:
      Vom Mittalater bis zur Gegenwart. Edited by Dieter Mehl.
      Dusseldorf: A. Bagel, pp. 291-306.
          Introduces the play, emphasizing its place within the con-
      text of seventeenth-century drama. (This entire collection is
      summarized in English and American Studies in German 3:15-16.)

12   GUNBY, D.C. "The Duchess of Malfi: A Theological Approach."
      In John Webster. Edited by Brian Morris. London: Benn, pp.
      178-204.
          Contends that The Duchess of Malfi is neither melodrama nor
      a drama of existential despair, but didactic and fideistic. Thus,
      Ferdinand is a demonic and antireligious figure and the play be-
      comes a conflict between good and evil, with the Duchess established
      as an emblem of virtue. The goal of the evil characters is to bring
      the Duchess to despair. In this role, Bosola functions as both
      tormentor and comforter, directing the thoughts of his victim to-
      wards eternity. As she attains grace, her brothers are doomed.
      Sees Antonio, seeking patience rather than salvation, as represent-
      ing the limits of stoicism. Concludes that the play as a whole
      asserts the power of God to destroy evil.

13   _____. "Webster: Another Borrowing from Jonson's Sejanus?"
      Notes and Queries, n.s. 17, no. 6:214.
          Suggests Webster may have borrowed from Sejanus Ferdinand's
      rebuke to the courtiers in 1.1. of The Duchess of Malfi.

14   GURR, ANDREW. The Shakespearean Stage, 1574-1642. Cambridge:
      Cambridge University Press, pp. 62, 149, 153, 169.
          Notes how Webster's "character" of a good actor reinforces
      Heywood's Apology in praising the moral potential of the theater.
      Also comments on Webster's relation with his audience (not very
      good) and includes his works in an appended checklist.

*15   HARTWIG, HEINZ. "Der Ausländer als Schurke im englischen Drama
      bis 1642." Ph.D. dissertation, University of Graz.
          Summarized in English and American Studies in German 3:33-35.

16   HENKE, JAMES. "Elizabethan-Jacobean Dramatic Bawdy: A Glossary
      and Critical Essay." Ph.D. dissertation, University of
      Washington, 303 pp. [Published as 1974.12.]
          Part 1 is a glossary of the bawdy wit of non-Shakespearean
      dramatists. Part 2 examines the dramatic function of that bawdy,
      covering twenty-eight plays with special emphasis on The White

Devil and A Trick to Catch the Old One. See Dissertation
Abstracts International 32 (1971):389A.

17   HERNDL, GEORGE C. The High Design: English Renaissance
     Tragedy and the Natural Law. Lexington: University of
     Kentucky Press, pp. 160-217.
          Argues that the ultimate reason for the darkness of Webster's
     plays is the absence of traditional natural law from his world-view.
     Virtue thus becomes a code morality, abstracted from--and often
     opposed to--nature. Webster's Machiavellian malcontents see and
     explain the world as evil. Finds in The White Devil a duel of
     villains, in which Vittoria and Brachiano respond to the world's
     lawlessness with a wild courage and grandeur. In The Duchess of
     Malfi there remain vestiges of the notion of the Duchess as a
     sinner and the action of the play as her retribution, but the play
     does not finally have this effect on us. Rather, we perceive more
     of a study in Renaissance psychology, especially the melancholic
     humor.

18   KOHLER, RICHARD C. "The Fortune Contract and Vitruvian
     Symmetry." Shakespeare Studies 6:311-26.
          Tests Frances Yates's theories of theater construction, based
     on the architectural principles of the Roman Vitruvius, using con-
     temporary descriptions, sketches, etc. Cites Webster briefly and
     in passing.

19   LAGARDE, FERNAND. "The White Devil: Esquisse de panorama
     critique." Etudes Anglaises 23, no. 4:415-24.
          Surveys Webster studies, in these categories: bibliographies,
     editions, background and sources, scholarship. A very selective,
     annotated listing.

20   MOORE, DON D. "The Duchess of Malfi by John Webster and R.H.
     Horne." In Essays in Honor of Esmond Linworth Marilla. Edited
     by Thomas A. Kirby and William J. Olive. Louisiana State
     University Studies, Humanistic Series, 19. Baton Rouge:
     Louisiana State University Press, pp. 166-73.
          Reports that Horne's version of Webster was quite popular
     c. 1850-75. The adaptation is not imperfectly Websterian; it is
     just wretched. There are several alterations (e.g., Bosola is a
     weaker character) and most of the play's sex is eliminated. Con-
     tends that Horne translated sting into sentimentality.

21   MORRIS, BRIAN, ed. John Webster. London: Benn, 228 pp.
          Includes 1970.1-2, 5-6, 8, 12, 22, 27-28, and 31.

22   MULRYNE, J.R. "Webster and the Uses of Tragicomedy." In John
     Webster. Edited by Brian Morris. London: Benn, pp. 131-55.
          Defines "tragicomedy" as neither comic scenes in tragedy,
     nor the opposite, but plays in which neither dominates; finds
     only Marlowe and Webster use tragicomedy thus defined. Contends

that Webster's plays were written in the service of no absolute,
and therefore in The White Devil, we can delight in the main characters yet affirm the morals they deny. Webster's deliberate culti-
vation of this moral ambivalence leads to the importance of self-
conscious theatricality and role playing, with Flamineo representing
the audience's open-mindedness to the action of the drama. Compares
the discontinuity of The Duchess of Malfi to that of Marat/Sade—a
deliberate jangle of styles, for which the Duchess provides the
only center.

23   ____, ed. John Webster. The White Devil. Lincoln: University
of Nebraska Press, 158 pp.
    In the introduction considers the text, sources, and histori-
cal background of the play. Finds the play thematically difficult
—it is unconventional and seems jerky and hard to define. But its
fragmentary action and language correspond to the moral anarchy it
depicts, in which conventional morals are overwhelmed by a primi-
tive value system of strength, cunning, and self-assertion.

24   NELSON, CONNY. "T.S. Eliot, Michelangelo, and John Webster."
Research Studies 38, no. 4:304-6.
    Notes that in the "Michelangelo couplet" of Prufrock, Eliot
alludes also to the tragic vision of Webster.

25   PRATT, SAMUEL M. "Webster's The White Devil, V. iv. 115."
Explicator 29, no. 2:Item 11.
    When Flamineo speaks of the "mase" of conscience, does he
mean "maze" (as bewilderment, as most editors believe)? Contends
it is more likely he means "mace"—the blow of conscience.

26   SAMPSON, GEORGE, and CHURCHILL, R.C. The Concise Cambridge
History of English Literature. Cambridge: Cambridge University
Press, pp. 267-69.
    A revision of 1941.15, with minor alterations.

27   SMITH, A.J. "The Power of The White Devil." In John Webster.
Edited by Brian Morris. London: Benn, pp. 69-90.
    Asks what makes the play more than a collection of theatrical
coups. Webster's speeches seem not to build a unity but to put in-
congruent things next to each other. Suggests that Webster is try-
ing to depict a world of random violence and ad hoc motivations in
which no absolutes are allowed to stand. Scenes of abrupt, shock-
ing violence are a principle of construction.

28   THOMPSON, PETER. "Webster and the Actor." In John Webster.
Edited by Brian Morris. London: Benn, pp. 21-44.
    Asks if the audience for Webster is growing—and what is
that audience? Surveys some reactions to twentieth-century productions. One problem is the constant comparison of Shakespeare
and Webster. Among the problems for actors: unclear character
motivations, and the withholding of information about the off-stage

lives of the characters. Considers special acting problems of
The White Devil.

29   TOKSON, ELLIOT H. "The Popular Image of the Black Man in
      Elizabethan Drama, 1550-1688." Ph.D. dissertation, Columbia
      University, 295 pp.
          Finds that the Elizabethan image of blacks was negative--
      they are depicted as deceitful, sexual, savage. Webster, along
      with most other dramatists, contributed to this negative, dehuman-
      ized, treatment. See Dissertation Abstracts International 32
      (1971):403-4A.

30   WADSWORTH, FRANK. "Webster, Horne, and Mrs. Stowe: American
      Performances of The Duchess of Malfi." Theater Survey 11:
      151-66.
          Reports that the first American production of The Duchess
      of Malfi was in 1857 in San Francisco, in Horne's version. It was
      an elaborate production, beginning a tradition of visual effects
      such as tableaux of the Duchess and Antonio in heaven. The most
      important influence on American performances of the play was prob-
      ably the success of Uncle Tom's Cabin.

31   WARREN, ROGER. "The Duchess of Malfi on Stage." In John
      Webster. Edited by Brian Morris. London: Benn, pp. 45-68.
          Suggests that the Duchess can be depicted as vivacious and
      witty, even urbane. The early scenes between her and Antonio
      should convey a genuine courtliness. Later, the scenes of corrup-
      tion and torture have fire and vigor. Argues a performance must
      convey this variety within the play. Also notes that Ferdinand
      must be played as a man of violent contrasts, and that the scene
      of the Duchess' death conveys both the fraility of humanity and
      an affirmation of human worth.

32   YOUNG, STEVEN C. "The Induction Plays of the Tudor and Stuart
      Drama." Ph.D. dissertation, University of California, Berkeley,
      399 pp. [Published as 1974.28.]
          Describes the use of the induction in fifty-nine English
      plays from 1497 to 1642. Notes several types of inductions, in-
      cluding the "extra-dramatic" as in The Malcontent. See
      Dissertation Abstracts International 32 (1971):991-92A.

                              1971

1   BAWCUTT, N.W. "Don Quixote, Part I and The Duchess of Malfi."
      Modern Language Review 66:488-91.
          Reports that an image from The Duchess of Malfi that had
      been noted in part 2 of Cervantes's work is also found in part 1.
      Several other items are borrowed, skillfully, from Cervantes.

2   BENTLEY, G.E. The Profession of Dramatist in Shakespeare's
     Time, 1590-1642. Princeton: Princeton University Press, pp.
     197-263.
          Notes, in this general description of the life of Elizabethan
     dramatists, that Webster's collaborative record indicates he was
     clearly a professional, and discusses the revisions of The Duchess
     of Malfi.

3   BERGERON, DAVID. English Civic Pageantry, 1558-1642. Columbia:
     University of South Carolina Press, pp. 201-6.
          Considers Webster in the section on Lord Mayor's shows,
     specifically the 1624 Monuments of Honour written for the instal-
     lation of Sir John Gore. Finds this a costly and opulent show,
     thematically unified by a focus on "honour" presented through
     historical personages, including the unique inclusion of poets.

4   BRODWIN, LEONORA L. Elizabethan Love Tragedy, 1587-1624. New
     York: New York University Press, pp. 253-307.
          Finds the characters in The White Devil more satiric than
     tragic. Webster employs Machiavellian satirists as antagonists
     to worldly lovers; thus, the tragic and satiric voices clash.
     Suggests that Vittoria and Brachiano seek to find compassionate
     fulfillment in a corrupt world and thus feel themselves innocent.
     They are measured not in terms of good and evil, but of integrity.
     The Zanche-Flamineo-Francisco affair is a parody of the genuinely
     redemptive quality of the central love story. But true Christian
     action proves finally impossible in a corrupt world, and only
     individual integrity provides final value. Argues that in The
     Duchess of Malfi, however, virtue replaces virtu, but the Duchess
     has less vitality than Vittoria. The play is a true tragedy of
     worldly love. The Duchess seeks moral health through love, while
     Bosola contends that love is meaningless. But the Duchess main-
     tains her identity through her faith in love, and Bosola is finally
     converted. Concludes that, in Webster's tragic world, men achieve
     dignity by attempting to realize a personal love within a malevolent
     universe.

5   GOREAU, ELOISE K. "Integrity of Life: Allegorical Imagery in
     the Plays of John Webster." Ph.D. dissertation, Rutgers
     University, 263 pp. [Published as 1974.10.]
          Suggests that "integrity of life" is the principal theme of
     Webster's two tragedies and they are set within a context of
     Christian orthodoxy, as revealed in the use of medieval allegori-
     cal imagery. Argues that the moral actions of princes provide the
     organization of The White Devil and The Duchess of Malfi. Concludes
     that Webster's imagery suggests he accepted the world view of
     Anglican Christianity with its division between the world and the
     spirit. See Dissertation Abstracts International 32 (1971):919A.

6   GUNBY, D.C. Webster: The White Devil. Studies in English
     Literature, no. 45. London: E. Arnold, 64 pp.

Offers a close, critical reading of The White Devil. Finds
Webster a slow, careful writer, true to these classical precepts:
truth of argument; dignity of persons; gravity and height of elocu-
tion; fullness and frequency of sentence. Suggests that his chief
themes are the illusory nature of courtly glory and the eventual
fall of evil. Suggests the play shows the final fall of evil and
includes a hopeful symbol of regeneration in Giovanni.

7   JONES, ELDRED. The Elizabethan Image of Africa. Folger Booklets
    on Tudor and Stuart Civilization. Charlottesville: University
    of Virginia Press for the Folger Shakespeare Library, pp. 45-48.
        Cites Zanche in The White Devil as a popular type and also
    notes that play's emblem of the Aetheopian washed white.

8   KING, THOMAS J. Shakespearean Staging, 1599-1642. Cambridge,
    Mass.: Harvard University Press, 163 pp., passim.
        Cites Webster often, giving publication data, textual notes,
    and printing information for several plays but not discussing their
    staging. This work is largely a modern playlist.

9   LAGARDE, FERNAND. "Webster et The Merchant of Venice." Caliban
    8:3-11.
        Identifies Webster's extensive borrowings (including place
    names, similar characters, the use of the University of Padua,
    central trial scenes, plus many verbal echoes) from The Merchant
    of Venice.

10 LANAHAN, WILLIAM F., Rev. "Rhetorical Characterization in
    Elizabethan Drama." Ph.D. dissertation, Fordham University,
    280 pp.
        Discusses Webster's utilization of rhetorical guidelines for
    the composition of characters. Suggests he created his own tri-
    partite format for characterization. See Dissertation Abstracts
    International 32 (1971):922-23A.

11 LEVER, J.W. The Tragedy of State. London: Methuen, pp. 78-97.
    [Excerpted: 1975.18.]
        Argues that The White Devil is well designed and constructed,
    with many familiar revenge play motifs, but also includes a current
    of sympathy that flows in the opposite direction: wrongdoers have
    color and vitality while the revengers are corrupt. Suggests that
    while the play has characters to admire, it has no heroes. Finds
    that The Duchess of Malfi reshapes the earlier play but with sharp
    differences. It is more closely related to English court politics.
    The Duchess and Antonio are not guilty of violating order, and the
    violence and evil are more personal. Identifies the theme of the
    play as the effect of power on the human heart and mind. It is
    the last of the great Jacobean tragedies of state.

12 LYONS, BRIDGET G. Voices of Melancholy. New York: Barnes &
    Noble, 189 pp., passim.

Cites Webster throughout, e.g., Flamineo and Bosola are men
of broken fortune, Bosola as a melancholy tool-villain type, and
Flamineo as a malcontent satirist/cynic. These characters are not
only manipulators but potential heroes, connecting melancholy and
satire.

*13   OKADA, YOICHI. "A Note on 'Ambiguity' in Webster's The Duchess
      of Malfi." Studies in English Literature (Japan) 48, no. 1:3-15.
      Source: MLA International Bibliography for 1972 1:Item 4396.

14   PERRY, GEORGE F. "A Study of the Image of Man in Jacobean City
      Comedy." Ph.D. dissertation, Fordham University, 178 pp.
      Notes that in city comedies, including the "Ho" plays, hus-
bands and wives engage in extramarital affairs, as upper-social-
strata men direct their lives to the flesh and to finances, and
lower class folk are bawds and knaves. All men, thus, are sensual
and materialistic. Finds this genre combines satire with realism.
See Dissertation Abstracts International 32 (1971):2067A.

15   PFEFFERKORN, ELI. "Irrational Man in the Jacobean Drama and in
      the Theatre of the Absurd." Ph.D. dissertation, Brown University,
      139 pp.
      Focuses on The Duchess of Malfi and The White Devil through-
out and especially in the final chapter, where the tragedies are
compared to The Birthday Party and The Homecoming by Pinter. Finds
both dramatists deny the possibility of rational motivations to
their characters and depict humans as savages. But Webster was
still bound by the law of causality and gives his characters a
gloss of verisimilitude; Pinter doesn't. Concludes that both
dramatists depict mankind as mocked by the heavens and crushed by
the forces of earth. The spiritual anguish of our times echoes
that found in the works of Jacobean artists. See Dissertation
Abstracts International 39 (1978):6746A.

16   ROLLE, DIETRICH. Ingenious Structure: Die dramatische Funktion
      der Sprache in der Tragödie der Shakespearezeit. Heidelberg:
      C. Winter, pp. 227-38.
      Focuses on the use of chains of imagery in Jacobean tragedies
to create artistic unity. The Duchess of Malfi uses images to create atmosphere and to mark changes of mood. Argues that Webster
also uses imagery to foreshadow the doom of his characters long
before they know it, e.g., through sinister images in opening
scenes and the turning of verbal imagery into actual physical
reality.

*17   YAMADA, AKIHIRO. "Eliot and Webster." English Studies (Japan)
      52:41-43.
      Source: MLA International Bibliography for 1971 1:Item 6264.

1972

1 AYERS, PHILIP J. "Degrees of Heresy: Justified Revenge and
Elizabethan Narratives." Studies in Philology 69, no. 4:461-74.
Discusses the Elizabethan perception of the morality of revenge as depicted in works including Webster's tragedies. Finds
that while most revengers were considered villains some were clearly presented as heroic and praiseworthy. Audiences, therefore,
were prepared for either possibility.

2 BATTENHOUSE, ROY. "Recent Studies in Elizabethan and Jacobean
Drama." Studies in English Literature 12:391-428.
A review article that mentions several studies that include
Webster material. Focuses especially on Ansari's book on imagery
(1969.2), which suggests Webster's images imply that human misery
is the result of the violation of traditional Christian morality.

3 BERGERON, DAVID M. "Medieval Drama and Tudor-Stuart Civic
Pageantry." Journal of Medieval and Renaissance Studies 2:
279-93.
Discusses the continuation of medieval dramatic traditions
(processional form, allegorical content, emblematic costume and
properties) in Renaissance street pageants, such as Webster's
Lord Mayor's show.

4 _____. Twentieth-Century Criticism of English Masques, Pageants,
and Entertainments: 1550-1642. San Antonio: Trinity University
Press, pp. ix-xi, 29-40.
Cites Monument of Honour (within the format of a general
checklist).

5 BERRY, RALPH T. The Art of John Webster. Oxford: Clarendon
Press, 174 pp. [Excerpted: 1975.18.]
Focuses upon the general theme in Webster's works that the
law must oppose evil. Argues that Webster criticism has been too
concerned with the issue of decadence; actually Webster's works
are "baroque" (depicting extreme states of emotion). Finds a number of analogies with the baroque visual arts, e.g., sensational-
ism, irony, grotesquerie, density of imagery, and the like. Image
clusters in The Duchess of Malfi, The White Devil and The Devil's
Law Case (the "most skillful" of the three plays) illuminate themes
of law and evil. In The White Devil, finds images of animality,
disease, devils, Machiavellianism, and the like. In The Duchess
of Malfi, each individual must generate his or her own values:
the knowledge discovered in the play is thus existential. Sees
The Devil's Law Case as satiric tragicomedy in which the themes
of law and evil are literal, not metaphorical. It depicts a conflict between civil law and natural law. Reviewed: 1973.6.

6 BODTKE, RICHARD. Tragedy and the Jacobean Temper: The Major
Plays of John Webster. Jacobean Drama Studies, 2. Salzburg:

Institut für Englische Sprache und Literatur, Universität
Salzburg, 246 pp.
Published version of 1957.4.

7   BRAENDEL, DORIS B. "The Limits of Clarity: Lyly's Endymion,
     Bronzino's Allegory of Venus and Cupid, Webster's The White
     Devil, and Boticelli's Prima-vera." Hartford Studies in
     Literature 4:197-215.
         Finds Boticelli and Lyly alike in structure, balance, char-
     acterization, and "color" of language. The prose-like poetry of
     The White Devil is presented as a contrast--irregular, images of
     violence, constriction, darkness, shadows, harshness, and savagery
     --as in Bronzino's painting. Sees the Jacobeans as more complex,
     closer to chaos, slightly pornographic, and of ambiguous morality.

8   CAMOIN, FRANÇOIS ANDRE. The Revenge Convention in Tourneur,
     Webster, and Middleton. Jacobean Drama Studies, 20. Salzburg:
     Institut für Englische Sprache und Literatur, Universität
     Salzburg, 141 pp.
         Published version of 1968.7.

9   DWYER, WILLIAM G. "A Study of John Webster's Use of Renaissance
     Natural and Moral Philosophy." Ph.D. dissertation, Syracuse
     University, 249 pp. [Published as 1973.5.]
         Investigates the relationship between Webster's seemingly
     ambiguous character portrayals and the religious and philosophical
     basis of his moral vision. Finds character motivations can be
     explained, in terms of Renaissance physiological psychology, as
     part of a pattern of the investigation of the human condition with-
     in the framework of humanistic and Christian ideals. Webster uses
     tragedy as a negative moral exemplum. In accord with the conserva-
     tive Christianity of his time, Webster believed in God's redemptive
     grace, complemented by human reason and faith. See Dissertation
     Abstracts International 32 (1972):4560A.

10   EMERSON, KATHY L. "Controlled Lighting at the Blackfriars'
     Theatre: The Evidence of John Webster's The Duchess of Malfi."
     Renaissance Papers, 1972, pp. 11-16.
         Finds that playhouse windows at indoor theaters could be
     shuttered prior to "nocturnal" plays and scenes, such as The
     Duchess of Malfi 2.3 (Bosola and Antonio's nighttime meeting),
     4.1 (Ferdinand's visit to the Duchess), and 5.2 (which employed
     torches, lanterns, etc., carried on and off stage).

11   FORKER, CHARLES R. "John Webster." Études Anglaises 25, no.
     2:286-89.
         A review article on Lagarde's John Webster (1968.21). Finds
     the book encyclopedic, even elephantine, asking if Webster merits
     such an extended commentary. Notes Lagarde's criticism is well
     balanced, historically oriented, conservative. The book's range
     is impressive--from biography through descriptive bibliography,

to scholarly discussion of thematic material. Finds Lagarde particularly sensitive to Webster's treatment of female characters.

12   FUZIER, JEAN. "La Tragédie de vengeance élisabéthaine et le
      théâtre dans le théâtre." _Revue des Sciences Humaines_ 145
      (January-March):17-33.
             Finds Webster's use of "theater within theater" unique.
      Discusses the spouse murder dumb shows and the scene of Brachiano's
      murder in _The White Devil_, and from _The Duchess of Malfi_, the dumb
      show horrors used to torture the Duchess and the masque of bed-
      lamites.

13   GRANT, GEORGE. "The Imagery of Witchcraft in _The Duchess of
      Malfi_." Ph.D. dissertation, Stanford University, 291 pp.
             Notes that while Webster is often praised for his imagery,
      frequently the images praised are in scenes condemned for sensa-
      tionalism. In _The Duchess of Malfi_, demonology and witchcraft are
      sources of the most sustained image pattern, which prepares us for
      the grotesque horrors of act 4. Ferdinand and the Cardinal attempt
      to damn the Duchess and instead entrap themselves, while their
      sister is scourged into salvation. Bosola is seen as representing
      the power of witchery to corrupt normal men. See _Dissertation
      Abstracts International_ 32 (1972):5737A.

14   GRIFFIN, ROBERT P. _John Webster: Politics and Tragedy_.
      Jacobean Drama Studies, 12. Salzburg: Institut für Sprache
      und Literatur, Universität Salzburg, 1979 pp.
             Published version of 1966.10.

15   GUNBY, D.C. "'In Her Effected': A Websterian Crux Resolved?"
      English Language Notes 10, no. 5:107-10.
             Suggests that the use of the word "effected" in Monticelso's
      prosecution of Vittoria in _The White Devil_'s trial scene probably
      means "perfected" and has a sexual innuendo.

16   _____, ed. _Three Plays: "The White Devil," "The Duchess of
      Malfi," and "The Devil's Law Case." By John Webster_. Baltimore:
      Penguin, 458 pp.
             Includes an introduction, texts, commentary, and notes. In
      the introduction suggests that _The Devil's Law Case_ is a deeply
      serious and underevaluated work. It demonstrates Webster's slow
      and careful composition. Argues that Webster's world was one of
      change and pessimism. His characters become lost in this world,
      but he does not. Finds that Webster believes in a moral, God-
      centered cosmos, in which good and evil struggle. In _The White
      Devil_, he presents evil-doers, in _The Duchess of Malfi_, more
      balanced characters, and _The Devil's Law Case_, a study of the
      redemption of Romelio.

17   HART, CLIVE, ed. _John Webster. The Duchess of Malfi_.
      Fountainwell Drama Series. Edinburgh: Oliver & Boyd, 144 pp.

Includes a critical introduction, textual note, commentary,
bibliography and glossary. In the introduction presents the facts
of Webster biography, the history behind Webster's plot, and the
play's literary sources. Finds the Duchess and Antonio not wholly
good--like everything else in the play, their appearances can be
deceptive. Also unclear are Ferdinand's motives. The Cardinal,
however, is a picture of pure, cold reason--a contrast to
Ferdinand's passion. Finds Bosola the play's most complex and
interesting character. He is highly ambiguous and not perfectly
brought-off since his avenging actions and his moral sense do not
always mesh. Argues that the play builds careful image networks
and is generally well constructed, but the conclusion of the play
does not live up to its early scenes.

18   HAWKINS, HARRIETT. Likenesses of Truth in Elizabethan and
      Restoration Drama. Oxford: Clarendon Press, pp. 15-17.
         Uses The Duchess of Malfi as an illustration of the way
modern critical dicta force readers to speak against their feel-
ings--we like the Duchess, but feel she has to be condemned for
violating degree and order. Contends that actually the tragedy
defends integrity and questions degree so that we are tending to
damn the Duchess for what Webster praised in her.

19   HOY, CYRUS. "Artifice and Reality and the Decline of the
      Jacobean Drama." Research Opportunities in Renaissance Drama
      13/14:169-80.
         Begins by defining the "baroque" as real feelings lavished
on unreal objects: in the case of Webster, intense feelings
aroused by sinister Italianate plots. Argues that, in general,
the plots of Jacobean tragedy are highly artificial, Senecan, and
based on stereotyped villainy. Finds that the artifice of Webster's
works in particular is clogged with moral parables and exotic
imagery unloaded from his commonplace book, yet his sensational
scenes are charged with real feeling.

20   _____. "On Editing Elizabethan Plays." Renaissance and
      Reformation 8:90-99.
         Includes a lament on the passing of the older sort of literary
editor who combined textual scholarship with commentary in one-man
versions such as Lucas's edition of Webster.

21   HUFFMAN, CLIFFORD, comp. "Tudor and Stuart Drama: A Bibli-
      ography, 1966-1971." Educational Theater Journal 27:169-78.
         Supplements Ribner's bibliography (1966.21). Includes
general studies, then works on specific dramatists including
Webster (pp. 177-78).

22   HUNTER, G.K. "Further Borrowings in Webster and Marston."
      Notes and Queries 19:452-53.
         Cites four Websterian borrowings: from Tacitus's Agricola,
Marston's Antonio's Revenge, Sylvester's Du Bartas, and Ovid's
Amores.

23 HUSSY, MAURICE. <u>The World of Shakespeare and His Contemporaries:</u>
    <u>A Visual Approach</u>. New York: Viking, 136 pp., passim.
        Mentions Webster--very passingly--in a study of the relation-
    ship between the visual arts and the drama. Examines maps, icons,
    emblems, paintings, and the like.

24 JURIS, ALLEN S. "Satire and the Problem of Evil in Jacobean
    Drama." Ph.D. dissertation, University of Wisconsin, Madison,
    182 pp.
        Argues Jacobean drama is distinguished from Elizabethan by
    its emphasis on the disintegration of the old social order. This
    leads to a revival of satire. Finds in Webster that the satiric
    condition is identical with the moral condition of the world.
    Bosola and Flamineo turn the satiric impulse into a psychological
    motivation. See <u>Dissertation Abstracts International</u> 33 (1972):
    725A.

25 KELLCHER, VICTOR M.K. "Notes on <u>The Duchess of Malfi</u>." <u>Unisa</u>
    <u>English Studies</u> 10, no. 2:11-15.
        Argues that criticism of <u>The Duchess of Malfi</u> simplifies it;
    actually the play is complex and subtle. Suggests that most of
    the major characters are difficult and ambiguous, including the
    Duchess.

26 KIRSCH, ARTHUR C. <u>Jacobean Drama Perspectives</u>. Charlottesville:
    University Press of Virginia, pp. 97-111.
        Sees <u>The White Devil</u> as deliberately disjunctive and non-
    continuous, thus calling attention to itself--we always watch
    observers observe. Also notes that this play, unlike <u>The Duchess</u>
    <u>of Malfi</u>, offers no clear moral guidelines.

27 KRAMER, MARY D. "The Roman Catholic Cleric on the Jacobean
    Stage." <u>Costerus</u> 2:109-17.
        Discusses the Cardinal in <u>The Duchess of Malfi</u> as an example
    of a cleric punished for the selling of his soul. Monticelso is
    another of this very popular type. Contrasts the earnest, righteous
    and dedicated Capuchin Friar in <u>The Devil's Law Case</u>.

28 LUISI, DAVID. "The Function of Bosola in <u>The Duchess of Malfi</u>."
    <u>English Studies</u> 53:509-13.
        Argues that Bosola's villainy seems inconsistent with his
    constant references to morals. Suggests that Webster has suspended
    psychology in order to affirm moral values so that he speaks through
    Bosola even before Bosola's repentance, thus rendering him somewhat
    inconsistent.

29 LYNCH, ROBERT E. "Popular Insurrection in Elizabethan and
    Jacobean Drama." Ph.D. dissertation, New York University,
    283 pp.
        Finds <u>Sir Thomas Wyat</u>, at the end of the Elizabethan period,
    has a less hostile view of insurrection than did earlier plays.

Moreover, <u>Appius and Virginia</u>, in 1625, depicts a total revolt
against a corrupt government with complete sympathy. Suggests
that the increasing acceptance of popular revolution was prophetic.
See <u>Dissertation Abstracts International</u> 32 (1972):5744A.

30   MOODY, JO ANN. "Britomart, Imogen, Perdita, The Duchess of
      Malfi: A Study of Women in English Renaissance Literature."
      Ph.D. dissertation, University of Minnesota, 244 pp.
           Notes that many Renaissance heroines united "female" traits
      (chastity, generosity, affection) with "masculine" adventuresome-
      ness and independence. The Duchess shows how these qualities can
      be possessed within a world of depravity. Notes the obvious in-
      fluence of the image of Queen Elizabeth on these figures. See
      <u>Dissertation Abstracts International</u> 33 (1972):1146-47A.

31   PINEAS, RAINER. <u>Tudor and Early Stuart Anti-Catholic Drama</u>.
      Bibliotheca Humanistica et Reformatorica, 5. Nieuwkoop: De
      Graff, pp. 12, 39-40.
           Finds <u>Sir Thomas Wyat</u> attempts to glorify a hero of
      Protestantism and nationalism.

32   SALOMON, BROWNELL. "Visual and Aural Signs in the Performed
      English Renaissance Play." <u>Renaissance Drama</u> 5:143-69.
           Attempts to apply semiology to presensational as well as
      rhetorical elements of the drama. Notes various types of theatri-
      cal "signs"--vocal tone, gesture, masque, make-up, music, sound
      effects, and the like, with examples from Webster and others.

33   SCHNEIDER, EVELYN S. "I. Glories and Glow Worms: A Study of
      the Juxtaposition of Opposites in Three Plays by John Webster;
      II. The Changing Image of Charles Brockden Brown as Seen by
      American Critics from 1815 to the Present; III. Action, Motion,
      and Being: The Technique of Kinesis in the Poems of e. e.
      cummings." Ph.D. dissertation, Rutgers University, 190 pp.
           Finds Webster's style juxtaposes opposites, such as virtue
      and corruption, in verbal imagery, stage emblems, action, and
      character. Illustrates this idea in the two tragedies and <u>The
      Devil's Law Case</u>, with special emphasis on act 4 of <u>The Duchess
      of Malfi</u> which features a heightened contrast between good and
      evil. See <u>Dissertation Abstracts International</u> 32 (1972):6943A.

34   SCHUMAN, SAMUEL. "The Ring and the Jewel in Webster's Tragedies.
      <u>Texas Studies in Literature and Language</u> 14:253-68. [Revised
      version of a section of 1969.29.]
           Finds that the emblematic use of rings and jewels in <u>The White
      Devil</u> and <u>The Duchess of Malfi</u> highlights, through the ambiguity of
      these symbols, the complex relationship between virtue and vice in
      Webster's tragedies. Argues that both the verbal and visual uses
      of these motifs ultimately suggest that Webster's universe is moral-
      ly chaotic. See 1980.34 for a related piece.

35   SHIRLEY, FRANCIS A., ed. <u>John Webster</u>. "The Devil's Law Case."
     Regents Renaissance Drama Series. Lincoln: University of
     Nebraska Press, 149 pp.
          In the short introduction to this edition, includes a dis-
     cussion of the date and stage history of the play. Argues that
     Webster seems to handle tragicomedy uneasily and with imprecise
     control, yet the play remains fascinating. Suggests that the main
     thread of the work is the scheming and downfall of Romelio, who
     dominates our interest. Reviewed: 1974.4.

36   STEADMAN, JOHN M. "Iconography and Methodology in Renaissance
     Dramatic Study: Some Caveats." <u>Shakespearean Research
     Opportunities</u> 7-8:39-52.
          Suggests that amateurs can easily overread emblematic and
     iconological possibilities in plays by Webster and his fellows.

37   _____. "Iconography and Renaissance Drama: Ethical and
     Mythological Themes." <u>Research Opportunities in Renaissance
     Drama</u> 13-14:73-122.
          Notes that Renaissance poets and painters inherited the same
     ethical and mythological traditions, and this spurred their rela-
     tionship as "sister arts." They also shared critical perspectives
     (e.g., Horatian goals), devices (e.g., allegory), and an interest
     in "synaesthetic" art forms such as emblems.

38   STEARNS, STEPHEN J. "A Critical Edition of Webster's <u>The White
     Devil</u>." Ph.D. dissertation, University of Washington, 266 pp.
          Focuses upon the actor, director, and reader. Finds that
     the play's moral vision is unified around the concept of an ordered
     universe governed by the special providence of a just God. Com-
     ments on the complexity and brilliance of Webster's dramaturgy,
     especially in sustaining the suspense of the last act. See
     <u>Dissertation Abstracts International</u> 33 (1972):441-42A.

39   STERNLICHT, SANFORD. <u>John Webster's Imagery and the Webster
     Canon</u>. Jacobean Drama Studies, 1. Salzburg: Institut für
     Englische Sprache und Literatur, Universität Salzburg, 193 pp.
          Published version of 1963.21.

40   TAMAIZUMI, UASUO. "Guise and Elizabethan Dramatists." <u>Studies
     in English Literature</u> (Japan), nos. 201-2, pp. 181-98.
          Cites Webster's lost play, but mostly discusses Marlowe and
     Chapman's <u>Bussy</u>.

41   WICKHAM, GLYNNE. <u>Early English Stages</u>. Vol. 2, <u>1576-1660</u>.
     London: Routledge & Kegan Paul, pt. 1:407 pp.; pt. 2:266 pp.,
     passim.
          Cites Webster frequently, e.g., for his use of the "emblematic
     tradition," and the pageantry and tournament of <u>The White Devil</u>.

*42   YAMAMOTO, HIROSHI. "The White Devil ni egakareta konran no sekai" [The world of confusion as shown in The White Devil]. English Literature and Language (Tokyo) 9:84-99.
      Argues that The White Devil depicts a world thrown into chaos.

1973

1   BECK, ERVIN, Jr. "Terence Improved: The Paradigm of the Prodigal Son in English Renaissance Comedy." Renaissance Drama 6:107-22.
      Studies comedies (including the "Ho" plays) in which rebel sons return to their parents.

2   BINDER, BARRETT F. "Tragic Satire: Studies in Cyril Tourneur, John Webster, and Thomas Middleton." Ph.D. dissertation, Tufts University, 305 pp.
      Argues that the works of Tourneur, Middleton, and Webster (especially The Duchess of Malfi) exhibit a conflict between tragic and satiric responses to a calamity, emphasizing the contrast between a bestial world and ideal values. While corruption is widespread, it seems less grand here than in tragedy; it is not so much that the heroes violate the moral order as that there is no moral order. Finds the cynical malcontent figure, such as Bosola, at the center of these works. See Dissertation Abstracts International 33 (1973):4331A.

3   BRADBROOK, MURIEL C. Drama in English: Comedies, 1558-1625. London: Chatto & Windus, pp. 234-36. [Revised version of The Growth and Structure of Elizabethan Comedy (London: Chatto & Windus, 1955).]
      Finds the "Ho" plays more comic than satiric, in spite of a certain sardonic tone.

4   BYERS, GEORGE F. "The Valiant Scot by J.W. (1637)--Critical Edition." Ph.D. dissertation, Indiana University, 334 pp.
      Includes a discussion of Howarth's suggestion (in 1969.16) that Webster wrote The Valiant Scot. See Dissertation Abstracts International 33 (1973):6343A.

5   DWYER, WILLIAM W. A Study of Webster's Use of Renaissance Natural and Moral Philosophy. Jacobean Drama Studies, 18. Salzburg: Institut für Englische Sprache und Literatur, Universität Salzburg, 206 pp.
      Published version of 1972.9.

6   ECCLES, MARK. "Recent Studies in Elizabethan and Jacobean Drama." Studies in English Literature 13, no. 2:374-406.
      Includes a review of Berry, 1972.5, finding it readable and important, especially for its treatment of verbal imagery, irony, and character. Notes Berry's emphasis on human evil in relation to law.

7   FORKER, CHARLES R.   "Love, Death and Fame: The Grotesque
     Tragedy of John Webster."   Anglia 91:192-218.
         Notes both the frequency and strength of horrors in the two
major tragedies, and finds that the effect of such Jacobean grotesquerie is one of strangely mixed comic horror and lyric sadness.
Webster's technique involves a touch of the surrealistic, as he
mixes the natural with the unnatural.   Also comments that Webster,
along with his interest in death, asserts the intensity and value
of love; these two abstractions are deeply embedded together in
both tragedies.   See 1975.12.

8   GRUSHOW, IRA.   "Bosola's Dirge in The Duchess of Malfi."
     Concerning Poetry 6, no. 2:61-62.
         Argues that although this poem is often treated by Webster
critics as ironic, it can be taken as a self-contained utterance,
complete with its own pattern of water imagery, which deals with
the impermanence of human life.

9   HANLEY, CECILE C.   "Jacobean Drama and Politics."   Ph.D. dis-
     sertation, Temple University, 234 pp.
         Discusses how Jacobean drama treats the decline in tradition-
al Renaissance concepts of state and how it attempts to combat
Machiavellianism and materialism.   The drama, including Webster's,
presents an image of growing social disorder, depicting corrupt
courts that reflect that of James I.   Finds that the drama also
views with suspicion the aspirations of the trading class to political power based on money.   Overall, the Jacobean drama is in-
tensely political.   See Dissertation Abstracts International 33
(1973):5680A.

10   HOLLAND, GEORGE.   "The Function of the Minor Characters in The
     White Devil."   Philological Quarterly 52:43-54.
         Argues that the minor characters provide a social context
for the judgment of the major figures of the play.   Thus, for example, Monticelso's reactions to Brachiano indicate the unsettling
effect of corruption in high places.   Suggests that Cornelia gives
an example of the preservation of moral standards; she is not just
a meddling woman, but a chorus and the ethical center of the play.
She shows that the acts of princes should be a moral guide to the
body politic.   Webster uses minor characters to make the audience
make moral decisions.

11   HORWICH, RICHARD.   "Wives, Courtesans, and the Economics of
     Love in Jacobean City Comedy."   Comparative Drama 7, no. 4:
     291-309.
         Finds the coupling of marriage and money a common factor in
the City Comedies: if they do not analyze, they do present a picture of mercantile interests.   Marriage becomes a testing ground
for new economic ideas.   Northward Ho uses many of the conventions
of this genre but fails to make explicit connections that would
give meaning to its themes.

12   JAMES, KATHERINE H. "The Widow in Jacobean Drama." Ph.D.
dissertation, University of Tennessee, 389 pp.
        Examines seventy Jacobean stage widows. Finds that, in
tragedies, these widows are often connected to themes of adultery
and husband murder as in The White Devil. The Duchess of Malfi is
unique in its presentation of an innocent remarriage that causes
death. Finds in The Devil's Law Case a typical pattern involving
a widow dealing with a wayward child. See Dissertation Abstracts
International 34 (1973):1246A.

*13 KITAGAWA, TEIJI. John Webster Kenkyu. Tokyo: Hokuseido.
        Source: MLA International Bibliography for 1973 1:Item 4427.

14   KOLIN, PHILIP C. "The Elizabethan Stage Doctor as a Dramatic
Convention." Ph.D. dissertation, Northwestern University,
290 pp.
        Comments on the two physicians in The Duchess of Malfi--the
madman in act 4 and the fool in act 5. Notes that Webster links
madness to medicine, and utilizes the doctors to highlight
Ferdinand's insanity. See Dissertation Abstracts International
34 (1973):3406A.

15   KROLL, NORMA. "The Democritean Universe in Webster's The White
Devil." Comparative Drama 7, no. 1:3-21.
        Finds Democritus a cornerstone of Webster's aesthetic theory
and practice: events are caused by an indifferent chain of random
action and human behavior is governed by neither self-interest nor
virtue, but an irrational tendency towards self-destruction. Finds
that Fortune swoops in The White Devil like the random swerving of
Lucretius's atoms. Democritean atomism also dominates the image
pattern of the play.

16   LAGARDE, FERNAND. "Pourquoi Flamineo alla-t-il à Padoue?"
Caliban 10:19-22.
        Asks why Flamineo was a student at the University of Padua.
Suggests that possibly that University's institutional avowal of
Aristotelian ethics casts ironic light on Flamineo's character as
a malcontent.

17   LEECH, CLIFFORD. "The Invulnerability of Evil." In
Shakespeare's Art: Seven Essays. Edited by Milton Crane.
Chicago: University of Chicago Press, pp. 151-68.
        Compares Webster to Shakespeare, in that the latter anguishes
over the question of the possibility of the elimination of evil,
while Webster has evil characters murder and be murdered relatively
casually.

18   _____. "Studies in Shakespearean and Other Jacobean Tragedy,
1972: A Retrospect." Shakespeare Survey 26:1-19.
        Notes that Brooke's view of Webster (1916.1) is no longer
ours. Cites and reviews several important studies, including those

of Lucas (1927.11) and Ellis-Fermor (1963.2; 1948.6) while sketch-
ing the large critical context of twentieth-century study of
Jacobean drama.

19   _____. "Three Times Ho and a Brace of Widows: Some Plays for
the Private Theater." In The Elizabethan Theatre III. Edited
by David Galloway. Hamden, Conn.: Shoestring Press, pp. 14-33.
    Notes that the "Ho" plays refer to each other and also pre-
suppose a knowledge of the doings of other theaters; they were
written for a kind of in-group. Westward Ho is a parody of the
"journeying" play, Eastward Ho parodies it, and Northward Ho
parodies both. Westward Ho is a tribute to city morality, while
at the same time making fun of the citizen class. Argues that
Eastward Ho is not a moral rebuttal but a continuation; it, too,
is a "play about plays." Comments that the general practice of
private theater plays was to mock widows' remarrying, and thus
Webster triumphed over prejudice in creating the heroic stature
of the Duchess of Malfi.

20   LEGGATT, ALEXANDER. Citizen Comedy in the Age of Shakespeare.
Toronto: University of Toronto Press, pp. 13, 135, 143, 149.
    Notes Webster/Dekker collaborations.

*21   LELL, GORDON. "'Ganymede' on the Elizabethan Stage: Homosexual
Implications of the Use of Boy Actors." Aegis 1:5-15.
    Source: MLA International Bibliography for 1973 1:Item 2895.

22   MAHANEY, WILLIAM E. Deception in the John Webster Plays: An
Analytical Study. Jacobean Drama Studies, 9. Salzburg:
Institut für Englische Sprache und Literatur, Universität
Salzburg, 188 pp.
    Published version of part 1 of 1967.14.

23   _____. John Webster: A Classified Bibliography. Jacobean
Drama Studies, 10. Salzburg: Institut für Englische Sprache
und Literatur, Universität Salzburg, 319 pp. [Originally part
2 of 1967.14.]
    A large and largely accurate classified bibliography. Cites
works in these categories: bibliographical and reference works;
literary history; biography; editions (collected and individual);
selections; text; authorship and dating (general and individual);
sources and borrowing (general, individual, and borrowings from
Webster); general criticism; criticism of Webster (general, dramatic
works, and nondramatic works); stage history; and historical background.

24   McLEOD, SUSAN H. "Dramatic Imagery in the Plays of John Webster."
Ph.D. dissertation, University of Wisconsin, 258 pp. [Published
as 1977.13.]
    Argues that, since Webster's plays are not long poems or ex-
tended metaphors, their imagery must be understood in a theatrical

context. Examines The White Devil, The Duchess of Malfi, and The Devil's Law Case in terms of the verbal and presentational images that give a unity to the plays. The White Devil focuses upon themes of courtly reward and punishment; The Duchess of Malfi features dramatic images of appearance vs. reality and of the diseased chaos of the court. The Devil's Law Case emphasizes tragicomic reversals. See Dissertation Abstracts International 33 (1973):4355A.

25   MULLANY, PETER F. "The Knights of Malta in Renaissance Drama." Neuphilologische Mitteilungen 74:297-310.
      Notes that between 1586 and 1611 there was much interest in the East. Finds Webster uses the Knights as a symbol of evil disguised as good in The White Devil. Also, Ercole in The Devil's Law Case is a Knight, but this seems insignificant.

26   O'DONNEL, C. PATRICK, Jr. "The Repertory of the Jacobean King's Company." Ph.D. dissertation, Princeton University, 413 pp.
      Presents material in three areas: an analysis of Henslowe's records of the King's chief competitors; a discussion of similarities between the King's Company and the Lord Admiral's Company; and an annotated bibliography of plays in the repertory. See Dissertation Abstracts International 34 (1973):736-37A.

27   PLATZ, NORBERT H., ed. English Dramatic Theories. Vol. 1, From Elyot to the Age of Dryden, 1531-1668. Tübingen: Niemeyer, pp. 46-47.
      Includes Webster's "To the Reader" from The White Devil in a collection of critical texts.

28   QUENNELL, PETER. A History of English Literature. Springfield, Mass.: G. & C. Merriam, pp. 100-101.
      Finds that Webster's plays are based upon a revenge rooted in implacable, deep-seated malice. Virtue is powerless, especially in The Duchess of Malfi. Judges that Webster's poetic treatment and atmosphere of brooding melancholy redeem potentially crude melodrama.

29   SEIDEN, MELVIN. The Revenge Motive in Websterian Tragedy. Jacobean Drama Studies, 15. Salzburg: Institut für Englische Sprache und Literatur, Universität Salzburg, 148 pp.
      Published version of 1956.26.

30   SHAW, SHARON K. "Medea on Pegasus: Some Speculations on the Parallel Rise of Women and Melodrama on the Jacobean Stage." Ball State University Forum 14, no. 4:13-21.
      Argues that Webster separated wise and noble women from terrible and vengeful ones. Although he achieved some moments of poetic beauty, his portraits of females tend to be extravagant and oversimplified. Finds Webster, overall, a "semi-great" dramatist.

31   WHITMAN, ROBERT F. Beyond Melancholy: John Webster and the
     Tragedy of Darkness. Jacobean Drama Studies, 4. Salzburg:
     Institut fur Englische Sprache und Literatur, Universitat
     Salzburg, 225 pp.
          In a revision of 1956.32 finds two traditions in Webster
     studies: those who find in his plays moral chaos and those who
     see moral vision. Argues that the plot of The White Devil is
     binary, not hierarchical: it chronicles the rise of Flamineo and
     the romance of his sister in a series of rises and falls, each of
     which stresses the worthlessness of the character's goals. The
     Duchess of Malfi, while less bleak, also focuses upon the ruin
     that awaits those who put their faith in beauty, wealth, power,
     and the like. Webster blends several theatrical and literary tra-
     ditions, and utilizes a wide range of sources to present this theme.
     Concludes that, although the plays firmly deny the value of worldly
     things, Webster still seems to admire the earthly vigor of his
     heroes.

32   WHITMARSH-KNIGHT, DAVID. "The Second Blackfriars: The Globe
     Indoors." Theatre Notebook 27:94-98.
          Describes the Second Blackfriars theater as a winter house
     for the King's Men from 1609-42. Sketches its dimensions, conclud-
     ing that the stage size was almost identical to the Globe, and thus,
     plays like The Duchess of Malfi transferred easily back and forth.

                              1974

1   BLUESTONE, MAX. From Story to Stage: The Dramatic Adaptation
     of Prose Fiction in the Period of Shakespeare and His Contempo-
     raries. Studies in English Literature, 70. The Hague: Mouton,
     341 pp., passim.
          Studies dramatic adaptations of prose fiction in the
     Renaissance, citing Webster frequently as a voluminous adapter of
     the lines of others, e.g., he uses seven passages from the Arcadia
     within thirty lines of The Duchess of Malfi.

2   BONI, JOHN. "Analogous Form: Black Comedy and Some Jacobean
     Plays." Western Humanities Review 28:201-15.
          Finds modern writers of black comedy (Heller, Pynchon, etc.),
     like the Jacobeans, fend off despair with laughter, admitting mean-
     ing only in individual laughter. Ghoulish humor such as the masque
     of madmen in The Duchess of Malfi and the anti-establishment satire
     of The White Devil seem quite contemporary. Bosola, a mixture of
     good and evil, appeals to our modern sense of character.

3   CHAMPION, LARRY S. "Webster's The White Devil and the Jacobean
     Tragic Perspective." Texas Studies in Literature and Language
     16:447-62. [Incorporated in 1977.3.]
          Argues that all the characters in the earlier tragedy are
     dominated by self-interest.

4　CHARNEY, MAURICE. "Recent Studies in Elizabethan and Jacobean
　　Drama." Studies in English Literature 14, no. 2:297-314.
　　　　Notes the appearance of The Devil's Law Case in the Regents
Renaissance Drama Series (1972.35), and that the University of
Salzburg's Jacobean Drama Studies series is making a helpful con-
tribution with its volumes, especially those on Webster.

5　CLAY, CHARLOTTE N. The Role of Anxiety in English Tragedy,
　　1580-1642. Jacobean Drama Studies, 23. Salzburg: Institut
　　für Englische Sprache und Literatur, Universität Salzburg, 251
　　pp., passim.
　　　　Argues that the loss of universal beliefs in the Jacobean
age led to a rise of skepticism, pessimism, melancholy, and anxiety.
Webster's Duchess is a symbol of the chaos and anxiety of the later
Renaissance.

6　COLLEY, JOHN S. "Music in the Elizabethan Private Theaters."
　　Yearbook of English Studies 4:62-69.
　　　　Notes that the induction to The Malcontent explains that
play has been adapted for adult actors "to abridge the not received
custome of musicke in our Theatre." Also notes that Dekker's public and private plays, including the "Ho" plays, seem musical.

7　DALLBY, ANDERS. The Anatomy of Evil: A Study of John Webster's
　　"The White Devil." Lund Studies in English, 48. Lund: Gleerup,
　　236 pp.
　　　　In the introduction, surveys critical reactions to Webster,
and notes the deeply divided opinions on his works. Focuses next
upon the plot of the play and its structure: each act depicts one
major event. Finds a number of parallels in the plot and concludes
that its pattern is one of crossed rising and falling destinies.
It is a well-balanced and tight structure. Comments on various
rhetorical devices, including the "asides," then considers the
play's characters, presenting a brief analysis of each. Analyzes
several categories of imagery (e.g., poison, disease, storms, etc.),
all of which mesh into a net of images focusing upon the reality/
appearance theme. The other main thematic focus of the play is
reward and punishment. Both these concepts point to a world of
evil. Finds that Webster's moral perspective is conventional but
unclear. Concludes with a discussion of the movement, during the
Elizabethan age, towards dramatic realism, and the place of The
White Devil in this progression—in it, traditionalism, symbolism,
and realism meet.

8　DAMISCH, ISABEL M. "Analyse des motifs religieux dans les
　　images des trois tragédies de Webster." Caliban 10:113-25.
　　　　Finds that Webster's religious imagery—biblical references,
themes of atheism, clerical characters, and the like—reflects his
theological ambiguity. Often, such images are presented with a
cynical tone, with religious ritual parodied and sacred elements
overwhelmed by profane ones. Webster's religious imagery per se

is trite; the subject does not seem of such interest to the dramatist.

9   FLAXMAN, ERWIN. "Ingenious Structure and the Action of Elizabethan Drama." Ph.D. dissertation, New York University, 133 pp.
    Considers various plot structures and devices in Elizabethan drama. Finds Webster's plays are informed by fantasies that are displaced throughout the action--plot fragments that alternately reveal and obscure. For example, Bosola in The Duchess of Malfi is a perverted mirror of Antonio. Both the major tragedies depict moral anarchy derived from sexual competition. See Dissertation Abstracts International 34 (1974):4197-98A.

10 GOREAU, ELOISE. Integrity of Life: Allegorical Imagery in the Plays of John Webster. Jacobean Drama Studies, 32. Salzburg: Institut für Englische Sprache und Literatur, Universität Salzburg, 194 pp.
    Published version of 1971.5.

11 HAMEL, GUY A. "Structure in Elizabethan Drama." Ph.D. dissertation, University of Toronto.
    Finds that a close-textured design is a characteristic of the Elizabethan drama, and an organically unified structure is not. The White Devil is structured around the presentation of conflictin points of view and the antagonisms of its characters. Both lead to Vittoria as the center of the play. See Dissertation Abstracts International 34 (1973):5101-2A.

12 HENKE, JAMES T. Renaissance Dramatic Bawdy (Exclusive of Shakespeare): An Annotated Glossary and Critical Essays. 2 vols. Jacobean Drama Studies, 39-40. Salzburg: Institut für Englische Sprache und Literatur, Universität Salzburg, 366 pp.
    Published version of 1970.16.

13 HOGAN, JEROME. "Webster's The White Devil, V. iv. 118-121." Explicator 33, no. 3:Item 25.
    Finds that the expression "maze of conscience" used by Flamineo refers to a state of confusion induced by guilt.

14 KARSTEN, DAVID P. "A Descriptive Study of the Sprecher Concept as Found in Selected Plays by George Chapman, Cyril Tourneur, and John Webster." Ph.D. dissertation, Michigan State University, 499 pp.
    Considers the relationship between mannerist art and Jacobean drama, including Webster's major tragedies, which reflect the same historical context and aesthetic biases as contemporary visual arts. See Dissertation Abstracts International 34 (1974):7917-18A.

15 KEYISHIAN, HARRY, comp. "A Checklist of Medieval and Renaissance Plays (Excluding Shakespeare) on Film, Tape, and Recording."

Research Opportunities in Renaissance Drama 17:45-58.
Lists a Caedmon record/tape of *The Duchess of Malfi*, and a
radio transcription of the same play from the BBC World Theatre
Series.

16   KUCHNERT, PHILIP G. "Will and Fate in Four English Renaissance
     Tragedies." Ph.D. dissertation, University of Utah, 159 pp.
     Argues that *Tamburlaine I* and *II*, *The Changeling*, and *The
     Duchess of Malfi* show human will in tragic conflict. Finds that
     the Duchess is virtuous, electing a fate of married happiness that
     is destroyed by the corrupted world in which she lives. Ferdinand,
     who loves incestuously, resents his sister's virtue. Concludes
     that the Duchess's torments and death are a feat of stoic endurance,
     showing the nobility and dignity of the human spirit that survives
     death and stands in opposition to the chaos of the world. See
     Dissertation Abstracts International 35 (1974):1626A.

17   LEECH, CLIFFORD. "The Incredible in Jacobean Tragedy." In
     Renaissance Studies in Honor of Carroll Camden. Edited by J.A.
     Ward. *Rice University Studies* (Special Issue) 60:109-22.
     Argues that the Jacobeans achieved a drama that, on the one
     hand, was obviously "invented" and on the other cleaves closely to
     life. Notes that Webster urges actors, in the *Characters* and the
     preface to *The White Devil*, to act naturalistically. Yet he is
     often accused of overdoing the theatrical dimension in his plays.
     Concludes that many of Webster's characters are not beyond belief
     and have a capacity to move an audience.

18   MORSBERGER, ROBERT E. *Swordplay and the Elizabethan and Jacobean
     Stage*. Jacobean Drama Studies, 37. Salzburg: Institut für
     Englische Sprache und Literatur, Universität Salzburg, 129 pp.,
     passim.
     Notes that *The White Devil* is one of the few Elizabethan
     plays featuring duelling at Barriers, a scene unnecessary for plot
     but which adds a spectacle. Cites Webster works intermittently.

19   OLIVER, HAROLD JAMES. "Literary Allusions in Jacobean Drama."
     In *Renaissance Studies in Honor of Carroll Camden*. Edited by
     J.A. Ward. *Rice University Studies* (Special Issue) 60:131-40.
     Argues that most of Webster's quotations from other litera-
     ture were not expected to be recognized and thus are not "allusions."

20   PENDRY, E.D. *Elizabethan Prisons and Prison Scenes*. 2 vols.
     Elizabethan and Renaissance Studies, 17. Salzburg: Institut
     für Englische Sprache und Literatur, Universität Salzburg, 385
     pp., passim.
     Cites *The Devil's Law Case*, *Appius and Virginia*, and the
     "Ho" plays, with no lengthy analysis.

21   PETERSON, JOYCE E. "A Counsellor For a King: A Study of the
     Morality Drama, Commonwealth Tragedy, and *The Duchess of Malfi*."

Ph.D. dissertation, University of Califoria, Irvine, 228 pp.
[Revised and published as 1978.24.]

Uses The Duchess of Malfi to illustrate the relationship between the moralities and the Renaissance "Commonwealth plays."
Notes that those who find Webster's work structurally weak fail
to understand its genre. The ethics of the play derive from the
equation of king and country. The Duchess falls because she
fails to put her country before her self. See Dissertation
Abstracts International 34 (1974):7718A.

22   STODDER, JOSEPH HENRY. Moral Perspective in Webster's Major
      Tragedies. Jacobean Drama Studies, 48. Salzburg: Institut
      für Englische Sprache und Literatur, Universität Salzburg,
      164 pp.

      Finds that the balance between good and evil in Webster's
plays is revealed in contrasts between his major characters.
Analyzes, in this context, Vittoria and the Duchess; Brachiano
and Antonio; Bosola and Flamineo; Ferdinand and Francisco. Concludes that Webster's plays are moralizing tragic satire, balanced
in their presentation of virtue and vice. All the evil characters
have some redeeming good, and all the good contain some small taint,
but the good die in faith and the evil in despair.

23   ____. Satire in Jacobean Tragedy. Jacobean Drama Studies, 35.
      Salzburg: Institut für Englische Sprache und Literatur,
      Universität Salzburg, 186 pp.
      Published version of 1964.36.

24   SULLIVAN, S.W. "The Tendency to Rationalize in The White Devil
      and The Duchess of Malfi." Yearbook of English Studies 4:77-84.
      Finds that Webster's villains always try to squirm out of
the moral responsibility for their acts, blaming their evil actions
on others. Flamineo is among the more open about his guilt, but
Bosola, Vittoria, and Brachiano all try to rationalize their actions.

25   URE, PETER. Elizabethan and Jacobean Drama: Critical Essays.
      Edited by J.C. Maxwell. New York: Barnes & Noble, 258 pp.,
      passim. [Reprint of 1948.14.]
      Webster is also mentioned throughout in other essays, e.g.,
as a writer of revenge tragedy or in the context of a discussion
of the morality of the "Ho" plays.

26   WATSON, GEORGE, ed. The New Cambridge Bibliography of English
      Literature. Vol. 1, 600-1660. Cambridge: Cambridge University
      Press, columns 1697-1703. [Revision of 1941.1.]
      For Webster, lists primary works, individual and collected,
and scholarly discussions.

27   WEST, MURIEL. The Devil and John Webster. Jacobean Drama
      Studies, 11. Salzburg: Institut für Englische Sprache und
      Literatur, Universität Salzburg, 319 pp. [Published form of

1957.29.]
Reviewed: 1976.20.

28 YOUNG, STEVEN C. The Frame Structure in Tudor and Stuart Drama.
    Elizabethan and Renaissance Studies, 6. Salzburg: Institut
    für Englische Sprache und Literatur, Universität Salzburg,
    189 pp.
       Published form of 1970.32.

                              1975

1   BARROLL, J. LEEDS, et al. The Revels History of Drama in
    English. Vol. 3, 1576-1613. London: Methuen, 526 pp., esp.
    pp. 394-403.
       Includes several sections of general interest on Jacobean
    society and literature, and Alvin Kernan, "The Plays of John
    Webster." Places Webster in the front rank of English dramatists.
    His characters, surrounded by sensational settings and plots, pro-
    duce a belief in the possibility of goodness and virtue in a life
    lived in the darkest of worlds. Finds The Duchess of Malfi his
    finest play. Discusses the plot, characters, and theme of the
    work, and concludes that the Duchess embodies humanistic values
    in a world that always moves toward ruin.

*2 BAYERL, FRANCIS JAMES. "The Characterization of the Tyrant in
    Elizabethan Drama." Ph.D. dissertation, University of Toronto.
       Considers portraits of the tyrant on stage in, among other
    settings, the Machiavellian drama, and finds the tyrant figure re-
    lated to revenger and malcontent characters. Cites the "tool vil-
    lains" of both tragedies. See Dissertation Abstracts International
    36 (1975):1516-17A.

3   BELTON, ELLEN ROTHENBERG. "The Figure of the Steward: Some
    Aspects of Master-Servant Relations in Elizabethan and Early
    Stuart Drama." Ph.D. dissertation, Columbia University, 502 pp.
       Studies dramatic portraits of the master-steward relation.
    For specific application to The Duchess of Malfi, see 1976.1. See
    also Dissertation Abstracts International 35 (1975):4415-16A.

4   BENSTON, KIMBERLY W. "The Duchess of Malfi: Webster's Tragic
    Vision." Gypsy Scholar 3:20-36.
       Suggests that The Duchess of Malfi asks two questions:
    should we understand ourselves as part of a world governed by
    forces beyond ourselves or can we know ourselves and act according-
    ly; and is there free will? Finds that the world of the Duchess
    is somber, brooding, and touched with magic and madness. The cen-
    tral metaphors of the play suggest that the world is a prison or
    madhouse. The figure of the Duchess stands against this madness
    and subjugation as a force of love and order. Act 5 tests whether
    the other characters of the play come close to the Duchess. Only

Antonio seems to learn from her as he approaches death, the only true testing time of life's values.

5   BERGERON, DAVID M. "Civic Pageants and Historical Drama." Journal of Medieval and Renaissance Studies 5:89-105.
     Finds that city pageants continued to present historical themes and characters after history plays were no longer being written. Webster's Monuments of Honour, for example, includes largely historical characters.

6   BRADBROOK, MURIEL C. "The Triple Bond: Audience, Actors, Author in the Elizabethan Playhouse." In The Triple Bond: Plays, Mainly Shakespearean, in Performance. Edited by Joseph G. Price. University Park: Pennsylvania State University Press, pp. 50-69.
     Discusses the importance of audience response as part of performance, noting that The Duchess of Malfi works within the older, public theater tradition but is also conscious of readers as a potential audience, as is evidenced by Webster's comments in the prologue to The White Devil.

7   BRENNAN, ELIZABETH M., ed. John Webster. "The Devil's Law Case." New Mermaids Series. London: Benn, 157 pp.
     A modern-spelling edition with introduction, notes, and textual appendices. In the introduction surveys Webster's life and career, then focuses upon the play, chronicling early perform- ances, sources, and critical history. Finds in the play's question ing of values a common theme of Jacobean drama, namely that of the uncertainties of man's relation to man--and woman. The specific issue of trust in women is raised in Webster's tragedies as well. In The Devil's Law Case, men turn out to be unreliable, within a harsh world of commerce and mercantilism. Suggests that the play affirms a basic Christian perspective, with sin punished and vir- tue rewarded.

8   CLARK, ANDREW. Domestic Drama: A Survey of the Origins, Antecedents, and Nature of the Domestic Play in England, 1500- 1640. Vol. 2. Jacobean Drama Studies, 49. Salzburg: Institut für Englische Sprache und Literatur, Universität Salzburg, pp. 317-22.
     Briefly discusses Westward Ho and Northward Ho, finding that they handle conjugal relations in a cynical attitude of ridicule and contempt. Thus, the plays differ sharply from Dekker's Shoemaker's Holiday.

9   DANIELS, RACHEL LEONA. "The Role of Dialectical Relationships in John Webster's The Duchess of Malfi." Ph.D. dissertation, University of Detroit, 143 pp.
     Finds that The White Devil is governed by dualisms, caused by the change in world-view (from that of a fixed and determined universe to one subject to change and human control) that took

place in Jacobean England. Webster affirms the value of Christian morality in that The Duchess of Malfi rejects a hierarchically ordered universe in favor of the rights of the person. The Duchess' death, thus, symbolizes a crisis of authority. Sees the play as dramatizing these two irreconcilable value systems, deriving from individual and hierarchical orders, and therefore structured with dialectic elements (man-woman, justice-mercy, etc.). See Dissertation Abstracts International 40 (1979):5872-73A.

10   EATON, WINIFRED KITTREDGE. Contrasts in the Representation of Death by Sophocles, Webster, and Strindberg. Jacobean Drama Studies, 17. Salzburg: Institut für Englische Sprache und Literatur, Universität Salzburg, 244 pp.
Published version of 1966.7.

11   EWBANK, INGA-STINA. "Webster, Tourneur, and Ford." In English Drama (Excluding Shakespeare): Select Bibliographical Guides. Edited by Stanley Wells. London: Oxford University Press, pp. 113-33.
The bibliography for Webster includes texts and critical studies (pp. 128-30). Observes in a brief introductory survey that, like the work of the dramatists themselves, criticism of these three playwrights varies widely. Finds two camps of contemporary Webster criticism: those who see him as confused and those who take him as a serious, usually moral, writer.

12   FORKER, CHARLES R. "The Love-Death Nexus in English Renaissance Tragedy." Shakespeare Studies 8:211-30.
Finds the relationship of love and death an especially strong theme in Elizabethan drama. An example is the entrance of Ferdinand into the Duchess' bedroom, disrupting tenderness with threats. Also finds Webster's imagery frequently necro-erotic. See 1973.7 for a related study focusing on Webster.

13   GANS, NATHAN ALFRED, Jr. "Tragic Space in Elizabethan and Jacobean Drama." Ph.D. dissertation, Yale University, 179 pp.
Argues that an enlarged cosmos diminished the role of man during the Renaissance, producing, paradoxically, a sense of claustrophobia that was reflected in the Jacobean drama. The Duchess of Malfi reflects this shrunken vision of man trapped in infinity. See Dissertation Abstracts International 35 (1975):4427A.

14   GOODWYN, FLOYD LOWELL, Jr. "Image Pattern and Moral Vision in John Webster." Ph.D. dissertation, State University of New York, Albany, 183 pp. [Published as 1977.5.]
Considers the relation of imagery to morality in the two major tragedies. Finds that Webster did not separate art and morality; he uses imagery to focus attention on the patterns of action and consequence in the plays. In The White Devil, images express the theme of dehumanization, and in The Duchess of Malfi they convey an atmosphere of ruin. Notes many theatrical species of

imagery--dumb show, masques, and the like--as important in the
definition of character and theme. See <u>Dissertation Abstracts
International</u> 36 (1975):3729-30A.

15   HANSEN, CAROL LOUISE. "Woman as Individual in English
     Renaissance Drama: A Defiance of the Masculine Code." Ph.D.
     dissertation, Arizona State University, 336 pp.
        Finds that female characters in the English Renaissance
     drama were often caught in the masculine code of the day, based
     upon antifeminist stereotyping. Those who defy this code die (in
     plays such as Webster's). Argues that he and his fellow dramatists
     asked the right questions regarding women in a male society, even
     if they could not come up with answers. Women could show defiance
     and emerge as individuals in their plays. See <u>Dissertation Abstracts
     International</u> 35 (1975):7867A.

16   HAWKINS, HARRIETT. "The Victim's Side: Chaucer's <u>Clerk's Tale</u>
     and Webster's <u>The Duchess of Malfi</u>." <u>Signs</u> 1, no. 2:339-61.
        Argues that modern critics try to discover a guilt to match
     the sufferings of victims in early literature. Actually, Webster
     wants us on the Duchess' side: if we feel she deserves her fate,
     we side with her brothers. Since the Duchess retains her integrity,
     she is a victor as well as a victim: she defines herself, retains
     her independence, and judges others. Finds that Webster attacks
     injustice, and the correct reading, uncorrupted by critical dogma-
     tism, judges the Duchess innocent.

17   HENKE, JAMES T. "John Webster's Motif of 'Consuming': An
     Approach to the Dramatic Unity and Tragic Vision of <u>The White
     Devil</u> and <u>The Duchess of Malfi</u>." <u>Neuphilologische Mitteilungen</u>
     76:625-41.
        Finds that the act of consuming is an overarching image pat-
     tern in the tragedies, encompassing other image structures such as
     poisoning, predators, etc. Both plays move from a heightened sexu-
     al passion to rage, and from an urge for revenge to insanity. The
     consuming image suggests that passion and rage are versions of in-
     sanity, and all lead to death. This image pattern provides a unique
     unity to the plays and helps explain Webster's tragic universe in
     which there are neither victors nor resolutions, only endurance
     with dignity.

18   HOLDSWORTH, ROGER V., ed. <u>Webster, "The White Devil" and "The
     Duchess of Malfi": A Casebook</u>. London: Macmillan, 256 pp.
        A collection of previously published material on Webster in
     three parts: short comments from 1617 to 1957; articles and essays
     from 1949 to 1972; and reviews of productions, 1919-71; plus an
     introduction and bibliography. Works included are cross referenced
     to this item.
        In the introduction notes that after a history of critical
     controversy, modern scholars seem agreed that Webster was and is
     a figure of some importance. Notes that he was ignored during the
     eighteenth century and reviews the critical traditions thereafter.

19   JENSEN, EJNER J. "The Boy Actors: Plays and Playing." Research Opportunities in Renaissance Drama 18:5-11.
        Comments that the children's plays were highly varied and brilliantly inventive. Also notes Webster's creation of in-house satirists, anatomizers of a diseased court system. Discusses Webster's consideration of the nature of women in Vittoria and the Duchess.

20   KANTAS, ALEXANDER A. "Enigmas of Justice: Marlowe to Ford." Ph.D. dissertation, University of Illinois, 372 pp.
        Considers Renaissance tragedies that challenge the traditional view of Christian justice. Finds Webster's tragedies show a depraved humanity, in which men mistrust will and reason, and lack all ethical restraints, mitigated only by the power of love that can lead to a desire for justice. See Dissertation Abstracts International 35 (1975):7257-58A.

21   LAWRENCE, ROBERT G., ed. Jacobean and Caroline Tragedies. London: Dent, pp. 184-89.
        In the introduction to The Cardinal, notes Shirley's extensive borrowings (in plot, character, structure, and language) from The Duchess of Malfi.

22   LOGAN, TERENCE P., and SMITH, DENZELL S., eds. "Other Dramatists." In The Popular School: A Survey and Bibliography of Recent Studies in English Renaissance Drama. Lincoln: University of Nebraska Press, pp. 250-74.
        An annotated bibliography that includes, in the section on Rowley, discussion of the authorship of A Cure for a Cuckold.

23   MAXWELL, BALDWIN. "The Attitude Toward the Duello in Later Jacobean Drama: A Postscript." Philological Quarterly 54: 104-16.
        Suggests that, after 1615, dramatists rejected dueling. The Devil's Law Case clearly repudiates such actions in its double-murder plot.

24   McLEOD, SUSAN H. "The Commendatio Animae and Brachiano's Death Scene in Webster's The White Devil." American Notes and Queries 14, no. 4:50-52.
        Argues that Brachiano's death scene is not a parody of extreme unction but of "commendatio animae," a Catholic liturgical ritual following the last annointing at the moment of death. The final cry of Vittoria parallels the final words of this rite.

25   MITCHELL, GILES, and WRIGHT, EUGENE P. "Duke Ferdinand's Lycanthropy as a Disguise Motive in Webster's The Duchess of Malfi." Literature and Psychology 25, no. 3:117-23.
        Asks why Ferdinand tortures his sister. Considers the evidence for an interpretation that stresses the incest motivation: there is a psychological relation between incest, lycanthropy,

and necrophilia, in that night walking is a symbol of freedom from
compulsions and heightened potency. Lycanthropia's cannibalism is
equated to oral sadism, and necrophilia is related to unresolved
Oedipal/incest feelings. Notes Ferdinand's sexual imaging of the
Duchess in the early scenes of the play. He does not seem to know
why he acts as he does. Later, he goes mad to obliterate memory,
hatred, and desire. Thus, there is a growing pattern of repression
throughout. Concludes that Webster's understanding of frustrated
incestuous desire and its relation to lycanthropia is modern and
exact.

26   MOORE, DON D. "John Webster." In The Popular School: A Survey
     and Bibliography of Recent Studies in English Renaissance Drama.
     Edited by Terence P. Logan and Denzell S. Smith. Lincoln:
     University of Nebraska Press, pp. 85-104.
          Surveys recent studies, including general criticism and
     scholarship on individual plays. Includes a selected bibliography.

27   OBAID, THORAYA AHMED. "The Moor Figure in English Renaissance
     Drama." Ph.D. dissertation, Wayne State University, 616 pp.
          Finds that Moors were depicted in terms of several stereo-
     types in English Renaissance literature, including confidants (such
     as Zanche) and princes and soldiers (as the disguised Mulinassar).
     Notes that Englishmen felt that black skin color reflected an in-
     nate evil, cruel, and treacherous nature. See Dissertation
     Abstracts International 35 (1975):4446A.

28   POTTER, LOIS. "Realism vs. Nightmare: Problems of Staging The
     Duchess of Malfi." In The Triple Bond: Plays, Mainly
     Shakespearean, in Performance. Edited by Joseph G. Price.
     University Park: Pennsylvania State University Press, pp.
     170-89.
          Notes that one difficulty in staging The Duchess of Malfi is
     the play's mixture of realism and convention. The Duchess and
     Antonio seem real characters, while Bosola comes from a nightmare.
     Describes several modern versions in which such a staging has been
     attempted. Suggests that the mixed style demands a mixed perform-
     ance in the theater.

29   RICE, NANCY HALL. "Beauty and the Beast and the Little Boy:
     Clues About the Origins of Sexism and Racism from Folklore and
     Literature." Ph.D. dissertation, University of Massachusetts,
     386 pp.
          Argues that hatred towards women and minorities is based on
     a fear of death and sexuality. The Duchess of Malfi presents in
     its heroine an image of beauty that must be destroyed--the Duchess
     is subjected to a sexist attack on her right to marry for love
     while maintaining her status. See Dissertation Abstracts
     International 36 (1975):875A.

30   WALKER, MELISSA GRAVES. "Scattered Fragments of Truth: John
      Webster and Renaissance Skepticism." Ph.D. dissertation, Emory
      University, 280 pp.
            Sees skepticism as a major philosophical position from the
      sixteenth century on. Presents The White Devil, The Duchess of
      Malfi, and The Devil's Law Case as embodying Montaigne's view that
      man has little chance to discover ultimate truths. The plays pre-
      sent rapidly changing perspectives that make it impossible to claim
      we really know a character at all. All three explore the inade-
      quacies of human knowledge, with the tragedies showing mankind
      defeated, and the tragicomedy suggesting the possibility of sur-
      vival in the darkness. See Dissertation Abstracts International
      35 (1975):7274-75A.

31   WANG, TSO-LIANG. The Literary Reputation of John Webster to
      1830. Jacobean Drama Studies, 59. Salzburg: Institut für
      Englische Sprache und Literatur, Universität Salzburg, 169 pp.
            Offers a detailed history of Webster's critical reputation,
      from his contemporaries through the revival of interest in the
      mid-nineteenth century, including playlists, adaptations, encyclo-
      pedia entries, and the vogue of specimen anthologies. Reviewed:
      1976.20.

32   WELD, JOHN. Meaning in Comedy: Studies in Elizabethan Romantic
      Comedy. Albany: State University of New York Press, p. 13.
            Sees the dance of madmen in The Duchess of Malfi as an example
      of a visual set piece "carrying a large burden of communication"
      through nonverbal symbolism.

33   WHITMAN, ROBERT F. "The Moral Paradox of Webster's Tragedy."
      PMLA 90:894-903.
            Argues that one reason many students have found Webster's
      plays obscure is the difficulty of ethical evaluation of his char-
      acters: "The judgments made by the realist-cynics are wholly at
      odds with those offered by the defenders of piety and virtue, and
      neither seem to bear much relationship to any of the values im-
      plicit in the action." Speculates we are meant to hold contra-
      dictory moral positions, e.g., those of Vittoria and Cornelia.
      Webster ignores conventional good and evil, and presents some vice
      in his most noble characters, some virtue in his darkest villains.
      He depicts a struggle between Apollonian and Dionysian systems
      that produces audience ambivalence.

34   ZIMMER, R.K. "The Emergence of the 'New' Woman on the English
      Stage." Kentucky Philological Association Bulletin, 1975, pp.
      25-31.
            Suggests that women play an increasingly important thematic
      role in Elizabethan plays. Webster's tragedies deal with the love-
      espousal-marriage relationship and the problems of women in it.
      Finds in The White Devil two loveless arranged marriages that are
      at the root of the tragedy. Sees Vittoria as not evil but a strong

personality forced into a misalliance that she can only escape
through evil actions. Webster's ambiguity toward her reflects that
of society toward such women. The same problem is illuminated in
The Duchess of Malfi: the Duchess is a vivacious and complex person, who is treated by her brothers as property.

1976

1   BELTON, ELLEN ROTHENBERG. "The Function of Antonio in The
     Duchess of Malfi." Texas Studies in Literature and Language
     18:474-85. [Originally part of 1975.3.]
         Notes that critics have found little to say about or admire
     in Antonio. Finds that he is not weak or dull, but a Christian
     stoic and Webster's ideal within the play, and, thus, at its philo-
     sophical center: he is not a killer and is capable of managing
     his feelings. Compares Antonio to Bosola: both are valiant and
     forced to be self-reliant, but Bosola is impatient, unlike Antonio.
     The Duchess shares his patience and, in her trials, relies upon
     his philosophy.

2   BEST, MICHAEL R. "A Precarious Balance: Structure in The
     Duchess of Malfi." In Shakespeare and Some Others: Essays on
     Shakespeare and Some of His Contemporaries. Edited by Alan
     Brissenden. Adelaide: Department of English, University of
     Adelaide, pp. 159-77.
         Sees the Aragonian brothers as governed by will uncontrolled
     by higher reason or conscience. The Cardinal exercises intelli-
     gence, Ferdinand, passion; the former is a Machiavel, the latter,
     a beast. Both are ruined by their imbalances. Argues that the
     Duchess, in contrast, combines wit and passion, and possesses
     strength and Christian confidence in salvation. Other characters,
     including Antonio and Bosola, are also variations on the theme of
     wit balanced with passion.

3   BUELER, LOIS WEST EATON. "The Dramatic Uses of Women in
     Jacobean Tragedy." Ph.D. dissertation, University of Colorado,
     332 pp.
         Suggests that Jacobean tragedies manipulate conventional
     treatments of women so as to achieve a dual exploration of the
     nature of authority and the nature of the psychological process of
     self-creation. Webster's women raise doubts about the traditional
     exercises of male authority. Finds that the male characters in
     his plays are fragmented and in conflict yet demand female obedi-
     ence. See Dissertation Abstracts International 37 (1976):2192A.

4   CHARNEY, MAURICE B. "Webster vs. Middleton, or the Shakespearean
     Yardstick in Jacobean Tragedy." In English Renaissance Drama:
     Essays in Honor of Madeleine Doran and Mark Eccles. Edited by
     Standish Henning et al. Carbondale: Southern Illinois
     University Press, pp. 118-27.

Comments upon the difficulties of using Shakespeare as a
yardstick for the Jacobeans: Swinburne, for example, saw
Shakespeare and Webster as great lyric poets who happened to write
plays. Finds that nineteenth- and twentieth-century critics also
make this comparison, sometimes criticizing Webster simply because
he differs from his predecessor. While there are many links between Webster and Shakespeare, there are many links between Webster
and everyone. They really should not be compared because Webster
is a satirist and not in the Shakespearean vein. His metaphysical
language, unlike Shakespeare's, moves our attention away from the
action; his plots are more episodic; his characters more Senecan.
Webster is more aptly compared to Marston or Tourneur, Middleton
to Shakespeare.

5   EDMOND, MARY. "In Search of John Webster." Times Literary
     Supplement, 24 December, pp. 1621-22.
         Provides important new biographical data. John Webster's
father and brother (John and Edward) lived in St. Sepulchre-
without-Newgate parish, and were in the cart, wagon, and coach
business. They were wealthy and respected. The dramatist was
probably the first-born son, born as early as 1571. John Webster,
Sr., left many records of business dealings. See 1980.8 for a
book based largely upon these biographical discoveries.

6   FORKER, CHARLES R. "Nathanael Richards' Messalina and The
     Duchess of Malfi." Notes and Queries, n.s. 23, no. 5/6:221-22.
         Finds that The Tragedy of Messalina (1634-36) imitates
Webster's major tragedies and other Renaissance dramas; like
Webster, Richards composed with a copybook nearby.

7   FRASER, RUSSELL W., and RABKIN, NORMAN, eds. Drama of the
     English Renaissance. Vol. 2, The Stuart Period. New York:
     Macmillan, pp. 431-515.
         An anthology that includes The White Devil and The Duchess
of Malfi. In the introduction to the volume, Fraser notes the
theme of integrity in the face of death as characteristic of
Webster. Finds that horror is the norm in his works and that he
pictures a life removed from morality: to move in his world is
to be destroyed. Reviewed: 1977.23.

8   HOGAN, FLORIANA. "Elizabethan and Jacobean Dramas and Their
     Spanish Sources." Research Opportunities in Renaissance Drama
     19:37-47.
         Cites The Duchess of Malfi in relation to Lope de Vega's El
Mayordomo de la Duquesa de Amalfi.

9   HONINGMANN, E.A.J. "Re-Enter the Stage Direction: Shakespeare
     and Some Contemporaries." Shakespeare Survey 29:117-25.
         Raises the issue of how modern editors should handle stage
directions--those of the author, of eighteenth-century editors,
etc. Cites as examples The Duchess of Malfi and The Devil's Law
Case, specifically for asides and "crypto-directions."

10   HOWSON, FRANK. "Horror and the Macabre in Four Elizabethan
     Tragedies: The Revenger's Tragedy, The Duchess of Malfi, The
     Second Maiden's Tragedy, The Atheist's Tragedy." Cahiers
     Elisabéthains, no. 10, pp. 1-12.
            Finds these plays pervaded by an obsessive fear of death--
     in dialogue, action, and visual representations. Thus, the death
     of the Duchess drives Ferdinand mad. His "vengeance" has been
     macabre, and he comes to see himself as corrupt. He becomes fas-
     cinated with corpses, as his brother becomes preoccupied with hell,
     especially in act 5. Argues that the death of the Duchess must
     have provoked a mounting horror in the audience, although she is
     less terrified of death than the play's other characters, thanks
     to her religion.

11   HOY, CYRUS. "Critical and Aesthetic Problems of Collaboration
     in Renaissance Drama." Research Opportunities in Renaissance
     Drama 19:3-6.
            Surveys the history of attribution studies, from their early
     excesses through twentieth-century reactions. Notes the differences
     between attribution scholarship and criticism. Sometimes, as in
     the Webster/Dekker collaborations, criticism has neglected works
     due to attribution problems.

12   KAYE, MELAINE. "The Sword Philippan: Woman as Hero in Stuart
     Tragedy." Ph.D. dissertation, University of California,
     Berkeley, 318 pp.
            Argues that Webster and other Jacobean dramatists center
     their tragedies on women because the Stuart period saw women as
     becoming increasingly powerless and thus able to depict a heroism
     grounded in romantic love. The women in Webster's major tragedies
     embody love, integrity, defiance, and endurance, all values that
     depend upon powerlessness. See Dissertation Abstracts International
     37 (1976):332-33A.

13   LAGARDE, FERNAND. "Webster à Salzbourg." Cahiers Elisabéthains,
     no. 10, pp. 45-63.
            A multiple review article, focusing upon the many books on
     Webster, or with important Websterian components, in the Jacobean
     Drama Studies series published by the Institut für Englische Sprache
     und Literatur, University of Salzburg. Finds that overall the
     series contributes to creating an understanding audience for
     Webster. (All the works reviewed are annotated herein.)

14   LORD, JOAN M. "The Duchess of Malfi: 'The Spirit of Greatness'
     and 'of Woman,'" Studies in English Literature 16, no. 2:305-17.
            Finds that students of the play have agreed on the centrality,
     but disagreed on the nature, of the Duchess. She is both natural-
     istic and conventional in that her responses to the action are both
     individualized and Senecan/stoic. Suggests that, as with other
     Webster characters, the Duchess enjoys role playing, and in the
     death sequence, her natural response and her sense of role unite

as she reacts to increasing horrors with increasing stoicism until death itself becomes ceremonial, yet highly personal.

15   PENNINGER, FRIEDA ELAINE. English Drama to 1600 (Excluding Shakespeare). American Literature, English Literature, and World Literatures in English: An Information Guide Series, 5. Detroit: Gale, pp. 335-39.
        Includes several general bibliographical sections and a short selection of secondary materials on Webster.

16   PRESTON, DENNIS R. "Imagery in The Duchess of Malfi." Studia Anglica Posnaniensia: An International Review of English Studies 7:109-20.
        Finds that Webster's use of imagery is traditional. Important images in The Duchess of Malfi include storms, disease, dramatic art, plant, and animal (especially bird) materials.

17   SCHOEN-RENE, ERNST WILLIAM. "The Malcontent Strain: A History of Malcontentedness in English Popular Drama from 1584 to 1614." Ph.D. dissertation, University of Washington, 302 pp.
        Shows that there were three periods of malcontent characters: the first were proto-malcontent types, e.g., vices; then, from 1584-95 a group of scholars, hermits, and overreachers. These evolved into the final, Websterian, satiric species in the 1590s. This strain develops from tool-villains to become panders, flatterers, spies, whose lives and actions, like those of both Flamineo and Bosola, are taken "in a mist." See Dissertation Abstracts International 37 (1976):1570A.

18   STILLING, ROGER. Love and Death in Renaissance Tragedy. Baton Rouge: Louisiana State University Press, pp. 224-46.
        Finds that Webster was like only Shakespeare and Ford among his contemporaries in his treatment of love: he builds plays on antiromantic situations, but his plots and characters develop from an earlier romantic tradition. Argues that the plays focus not upon the destructive power of eros but on the efforts of lovers to carve out a place within a hostile world. Notes that Webster was fascinated with women, almost to the point of being a feminist. Considers the tragedies individually: The White Devil shows the divorce of energy and morality but is a moral play. Still, it reveals Webster as more a psychologist of eros than a moralizer. The Duchess of Malfi features themes of generosity and love within a romantic marriage, disrupted by Ferdinand, who is both incestuously lustful and violently anti-erotic.

19   WEISS, ADRIAN. "Webster's Induction and Prologue to The Malcontent." Papers of the Bibliographical Society of America 70:103-7.
        Discusses evidence that the prologue must be dated before 1604 and that the play may have been written in four stages: the first quarto; the augmented quarto; the prologue; and Webster's

induction. In the induction, Webster shows he knows the play but
not the prologue.

20   YOUNG, DAVID. "Recent Studies in Elizabethan and Jacobean
      Drama." Studies in English Literature 16:333-48.
         Reviews two recent works in the Salzburg Jacobean Drama
      Studies series: Wang's survey of early Webster criticism (1975.31)
      and West's The Devil and John Webster (1974.27). Finds the first
      readable, crisp and lively, the second a compendium of interesting
      lore, carried a bit too far.

                                  1977

1   BENNETT, ROBERT B. "John Webster's Strange Dedication: An
      Inquiry into Literary Patronage and Jacobean Court Intrigue."
      English Literary Renaissance 7, no. 3:352-67.
         Asks why Webster dedicated A Monumental Column (on the death
      of Prince Henry) to the Prince's rival, Robert Carr, who had even
      been linked to rumors of an assassination attempt on the Prince.
      Carr stood for all that was profligate in the Jacobean court,
      Henry for sobriety. Suggests that the dedication is ironic, sa-
      tirical, and cynical.

2   BLISS, LEE. "Destructive Will and Social Chaos in The Devil's
      Law Case." Modern Language Review 72, no. 3:513-25.
         Finds that Romelio is like Flamineo in his vitality and
      cynicism, and both are self-deluded fools, overvaluing their own
      manipulative intelligence. The play is full of others who attempt
      to manipulate their fellows and fail. This theme is reinforced by
      many references to the theater and to role playing. Another im-
      portant idea in the play is that the destruction of family bonds
      leads to social decay. These serious components are not dissi-
      pated by the play's comic conclusion, which is deliberately made
      unsatisfactory.

3   CHAMPION, LARRY S. Tragic Patterns in Jacobean and Caroline
      Drama. Knoxville: University of Tennessee Press, pp. 119-51.
      [Incorporates 1974.3.]
         Notes that controversy still surrounds the issue of the moral
      value and structural coherence of Webster's two major tragedies.
      Finds that these works present a morally ambivalent world, where
      choices are not clear. In The White Devil, all the major charac-
      ters act out of self-interest. The only virtuous characters are
      destroyed, while those who gain power all prove corrupt. It is
      against this grim backdrop that Vittoria's tragedy develops. She
      progresses from a courtesan to a woman with a sense of value and
      responsibility: while others around her decay, she grows in forti-
      tude. Finds that The Duchess of Malfi operates in this same bleak
      setting but with a protagonist who is not morally flawed: her
      tragedy is more clearly caused by social and external forces.

Similarly, Bosola is like Flamineo, but adds a dimension of moral
conscience as a result of his exposure to the Duchess.

4   FELPERIN, HOWARD. Shakespearean Representation: Mimesis and
     Modernity. Princeton: Princeton University Press, pp. 171-91.
        Argues that Webster consciously deconstructs Shakespeare's
     piety as well as his romantic or subjective aspect: his is a con-
     sistent and coherent revision of Shakespeare. The White Devil is
     full of characters making moral pronouncements; too, the virtuous
     characters often have to pretend to be evil, rather than the
     (Shakespearean) reverse. Concludes that all this posturing and
     theatricalization of morality is anti-Shakespearean, that there
     is no "reality" to Webster's "selfs" beyond appearance.

5   GOLDWYN, FLOYD LOWELL, Jr. Image Pattern and Moral Vision in
     John Webster. Jacobean Drama Studies, 71. Salzburg: Institut
     für Englische Sprache und Literatur, Universität Salzburg, 143 pp.
     Published version of 1975.14.

*6 GRACE, DERMOT BERTRAND. "The Bosola Context." Ph.D. disserta-
     tion, University of Toronto.
        Presents Bosola as a malcontent, within the context of other
     Elizabethan dramatic malcontents. These figures develop out of
     philosophical and formal aspects of Senecan tragedy in interaction
     with a growing interest in Machiavellianism. The malcontent char-
     acter emerges as a satirist as the vice of the morality play dis-
     appears. Discusses the varieties of malcontents in different
     Renaissance dramatists, returning to Bosola in The Duchess of Malfi,
     who represents a culminating point in the tradition. See
     Dissertation Abstracts International 37 (1977):6495-96A.

7   GRAVES, ROBERT BRUCE. "English Stage Lighting: 1575-1642."
     Ph.D. dissertation, Northwestern University, 380 pp.
        Traces the different effects of candlelit and sunlit plays
     on Renaissance public and indoor stages. Finds that the conventions
     of lighting were remarkably similar indoors and out, with artificial
     illumination playing less of a role than previously thought. Con-
     cludes with a look at The Duchess of Malfi, 4.1 (the dead man's
     hand scene), that while often assumed to require darkness, would
     actually work best if the audience saw it in its entirety. See
     Dissertation Abstracts International 37 (1977):3987-88A.

8   HOLDSWORTH, ROGER V. "Another Echo of Hamlet in The White Devil."
     Notes and Queries, n.s. 24, no. 3:204-5.
        Suggests that a speech by Flamineo (5.3. 206-12) declaring
     his intention to meet Brachiano's ghost recalls act 1, scenes 1
     and 2 of Hamlet.

9   JOHNSON, PAULA. "Jacobean Ephemera and the Immortal Word."
     Renaissance Drama, n.s. 8:151-71.
        Notes that Webster's Lord Mayor's show, when printed,

contained descriptions of the theatrical devices used in its
presentation. Briefly analyzes <u>Monuments of Honour</u>, noting that
Webster was conscious of his literary precedents and that the
printed text asserts an authorial presence. Finds Webster was
attentive to the balanced demands of cost and spectacle, and sup-
plies "iconological exegesis." Concludes that Webster's is the
last Lord Mayor's show to try to link its visual features to time-
less significances.

10   JORDAIN, V.L. "Webster's Change of Sidney's 'Wormish' to
      'Womanish.'" <u>Notes and Queries</u>, n.s. 24, no. 2:135.
          Discusses Webster's borrowing and alteration of a line from
      Sidney in <u>The Duchess of Malfi</u>, 5.5. Argues that the usage does
      not make sense unless it has a proverbial, as well as a literary,
      source.

11   KING, ROBERT PETER. "Theatrical Playmaking in Elizabethan
      Revenge Tragedy." Ph.D. dissertation, New York University,
      185 pp.
          Considers the play-within-a-play as a device for blood re-
      venge in, among other settings, Bosola's revenge in <u>The Duchess of
      Malfi</u> and "Mulinassar's" in <u>The White Devil</u>. Also finds the tor-
      ture of the Duchess a "playlet," and uses the same term to describe
      the trial of Vittoria. Suggests that this device is used to avoid
      some of the moral implications of revenge. See <u>Dissertation
      Abstracts International</u> 37 (1977):5852-53A.

12   LOGAN, TERENCE P., and SMITH, DENZELL S., eds. "Other Drama-
      tists." In <u>The New Intellectuals: A Survey and Bibliography
      of Recent Studies in English Renaissance Drama</u>. Lincoln:
      University of Nebraska Press, pp. 323-40.
          Sections on William Alexander and William Barkstead cite
      studies of Webster's debts to both authors.

13   McLEOD, SUSAN H. <u>Dramatic Imagery in the Plays of John Webster</u>.
      Jacobean Drama Studies, 68. Salzburg: Institut für Englische
      Sprache und Literatur, Universität Salzburg, 179 pp.
          Published form of 1973.24.

14   MEHL, DIETER. "Emblematic Theatre." <u>Anglia</u> 95:130-38.
          Asks if Elizabethan theater was primarily visual or aural.
      Notes that dumb shows show a strong desire for visual effects, but
      argues it is also possible to overread iconographic, as well as
      verbal, subtleties. Finds no break between early dramatic specta-
      cles and Webster's visual rituals. He was one of a company of
      stylized, pageant-filled dramatists. Concludes with a lament over
      our lack of knowledge of Elizabethan production practices. See
      1969.26, 29.

15   MIRENDA, ANGELA MARIE. "The Noble Lie: Selfhood and Tragedy
      in the Renaissance." Ph.D. dissertation, Pennsylvania State

University, 213 pp.

Suggests that the somewhat credulous humanism of the Elizabethans believed art could transcend reality, but the Jacobeans were more skeptical. This leads to a movement from Elizabethan tragedies in which heroes transcend death to a seventeenth-century sense that death is inexplicable, which leads in turn to tragicomedy. Webster's Duchess is the ultimate in human heroes, totally self-possessed, clever, and good. Finds that the Duchess achieves transcendence by looking within herself rather than to any outside agency. See Dissertation Abstracts International 38 (1977):2815A.

16 MULLANY, PETER F. Religion and the Arifice of Jacobean and Caroline Drama. Jacobean Drama Studies, 41. Salzburg: Institut für Englische Sprache und Literatur, Universität Salzburg, 184 pp., passim.

Cites Webster, e.g., for his achievement of moral significance in The Duchess of Malfi through the interplay of character and action. Notes how elsewhere he utilizes straightforward moralizing didacticism. Finds that both the tragedies show revenge disapprovingly. Webster was centrally concerned with the religious implications of human actions.

17 NORDFORS, MARIANNE. "Science and Realism in John Webster's The Duchess of Malfi." Studia Neophilologica 49:233-42.

Observes that to most critics, The Duchess of Malfi involves a pattern of integrity, centering upon the unique heroic figure of the Duchess, who is full-bodied and vital. Bosola comments on the action with an almost medical realism, and elsewhere also the play is characterized by an almost scientific objectivity. Suggests the possibility that Bosola is an autobiographical portrait.

18 SHAPIRO, MICHAEL. Children of the Revels: The Boy Companies of Shakespeare's Time and Their Plays. New York: Columbia University Press, 313 pp., passim.

Cites Webster in passing. Notes that the "Ho" plays were written for the boy companies.

19 SIMON, ROSE ANNE. "The Courtly Labyrinth: Renaissance Courtiership and Jacobean Drama." Ph.D. dissertation, University of Rochester, 469 pp.

Contrasts Castiglione's platonic and ideal courtier (who combined altruism and patriotism) with Machiavelli, who was seen as the opposite. Jacobean plays, including Webster's, often focus on the relationship between a Prince and a courtier, asking if the love between them is genuine or feigned. See Dissertation Abstracts International 38 (1978):770A.

20 SPIKES, JUDITH DOOLIN. "The Jacobean History Play and the Myth of the Elect Nation." Renaissance Drama, n.s. 8:117-49.

Discusses Sir Thomas Wyat as a treatment of Elizabethan current events, since Wyat's rebellion was seen as parallel to the

Essex rebellion. The play raises the delicate question of the
rebellion by a good Protestant against a lawful, Catholic sovereign.

21   STAGG, LOUIS CHARLES. Index to the Figurative Language of the
     Tragedies of Shakespeare's Chief Seventeenth-Century Contempo-
     raries: Chapman, Heywood, Jonson, Marston, Webster, Tourneur,
     and Middleton. Ann Arbor: University Microfilms International
     for the Memphis State University Press, 520 pp., esp. pp. 291-361.
     [Expanded version of 1967.24.]
        An alphabetical list of images, with reference to plays (e.g.,
     "Anchor (Ancor): Then cast ancor [--as ship in storm]. WD, V. vi.
     249."). Also cross-references indices by subject (e.g., nature,
     learning, etc.).

22   TABB, MARGARET MIKESELL. "The Female Protagonist in Jacobean
     Tragedy." Ph.D. dissertation, University of Connecticut, 599 pp.
        Finds that tragedies with female protagonists in the Jacobean
     period focus upon love and marriage, and have different themes and
     conventions than other tragedies. Women in these plays are defined
     by their sexual relationships. Finds that The White Devil and The
     Duchess of Malfi concern the demise of the family and the rise of
     financial considerations as a basis for marriage, and thus depict
     the degeneration of traditional values. Concludes that Jacobean
     dramatic women reflect, and do not form, their world. See
     Dissertation Abstracts International 37 (1977):5857A.

23   TURNER, ROBERT Y. "Recent Studies in Elizabethan and Jacobean
     Drama." Studies in English Literature 17, no. 2:333-57.
        Comments upon the anthology edited by Fraser and Rabkin
     (1976.7) and Fraser's suggestion that Webster's dramas depict an
     amoral world.

                              1978

1   ADAMS, ROBERT P. A Companion to Shakespeare: The Non-
     Shakespearean Elizabethan Drama: An Introduction. Washington:
     University Press of America, pp. 134-56.
        Chapter 10 is entitled "Dear Beauteous Death, The Jew of the
     Just," and concerns The White Devil. Reviewing the drama since
     1585, finds a major change around 1600 from conservativism to
     skepticism. Presents Webster's art as a strange, nonnaturalistic
     nightmare depicting the collapse of traditional values through the
     story of Vittoria.

2   BARRANGER, MILLIE SLATER. "The Shape of Brecht's The Duchess
     of Malfi." Comparative Drama 12:61-74.
        Reports that Brecht adapted Webster's tragedy in 1933 while
     he was living in the U.S. in exile. He collaborated with Auden,
     to whom the version is usually credited. Brecht wrote new scenes,
     transposed scenes from other plays, and refocused Webster's themes

and characters in order to highlight Marxist theory. Argues that
he attempted, in the style of the silent cinema, to make the story
more intelligible. His most notable changes were in the prologue,
plot, character, and theatrical elements of the work.

3   BERGERON, DAVID M. "The Wax Figures in The Duchess of Malfi."
     Studies in English Literature 18, no. 2:331-39.
         Suggests that the wax figures are not gratuitous horrors but
     central in the play's progressive development since they attack
     the Duchess' reason for living (her love for Antonio and the chil-
     dren). Comments on sources and analogues of this scene. Notes
     that life imitates art since the real children are later dead.
     Like the dead man's hand, these figures show the movement from love
     and hope to death. Finds that there is a recurrent theme of funer-
     ary effigies throughout the play, of which this group is center.
     They are prophetic images and part of a pattern in which all things
     move towards the grave.

4   BERGGREN, PAULA S. "Womanish Mankind: Four Jacobean Heroines."
     International Journal of Woman's Studies 1:439-62.
         Contends that Stuart tragedy reflects a loss of confidence
     taking place in English society under King James. It depicts young
     women under attack rather than focusing upon oversize male heroes.
     Vittoria and the Duchess subvert a conservative and patriarchial
     society by consulting their own desires before the values of so-
     ciety. Vittoria shows how style can make evil attractive, while
     the Duchess is more virtuous--her only crime may be her femininity.

5   BLANTON, CYNTHIA LANHAM. "A Perspective that Shows Us Hell:
     Form and Vision in Webster's Major Tragedies." Ph.D. disserta-
     tion, Princeton University, 296 pp.
         Notes critical disagreement regarding the theatrical value
     of Webster's tragedies. Argues that Webster makes use of medieval
     and early Elizabethan dramatic forms, especially borrowing from
     Marlowe and Kyd. Finds three major issues of stagecraft that need
     discussion: characterization and motivation; structure as a re-
     flection of meaning; and potential audience response. Both the
     dramas rely heavily upon theatrical illusion: The Duchess of Malfi,
     especially, uses other theatrical genres such as romantic comedy.
     Both works provide a way of accommodating and defining a hostile
     and illogical world. See Dissertation Abstracts International 38
     (1978):4174-75A.

6   BRUCHER, RICHARD. "Esthetic Violence in Elizabethan and Jacobean
     Tragedy." Ph.D. dissertation, Rutgers University, 235 pp.
         Explores the mature and effects of Renaissance stage violence.
     Such violence, as a dramatic illusion, is all "esthetic." Also, it
     is often witty or histrionic. Finds Webster uses aesthetic vio-
     lence and ritual to depict the deranged minds of his characters
     and to involve the audience in the bizarre moods of the plays.
     Webster's horrors are not relieved by morality or comic effects--

they depict instead the collapse of sane values. See <u>Dissertation Abstracts International</u> 39 (1979):6772A.

7   CANDIDO, JOSEPH DOMINIC. "Renaissance Biographical Practice and the Tudor Biographical Play." Ph.D. dissertation, Indiana University, 324 pp.
    Notes that <u>Sir Thomas Wyat</u>, by Webster and Dekker, is among the dramatic biographies of major Tudor figures. This, and similar plays, adopt and adapt the ideas and techniques of such prose biographies as Walton's <u>Lives</u>. See <u>Dissertation Abstracts International</u> 38 (1978):6739A.

8   CARSON, NEIL. "John Webster: The Apprentice Years." In <u>Elizabethan Theater VI</u>. Edited by G.R. Hibbard. Hamden, Conn.: Archon, pp. 76-87.
    Shows Webster's later style and genius developed out of his apprentice period. Notes that Webster and Dekker were much different individuals, and their collaboration is surprising. Webster's early work seems to try to satisfy both the realistic aims of the public companies and the goal of deliberate artifice in the boy companies. The mature Webster's works show the same tension between naive and self-conscious artistry, achieving a metaphysical "yoking" effect.

9   CAUTHEN, I.B., Jr. "An Unpublished Letter by T.S. Eliot (1962)." <u>Yeats-Eliot Review</u> 5, no. 1:223.
    Reports that Eliot acknowledged Webster as a source for <u>A Game of Chess</u>, 11. 117-26 (specifically, act 5 of <u>The White Devil</u>).

10 CORNELIA, MARIE. <u>The Function of the Masque in Jacobean Tragedy and Tragicomedy</u>. Jacobean Drama Studies, 77. Salzburg: Institut für Englische Sprache und Literatur, Universität Salzburg, 162 pp.
    Published version of 1968.8.

11 DAVIDSON, RICHARD B. "Anonymous Plays." In <u>The Later Jacobean and Caroline Dramatists: A Survey and Bibliography of Recent Studies in English Renaissance Drama</u>. Edited by Terence P. Logan and Denzell S. Smith. Lincoln: University of Nebraska Press, pp. 210-27.
    Presents bibliographical data on some possible Webster attributions.

12 DIEHL, HUSTON. "Iconography and Characterization in English Tragedy 1585-1642." <u>Comparative Drama</u> 12, no. 2:113-22.
    Argues that characters in Renaissance plays fused realism with symbolism: the individual embodied the universal, especially in visual presentations. Notes Webster's stress on visual matters in the "character" of "An Excellent Actor." Comments upon Webster's use of such visual elements as emblems, disguise, portraits, and the like.

13 GRAVES, ROBERT BRUCE. "<u>The Duchess of Malfi</u> at the Globe and the Blackfriars." <u>Renaissance Drama</u>, n.s. 9:193-209.

Notes that The Duchess of Malfi was performed both indoors
and out. Compares the possible stagings of the "dead man's hand"
scene, and concludes that it was probably not intended to be done
illusionistically--in actual darkness--in either theatrical venue.
In fact, both public and indoor theaters would be in moderate darkness by act 4 of this play, which is how the scene would play best.
Also discusses Webster's more general use of torches and their re-
moval to signify light and darkness, and finds that this was usually
a symbolic, rather than literal, stage effect.

14 HALL, ELIZABETH J. "A Study of the Change in Attitude Towards
   Blood in the Renaissance Drama 1589-1642." Ph.D. dissertation,
   University of Kentucky, 243 pp.
      Argues that blood, in language and in action, was a central
and sacred substance in the Renaissance drama. Discusses twelve
plays of the period. Webster (and others) alter the "sacramental"
use of blood of the early and Shakespearean dramas. He shows characters and worlds no longer dependent upon the former codes that
were symbolized by blood. Finds that the period shows an increasing lack of respect for blood, as the coherence of social order
decayed. See Dissertation Abstracts International 40 (1979):3315-
16A.

15 HALSALL, TONY. "The Collaboration of Dekker and Webster in
   Westward Ho and Northward Ho." Papers of the Bibliographical
   Society of America 72 (1st Quarter):65-68.
      Supports an attribution of the "Ho" plays of roughly 60% to
Dekker and the rest to Webster, based upon the uses of names in
ways characteristic of the two authors.

16 JENSEN, EJNER J. "Lamb, Poel, and our Postwar Theater:
   Elizabethan Revivals." Renaissance Drama, n.s. 9:211-32.
      Discusses "Lamb's revival" of interest in the Elizabethan
drama, noting that Lamb cited scenes in 1808.1 for their isolated
dramatic effect, not their overall place within dramas. He was
interested in curiosities, antiquarianism, and the like. Also, he
saw the older dramatists mostly as poets, not men of the theater.
Finds that a second revival, headed by Poel, focused upon the stage,
beginning with the 1892 production of The Duchess of Malfi (which
was not very successful). Concludes that today we are seeing another
revival that originates in the kinship of our world to that of the
Elizabethan drama: contemporary theater has taught us to appreciate
Webster's tragedies. Reviews several productions beginning in 1945.

17 KINNEY, ARTHUR F. "Recent Studies in Elizabethan and Jacobean
   Drama." Studies in English Literature 18, no. 2:361-418.
      Reviews several recent studies of Webster, noting the stress
on the dramatist's emphasis of horror, waste, and intense theatricality.

18 KLINCK, DENNIS R. "Calvinism and Jacobean Tragedy." Genre 11
   (Fall):333-58.

Sees Bosola in The Duchess of Malfi as a malcontent, cynically aware of human depravity and capable of the worst sort of criminal behavior--but with moral sensitivity as well: his "natural" virtue attempts to redeem itself, ineffectively. Finds that he experiences a true awakening of conscience, tries to atone, and only confirms his condemnation.

19 LEVY, BEVERLY SAUER. "The Theater of God's Judgment: Revenge Tragedy and the Renaissance Worldview." Ph.D. dissertation, Brandeis University, 193 pp.
    Argues that revenge tragedies use the dramatic metaphor to show the world as God's theater. Webster cited passim; the focus is on Kyd, Tourneur, and Shakespeare. See Dissertation Abstracts International 38 (1978):7347A.

20 LOGAN, TERENCE P., and SMITH, DENZELL, eds. "Other Dramatists." In The Later Jacobean and Caroline Dramatists: A Survey and Bibliography of Recent Studies in English Renaissance Drama. Lincoln: University of Nebraska Press, pp. 228-59.
    Webster is cited, but never the object of major attention, in this bibliographical study.

*21 MaCDONALD, ROGER ALFRED. "The Widow: A Recurring Figure in Jacobean and Caroline Comedy." Ph.D. dissertation, University of New Brunswick.
    Discusses thirty-five comedies containing widows, especially focusing upon the suitor-pursues-widow motif. Includes much information concerning attitudes towards widows, remarriage, etc., but little specifically directed to Webster. See Dissertation Abstracts International 39 (1978):1594A.

22 McCONNELL-DERKSEN, DOROTHY DIANE. "The Theme of Right Reason in Jacobean Tragedy." Ph.D. dissertation, University of Toronto.
    Finds that the Jacobean drama moved away from the idea of "right reason," which seemed useless and/or limited. Includes a discussion of the issue of the value and authority of such reason in The Duchess of Malfi, and of Webster's cynicism. See Dissertation Abstracts International 39 (1978):2295A.

23 MATSON, M.N. "The Hamilton Collection in Stockholm." Research Opportunities in Renaissance Drama 21:53-60.
    Notes that this Swedish collection includes a 1623 edition of The Devil's Law Case and a 1640 The Duchess of Malfi.

24 PETERSON, JOYCE E. Curs'd Example: "The Duchess of Malfi" and Commonwealth Tragedy. Columbia: University of Missouri Press, 122 pp. [Revision of 1974.21.]
    Argues that critical readings that see the statement "I Am Duchess of Malfi still" as heroic are misguided. Actually, The Duchess of Malfi is in the moral play/commonwealth tragedy tradition, wherein a monarch and his state suffer due to the neglect of

social duties for personal pleasure. The Duchess is guilty of
this infraction in her affair with Antonio and brings upon herself
and her society all the ills of the tragedy. Reviewed: 1979.23.

25   PFISTER, MANFRED. "Neue Jacobean Drama Studies aus Salzburg."
      Archiv für das Studium der Neueren Sprachen und Literatur 215:
      92-99.
          Reviews several of the Jacobean Drama Studies series volumes,
      including some (herein annotated separately) that deal with Webster.

26   ROSENFELD, HARVEY. "Roman Catholic Churchmen in Elizabethan
      Drama." Ph.D. dissertation, St. John's University, 385 pp.
          Finds that over fifty clerics appear in Elizabethan plays,
      of which only about twenty are positive portraits. The most common
      negative images of Catholic clerics are in plays dealing with Spain,
      but Italianate dramas also feature such villains, often (as in both
      Webster's major tragedies) with the clergymen participating avidly
      in affairs of state. See Dissertation Abstracts International 38
      (1978):4186A.

27   SABOL, ANDREW J., ed. Four Hundred Songs and Dances from the
      Stuart Masque. Providence: Brown University Press, pp. 18,
      553, 579, 598, 618.
          Notes dramatists' use of masque materials, e.g., Webster's
      The Duchess of Malfi with its madmen's utterances that focus that
      tragedy's grim humor. Notes also some specific masques that
      Webster may have had in mind when he has Ferdinand say "I'll send
      her masques of common courtesans."

28   SAXON, PATRICIA JEAN. "The Limits of Assertiveness: Modes of
      Female Identity in Shakespeare and the Stuart Dramatists."
      Ph.D. dissertation, University of Texas-Austin, 276 pp.
          Finds three types of assertive women in Elizabethan plays:
      manly women; gaming and sexually posturing women; and "spunky"
      comic heroines. Examines Vittoria and other Stuart heroines in
      terms of these three types. In Jacobean drama, sex comes to serve
      the drive for power and women are seen more and more as prostitutes.
      See Dissertation Abstracts International 30 (1978):7349-50A.

29   SPEAR, JEFFREY L. "'The Burial of the Dead': Eliot's Corpse
      in the Garden in a Christian Context." American Literature 50,
      no. 2:282-85.
          Presents Webster as a source for the "stetson" passage at
      the end of the first section of The Wasteland. Specifically notes
      Cornelia's "Dirge," which can be read as a Christian document.

30   SUTHERLAND, SARAH P. "Masques in Jacobean Tragedy." Ph.D.
      dissertation, Columbia University, 211 pp.
          Studies six Jacobean plays with masques, including The
      Duchess of Malfi, wherein Duke Ferdinand tries to drive the Duchess
      insane through the masque of madmen; she retains her sanity and her

brothers are snared in their own masque. Finds that all Jacobean
masques yoke together the decorum of courtly celebration with the
indecorum of mayhem, madness, and murder, illuminating a particularly Jacobean sensibility. See <u>Dissertation Abstracts International</u>
39 (1978):2303A.

31   VILLAREJO, OSCAR M. "Shakespeare y los dramaturgos compañeros
     suyos. Las Fuentes españolas de varias de sus obras." <u>Revista</u>
     <u>de Archivos, Biblioteras y Museos</u> 78:829-67.
          Discusses Lope de Vega's influence on Shakespeare and the
     possibility of his influence on <u>The Duchess of Malfi</u>.

32   VOYTOVICH, EDWARD ROBERT. "Tragedy and Eschatology: <u>Arden of</u>
     <u>Feversham</u> to <u>The Broken Heart</u>." Ph.D. dissertation, Syracuse
     University, 284 pp.
          Argues that, over the course of the Renaissance drama, retri-
     butive justice becomes increasingly dispensed in this life rather
     than the next; death is an end, and a secular virtue based on inner
     strength replaces Christian morality. <u>The Duchess of Malfi</u> and
     similar works present a vision of man increasingly alone in an in-
     creasingly secular eschatological universe. See <u>Dissertation</u>
     <u>Abstracts International</u> 38 (1978):4855A.

                              1979

1   ADAMS, ROBERT M., ed. <u>The Duchess of Malfi</u>. In <u>The Norton</u>
     <u>Anthology of English Literature</u>. 4th ed. 2 vols. Edited by
     M.H. Abrams et al. New York: Norton, 1:1236-1315.
          Includes <u>The Duchess of Malfi</u>, with a very short introduction.
     Finds Webster second only to Jonson among Shakespeare's contempo-
     raries. He is a poet of moods, especially melancholy, of which
     Bosola is a fine example. Notes Webster's fascination with de-
     generate Italianate courts. Concludes that the Duchess is a free
     and positive woman.

2   ARDEN, JOHN. "Rug-Headed Irish Kerns and British Poets." <u>New</u>
     <u>Statesman</u>, 13 July, pp. 56-57.
          Cites Webster as one of several authors who held deep-seated
     and obsessed hostility to Irish life.

3   BASHIAN, KATHLEEN RYNIKER. "Rhetoric as an Act of Self Defense:
     An Analysis of Trial Scenes in the Works of Peele, Shakespeare,
     Webster, and Massinger." Ph.D. dissertation, New York
     University, 237 pp.
          Analyzes four trial scenes, including that in <u>The White Devil</u>,
     in which protagonists serve as their own defense attorneys. Studies
     sources, rhetoric, logic, and poetry. Considers the legal aspects
     of the scenes, including, in Webster's case, the law of adultery.
     Finds that <u>The White Devil</u> was influenced by Cicero and the rhe-
     torical theories of Petrus Ramus. See <u>Dissertation Abstracts</u>
     <u>International</u> 40:1476-77A.

4   BRADBURY, GAIL. "Webster's 'Lapwing': A Significant Allusion
      in The White Devil." Notes and Queries, n.s. 26:148.
        Finds that specific bird allusions in The White Devil illumi-
nate character. Brachiano's reference to his son as a "lapwing"
(2.1. 128-29) alludes to both precocity and deceit or cunning.
Notes that later, Flamineo compares him to a raven and an eagle.
Concludes that the young prince may be covering up a cunning and
cruel nature.

5   BROOKE, NICHOLAS. Horrid Laughter in Jacobean Tragedy. New
      York: Harper & Row, 135 pp., esp. pp. 26-69.
        Discusses a line of plays from Kyd through Webster ending in
stylized masques of grotesque violence. In both of Webster's tragedies, finds the same pattern of characters: female heroes, "great
men," and caustic commentators. In The White Devil, these characters
shift within a complex plot, with Vittoria being especially ambiguous.
Notes that the play's dumb show will provoke laughter, while the
trial scene will demonstrate Vittoria's magnificence. Finds
Cornelia is the work's "normative" conscience, the voice of conventional Christian morality, from which the play departs. Stresses
the humor of Flamineo's mock death. At the work's conclusion, horror and laughter are brilliantly controlled.
        Finds that The Duchess of Malfi contrasts the domestic virtue
of the Duchess and Antonio with the madness of the great, especially
when Ferdinand changes from a secretive dormouse into a wolf. Notes
also the theatrical shows within the work, which are grotesque and
contrast with the dignity of the Duchess' death scene. The piling-
up of bodies at the conclusion is mirth-provoking, and laughter
here cannot and should not be suppressed. Concludes that both
tragedies are about death, but The Duchess of Malfi is also about
the possibilities of life. Reviewed: 1981.14, 22.

6   BRUDER, HARRY. "Analogic Form and Webster's White Devil."
      Publications of the Arkansas Philological Association 5, nos.
      2 and 3:41-47.
        Observes that critics find The White Devil both successful
and seriously flawed, often in comparison with other works such
as Hamlet. Actually, the function of the play is to confound the
audience, especially in its reaction to Vittoria in, for example,
the trial scene wherein she is guilty, but the trial itself is a
mockery of justice. The play deliberately denies audience certi-
tude through three techniques: 1) soliloquies that do not explain
character motivation, 2) irony that "takes in" the audience as well
as the characters, and 3) the failure of the play to provide an
internal norm or moral center.

7   BURGESS, JUDITH LIVINGSTON. "The Trickster in Elizabethan-
      Jacobean Drama: The Development of a Western Archetype." Ph.D.
      dissertation, Stanford University, 349 pp.
        Discusses the history of dramatic tricksters--parasites,
tricky slaves, vices, etc., and their use in comedy and tragedy

including Webster's tragedies. The same traits tend to recur in all the trickster types, and the Elizabethan-Jacobean version has become an archetype down to the present day. Characters like Flamineo let us laugh at, and evade, oppressive authority without open rebellion. See Dissertation Abstracts International 39:7352A.

8   CHARNEY, MAURICE. "Shakespeare--and the Others." Shakespeare Quarterly 30:325-42.
       Notes that Shakespeare needs to be considered among, not isolated from, his contemporary dramatists. Cites Webster throughout. The Duchess of Malfi has less sense of the tragic than Shakespeare's works, and demonstrates Webster's interest in "detached eloquence," e.g., Flamineo's death speech.

9   CORBALLIS, RICHARD, and HARDING, J.M., comps. A Corcordance to the Works of John Webster. 4 vols. Jacobean Drama Studies, 7. Salzburg: Institut für Englische Sprache und Literatur, Universität Salzburg, 1890 pp.
       A computer-generated concordance, citing each word with the line in which it appears plus play, act, and scene. Vol. 4 includes Sir Thomas Wyat. (Only vol. 4 has been seen; it was actually published prior to vols. 1-3.)

10   COURTADE, ANTHONY EDWARD. "The Structure of John Webster's Plays." Ph.D. dissertation, Indiana University, 200 pp.
       Studies the structure of The White Devil, The Duchess of Malfi, and The Devil's Law Case, finding that Webster's structural sense is clearly based upon Jacobean dramatic conventions. Departures from expectation are designed to achieve dramatic effect--they are not structural flaws. Finds in The White Devil a multiple focus on one topic--the effort of the individual to survive in a world of corruption and hypocrisy: Vittoria is guilty, but less so than her persecutors. Sees the heroine of The Duchess of Malfi as stronger and more dominant. She suffers harsh punishment for breaking social and political restraints. Personal integrity seems the only worthwhile path in a world of cruelty and corruption that tests the princely nature of the protagonist. The Devil's Law Case utilizes the same structure, in spite of its generic difference. Social intercourse is impossible, but the work's ending is optimistic. Concludes that Webster's structures hold a mirror up to those imperfections that mask true human beauty. See 1980.13; Dissertation Abstracts International 40 (1979):1749A.

11   COUTON, MARIE. "La Duchesse d'Amalfi: Deux récits d'une histoire tragique." Confluents 5, no. 1:27-46.
       Compares the English versions of the story of the Duchess of Malfi of Painter and Webster, with special emphasis on characerization, plot, and the manner in which the two authors utilize different structures to recount the same history.

12   DUER, LESLIE. "The Landscape of Imagination in The Duchess of
      Malfi." Modern Language Studies 10 (Winter, 1979-80):3-10.
          Finds very little actual landscape in the play, but much
      landscape imagery--trees, ponds, droplets, etc. Concludes that
      this imagistic landscape is generally surreal, distorted and wild,
      a moral wilderness that prepares us for actual physical symbols
      such as the dead man's hand.

13   FITZ, L.T. "Humanism Questioned: A Study of Four Renaissance
      Characters." English Studies in Canada 5:388-405.
          Studies Tamburlaine, Faustus, Angelo, and Ferdinand. In The
      Duchess of Malfi, Ferdinand is opposed, platonically, to the physi-
      cal, especially sex (notes this is an alternative to the "incest"
      reading of this character). His hypocrisy is internal: he tries
      to deceive himself. Since he cannot ascend, he descends to beastli-
      ness. The play sees the neoplatonic ideal of ascent as impossible.
      The Duchess offers a healthy alternative in her relationship with
      Antonio.

14   GLOE, ESTHER MATHILDA. "The Influence of the English Work Laws
      on the Drama of the Period from 1563 to 1642." Ph.D. disserta-
      tion, Oklahoma State University, 387 pp.
          Mentions Webster occasionally, particularly in the context
      of the "Ho" plays. See Dissertation Abstracts International 40
      (1980):6290A.

15   GODSHALK, W.L. "Shakespeare's 'Honey-Stalks': Webster's
      'Honey-Dew.'" Notes and Queries, n.s. 26:114-15.
          Considers Webster's use of "honney-dew" in The Duchess of
      Malfi (1.1. 340-42). Finds that Webster's source may be
      Shakespeare's "honey-stalks" in Titus Andronicus (4.4. 89-93).

16   HAPPÉ, PETER. "The Vice: A Checklist and An Annotated Bibli-
      ography." Research Opportunities in Renaissance Drama 22:17-35.
          Includes citations of Eastward Ho and The White Devil (in
      which Flamineo is considered a "vice" character).

17   HASSEL, R. CHRIS. Renaissance Drama and the English Church Year.
      Lincoln: University of Nebraska Press, 215 pp., passim, esp.
      pp. 52, 179-83, 209.
          Comments that The Duchess of Malfi was performed on the festi-
      val day of St. Stephen in 1630, and appropriately, since the Duchess
      is a martyr like the Saint. Finds the contrast to Webster's Vittoria
      marked, and notes that The White Devil was not performed in conjunc-
      tion with any religious festival.

18   HERRING, HENRY. "The Self and Madness: Marlowe's Edward II and
      Webster's The Duchess of Malfi." Journal of Medieval and
      Renaissance Studies 9:307-23.
          Notes that the late sixteenth- and early seventeenth-century
      drama sometimes measures a person's value by the standard of

personal integrity, under an assault attempting to provoke madness.
Sees Webster's creation of such a world as closer to despair than
Marlowe's vision, in that the strong Duchess cannot save society
through her integrity--only her self. Concludes that Webster's
is a fictional universe of individual and social duplicity and rift.
The Duchess is a stronger character than Marlowe's Edward II, yet
all she can salvage is her sanity and selfhood.

19   HILLMAN, RICHARD W. "Meaning and Morality in Some Renaissance
     Revenge Plays." University of Toronto Quarterly 49:1-17.
     Sees Webster using revenge to show individuals finding a
meaning to life that makes death itself superfluous, especially in
The White Devil, where Francisco and Ludovico's revenge is identified with the ultimate meaning of life and the transcendence of
death. Both characters seem to cherish revenge for its own sake,
more than an actual redress of any deeply felt wrongs. Thus,
Webster implies that life is meaningless, transient, slippery, and
without absolutes.

20   HOWARD, TONY. "Census of Renaissance Drama Productions."
     Research Opportunities in Renaissance Drama 22:73-85.
     Includes reviews of The Duchess of Malfi done in London and
at the Birmingham Repertory Theatre; and The White Devil at
Washington's Kennedy Center (with comments upon the latter as "an
appalling production" by Susan H. McLeod).

21   JOCHUM, KLAUS PETER. Discrepant Awareness: Studies in English
     Renaissance Drama. Neve Studien zur Anglissik und Amerikanistik
     13. Frankfort: Lang, 310 pp.
     Finds Webster's complexity in the tragedies almost Shakespeare-
ean: both make use of "discrepant awareness." Analyzes the "in-
formational strategy" of the plays. Finds that The White Devil
features a moral chiaroscuro, based upon what the characters do
and do not know, and how they get their information. For example,
Brachiano believes the false letter written by Francisco concerning
Vittoria's infidelity. Finds the handling of information in the
play rather loose, adding to the work's sense of moral ambiguity.
In The Duchess of Malfi, the process is neater: the brothers dis-
cover the truth about the Duchess' wedded state at the play's mid-
point.

22   LEVIN, RICHARD. New Readings vs. Old Plays: Recent Trends in
     the Reinterpretation of English Renaissance Drama. Chicago:
     University of Chicago Press, 277 pp.
     Cites Webster intermittently in a study of contemporary re-
interpretation. Uses The Duchess of Malfi as an example of the impulse to compare characters--here, Julia and the Duchess--who are
really incomparable. Also discusses the issue of the relative
harshness of contemporary and Elizabethan attitudes towards remarriage. Considers The White Devil as a target of critical efforts to see imagery as a unifying force; of current impulses

towards ironic readings; and of the efforts to "refute the ending" by considering Giovanni an evil character. Reviewed: 1980.32.

23 McELROY, BERNARD, Jr. "Recent Studies in Elizabethan and Jacobean Drama." SEL: Studies in English Literature 1500-1900 19:327-57.
     Includes a review ("unconvincing") of Peterson, 1978.24.

24 McELROY, JOHN F. "The White Devil, Women Beware Women, and the Limitations of Rationalist Criticism." SEL: Studies in English Literature 1500-1900 19:295-312.
     Notes that many critics dismiss Webster as chaotic, especially in comparison with Middleton. Finds this a "rationalist reduction" that denies the fluidity of the dramatic experience. Webster deliberately tries to render his audience intellectually and emotionally unsettled. Demonstrates this thesis in the case of Flamineo, a deeply split character, to whom we react in multiple and complex ways.

25 MATHIESON, BARBARA JEAN OFFUTT. "Patterns of Mysogyny in Jacobean Tragedy." Ph.D. dissertation, Stanford University, 306 pp.
     Finds that Jacobean dramatists often mix praise and scorn of women, frequently by having one character vent a private hatred that can contrast with the final dramatic statements of the imagery and structure of the play. In The White Devil and similar works, female adultery informs the plot, and shows a fear of the destructive power of female sexuality. In The Duchess of Malfi, Webster shows the psychological link between mysogyny and melancholy. See Dissertation Abstracts International 40 (1980):4055A.

26 MROCZKOWSKA-BRAND, KATARZYNA. "Overt Theatricality and the Theatrum Mundi Metaphor in Spanish and English Drama, 1500-1640." Kwartalnik Neofilologiczny (Warsaw) 26:201-14.
     Concludes that seventeenth-century English and Spanish drama emphasizes the role-playing aspect of the medieval theatrum mundi metaphor (e.g., Webster's Bosola). Cites Webster briefly.

27 PFEIFFER, K. LUDWIG. "Zur Theorie des Tragischen in der Tragödie der Stuart-Zeit." Germanische-Romanische Monatsschrift 29:170-84.
     Includes discussions of both Vittoria and the Duchess as representative of female Jacobean tragic heroines--tortured and tormented, but strong and retaining their personal integrity.

28 PREAUX, ALAIN. "Le Motif des frères ennemis dans la littérature élizabéthaine et jacobéene et dans le Sturm und Drang." Revue de Littérature Comparée 53:470-89.
     Finds that, by the time of Webster, enemy brothers had become a symbol of a morally inexplicable society. For example, Flamineo, who kills his brother Marcello, is a malcontent type, who is willing

to use all means to raise himself within a corrupt society. Sees
in the use of this motif echoes of the story of Cain, as well as
biblical values. In The Duchess of Malfi, two corrupt brothers
fight with their virtuous sister.

29   SALOMON, BROWNELL. Critical Analyses in English Renaissance
     Drama: A Bibliographic Guide. Bowling Green: Bowling Green
     State University Popular Press for the Bowling Green State
     University Center for Bibliography, 153 pp.
        An annotated, highly selected, secondary bibliography, in-
     cluding nineteen items (numbers 429-447) on Appius and Virginia,
     The Devil's Law Case, The Duchess of Malfi, and The White Devil.

30   SHAW, CATHERINE M. "Some Vanity of Mine Art": The Masque in
     English Renaissance Drama. Jacobean Drama Series 81. Salzburg:
     Institut für Anglistik und Amerikanistik, Universität Salzburg,
     pp. 426-28.
        Discusses the Masque/Antimasque of Madmen in The Duchess of
     Malfi as a visual representation of chaos and disharmony, specifi-
     cally, of the madness into which Bosola attempts to drive the
     Duchess.

31   SPIVACK, CHARLOTTE. "The Duchess of Malfi: A Fearful Madness."
     Journal of Women's Studies in Literature 1:122-32.
        Observes that the Jacobean period saw women as heroes for the
     first time in the history of the English stage. The Duchess is one
     of the greatest. She is trapped, physically and psychologically, by
     men. Finds also that the Duchess is caught between "greatness" and
     "woman" or the spirit of femininity. When tortured, it is she who
     transforms her tortures. She is a wife and mother, as well as a
     political ruler, a complete woman with integrity and the power to
     transform others.

*32 SQUARZINA, LUIGI. "Le Strutture del teatro elisabettiano-
     giacobeo." In Shakespeare e Jonson: Il teatro elisabettiano
     oggi. Edited by Agostino Lombardo. Rome: Officina, pp. 19-50.
        Concerns stage design. Source: MLA International Bibliography
     for 1981 1:Item 615.

33   STEIN, THOMAS MICHAEL. Formen und Funktionen des Kommentars in
     der Tragödie der frühen Stuart-Zeit. European University Studies
     14, no. 66. Frankfort: Lang, 238 pp.
        Considers dramatic commentary and commentators in several
     Jacobean dramatists, most importantly Webster. Discusses fore-
     shadowing in The White Devil in Cornelia's prophetic speeches; de-
     ceptive comments by villains in both tragedies; and how stage ac-
     tion, especially in The Duchess of Malfi, corrects such distortions
     and is the source, along with imagery, of "true" comments.

34   WHITNER, STEPHEN MITCHELL. "Revenge and Society on the English
     Stage: 1562-1642." Ph.D. dissertation, Emory University, 268 pp.

Discusses the political importance of revenge during an age
in which Englishmen came to see themselves not as subjects but as
sharers in the governing process. Revenge plays mirror this movement, from prince-revengers to citizen revenge heroes. In The
Duchess of Malfi, false princes rule the world, while the true
prince figures are killed before revenge can occur. Concludes
that the only fulfillment found in the play comes from internally
glimpsed turth. See Dissertation Abstracts International 40 (1979):
1489A.

1980

1   BAKER, SUSAN C. "The Static Protagonist in The Duchess of Malfi."
    Texas Studies in Literature and Language 22:243-57.
        Suggests that a central feature of The Duchess of Malfi is
    its static heroine: the Duchess does not change or develop. This
    puts the play in a line of "static protagonist" dramas in which an
    early choice is made, then defended throughout the action: here,
    the Duchess refuses to obey her brothers, an act that defines her.
    For the major part of the play, she defends her integrity. Sug-
    gests that the chief image of the work is the radiating light of
    the Duchess. Finds also that Bosola's allegiance to sinful "duty"
    parallels the Duchess' stasis. Concludes that it is Bosola and
    the audience who change during the play, not the Duchess.

2   BELSEY, CATHERINE. "Emblem and Antithesis in The Duchess of
    Malfi." Renaissance Drama, n.s. 11:115-34.
        Sees the play as poised between the emblematic tradition of
    the medieval stage and a later realism. The emblem heritage gives
    the play its structure--a relationship between concepts organized
    by a debate/antithesis polarity. The work often has static dialog
    filled with emblematic imagery. Concludes that its quasi-realistic
    surface often falls into sententiae, meditations, and fables, and
    a series of neat antithesis: abstraction prevails over actuality.

3   BERGERON, DAVID M. "Webster's Allusion to The Second Maiden's
    Tragedy." English Language Notes 17 (June):253-55.
        Asserts that, in The Duchess of Malfi 4.1. 58-69, Webster re-
    fers to The Second Maiden's Tragedy 4.3. 110-14, both being scenes
    of realistic presentation of dead or waxen bodies.

4   BERGGREN, PAULA S. "Spatial Imagery in Webster's Tragedies."
    SEL: Studies in English Literature 1500-1900 20:287-303.
        Suggests that Webster's tragedies are patterned by explicit
    verbal and visual spatial imagery. Specifically, the works' char-
    acters attempt to enlarge the enclosed spaces in which they are
    confined, to assert their wills against the repressions of conven-
    tion. In The White Devil, most of the characters, except Flamineo,
    are unsuccessful in this effort. In The Duchess of Malfi, there
    is a reversal, and physical confinement can be coterminal with
    spiritual freedom.

5   BERRY, RALPH T.   "Masques and Dumbshows in Webster's Plays."
     In The Elizabethan Theatre 7.   Edited by G.R. Hibbard.   Hamden,
     Conn.:   Archon, pp. 124-46.
        Discusses the two dumb shows in The White Devil, both of
which depict the murder of unwanted spouses.   Both are effective
theatrically.   Also suggests that the play's scene at the Barriers
is a masque, reminiscent of Jonson's "Prince Henry's Barriers."
In The Duchess of Malfi, finds more masque, less dumb show.   The
scene of the installment of the Cardinal is an effective dumb show,
telescoping the action.   The madmen are an antimasque within a
parody of a masque, in which the entire presence chamber scene is
a ritualistic inverted epithalamion.   This scene depicts the chaos
of the entire world, and challenges glory, state, etc.   The Devil's
Law Case modifies the other plays--its theme is law infringed.
Finds that the dumb shows of the tragicomedy are less related to
plot, but that all three shows in the play challenge ceremony,
order, and hierarchy.

6   BOERNER, DOROTHY PAYNE.   "The Trial Convention in English
     Renaissance Drama."   Ph.D. dissertation, University of Maryland,
     300 pp.
        Discusses the history of trials upon the English stage, their
staging, varieties, etc.   Notes the character of Appius in Appius
and Virginia is determined by his role as a judge.   Also comments
that the trial is at the structural center of The White Devil.   In
general, trials in Renaissance drama reflect dramatic and social
truth, not actual legal practice.   See Dissertation Abstracts
International 42 (1981):709-10A.

7   BOURGY, VICTOR.   "La Fantôme sur la scène élisabéthaine et
     jacobéene: De l'illusion à l'illusionisme."   In La Mort, le
     fantistique, le supernaturel du XVIe siècle à l'époque romantique.
     Actes du Colloque.   Lille: Université de Lille, Centre de
     Recherches sur l'Angleterre des Tudors à la Régence, pp. 135-47.
        Cites the two ghost scenes in The White Devil to illustrate
real and imagined supernatural spirits.

8   BRADBROOK, MURIEL C.   John Webster: Citizen and Dramatist.
     New York: Columbia University Press, 218 pp.
        Presents Webster in accord with the findings of Mary Edmond
(1976.5), as the son of a wealthy coach-maker in West Smithfield.
Discusses this geographical and social context, including a careful historical discussion of the neighborhood and the trade, and
probable school experiences at the merchant-taylor's school and
the Middle Temple.   Suggests two contemporary stories that shaped
Webster's image of the court: the dark tale of the love-life of
Penelope Rich, and the influential London legend of Antonio Perez,
a Spanish spy.
        In a second section, considers Webster the dramatist.   The
"Ho" plays and Sir Thomas Wyat dramatize for the London citizenry
their own lives.   The White Devil has at its heart a woman and her

servant. Notes the importance of dreams, mimes, epigrams, and
pictures, with special stress on borrowings and visual elements.
The Duchess of Malfi is a superior drama, and a popular one in the
theater. Examines the social, psychological, and theatrical background of the play. Presents The Devil's Law Case as a vehicle for
the bravura display of the talents of the actor Perkins, and describes Appius and Virginia as a play for boys--clear and simple,
and about honest men and villains. Concludes by noting that modern
critical interest shows Webster is still very much alive. Reviewed:
1981.14, 22.

9   BUELER, LOIS WEST EATON. "Webster's Excellent Hyena."
     Philological Quarterly 59, no. 1:107-11.
         Contends that when Ferdinand calls the Duchess a "hyena" it
     is emblematic of her and her brothers, since the animal was often
     seen as hermaphroditic, hence sexually changeable, and thus tricky
     and crafty, sexually fluctuating. Also, the image points to the
     Duchess' man-like vigor and strength, within a woman's body.

10   BURROWS, MAIDWYN DENISE JONES. "The Dramatic Functions of the
     Doctor in Elizabethan and Early-Stuart Drama." Ph.D. disserta-
     tion, Texas Technical University.
         Mentions passingly, within a large general study, stage doc-
     tors in Webster and many others, as important in setting the tone
     of the plays in which they appear. See Dissertation Abstracts
     International 41 (1981):3115A.

11   CANDIDO, JOSEPH DOMINIC. "Katherine of Aragon and Female
     Greatness: Shakespeare's Debt to Dramatic Tradition." Iowa
     State Journal of Research 54:491-98.
         Demonstrates that Shakespeare derived his character of
     Katherine of Aragon not just from Holinshed, but from Webster's
     Vittoria and the Duchess, and other contemporary stage women. Sug-
     gests that there is a type of spirited and individualistic, aristo-
     cratic "great" woman. Notes that Jane, the heroine of Sir Thomas
     Wyat, is also cut from this same cloth. Concludes that all these
     heroines combine assertiveness, suffering, and a sense of self-
     definition.

*12 CHAPPA, RITA MANUELA. "La Technica theatrale in The Duchess of
     Malfi di John Webster." Acme 33, no. 3 (September-December):
     371-87.
         Source: MLA International Bibliography for 1981 1:Item 1992.

13   COURTADE, ANTHONY EDWARD. The Structure of John Webster's Plays.
     Jacobean Drama Series, 97. Salzburg: Institut für Anglistik
     and Amerikanistik, Universität Salzburg, 172 pp.
         See 1979.10.

14   DACRE, KATHLEEN. "The People's Theatre of Elizabethan and
     Jacobean England." Ph.D. dissertation, New York University,
     291 pp.

Notes that civic, processional performances reached a zenith in Lord Mayor's shows such as Webster's <u>Monuments of Honour</u>. See <u>Dissertation Abstracts International</u> 41 (1981):4887A-88A.

15 DIEHL, HUSTON. "The Iconography of Violence in English
    Renaissance Tragedy." <u>Renaissance Drama</u>, n.s. 11:27-44.
        Cites Webster intermittently in a discussion of violence and
    its accoutrements as visual symbols. For example, the trampling
    of Flamineo in <u>The White Devil</u> is presented as a metaphor of the
    punishments of hell.

16 DOEBLER, BETTIE ANNE. "Continuity in the Art of Dying: <u>The</u>
    <u>Duchess of Malfi</u>." <u>Comparative Drama</u> 14, no. 3:203-15.
        Finds that Webster utilizes the old <u>ars</u> <u>moriendi</u> tradition
    to lend comfort in the dying scenes of act 4 of <u>The Duchess of</u>
    <u>Malfi</u>. He "orchestrates a fearful comfort" in death scenes that
    would bring to the minds of the audience the devotional wood cuts
    depicting the temptations to despair.

17 FEINBERG, ANAT. "Observation and Theatricality in Webster's
    <u>The Duchess of Malfi</u>." <u>Theater Research International</u> 6, no.
    1:36-44.
        Affirms that the play is filled with images related to sight.
    All within <u>The Duchess of Malfi</u> are observers and/or observed,
    especially Bosola, the spy. Such observation can cause suffering,
    but it can also lead to knowledge. Webster sees the world as a
    stage, to be watched, and the play's characters recognize that
    they are "actors" in a "tragedy."

18 FORKER, CHARLES R. "<u>Westward Ho</u> and <u>Northward Ho</u>: A Revalu-
    ation." <u>Publications of the Arkansas Philological Association</u>
    6, no. 2:1-42.
        Notes that the Webster/Dekker city comedies have been under-
    valued, probably due to a certain generic flatness, especially of
    character. The works are playful, hurried, game-like, and self-
    consciously theatrical, especially in the parody of Chapman in
    <u>Northward Ho</u>'s Bellamont. Finds the plays ambiguous about the
    middle-class city morality they depict. Concludes with a discus-
    sion of their "faint adumbrations" in the later dramas.

19 HALLETT, CHARLES A., and HALLETT, ELAINE S. <u>The Revenger's</u>
    <u>Madness: A Study of Revenge Tragedy Motifs</u>. Lincoln:
    University of Nebraska Press, 349 pp., passim, esp. pp. 265-96.
        Finds <u>The Duchess of Malfi</u> closely linked to the revenge tra-
    dition through Webster's use of madness, and his use of an innocent
    hero (the Duchess) who suffers a head-on collision with evil, caus-
    ing her world to go mad. Webster uses madness to test the Duchess,
    who does not change. Like the revenge play heroes, she journeys
    through madness into self-discovery. At the play's conclusion,
    she is close to sainthood. Asserts that Ferdinand is the actual
    revenger of the drama, but a mad one with no quest for justice.

Notes that Bosola, like Flamineo, is a typical revenge tragedy tool villain.

20 HARDIN, RICHARD F. "Chapman and Webster on Matrimony: The Poets and the Reformation of Ritual." Renaissance and Reformation n.s. 4:65-73.
     Finds that as religion waned in importance, marriage became secularized (around 1600), including in literature. In The Duchess of Malfi the Duchess' ceremony, while secular, is clearly morally superior to the brutality of her brothers. Other symbols, including the conversion of the Cardinal and the ruined abbey, also point to the degeneration of religion in Webster's age.

21 HAWKINS, HARRIETT. "The Morality of Elizabethan Drama: Some Footnotes to Plato." In English Renaissance Studies Presented to Dame Helen Gardner in Honour of Her Seventieth Birthday. Edited by John Carey. Oxford: Clarendon Press, pp. 12-32.
     Finds that The Duchess of Malfi shows the injustice of certain narrow orthodox moral assumptions, specifically, those concerning marriage.

22 HOLDSWORTH, ROGER V. "The Revenger's Tragedy, Ben Jonson, and The Devil's Law Case." Review of English Studies, n.s. 31: 305-21.
     Uses parallel passages to attempt to date The Devil's Law Case. Specifically, 2.1. 130 ff. in Webster's work is paralleled to 2.4. 33-37 in The Devil is an Ass. Jonson, in turn, probably borrowed from The Revenger's Tragedy (105-6) 2.1. 199 ff.

23 HOWARD, TONY. "Census of Renaissance Drama Productions." Research Opportunities in Renaissance Drama 23:55-71.
     Includes comments by Jacqueline Pearson on a production of The Devil's Law Case at York Theatre Royal (textually straightforward and vigorous); R.V. Holdsworth's notes on The Duchess of Malfi in Cambridge and Manchester; and upon a version of The White Devil at the University Theatre, Manchester (a loud and lurid melodramatic effort).

24 HOY, CYRUS. "Masques and the Artifice of Tragedy." In Elizabethan Theatre 7. Edited by G.R. Hibbard. Hamden, Conn.: Archon, pp. 111-23.
     Briefly cites The White Devil for its brutal exploitation of the masque by the murderers who manage the finale; and The Duchess of Malfi with its grotesque revels of lunatics.

25 KIRSCH, ARTHUR C. "Jacobean Theatrical Self-Consciousness." Research Opportunities in Renaissance Drama 23:9-13.
     Contends that early in the seventeenth century, English drama lost its serious purpose and energy. Sees in Webster's plays a "travesty of tragic form," and "exhibitionism" that can not be justified by claims of "self-consciousness."

26   KOLIN, PHILIP C. "The Names of Whores and Their Bawds and
     Panders in English Renaissance Drama." Midwestern Journal of
     Language and Folklore 6:41-50.
          Notes "Julia" used as the name of a whore in The Duchess of
     Malfi and elsewhere; also discusses the names of whores and panders
     in the "Ho" plays.

27   LANGMAN, F.H. "Truth and Effect in The Duchess of Malfi."
     Sydney Studies in English 6 (1980-81):30-48.
          Finds that, generally, the modern positive revaluation of
     Webster's structural skills is legitimate, but it needs to be
     tempered. The dramatist does sometimes write for effect, for sen-
     sationalism, aiming for much excitement but with little substance.
     Cites as an example of this tendency the handling of the "waxworks"
     scene. Concludes that often excellent ironic touches are lost by
     the impulse towards theatrical spectacle, and that the tragedy un-
     folds without an examination of its deeper causes.

28   LEE, WILLIAM LAMBORN. "Interpreting Insane Characters in King
     Lear, The Duchess of Malfi, Rasselas, and As I Lay Dying: To-
     wards a Theory." 2 vols. Ph.D. dissertation, Yale University,
     790 pp.
          Attempts to apply the standards of the authors' cultures--
     not Freud--to the fictive insane. Finds that The Duchess of Malfi
     employs demonological and melancholic images of insanity, both of
     which create a unifying effect within the play, and provoke sensa-
     tionalism. Bosola mirrors the madness that the Duchess withstands.
     Finds also that Ferdinand's insanity, while tragic, is undermined
     by a sensational comic scene with the Doctor. A similar undermin-
     ing through comedy takes place in the masque of madmen. Altogether,
     finds six different kinds of madness in this ragged but power trage-
     dy. See Dissertation Abstracts International 41 (1980):2094A.

29   LEZBERG, AMY KIRK. "The Jacobean Tragedy of Dual Protagonists."
     Ph.D. dissertation, Boston University, 315 pp.
          Discusses The White Devil as one of a group of plays with
     "duteragonists"--paired heroes whose relationship denies the tenets
     of the surrounding moral universe. Flamineo and Vittoria conspire
     at adultery to achieve separate ambitions. Only in their dying
     moments do they acknowledge their consanguinity of spirit as well
     as blood.

30   LUTZE, LOTHAR. John Websters Tragödienstil als Ausdruck der
     Leidenschaftlichkeit. Jacobean Drama Studies, 84. Salzburg:
     Institut für Anglistik und Amerikanistik. Universität Salzburg,
     189 pp.
          Briefly surveys Webster's life and works, then focuses upon
     questions relating to his tragic style, especially issues of at-
     mospherics, sensory intensity, use of antithesis, and the like.

31   McLEOD, SUSAN H. "Duality in The White Devil." SEL: Studies
      in English Literature 1500-1900 20:271-85.
         Notes the common complaint that Webster's plays are "form-
      less." Contends that actually, The White Devil has as an organiz-
      ing principle the duality implied by the title. Finds the play
      filled with doubles, with repetitions of action and imagery, and
      with pairings of characters (e.g., Isabella and Zanche). Vittoria
      herself is torn between "whiteness" and deviltry.

32   ORNSTEIN, ROBERT. "Recent Studies in Elizabethan and Jacobean
      Drama." SEL: Studies in English Literature 1500-1900 20:345-65.
         Discusses Levin, 1979.22, and several other general studies
      that include consideration of Webster.

33   PEARSON, JACQUELINE. Tragedy and Tragicomedy in the Plays of
      John Webster. Totowa, N.J.: Barnes & Noble, 151 pp.
         Considers Webster's tragedies within the context of his
      tragicomic works, specifically The Devil's Law Case and A Cure for
      a Cuckold (a collaborative effort with Rowley). Finds all four
      plays demonstrate the incoherences of life. Tragicomedy is the
      form that most fully explores the clash of extremes of the human
      condition. Discusses the history of tragicomic form and its nature
      and unique strengths. Pays special attention to the endings of
      works. The White Devil presented as a tragedy that makes its final
      statement in the language of comedy. The Duchess of Malfi is more
      orthodox but still uses comic and tragicomic methods. Both plays
      include tragedy and "anti-tragedy," which expands and tests the
      tragic structure through ambiguity, irony, theatrical self-con-
      sciousness, and self-critical rhetoric. The works, thus, undermine
      themselves. Finds The Devil's Law Case, with its happy ending, has
      as its world that of the tragedies, only slightly modified away
      from the court, towards mercantilism. The collaborative A Cure
      for a Cuckold undermines its comedy, in turn, through irony and a
      subdued use of comic language. It, too, features clashing tones,
      ambiguity, etc. Concludes that Webster's career was one of working
      to force contrasting extremes within a single dramatic structure.
      Reviewed: 1981.14, 22.

34   SCHUMAN, SAMUEL. "'Theatre of Fine Devices': The Visual
      Imagery of Webster's Tragedies." Renaissance and Reformation,
      n.s. 4:87-94.
         Finds The White Devil features disguises utilizing the colors
      of black, white, and red for ironic value reversals that are re-
      flected as well in the work's title and in the stage picture of
      the trial scene. Visibilia in The Duchess of Malfi include the
      disguises of Bosola and the lycanthropic Ferdinand. Concludes
      both tragedies demonstrate Webster's preoccupation with the "false
      show," in which normalcy and convention are deceptive. See 1969.29,
      1972.34.

35   SPINRAD, PHOEBE S.   "Coping with Uncertainty in The Duchess of
     Malfi." Explorations in Renaissance Culture 6:47-63.
        Suggests that, in The Duchess of Malfi, it is the characters
     and the audience who are uncertain, not the drama's fictive uni-
     verse. Discusses Antonio and Bosola's difficulties in confronting
     and understanding life and death. Ferdinand, too, cannot face the
     realities of his universe, especially in the area of sex, and
     flees into the darkness. The Duchess's death, though, seems less
     unsure, and is thus a spiritual victory. The Cardinal, too, dies
     without doubt or fear. Thus, the play asks more questions than it
     answers.

36   WHARTON, J.F. "'Fame's Best Friend': Survival in The Duchess
     of Malfi." In Jacobean Miscellany I. Jacobean Drama Series,
     95. Salzburg: Institut für Anglistik und Amerikanistic,
     Universität Salzburg, pp. 18-33.
        Contends that the family context of the Duchess seems at
     first to be important, unlike most Jacobean plays. As she comes
     to know herself under torture in the later scenes of the play, her
     behavior becomes a "performance," and she sees herself as isolated.
     Finds the Duchess exhibits an "arrogant meekness," and her final
     victory is a purely personal one. Thus, while the play celebrates
     innocence, it shows innocence broken in both Antonio and Bosola,
     as well as the Duchess. Concludes that what finally counts is the
     victim's subjective energy: "Everything becomes a matter of opin-
     ion," and the Duchess finally looks unsettlingly indistinguishable
     from Vittoria.

37   _____. "'Yet I'll Venture': Moral Experiment in Early Jacobean
     Drama." In Jacobean Miscellany I. Jacobean Drama Series, 95.
     Salzburg: Institut für Anglistik und Amerikanistik, Universität
     Salzburg, pp. 3-17.
        Suggests Jacobean drama, in its gleeful asking of ultimate
     questions, can be a quest for moral disorder: it is filled with
     "moral experiments." Sees characters such as Flamineo as stressing
     the absolute isolatedness of the individual. Concludes that
     Shakespeare recoiled from such experimentation, and affirmed a
     revived faith.

38   WHITESIDE, GEORGE. "John Webster: A Freudian Interpretation
     of His Two Great Tragedies." In The Analysis of Literary Texts:
     Current Trends in Methodology. The 3d and 4th York College
     Colloquia. Edited by Randolph D. Pope. Ypsilanti: Bilingual
     Press, pp. 201-11.
        Suggests that Flamineo and Ferdinand are both sexually at-
     tracted to their sisters. Proposes that, in Webster's works, cer-
     tain men feel towards sisters as little boys do towards their
     mothers: Oedipal. The White Devil dramatizes the disastrous con-
     sequences of failing to curb illicit passions. In the play, all
     women are saints (Isabella) or whores (Vittoria)--the two aspects
     of the "mother figure." Finds in The Duchess of Malfi that the

Duchess combines both images of the mother, unlike Vittoria. In
both dramas there are a number of "son figures," and in both, the
mother figure is killed after her good aspect seems lost.

*39   YAMAMOTO, HIROSHI. "The Moral Vision of The Duchess of Malfi."
       Eibungaku to Eigogaku 15:88-110.
          Source: MLA International Bibliography for 1980 1:Item 5940.

                              1981

1   BECKERMAN, BERNARD. "The Use and Management of the Elizabethan
     Stage." In The Third Globe. Edited by C. Walter Hodges, S.
     Schoenbaum, and Leonard Leone. Detroit: Wayne State University
     Press, pp. 151-63.
        Notes that the horror display in The Duchess of Malfi seems
     to require a "discovery space."

2   BEVINGTON, DAVID. "The Use of Contemporary History in the Greek
     and Elizabethan Theatres." Proceedings of the Comparative
     Literature Symposium (Lubbock, Texas) 12:31-50.
        In a very general study, compares the uses of topicality in
     Renaissance Drama (e.g., Webster's use of contemporary Italian his-
     tory) with that of the classical Greek theater.

3   BRADBROOK, MURIEL C. "The Politics of Pageantry: Social Impli-
     cations in Jacobean London." In Poetry and Drama, 1570-1700:
     Essays in Honour of Harold F. Brooks. Edited by Antony Coleman
     and Antony Hammond. London: Methuen, pp. 60-75.
        Discusses the history and procedures of Lord Mayor's shows,
     with a special emphasis on merchant-taylor's shows, including those
     by Munday, Dekker, and Webster. In the discussion of Monuments of
     Honour, notes the theme of attempting to unify the past and the
     present. Observes that the sixteen-year-old Milton may have par-
     ticipated in Webster's show!

4   BRINES, OSBORNE ALLEN, II. "The Machine-Readable Text as an Aid
     to the Study of John Webster's The Duchess of Malfi." Ph.D.
     dissertation, University of Colorado, 1107 pp.
        Utilizes the electronic encoding of the text to produce a
     concordance. Studies the technology of this process, using The
     Duchess of Malfi as an example. An encoded text of the Lucas ver-
     sion is developed, generating a concordance and "other retrievals."

5   CHILLINGTON, CAROL. "Playwrights at Work: Henslowe's not
     Shakespeare's Sir Thomas More." English Literary Renaissance
     11 (Winter):439-79.
        Claims that the disputed portions of Sir Thomas More were
     written by Webster. See 1981.6, 17.

6   CYR, GORDON C. "'Shakespeare' vs. Webster as More's Author:
     A Heretical View." Shakespeare Newsletter 31, nos. 4-5:27.
          Responds to 1981.5, affirming the possibility that the Earl
     of Oxford was the author of Sir Thomas More and perhaps other
     Shakespearean dramas. Appears somewhat tongue-in-cheek. See also
     1981.17.

7   DOYLE, CHARLES CLAY. "John Webster's Echoes of More." Moreana
     70 (June):49-52.
          Notes Webster's use of The History of King Richard III and
     More's Epigrams. Elaborates on the findings of Dent, 1960.12.

8   DREW-BEAR, ANNETTE. "Face-Painting in Renaissance Tragedy."
     Renaissance Drama, n.s. 12:71-93.
          Finds that a basic image of The White Devil is the black-
     faced devil with the white-painted face, pointing to the theme of
     deception. Cardinal Monticelso accuses Vittoria of painting her
     face red and white. Also notes that Francisco, in an image of
     moral and political corruption, paints his face black to murder
     Brachiano, whose death comes by poison on his face. The Duchess
     of Malfi also uses face-painting to emblematize corruption and
     mortality.

9   FUZIER, JEAN, and MAQUIN, JEAN-MARIE. "Archetypal Patterns of
     Horror and Cruelty in Elizabethan Revenge Tragedy." Cahiers
     Elisabethains, no. 19 (April), pp. 9-25.
          Surveys several classical archetypes of horror, for example,
     incest and cannibalism, that find their ways into Jacobean revenge
     tragedy. Does not include The Duchess of Malfi among the "incest
     plays." Cites the strongly cannibalistic imagery of Ferdinand's
     speeches in that work.

10   HELLENGA, ROBERT R. "Elizabethan Dramatic Conventions."
     Renaissance Drama, n.s. 12:27-49.
          Notes that modern psychology cannot resolve the differences
     between realistic character portrayal and unrealistic literary con-
     vention. In The Duchess of Malfi, for instance, we seek but will
     not find a "real" Duchess--but she herself asserts her final identi-
     ty in terms of role: "I am Duchess of Malfi still."

11   IDE, RICHARD S. "Elizabethan Revenge Tragedy and the Providen-
     tial Play-within-a-Play." Iowa State Journal of Research 56,
     no. 1:91-96.
          In a general discussion of the revenge tradition, with little
     material on Webster, discusses the providential play-within-a-play
     to document the generic chain of influence in revenge plays from
     1600 to 1611.

12   No entry.

13   LAKE, D.J. "Webster's Additions to The Malcontent: Linguistic
      Evidence." Notes and Queries, n.s. 28:153-56.
           Notes that Webster is generally acknowledged to have written
      the induction and Marston the additions to the third edition of
      The Malcontent. Compares the language of the additions to known
      Webster and Marston works, and concludes that Webster wrote addi-
      tions numbers 4, 6, 7, 8, and 10, while Marston was the author of
      numbers 1, 2, 3, 5, 9, and 11.

14   LEGATT, ALEXANDER. "Recent Studies in Elizabethan and Jacobean
      Drama." SEL: Studies in English Literature 1500-1900 21:333-68.
           Includes reviews of Brooke, 1979.5; Bradbrook, 1980.8; and
      Pearson, 1980.33.

15   LEINWAND, THEODORE BART. "London Triumphing: Jacobean City
      Comedy 1603-1613." Ph.D. dissertation, Johns Hopkins University,
      362 pp.
           Discusses the relationship of city comedies, such as the "Ho"
      plays, to extratheatrical reality. Discovers that what is drama-
      tized is not reality, but real perceptions of city life. Also in-
      cludes a brief discussion of Lord Mayor's shows including Monuments
      of Honour.

16   MAGUIN, JEAN-MARIE. "Stratégie de l'emblème et stratégie du
      théâtre: De quelques interludes de l'image et du language dans
      la production du sens." In Emblèmes et devices du temps de la
      Renaissance. Edited by Marie-Thérèse Jones-Davies. Paris:
      Touzot, pp. 107-19.
           Compares the allegorical tableau in The White Devil, act 2,
      scene 3 to an emblem.

17   MARDER, LOUIS. Review of Chillington, 1981.5. Shakespeare
      Newsletter 31, no. 2:9-10.
           Finds Chillington's thesis attributing portions of Sir Thomas
      More to Webster to be convincing and impressive. See 1981.6.

18   MIKESELL, MARGARET L. "Matrimony and Change in Webster's The
      Duchess of Malfi." Journal of the Rocky Mountain Medieval and
      Renaissance Association 2:97-111.
           Finds that the old and new views of marriage come into con-
      flict in The Duchess of Malfi. The old vision, endorsed by the
      Aragonian brothers, is fiscal, arranged, and dynastic. The new
      marriage is a love relationship. Webster sides with the Duchess
      in favor of the new over the old. To some extent, too, this repre-
      sents a conflict between aristocratic and middle-class values.

19   ORGEL, STEPHEN. "The Renaissance Artist as Plagiarist." ELH
      48, no. 3:476-95.
           Raises the issue of "imitation" vs "plagiarism" in Renaissance
      literary and visual arts. Asks when imitation becomes plagiarism in
      artists such as Inigo Jones, Ben Jonson, and John Webster?

20   PIKOULIS, JOHN. "Palgrave and Eliot." Notes and Queries, n.s.
     28:432.
          Comments upon Eliot's use of Webster's song "Call for the
     robin-redbreast and the wren" juxtaposed with Shakespeare's similar
     ditty from The Tempest.

21   PUTT, S. GORLEY. The Golden Age of English Drama. Cambridge:
     D.S. Brewer; Totowa, N.J.: Rowman & Littlefield, pp. 128-54.
          Notes Webster's striking phrase making and his Italianate
     horror-filled plots, but also his broader, human message, which
     includes a potentially rebellious castigation of the ruling class.
     Outlines the plots of The White Devil and The Duchess of Malfi, and
     comments upon them: Vittoria is as bold as her lover is ruthless;
     The Duchess of Malfi is like "a puzzling piece of apparently eccen-
     tric lethal machinery whose . . . parts are made of precious stones."
     Notes the usefulness of the concept of the "baroque" as a way to
     understand the tragedies. Concludes that our recent bloody past
     authenticates the gruesomeness of Webster's drama.

22   _____. "Mirth in Funeral." English 30, no. 138:291-96.
          Reviews Pearson, 1980.33; Brook, 1979.5; and Bradbrook,
     1980.8. Finds Pearson's analysis of the tragicomic genre and of
     the four plays to be useful; Brooke's study displays a light, deft,
     artistry; and Bradbrook's work, while at times using a rather dense
     prose style, is a helpful recreation of Webster's world.

23   SELZER, JOHN L. "Merit and Degree in Webster's The Duchess of
     Malfi." English Literary Renaissance 11:70-80.
          Considers the relationship between intrinsic merit and in-
     herited status. The Duchess promotes the primacy of worth over
     degree, while her brothers rule solely on the basis of degree.
     Bosola is in the middle of this conflict. The last act affirms
     the value of individual merit over inherited station.

24   SHAPIRO, MICHAEL. "Annotated Bibliography on Original Staging
     in Elizabethan Plays." Research Opportunities in Renaissance
     Drama 24:23-49.
          Annotates works on playhouses and staging techniques (acting,
     pace, music, lighting, costume, props, deployment of actors on
     stage) from 1576 to 1642. Many of the works cited concern Webster.

*25 VENET, GISELE. "Justice et structure tragique: Webster." In
     Société française Shakespeare: Actes du congrès 1980. Edited
     by Marie-Thérèse Jones-Davies. Paris: Touzot, pp. 61-69.
          Source: MLA International Bibliography for 1981 1:Item 1998.

26   WELLS, SUSAN. "Jacobean City Comedy and the Ideology of the
     City." ELH 48, no. 1:37-60.
          Considers the genre of the "Ho" plays within the context of
     Mikhail Bakhtin's definition of the marketplace as a location where
     the lower bodily rights are legitimated--a locus of license.

Contrasts this with the emerging commercial marketplace, where
all is commodity.

Index

Abrams, Sherwin F., 1955.1
Academiarum Examen, 1820.1, 3;
    1898.2
Adams, Henry Hitch, 1943.1
Adams, Joseph Quincy, 1906.1;
    1917.1
Adams, Martin, 1950.1
Adams, Robert M., 1979.1
Adams, Robert P., 1978.1
Adams, Thomas, 1947.5
Adams, W. Davenport, 1904.1
Adaptations of Webster's Plays,
    1696.1; 1707.1; 1735.1;
    1850.1-2; 1851.2-3; 1885.2;
    1933.5; 1934.6; 1951.12;
    1961.12
Africa, Africans, Blacks,
    1965.11; 1970.29; 1971.7;
    1975.27
Agate, James, 1925.1; 1935.1;
    1943.2
Aggeler, Geoffrey, 1967.1
Aitken, George A., 1889.1
Akrigg, G.P.V., 1944.1; 1948.1-2;
    1950.2; 1954.1; 1959.1
Albright, Evelyn May, 1927.1
Albright, Victor E., 1909.1
Alden, Raymond M., 1914.1
Alden, Rose, 1920.1
Alexander, Nigel, 1970.1
Alexander, William (source),
    1966.26; 1977.12
Allen, Don Cameron, 1941.1
Allen, J.W., 1903.5
Allen, Richard O., 1969.1
Alleyn, Edward (actor), 1962.3
Allibone, S.A., 1871.1

Allison, Alexander, 1964.1
Anderson, Marcia Lee, 1937.1;
    1939.1-2
Ankebrand, Hans, 1906.2
Ansari, K.H., 1969.2; 1972.2
Anscombe, Alfred, 1913.1
Antonio (character, The Duchess of
    Malfi), 1694.1; 1808.1; 1818.1;
    1823.1; 1884.2; 1898.1; 1901.2;
    1909.12; 1937.6; 1944.6;
    1945.6; 1946.1; 1952.5;
    1956.17, 22, 31; 1960.19, 21;
    1962.1, 23; 1963.25; 1968.21,
    23; 1969.14; 1970.12, 30-31;
    1971.11; 1972.10, 17; 1974.22;
    1975.3-4, 28; 1976.1-2;
    1978.24; 1979.5, 13; 1980.35-36
Anything for a Quiet Life (play),
    1886.4; 1911.3; 1921.8;
    1922.7, 11; 1927.11; 1928.1, 7;
    1930.6; 1937.2; 1958.1; 1959.12;
    1960.22
Appius and Virginia (play)
-Bibliographical material, dating,
    emdations, text, 1884.1;
    1896.2; 1905.6; 1911.3;
    1913.3, 9, 11; 1916.1; 1921.2;
    1922.7; 1924.8-9; 1927.7, 9;
    1929.8; 1931.3; 1934.8; 1939.4;
    1957.13; 1963.21; 1966.22;
    1967.11; 1969.2, 27; 1979.29
-Editions, 1830.2; 1927.11
-General and miscellaneous, 1656.1,
    3; 1661.1; 1719.1; 1750.1;
    1807.1; 1808.1; 1814.1; 1820.3;
    1823.2; 1839.1; 1859.1; 1874.1,
    2; 1875.2; 1885.1; 1886.3;

255

1972.10, 13, 17, 24, 28;
1973.2, 8; 1974.2, 9, 22, 24;
1975.2, 28; 1976.1-2, 17;
1977.3, 6, 11, 17; 1978.18;
1979.1, 26, 30; 1980.1, 17,
19, 28, 34-36; 1981.23
Boulton, Marjorie, 1960.2
Bourgeois, A.F., 1914.3-5;
1915.1
Bourgy, Victor, 1980.7
Bowden, W.R., 1951.2
Bowers, Fredson Thayer, 1937.3;
1940.2; 1955.6
Boyce, Benjamin, 1947.1
Boyer, Clarence Valentine,
1914.6
Brachiano (character, The White
Devil), 1833.1; 1897.3;
1906.2; 1908.5; 1913.6;
1916.2; 1927.11, 18; 1931.6;
1940.5; 1947.9; 1948.10;
1951.7, 12; 1952.3; 1956.13;
1960.10; 1961.10; 1962.12;
1963.9, 18; 1965.2, 7, 21,
24; 1966.15-16; 1968.21;
1969.27, 33; 1970.17; 1971.4;
1972.12; 1973.10; 1974.22,
24; 1975.24; 1977.8; 1979.4,
21; 1981.8, 21
Bradbrook, Muriel C., 1932.2;
1947.2; 1952.3; 1962.3;
1965.3; 1973.3; 1975.6;
1980.8; 1981.3, 14, 22
Bradbury, Gail, 1979.4
Bradford, Gamaliel, 1921.1
Bradner, Leicester, 1956.3
Braendel, Doris B., 1972.7
Brecht, Bertolt, 1968.2; 1978.2
Breen, Robert S., 1937.4
Brennan, Elizabeth M., 1958.2;
1963.2; 1964.8; 1966.1;
1970.6; 1975.7
Brereton, John Le Gay, 1905.1;
1906.5; 1909.2; 1948.4
Brettle, Robert E., 1927.5
Bridges, Adams W., 1957.6
Briggs, Katherine Mary, 1962.4
Briggs, William Dinsmore, 1927.6
Brines, Osborne Allen II, 1981.4
Brissenden, Alan J., 1962.5
Broadus, Edmund K., 1935.2

Brockett, Oscar G., 1968.6
Brodwin, Leonora L., 1971.4
Bronzino, Il (painter), 1972.7
Brooke, C.F. Tucker, 1911.1;
1948.5
Brooke, Donald, 1945.3
Brooke, Nicholas, 1979.5; 1981.14,
22
Brooke, Rupert, 1913.3-4; 1916.1,
6; 1918.1; 1924.8-9; 1955.3;
1956.27; 1957.14; 1963.15;
1966.22; 1973.18
Brooke, Stopford A., 1897.1
Brown, Arthur, 1960.3-4; 1961.5
Brown, Ivor, 1960.5
Brown, John Russell, 1951.3;
1952.4; 1954.2; 1956.4; 1957.7;
1958.3; 1960.6-7; 1961.6;
1962.6; 1964.9; 1969.15
Browning, D.C., 1958.5
Browning, Robert (poet), 1929.10
Brucher, Richard, 1978.6
Bruckl, O., 1965.4
Bruder, Harry, 1979.6
Bryant, J.A., 1956.5
Brydges, Sir Samuel Egerton,
1810.1
Buchan, Moyra J., 1966.3
Buchon, Jean A., 1828.1
Buckle, Reginald W., 1967.2
Bueler, Lois West Eaton, 1976.3;
1980.9
Buland, Mable, 1912.1
Bullen, A.H., 1924.2
Burgess, Judith Livingston, 1979.7
Burrow, Maidwyn Denise Jones,
1980.10
Burton, E.J., 1960.8
Bush, Douglas, 1945.4
Bush, Geoffrey, 1956.6
Busino, Orazio, 1617.1
Butler, E.M., 1917.2
Butler, Pierce, 1916.2
Byers, George F., 1973.4
Byron, George Gordon, Lord,
1901.1

Calderwood, James L., 1962.7
Calish, Edward N., 1909.4
Camden, Charles Carroll, 1952.5
Camille, Georgette, 1941.5

Evans, Sir Benjamin Ifor, 1948.7
Evans, G. Blakemore, 1959.5;
 1963.7
Everitt, E.B., 1964.11
Ewbank, Inga-Stina, 1970.8;
 1975.11. See also Ekeblad,
 Inga-Stina
"An Excellent Actor." See
 Characters

Fahey, G.B., 1960.16
Fairholt, Fredrick W., 1843.2
Fair Maid of the Inn, The (play),
 1886.1; 1890.4; 1915.5;
 1927.11-12, 14; 1928.8;
 1930.7; 1938.2; 1948.16;
 1955.21; 1956.16; 1959.15;
 1965.16; 1966.22
Farnham, Willard, 1950.7; 1951.16
Feather, John, 1970.9
Feinberg, Anat, 1980.17
Feldman, A. Bronson, 1956.13
Fellheimer, Jeanette, 1935.3
Felperin, Howard, 1977.4
Felver, Charles S., 1963.8
Fenton, Doris, 1930.3
Ferdinand (character, The Duchess
 of Malfi), 1914.10; 1943.11;
 1947.8; 1948.1, 10; 1951.1,
 12; 1952.18; 1956.12, 29;
 1957.24; 1959.3; 1960.21;
 1962.7, 20-21, 23; 1963.2;
 1964.1, 22, 31, 38; 1968.18,
 25; 1969.13; 1970.1, 8, 12-
 13, 31; 1972.10, 13, 17;
 1973.14; 1974.16, 22;
 1975.12, 25; 1976.2, 10, 18;
 1978.27, 30; 1979.5, 13;
 1980.9, 19, 28, 34-35, 38;
 1981.9
Fieler, Frank B., 1967.9
Fisk, Viva K., 1968.9
Fitz, L.T., 1979.13
Fitzjeffrey, Henry, 1617.1;
 1933.6
Flamineo (character, The White
 Devil), 1863.1-2; 1865.1;
 1883.1-2; 1906.2; 1909.1;
 1919.5; 1927.11; 1928.3, 5;
 1933.2, 9; 1936.8; 1937.5, 7;
 1939.11; 1943.11; 1948.9;

1950.13; 1951.4, 7, 12; 1952.3;
 1953.1, 6; 1956.5; 1957.4-5;
 1958.1; 1959.8; 1960.11, 19;
 1961.4, 15-16; 1963.2, 9, 22;
 1964.36; 1965.2, 14, 17-18,
 22; 1966.2, 4, 6, 15; 1969.11,
 26, 33; 1970.22; 1971.4, 12;
 1972.24; 1973.16, 31; 1974.13,
 22, 24; 1975.2; 1976.17;
 1977.2-3, 8; 1979.4-5, 7-8,
 16, 24, 28; 1980.8, 15, 19,
 29, 37-38
Flaxman, Erwin, 1974.9
Fleay, F.G., 1884.1; 1886.1;
 1890.1; 1891.1; 1906.1, 10;
 1914.4
Fletcher, John (dramatist), 1635.1;
 1656.2; 1833.1; 1890.4; 1899.1;
 1905.6; 1915.3; 1927.11, 14;
 1930.7; 1931.10; 1943.8;
 1955.8; 1956.16, 23; 1960.7;
 1962.15; 1970.5
Fletcher, Robert, 1895.3
Florence (character, The White
 Devil), 1952.3; 1965.11;
 1971.4; 1974.22; 1979.19, 21;
 1981.8
Florio, John (source), 1958.13
Fluchère, Henri, 1934.1; 1948.8
Foakes, R.A., 1602.1; 1952.8;
 1955.11; 1970.10
Fogel, Ephim, 1966.8
Ford, John (dramatist), 1623.1;
 1798.1; 1839.1; 1890.3; 1908.9;
 1917.1; 1922.9; 1926.1;
 1927.14; 1935.9; 1936.7;
 1952.12; 1955.12, 21; 1956.16;
 1957.19; 1975.11; 1976.18
Forker, Charles R., 1964.12;
 1965.6; 1967.10; 1968.10;
 1969.8-9; 1972.11; 1973.7;
 1975.12; 1976.6; 1980.18
Forsythe, Robert Stanley, 1914.7
Foss, Katherine A., 1929.4
Foster, Francis, 1912.2
Foxe, John (source), 1958.20
France, French, Frenchmen, etc.,
 1926.3; 1941.13-14; 1960.14;
 1963.5, 10
Francisco (character, The White
 Devil). See Florence

1968.12, 21; 1969.9; 1970.16;
1971.10; 1974.14, 19; 1979.3,
9; 1980.26; 1981.21. See
also Imagery; The Duchess of
Malfi-Language; The White
Devil-Language
Larkin, Daniel, 1958.14
Lauschke, Johannes, 1899.2
Law, Lawyers, 1905.4; 1906.4, 12;
1908.2; 1913.7; 1926.2;
1934.3, 5; 1942.1; 1958.14;
1964.14, 25; 1970.7; 1972.5;
1973.6; 1974.20; 1979.3;
1980.5-6. See also Arraignment of Vittoria
Lawrence, Robert G., 1975.21
Lawrence, William J., 1912.5;
1913.5; 1919.4; 1922.4;
1927.10; 1935.6
Layman, B.J., 1959.8
Lebèque, R., 1950.9
Lee, Nathaniel (dramatist),
1956.8
Lee, Sidney, 1885.1
Lee, Vernon. See Paget, Violet
Lee, William Lamborn, 1980.28
Leech, Clifford, 1941.12; 1947.6;
1950.10; 1951.12; 1955.18;
1957.19; 1958.15; 1959.9;
1962.14-15, 20; 1963.15-16;
1964.10, 17, 19, 21-22, 38;
1965.2, 14; 1969.19; 1973.17-
19; 1974.17
Leggatt, Alexander, 1973.20;
1981.14
Legois, Émile, 1924.6
Leinwand, Theodore Bart, 1981.15
Lell, Gordon, 1973.21
Leone, Leonard, 1981.1
Leopold, H., 1933.10
Lever, J.W., 1971.11
Levin, Harry, 1969.21
Levin, Richard, 1979.22; 1980.32
Levy, Beverly Sauer, 1978.19
Lewes, G.H., 1896.4
Lewis, George L., 1961.13
Ley, William (printer), 1656.3;
1938.5; 1975.31
Lezberg, Amy Kirk, 1980.29
Liebe, Carl, 1907.4
Lievsay, John Leon, 1955.19

Liljegren, S.B., 1958.16
Lindabury, Richard Vliet, 1933.5
Linthicum, M. Channing, 1930.6
Littleton, Taylor D., 1960.18
Lockert, Lucy, 1915.3
Lodovico (character, The White
Devil), 1952.3; 1962.12;
1965.2; 1979.19
Loftis, John, 1969.22
Logan, Terence P., 1975.22;
1977.12; 1978.20
Lord, Joan M., 1976.14
Lord Mayor's Shows. See Monuments
of Honour
Lovett, R.M., 1902.3
Lowell, James Russell, 1892.4
Lucas, F.L., 1922.5; 1924.7;
1926.5-6; 1927.11-12; 1928.2,
4, 7; 1933.6; 1945.7; 1953.5;
1954.10; 1956.17; 1958.17-18;
1959.3; 1972.20; 1973.18
Luecke, James Marie, O.S.B.,
1964.23
Luisi, David, 1972.28
Lutze, Lothar, 1956.18; 1980.30
Lynch, Robert E., 1972.29
Lyons, Bridget G., 1971.12

M., H., 1818.1-2
M., J., 1833.1
McCollom, William Gilman, 1944.5;
1957.21
McConnell-Derksen, Dorothy Diane,
1978.22
McCullen, Joseph J., 1948.10;
1951.13; 1952.15
McDonald, Charles O., 1966.17;
1967.20
MacDonald, Roger Alfred, 1978.21
McElroy, Bernard, Jr., 1979.23
McElroy, John F., 1979.24
McGinn, Donald Joseph, 1938.10
Macgowan, Kenneth, 1955.20
Machiavelli, Machiavellian, etc.,
1897.3; 1906.7; 1914.6; 1921.6;
1925.2; 1927.11; 1928.5; 1938.7;
1939.11; 1943.3; 1948.8;
1949.6; 1951.12, 22; 1955.24;
1956.2, 12, 21; 1957.4; 1959.8;
1960.11; 1964.1, 32, 36;
1966.10; 1967.6; 1968.9, 21;